An Introduction to
LINGUISTICS

An Introduction

to LINGUISTICS

BRUCE L. LILES

University of Missouri–St. Louis

PRENTICE-HALL, INC., Englewood Cliffs, New Jersey

Library of Congress Cataloging in Publication Data

LILES, BRUCE L
    An introduction to linguistics.

    Bibliography: p.
    Includes index.
    1. Language and languages. 2. Grammar, Comparative
and general. I. Title.
P106.L53   410   74-23249
ISBN 0-13-486134-5
ISBN 0-13-486126-4 pbk.

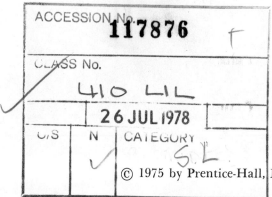
© 1975 by Prentice-Hall, Inc., *Englewood Cliffs, New Jersey*

Printed in the United States of America

10 9 8 7 6 5 4 3 2 1

PRENTICE-HALL INTERNATIONAL, INC., *London*
PRENTICE-HALL OF AUSTRALIA, PTY. LTD., *Sydney*
PRENTICE-HALL OF CANADA, LTD., *Toronto*
PRENTICE-HALL OF INDIA PRIVATE LIMITED, *New Delhi*
PRENTICE-HALL OF JAPAN, INC., *Tokyo*

Contents

2 SYNTAX

4 ACQUISITION, CHANGE, VARIATION

Preface

Any work with the word *introduction* in the title should have two characteristics. First, it should not assume any detailed background; and second, it should not exhaust the subject. This book does not presuppose any previous knowledge of formal studies in grammar on the part of its readers. It does assume that they are fluent in English, but not necessarily native speakers. People who speak a language fluently have a great deal of implicit knowledge about this language, but if they are asked why they understand a sentence in a given way or how they form a given structure such as a relative clause or a question, they may answer incorrectly. They are able to form these structures without mistakes, and they understand them perfectly when someone else uses them; yet they are not able to explain what they are doing. The purpose of linguistic investigation is to make explicit this knowledge which fluent speakers have of a language. This book, therefore, assumes that its readers speak English with ease, but it does not assume that they have had any formal training in discussing its structure.

As for the second point, there is no topic in this book which is exhaustively covered. With the present state of knowledge, it is impossible to write a complete grammar of English or of any other language. We have, therefore, selected a few structures in English and other languages to illustrate the systems that exist. Instead of starting with transformations which apply to simple sentences and then building up to larger sentences, we have devoted most of the discussion in the section on syntax to those sentences which traditional grammarians called complex. These structures provide better opportunities for revealing the nature of a person's knowledge of language than do the shorter ones. Pedagogically, they are more palatable to people receiving their first exposure to linguistics than are such structures as negatives, questions, and passives—which involve some of the most complicated transformations possible and which have many aspects that are poorly understood.

Although no topic is covered exhaustively, there is enough detail given on each one so that readers will gain a better understanding of what the study of language is about than they would with a hasty sweep of the areas of investigation. Because of this decision to go into some topics with a moderate amount of depth, it has not been possible to cover all areas of linguistic study. Nor have all approaches to linguistics been employed. There is, for example, no mention of tagmemics or stratificational grammar since these approaches have had little impact upon research as a whole, and current publications utilizing these approaches are scant. Nor is there much discussion of structural grammar beyond that found in Chapter 11, since this approach has been shown inadequate for the goals of current linguistic research. The generative-transformational model has been used throughout since it is the framework within which most linguistic scholarship is now conducted; it also provides a model which permits us to discuss syntax, phonology, change, and dialectology from a consistent, unified standpoint. Along with the transformational model, we make frequent references to traditional grammar, which to the current generation of linguists is not the ogre that it was to those of the 1940s and 1950s.

Perhaps the ideal introduction to linguistics would be one which drew examples from languages from all parts of the world, without giving any one more attention than others. This procedure would give a clearer picture of language possibilities than one which is limited to structures in a single language or a group of those which are closely related. Certainly, provincial myopia has no place in scholarship. In spite of these advantages, this book draws most of its examples from English. The main reason for this restriction is pedagogical. Whereas the future linguist is usually delighted with exercises from exotic languages, the prospective English teacher and the general reader are often terrified by them. Furthermore, for material from languages which readers do not know, they are dependent upon the information given in the text and can only hope that it is accurate and not skewed in some way. For a language which they speak themselves, they can test the statements in the book and provide additional examples to insure that the structures given are truly representative. Another reason for using primarily English examples is that this is the language which has been studied most intensively. Although there are many analyses of various aspects of a large number of languages in all parts of the world, most of these are not penetrating enough for the kind of work which linguists in the 1970s demand. In a great many places in this book, however, there are examples drawn from languages other than English. These were usually selected because they are the languages with which readers are most likely to be familiar and because they have been studied from the standpoint of current methodology.

Rules are stated informally throughout the book. There is currently much controversy over their form, and debates over them are best left for more advanced studies. The writing of rules is unquestionably a vital aspect of linguistic investigation, but the great attention given in the past to their formal representation has been more of a hindrance than an aid to students who were beginning their study of linguistics.

In Part 1 we try to determine what language is and how it differs from other means of communication. If we are to study language, our first task is to determine the limits of the field. We then proceed to the study of sentence structures, or syntax, in Part 2. This section begins with analyses which are fairly close to the surface and proceeds to those which are more abstract and complex. This approach is essentially the direction studies in syntax have taken since the later 1950s. In Part 3 we look at the sound patterns of language, following the same progression from surface to abstract as we did in syntax, and also using the same grammatical model. In both syntax and phonology, we see that there is much which a person knows about language that is not obvious from the actual spoken or written form which it takes. Our task is to account for this knowledge. Finally, in Part 4 we see how the systems we have been examining may vary among speakers of a language or from one time period to another. We also look for universal features found among languages throughout the world. Language is systematic, but it does not remain static, nor is it uniform among all speakers. If we are to avoid a distorted view of language, we must include a study of variation.

I would like to thank my colleagues and students who have read and offered comments on parts of this manuscript. Special thanks go to the anonymous reviewers provided by my editor.

BRUCE L. LILES

St. Louis, Missouri
March 1974

part 1

Language
and
Communication

chapter 1

The Uses of Language

We are seldom conscious of the objects that we see every day. We may easily remember the redwoods in California or the old oaks heavy with moss that we saw while we were on vacation in Louisiana, and yet we may not be aware of the trees we pass every day on our way to work. Whereas we can remember a birthday dinner for weeks, on an ordinary day we may have trouble remembering what we ate an hour ago. We may be so unconscious of our clothing that upon receiving a compliment about our shoes we have to check to see which ones we are wearing, but at the same time we may remember quite well what we wore to a party a month before. It is only when something happens to make ordinary objects and events exceptional that we notice them: A tree we pass every day is struck by lightning, the Brussels sprouts we had for lunch give us indigestion, or the shoes we are wearing are too tight.

The same tendency exists with reactions to language. We are surrounded by speech and writing throughout our waking hours; we even engage in conversation in our dreams. Because language is so common to us, we may not notice it any more than we do batting our eyes, swallowing, or shifting our legs to a more comfortable position. It is only when our own language is misunderstood or we find someone else's unusual that we become aware of it. Although language is usually accepted without special attention, it is man's most valuable possession. We should, therefore, try to understand its uses and features.

A person working alone can arrive at a great many new ideas; but if one is able to pool this information with that accumulated by others, each of us will have access to a much larger body of knowledge than if we had to depend solely upon our own experiences. Someone else can warn us that the limb we are sitting on is about to break, that a car is coming our way, that our clothing is on fire, that we are standing on a rattlesnake, or that some other source of danger is present. We can then react as though we personally had seen the evidence. Transfer of information from one person to another does not have to be a warning. It can be the news that a local music store has all records on sale for half price or that the neighbors have a new car. Although some of these ideas could be exchanged by gestures and yells, most of them depend upon the use of words joined into sentences.

Without language, civilization would not be possible. There has to be a great deal of communication extending beyond grunts and gestures before people can agree to divide their chores and cooperate in community living on a scale more complex than that found among animals and insects. Because verbal agreements have been reached, some people can specialize in farming, others in making clothes, still others in caring for the sick, and so on. For the community to continue functioning, frequent interchanges of information through the use of language are essential.

Language also permits knowledge to be transmitted to succeeding generations. In this way, each group of people does not have to discover *de novo* how to make fire, grow vegetables, or make permanent-press fabrics. People can begin with the knowledge accumulated by their predecessors and add new knowledge to it. Thus civilizations can progress from one level to another.

The use of language as a means of imparting information is so obvious that we do not need to develop the idea further. However, one may argue that language does not always succeed in communicating. Certainly if no one is listening or if the speaker is incoherent, there is no transfer of ideas. The same is true if someone speaks Italian to a person who understands only Japanese. In addition, there is the problem of the garrulous bore who can spout sentences indefinitely and never really say anything of importance. Nonetheless, in each of these instances and in others like them, the *intention* is to communicate information.

There have been a number of attempts to classify the uses of language. Most linguists list from three to five functions, the exact number varying more with their manner of grouping than with the uses which they recognize. All include an **informative** function. Language used in this way gives information that can be crucial or trivial, true or false. As the name suggests, its purpose is to inform. It can be an account of Mr. Crumpton's insomnia, a discussion of the oral formulaic passages in *Beowulf*, or a description of Niagara Falls. It does not matter if the speaker or writer is mistaken, lying, or being truthful and exact—in any case he is attempting to provide information.

A second use of language can be called **phatic communion,** following the term introduced by the anthropologist Bronislaw Malinowski. With this use of language there is no intention of exchanging facts. A greeting such as "How are you?" is relatively empty of content, and any answer other than an equally empty "Fine" or "Very well, thank you" comes as a surprise. Nor is there any reason for elation when one is told "It was nice seeing you again" or "I'm glad I met you." Everyone to whom we write a letter is not necessarily "dear" to us, any more than we belong to the addressee when we close a letter with "yours truly." These are all formalities similar to a smile, a wave, or a shaking of hands. It was because people intended "God be with you" as nothing more than a conventional greeting that it was allowed to become "Good-bye." The speaker does not intend to impart new information, but rather to demonstrate his own politeness and general attitude toward the other person when he gives a conventional greeting. Similarly, discussions of the weather usually do more for establishing rapport than for informing. The weather is a safe topic, one on which people usually agree and for which neither speaker nor listener can be blamed if it is unpleasant.

Another example of the use of obvious information occurs when a person stops to help someone whose car is parked on the shoulder of a freeway with the hood raised. The opening statement "Are you having car trouble?" should not be accepted with exasperation. The speaker is not being obtuse, but merely careful in leading up to an offer of help. Most people are very sensitive about being rebuffed and begin conversations with strangers on safe grounds. We have exposed no vulnerable points if we begin with relatively safe topics which have no direct reference to ourselves. Such uses of language as conventional greetings, comments about the weather, and small talk at parties do not impart new and important ideas. Nevertheless, they do express the speaker's attitudes. They show that people are still on speaking terms with each other and that a certain amount of courtesy can be expected if the conversation shifts to the use of informative language.

It should not be assumed that phatic communion exists only between strangers and people who know each other only casually. Even among friends a certain amount of chitchat at the beginning of a conversation can serve a useful function. If they are talking over the telephone, it establishes that the connection is good and that the listener can hear over any disturbances around him. Before the beginning of a conversation we may be thinking about something else or listening to music or another conversation. A small amount of phatic communion gives us time to adjust our attention to the new subject.

It also permits strangers to become accustomed to each other's voices. In addition, it can provide people with the confidence and encouragement necessary for proceeding with more serious conversation, or it can merely provide them with the feeling that they have associated with other people on a compatible basis. Used properly, this kind of language can provide smooth introductions to other kinds of communication or make waiting for a bus or the doctor agreeable. Used in excess, it can lead to boredom; there are, indeed, people who are content to continue with it ad nauseum. At the opposite extreme are those who have no gift for small talk, either because they have not developed the art, or else they feel that everything they say should always be full of meaning. By their reticence they may suggest indifference or even hostility.

A third use of language, the **expressive,** reveals feelings. Although some linguists combine this function with phatic communion, there are differences in purpose. If a person says, "Isn't it a beautiful day!" he may be merely breaking silence; on the other hand, he may be giving a genuine expression of feeling. If he is just breaking silence, he is using phatic communion; if he is giving his feelings, he is being expressive. Obviously the two may be combined. Two people who have passed the "How are you?"

stage and have proceeded into a serious conversation no longer have an immediate need for phatic language. Yet if they walk outside, one of them may be amazed by the sunshine and the pleasant temperature. His statement "Isn't it a beautiful day!" is a true expression of emotion, not a demonstration of courtesy and friendliness. Much literature serves an expressive function; lyric poetry is the most obvious example, but other forms of poetry and prose can demonstrate this function as well. Because of this use of language, it is possible for us to learn how other people have felt when they were exposed to death, love, beauty, leprosy, injustice, or Mont Blanc.

Finally, there is **directive** language, which affects another person's thought or behavior, causing him to do or not to do something. Of course, the person may ignore the direction, but the purpose of the language remains the same. It can be a question, whereby the speaker is requesting an answer from the listener, or it can be a command such as "Open the door." Sometimes there is little difference between a question and a command, as in "Would you pass the salt?" and "Pass the salt." The difference between the two utterances is one of politeness rather than function. A scale of politeness can be seen in the following sentences:

1.1   Wait in the outer office.
1.2   Wait in the outer office, please.
1.3   Would you wait in the outer office?
1.4   Would you mind waiting in the outer office?
1.5   Would you like to wait in the outer office?

Although tone of voice, facial expressions, and general posture of the speaker can add to the politeness or rudeness of any of the sentences, it is possible to keep these features constant for all of them. Spoken courteously, these sentences all mean the same thing: that the addressee should wait in the outer office. Whether expressed as a question or a command, this use of language is clearly directive, not informative, phatic, or expressive.

Directive language is not always formed as questions or commands. A salesman, clergyman, or politician who is trying to be persuasive will probably not say, "Buy this dress," "Do not gamble," "Give money," or "Vote for me." He may be more tactful and disguise his purpose with informative or expressive language: "This dress is certainly becoming on you" or "I would really appreciate your vote."

In most cases language combines two or more of these functions. A statement such as "I'll see you tomorrow at 2:30 in front of the library" can be both informative and directive. Certain political meetings, church services, and pep rallies can be both directive and expressive as people are singing together, repeating ritualistic statements, and reassuring one another. A person who admires someone's new car may be expressing genuine emotion; at the same time he may be engaging in a bit of phatic conversation or even directive language if he is hinting for a ride. A salesman normally gives information about his product as he is trying to persuade the customer to buy it.

Since the purpose of language is to communicate, it may be asked if the words *language* and *communication* are not synonymous. Like many other words which occur widely, *language* has been used with various meanings:

"the language of computers," "silent language," "body language," "sign language," "the language of art," and others. Such a broad use of the term is undesirable for the student of language. Every discipline needs definite limits, unless we ambitiously accept the whole world as our area of investigation. Since there are many ways in which people may communicate with one another, we should begin by separating them and deciding which ones we wish to study.

As a start let us see if there are alternate means of providing information, establishing rapport, expressing emotions, and directing others than we have discussed so far. Most information needs words for its transmission, but there are some elementary ideas that can be conveyed by gestures. For example, by nodding or shaking the head, we can signal "yes" or "no." Phatic communion can function without words easier than the transmission of information can. A warm smile, in fact, can inspire more confidence than the sentence "How are you?" Some people can look so sympathetic that they seem to be actually helping others talk. Others can discourage conversation with their expressions. For expressive communication, movements of the face and body can often be more effective than words. It is rare that words can express boredom, hatred, love, or astonishment as well as the face can. For directive communication, we can stop someone with a stern facial expression or elicit a comment with a look of puzzlement; we can use hand signals to tell someone to come forward, to turn left, to stop, to be quiet, to stand up, and the like.

Each of the uses we found for language can be performed by gestures and facial expressions as well. Rather than trying to decide whether we should make *communication* and *language* synonyms or whether we should restrict our use of the terms, let us distinguish between **verbal** and **nonverbal** communication. Verbal communication is that which uses words. All other is nonverbal. Hence, such expressions as "Go home," "They saw us," "Yes," and "Here" are examples of verbal communication, whereas gasps, groans, laughs, frowns, and nods are nonverbal. In Chapter 2 we will examine the most important aspects of nonverbal communication. Then in Chapter 3 we will compare these aspects with those of verbal communication so that we can determine exactly what a person who is investigating *language* is really studying.

Suggested Reading

COPI, IRVING M., "The Uses of Language," in *Introduction to Logic,* by Irving M. Copi. New York: Macmillan, Inc., 1953.

HAYAKAWA, S. I., *Language in Thought and Action,* 3rd ed. New York: Harcourt Brace Jovanovich, Inc., 1972.

JAKOBSON, ROMAN, "Closing Statement: Linguistics and Poetics," in *Style in Language,* ed. Thomas A. Sebeok. Cambridge, Mass.: The M.I.T. Press, 1960.

MALINOWSKI, BRONISLAW, "The Problem of Meaning in Primitive Languages," in *The Meaning of Meaning,* by C. K. Ogden and I. A. Richards. New York: Harcourt Brace Jovanovich, Inc., 1956.

WHATMOUGH, JOSHUA, *Language: A Modern Synthesis.* New York: St. Martin's Press, Inc., 1956.

Nonverbal Communication

Verbal communication is our most powerful means of exchanging information, yet it is not the only means. Accompanying any act of speech, there are various facial expressions and bodily movements as well as vocal characteristics such as varying degrees of loudness and speed. The value of such nonverbal acts becomes obvious on occasions when we need to confront a person face to face rather than just send a memorandum or a letter. We do not like to talk to a person whose back is turned or who is blocked from view by some object. Except for cases of seduction and certain kinds of scheming, we normally do not like to converse in a dark room; we want to see the person we are talking to.

Our interpretation of what another person says is determined by a number of features. Usually we do not separate verbal and nonverbal acts in our minds, but rather concentrate on the overall effect of what we think the other person is trying to communicate. Yet we have the ability to make such a distinction even if we are not aware of which features actually signal the information. For example, some people can give a compliment or extend an invitation, and we know that they do not really mean what they are saying but rather are just being polite. We may recognize that a mother is trying to convince herself when she says she is happy that her sixteen-year-old daughter is getting married. We can say "You idiot" so that we either insult the other person or express endearment.

All sources of information are not deliberate communicative acts. It is true that we learn something from and base judgments on hair coloring, watery eyes, bruised foreheads, wrinkled necks, and the like; but if we included sources of information such as these as communication, our field of inquiry would have no limits. We would also be dealing more with psychology and anatomy than with language.

Similarly, it is possible to communicate some ideas by merely remaining silent. The old expression "Silence means consent" in many instances holds true. For example, a child may tell his mother that he is going outside to play, or one friend may tell another to wait for him in the car. In either case a reply is unnecessary unless it is negative. Silence can mean consent, but it can also mean "I understand" without necessarily indicating agreement. Under other circumstances silence may indicate that the intended listener did not hear the speaker. At still other times it can signal rudeness, such as when a question is not responded to. There is usually room for considerable misunderstanding over silence. Although most of the ideas communicated by silence could also be expressed by sentences, we will not be referring to a "language of silence." As a device for communication, silence is not structured in any systematic, precise manner.

Of more interest to us are the facial expressions and various body movements which people use in place of language or along with it. Many of these are involuntary and are apparently instinctive since they are found among people all over the world. Certain facial expressions clearly indicate fright, pain, boredom, ecstasy, and a few other emotions. Even a visitor from a radically different culture would not need an interpreter to explain these expressions. We learn most of our gestures, however, from our cultural environment. People in some countries have been said to "speak with their hands"; that is, they customarily have a great deal of body motion when they are speaking. There is also much variation among people within a given culture, some of them being "poker-faced" and using very few facial motions and others being much more "vivacious." Even in the motions of a single individual there is much variation, depending upon whether he is bored or excited. Most of these gestures and facial expressions, though expressive of emotions, are not referential.

In addition to involuntary facial expressions, there are other motions which are symbolic. These obviously have to be learned. For example, children do not instinctively know what the sound of clapping hands means, but they learn that if it is accompanied by a smile they are being applauded for doing something clever. On the other hand, if one or two claps are accompanied by a stern facial expression, they are being reprimanded. Later they learn that clapping after certain programs indicates pleasure or politeness. On other occasions it may mean agreement with a statement made by a speaker or pleasure at the entrance of a celebrity, or it may be used as an accompaniment to music. In some cultures it may mean that a servant or other subordinate is being called.

Other gestures include those used by a policeman for directing traffic, by a driver for signaling a turn, or by anyone to indicate "Be quiet," "Come here," "Thumbs down," and the like. Other systems, such as semaphore, are based directly on language and are, therefore, different from the gestures we are discussing.

Nonverbal Communication Used in Place of Language

Probably the most complex forms of nonverbal communication used independently of language are mime, ballet, and interpretive dancing. These art forms can express emotions and relate events that are often quite lengthy and involved. Facial expressions and bodily motions that at other times accompany language are used, and they are usually exaggerated to prevent misunderstanding. Painting and sculpture, too, often capture the facial expressions and body positions which signal grief, happiness, despair, and the like, communicating without language.

It is sometimes difficult to communicate by means of language because of distance or noise; as a result, people have developed systems of conventional signals that do not depend upon specific words for their interpretation. A ground controller uses such signals to direct airplanes moving to an unloading gate or those landing on an aircraft carrier. A policeman may direct traffic by means of a few conventionalized signals. A more extensive set of motions is used by sports referees and underwater swimmers. There are many systems of conventional signals such as these that have no specific reference to language, unlike some sign languages such as those used by the deaf to spell out words. A person who understands the conventions of a traffic-control officer or a sports referee can follow the directions even if he and the person making the signals do not speak the same language.

In addition to systems of signals, there are isolated ones, such as an upraised hand with the palm out, meaning "Stop." Other hand motions signal "Come here," "Be quiet," "In that direction," "Good-bye," and the like. Motions of the head mean "Yes" or "No." Like the systems of signals, these are conventional and may be completely arbitrary, although many of them are closely related to the idea conveyed, such as a hand motion to the left to indicate that the driver is to move in that direction.

If we consider the messages that can be conveyed by means of signals such as these, whether within a system or isolated, the number is extremely small compared with the message potential of language. A policeman directing traffic or a service station attendant helping someone park on the grease rack has only a few messages that he can convey with his hand motions. A person thumbing a ride can signal only one idea. Moreover, new signals are added to one's repertoire only rarely. Language, on the other hand, adds words readily; some of them, such as *nonbreakfaster,* are immediately understandable by anyone who is fluent in the language, and they may not even be recognized as new. More productively, the rules for forming sentences in any language allow an unlimited number of sentences to be created, almost all of them new to any person. Except for such trivial examples as motions meaning "Be quiet and come here," it is not possible to combine conventionalized nonverbal signals into new messages. Whereas the elements of language constitute an open system that may be extended at will and permits an unlimited number of combinations, the elements of nonverbal signals are part of a closed system that permits only a few combinations.

Eye movements are less conventionalized than most hand signals, but they also convey information. Unless we are trying to catch someone's attention, we stare at him only when he is unaware of our doing so, such as when his back is turned, his eyes are closed, or he is not looking in our direction. If we are caught staring, we rapidly look away and sometimes even apologize. Children as young as six or seven have usually learned this form of social behavior. Another instance of such behavior occurs when people are walking toward each other. They are free to look so long as they are quite far apart, but when they reach a crucial point, they look at some other object—perhaps a blank wall or the sidewalk—or they approach with unfocused eyes. As they come closer, to the point at which their voices will carry without shouting, they look at each other only if they are planning to speak. If they are not going to speak, they continue not looking until they have passed. Likewise, if people are jammed together in an elevator, subway, or waiting area, they are careful not to look at others who might be aware of them unless they are trying to attract their attention.

This type of eye movement generally reflects politeness and respect for the other person, or at worst simply the impersonal character of modern life. But such eye behavior can also reveal distinctly negative attitudes. By not really looking at people, we can snub them, and if we are afraid unsavory characters are about to ask us for money, we are careful not to see them. The reaction of other people is usually that we have "looked right through them" or "treated them as though they didn't exist." On the other hand, if we stare at people who are within the forbidden distance, we are either being consciously rude or else indicating that we consider them incapable of feeling, as animals or statues would be.

If people lock eyes, the meaning is often sexual availability. Other clues, such as clothing, posture, and locale, indicate whether an exchange of money is expected or not. Like many other nonverbal signals, locked eyes have to be interpreted in context. If the eyelids are tensed and narrowed slightly, the meaning may be hostility rather than availability. Also, under certain circumstances people lock eyes to indicate a mutual feeling of amusement, annoyance, or shock over some event that they are both experiencing.

In addition to eye movements which signal politeness, respect, sexual availability, hatred, and mutual feelings, there are those which serve as traffic signals. When people who are meeting are within eight or ten feet of each other, one of them looks in the direction in which he is intending to pass in order to avoid collision. If the other person receives the signal and agrees to abide by it, he moves to the opposite side. Usually people are unaware of how these maneuvers are made even though they may practice them very adroitly many times a day. People who are constantly bumping into others even when there is adequate space for passing usually have not mastered these eye signals, and their collisions are caused more by their failure to follow conventions than by any lack of coordination. Those few people who stick to the center of any sidewalk or hallway, refusing to yield, are obviously destroying the possibility for communication by ignoring any eye signals they may receive.

Within recent years much has been written about the space which birds, animals, and humans feel to be theirs. Whether this is the territory claimed as a home or the space enveloping a person, people communicate information by respecting or violating it. There are, for example, prescribed distances to be maintained for passing in a hallway, standing and watching a fire, or any other occasion for which people come together. When these distances are not observed, people begin feeling crowded even though they are not actually touching. Although theaters and classrooms are normally equipped with individual seats, it often makes us uncomfortable if a stranger takes the seat next to ours when the room is not crowded and seats have not been assigned. There have been a number of interesting experiments conducted by psychologists in which the researcher sits closer than normal to a person on a park bench or intrudes on his space in some other way. The subject almost invariably becomes disturbed and leaves. Only when crowding is unavoidable do people not interpret it as an attack. In such cases, as in an elevator or in a waiting area, they hug their arms as closely as possible to their bodies and try to shrink. Except for such unavoidable contacts, intrusion on someone's personal space is normally interpreted as an act of either hostility or endearment. In fact, it is felt to be the same as actually touching; and in a sense it is, if we think of this space as an extension of the person's body. By merely coming too close, we can signal endearment or hostility even if we do not go so far as to kiss, caress, shove, or hit the other person. The difference between actually touching and intruding on personal space is one of degree rather than a difference in the nature of the message signaled.

A complete discussion of human nonverbal communication would include descriptions of the facial movements which accompany laughing, frowning, crying, looking puzzled, and the like. Each of these motions signals information and is not dependent upon language. Also, such devices of self-presentation as the nature and condition of clothing, hair styling, cleanliness, and posture convey information about one's social status, occupation, degree of masculinity or femininity, and overall personality. Unlike height, sex, and skin coloring, these characteristics can be altered at will, and through them people are consciously or unconsciously saying something about themselves. For a book such as this one, an extended treatment of such matters would be impractical since our primary concern is language. By giving a brief account of them, however, we are able to place language in perspective, showing how it differs from other means of communication.

Controlling Relationships during Verbal Exchange

Although nonverbal communication is much more restricted than language is in the messages it can signal, it is more pervasive. It often exists without language, yet it also normally accompanies verbal communication. When both are found together, nonverbal signals serve the function of reinforcing verbal communication, providing cues which emphasize ideas or focus on their proper interpretation. Fitting between nonverbal signals which are used to replace language and those which reinforce it are signals in a third group: those which control the relationships between people who are communicating. Among these are the motions which set off certain people as members of a group and exclude others, those which establish certain individuals as dominant and others as subordinate, those which help to determine the formality of the situation, and those which signal the beginning or ending of a conversation.

It would be hard to imagine a more tightly knit conversational group than a football team in a huddle. They form a close circle and even place their arms around one another. In this way they are insuring the inclusion of all members who belong and the exclusion of all others; more importantly, they are able to speak softly enough to prevent outsiders from overhearing. Two people on a date frequently form a similar unit to whisper secrets and endearing phrases. Although less tightly knit, groups of people in theater lobbies or at parties stand in circles which include the participants and exclude all others. Even though they do not actually touch one another, the individuals in these groups stand close enough together that another person cannot enter the circle unless the others widen it and make room for him. If he is not welcome, he has to remain on the outside. After struggling to understand the bits of conversation which reach him, he will probably give up and move to another group. The circle unites the participants and excludes others; in fact, it is usually impossible for someone outside the group to listen to what is being said.

People may form circles while sitting as well as while standing. They do not normally arrange their chairs in a perfectly round pattern, but they compensate for this by adjusting their body positions. In addition, they may cross their legs so as to lock in the members of the group and keep others out. The positioning of bodies is especially apparent at a small square table if three people are talking and an intruder sits in the fourth chair. The two sitting on each side of him will angle their bodies facing the other member of their group. They may even use their arms to shut him out, for example, placing the elbow of the arm nearest the intruder on the table and laying that arm flat or else propping up the head with it.

Other motions serve the function of establishing the relative status of the members of a group. In many countries there is a belief in the equality of all people, and there is good reason to try to carry out this belief in matters of law, courtesy, humanitarianism, and the like. In most of their relations, however, and especially in verbal exchanges, people usually establish a ranking of dominance and subordination. Such ordering is commonplace among most animal species, and it becomes obvious among humans with their clubs, military organizations, and groups in which certain members are the leaders. A pecking order usually exists also among people gathered to talk even though they may not be conscious of it. Since one sign of dominance is being physically higher than others, like a monarch on a dais, a person unsure of his status may sit up as straight as possible or even stand while the others are sitting. Thus we find some people kneeling, bowing, curtsying, or even prostrating themselves before others. Two people arguing may even look like two roosters as they stretch their necks in an attempt to rise above the other. Usually the leader is the one who is first to sit down, rise, light a cigarette, or cross his legs.

Status signals are much less rigid than are the principles governing language. For example, a person who is secure in his position as the dominant member of the group may slouch down in his chair or lie on the floor. He may even talk less than the others. These actions, of course, are akin to inverted snobbism. He is going to opposite extremes to show that he does not have to depend on the conventional signals for his position. Another example can be seen in some family units with the father occupying the largest, most comfortable chair and frequently being asked for advice or decisions. In reality the small, reticent, timid-looking wife may be tyrannically wielding the whip. She is the one who is actually making the decisions and whom the others are following in sitting down, crossing their legs, and the like. In still other situations a person who does not rise when a waiter, employee, or other person enters is maintaining his superior position even though he is physically lower than the other person. Since he does not move from his chair, no one could believe that he is offering it to the other person.

An especially revealing signal of rank is eye contact. The dominant person will give a bold, unwavering look, whereas the very shy subordinate will hardly look another person in the eye. In some cultures children and servants are taught to show respect by not looking directly at their superiors. Sometimes children make a game of seeing who can outstare an opponent. In this situation the dominant one wins, although the children normally do not interpret the results in this manner. As with other actions, once the relative status is firmly established, the dominant person may no longer feel the need for controlling the situation with his eyes and may scarcely look at the other one.

Invading the personal space of others and even touching them can be a signal of rank even more noticeable than eye movements. Teachers often feel free to pat children on their shoulders, backs, or heads, but they would be offended if the actions were reciprocated. Some women, especially those of less than average height, are annoyed by people who feel free to pat them on the top of the head. Women secretaries have complained that some male bosses frequently touch them even when no sexual advances are intended. If they ever patted back, the action would definitely be looked upon as a brazen attack and as petting rather than patting. After all, there are differences in salary and employment status. There may be additional ones in age and education. For some people sexual differences are an equally strong source of inequality.

In one American college the Dean of Women obtained the reputation of being a martinet. Girls who were caught cheating, stealing, or appearing in public with their hair in curlers were unfailingly summoned to her office. They dreaded these confrontations, primarily because of the seating arrangement. What the Dean apparently did was sit on the periphery of the personal space boundary and on crucial words lean forward and enter the personal territory. Although she did not actually touch the girls, they had the sensation of being repeatedly jabbed. Strong reprimands are frequently delivered in this fashion, whether by teachers, parents, or sergeants in basic training units. An especially good illustration can be seen if one shakes his index finger at a person from a distance of six feet and then moves closer to a distance of six inches and shakes it. The actions are usually more unpleasant than the actual words that accompany them.

Closely connected to the property of dominance in a relationship is that of formality. The stronger the dominant-subordinate pattern is, the greater the degree of formality. It would be hard to imagine a more formal situation than that of a monarch on a throne giving an audience to a kneeling subject. At the opposite end of the scale, two people who consider themselves approximately equal in rank can engage in very informal conversations.

In most classrooms the teacher is the dominant member; he or she, therefore, determines the degree of formality that will exist. For large classes there is always considerable formality: the teacher stands on a platform, separated from the class by a lectern and physical space; he or she is the only one allowed to speak, and may even use a microphone. Because of the size of the group, there is little opportunity for reducing formality; any approaches to informality have to come from the nature of the lecture itself. For smaller groups the teacher can choose how formal or informal the class will be. By standing behind a lectern and never moving, the teacher establishes dominance over the class both by distance and height, and ensures a highly formal situation. The distinction of height can be maintained while lessening that of distance if the teacher walks around in front of the class. Both distance and height can be reduced if he or she stands in front of the teacher's desk and leans back or even sits on it. Sitting behind the desk places the teacher on the same height as the students (provided that the desk is not on a platform), but it provides a maximum of distance. The most informal arrangement occurs when the teacher sits in the same kind of chair or desk as the students do and is no farther from them than they are from one another. This is the typical seminar arrangement, in which everyone is seated around a table or in student desks arranged in a circle.

In an interview or conference varying degrees of formality can be provided, depending upon how unequal the participants are (or perceive themselves to be). Two people are at the greatest distance if they talk across a large desk; the distance is lessened if the interviewee sits at the side of the desk. In some offices there are easy chairs so that people can move away from the desk and sit in a more informal setting. Posture, too, is adjusted according to the formality of the situation. On the most formal occasions people sit stiffly on the edge of a chair, in the position that was cultivated by tightly corseted women in the past. For less formal situations they may sit back in a relaxed position. Or they may sit on the base of their spine with their legs sprawled out or even slung over an arm of the chair.

The dominant person not only determines the degree of formality of a conversation; that person also terminates the conversation. He may lean forward in his chair, start shuffling papers, look at his watch, or even rise. In some situations he may turn and start talking to someone else.

It should be emphasized that nonverbal acts are not the only devices which determine relationships. Language itself varies according to the formality of the situation and the relative status of the individuals involved. In extremely formal situations between people of radically different social status, there are characteristic honorifics such as *sir, your majesty, your honor,* and the like which are seldom found elsewhere. These words, along with a type of language which is formal in other characteristics such as its avoidance of slang, coexist with spatial distance and differences in height. At the opposite end of the scale, as people are sitting at the same height and lounging in relaxed postures, they are calling each other by their first names, omitting honorifics, using a great deal of slang or shop talk, and generally avoiding sentence structures, words, and pronunciations which belong to formal speech. We shall return to this topic in Chapter 15 after we have learned enough about the various aspects of language to enable us to discuss contextual styles systematically.

Nonverbal Signals That Accompany Language

At the beginning of this chapter we spoke of the close interrelationship between verbal and nonverbal communication. It is because nonverbal signals are only partially included in writing that we often feel we do not know what a person really thinks about a subject unless we confront him face to face. As an example, we can consider "You stinker!" or "You silly ass!" There is no way to punctuate either expression to show whether the writer felt anger or amusement. When spoken, expressions such as these are normally unambiguous; in fact, the listener even knows how angry or how amused the speaker is. Nonverbal signals provide part of the actual content of the message. They can also emphasize the verbal aspect of communication: "We were *really* impressed." Or they can contradict the verbal act, as when a person describes something as "good" or "interesting" and it is obvious that he does not mean it. Whenever verbal and nonverbal signals contradict each other, we assume that the nonverbal clues are the more reliable and accept them as giving the real meaning. It is much easier to give misinformation verbally than nonverbally. For example, "Isn't this exciting" and "Isn't this boring" are equally easy to say in a neutral tone of voice, but it takes considerable effort to sound convincing for either sentence unless the speaker is actually experiencing the emotion. Most people find it easier to lie when they are writing than when they are speaking, even though they may use the same words and sentence structures in both instances.

Nonverbal signals which accompany language are usually classified under two headings: **paralanguage** and **kinesics.** Paralinguistic signals are those which are popularly called tone of voice; kinesic signals are the various motions made by the head, hands, and other parts of the body. Although both kinds of signals are an indispensable accompaniment to language, research on this aspect of communication has been scant. There is currently no scholarly framework within which nonverbal signals can be discussed. As a result, most of what follows is suggestive rather than explicit and anecdotal rather than systematic or explanatory.

All spoken sentences are uttered with characteristic patterns of stress and pitch. At one time it was thought that stress is mainly dependent upon the degree of loudness and force with which a person speaks, but recent studies have shown that it is more intimately connected with pitch than was originally thought; we will, therefore, not try to separate the two. With normal intonation a person in saying "He went to town" will have heavier stress on *town* than on any other word. Accompanying this heavy stress is a rise in the pitch level, followed by a lowering of pitch and a fading of the voice. If we want to express disbelief, anger, or other emotion over the fact that town is the place he went, we may increase both the level of stress and the height of pitch on *town*. In so doing, we are not using distinct paralinguistic signals but rather those which are normally present, only in a different degree. We can draw an analogy between stress and pitch in speech and the volume on a radio. We usually speak of a radio as being merely "too loud," "normal," or "too soft," although we can alter the loudness by continuous degrees as we turn a knob; there are not just three states. Similarly, we often speak of "normal stress" and "emphatic stress" when there is an unbroken range. We signal our degree of anger, amazement, and other emotions by altering our degree of stress and pitch. This is also the means by which we show contrast: "I didn't say that she was *pass*ionate; I said she was *com*passionate!"

For another example we can look at the duration of time we hold a vowel. In normal speaking, the vowel in *bed* is longer than the one in *bet,* as we can easily discover by saying "I'm going to bet" and then "I'm going to bed." In English a vowel before a [d] is held longer than one before a [t]. If a person wishes to emphasize *bed,* he will increase this vocalic duration while he is increasing the pitch and stress levels. For example, if he is asked, "Are you going to the party?" he may respond, "No, I'm going to *bed.*" Increased duration can have varying meanings, depending upon the context. A slightly different meaning from that found in "I'm going to *bed*" can be found in "They *lied*" when the vowel in *lied* is prolonged. As with stress and pitch, vocalic length is a feature which is found normally in speech; it can be intensified to express a range of emotions.

Other features such as overall volume, tempo, and tenseness of the speech-producing apparatus can likewise be increased or decreased to provide information. The lack of an adequate framework for discussing such paralinguistic features becomes obvious when we find playwrights giving such cryptic directions as "angrily" or "with amazement." Most of the time they give no instructions about nonverbal signals, depending upon the actors to work out their own. This reticence gives the actors much freedom of interpretation. For example, Hedda Gabler has been played both as a cold, outwardly passionless, but firm woman and as one who is loud, vulgar, and outgoing.

A good example of the wide range of meanings which one can achieve by means of paralinguistic features is given by Roman Jakobson (1960:354).[1] He reports that an actor at Stanislavskij's Moscow Theater at his audition had to make forty different messages from the phrase *segodnja vecherom,* "this evening." At a later time Jakobson asked him to repeat the exercise for a controlled experiment. The actor used the same phrase and wrote down fifty different situations in which it might be used. He then read the phrase fifty times into a tape recorder, each reading reflecting one of his

[1] Following the style found in virtually all current publications in linguistics, we refer to a work by the author, date of publication, and page number. Hence, *Jakobson (1960:354)* is a citation from a work by Jakobson which was published in 1960. The page cited is 354. Full references are to be found in the bibliography at the end of this book.

situations. The recording was then played to a number of native speakers of Russian, who were able to give the correct situation for most of the utterances. Even a speaker of English who has no special talent for acting can usually say "Hello" or some similar word or phrase in at least a dozen distinctive ways, clearly indicating surprise, disgust, amusement, and so forth. Experiments such as these clearly show that the differences in meaning are brought about by paralanguage, not by kinesic signals or verbal language.

Our desire to hear a person express his or her ideas rather than just read a written account of them reflects our dependence upon paralanguage in ascertaining the speaker's full meaning. The fact that we also want to see the person who is speaking shows that we need kinesic signals as well. We are alert to various motions of the mouth, nose, eyes and eyebrows, head, hands, arms, and other parts of the body. We also learn that all of these motions do not necessarily have any bearing on the message that is being transmitted. After all, we do squint our eyes because of the sun, scratch our head because it itches, or shift our position because we are uncomfortable. In addition, most people make many movements which do not signify anything. They make these same movements even when they are not talking or listening. It is rare for a person who is not paralyzed to remain totally motionless for extended periods of time. We learn to disregard movements such as these and those which result from physical causes not related to the message.

The eyes reflect a great deal of a person's attitude toward the message that he is uttering or listening to. If his pupils are dilated and his eyes are sparkling and focused on an object or person, he is extremely interested in the subject being discussed. He further shows his interest or lack of it by the direction in which he looks. We learn to associate truthfulness, honesty, and sincerity with an unabashed look at the other person; and we associate embarrassment, discomfort, and lying with avoiding the other person's eyes. We realize how much we notice the eyes when we talk to people who are wearing dark glasses, especially if they keep them on indoors.

Unless people are engaged in some task which they have to watch closely, they look intermittently at each other. The speaker reflects his true attitude toward his subject by his eyes. When he pauses he also indicates whether he is willing to be interrupted or not. If he looks directly at the listener during a pause, he is willing to yield; if he looks away, he is merely pausing and does not wish to be interrupted. Much of his looking at the other person is for the purpose of receiving feedback to his statements. A person who is listening normally looks at the other person about twice as much as he does when he is speaking. He is, in effect, directing the speaker, signaling him that he is bored or interested, that he is getting the point more rapidly than the speaker is talking or that he is having trouble understanding, that he agrees or disagrees, and so forth. Although there is much variation among people as to the amount of time they look at people with whom they are talking, it rarely interferes with our ability to use this device for inferring information.

The eyes by themselves are actually quite limited in the amount of information they can give. Although it may appear to do so, this statement does not contradict the evidence we presented in the last two paragraphs. It is true that authors of medical textbooks that contain pictures often find a wide black line across the eyes of a patient sufficient for concealing his identity. On the other hand, a mask two inches in width can also hide a person's identity, despite holes that reveal the eyes. Even more expressive than the eyeballs is the surrounding area. To show amazement, a person moves his eyelids so that they are as wide apart as possible; to limit the focus for concentration or firmness, he narrows them to a slit. Although we speak of opening and squinting the *eyes,* it is actually the *lids* which we move. In addition, the brows and forehead do not remain motionless, but contribute to our overall impression of the "language" of the eyes.

The rest of the face is also important in communication. To a lesser degree, a person uses his nose to signal information, dilating it or "crinkling" it up. And he uses his mouth to smile, frown, gawk, smirk, and the like. The entire head is nodded or shaken to indicate agreement, disagreement, or astonishment. It can be cocked to one side. It is the combination of these motions with those of the eyes that a person looks for in someone with whom he is talking.

It is not necessary for us to go into detail about the motions of the shoulders, arms, hands, and legs, since the use of kinesic signals has been adequately suggested in the preceding paragraphs. A number of figures of speech have their origin in paralanguage and kinesic signals: *Don't get in a huff, Grit your teeth, Keep a stiff upper lip, Don't shrug it off, Don't sweat it, Chin up,* and the like.

Some people have speculated that nonverbal communication preceded language in man's evolution. We have absolutely no way to test this idea since all people, including the most primitive savages, have fully developed languages. Nor are there any reliable records of ancient people who relied exclusively upon gestures and grunts for communication. At an earlier time when linguists were less particular about evidence, there were quite a few fanciful theories invented for the way man developed language out of his already existing nonverbal communication system. These theories were eventually given the delightful names of *bow-wow, ding-dong, yo-he-ho, woo-woo,* and so forth, depending upon whether language was thought of as beginning with attempts to imitate sounds in nature, with automatic, natural responses to stimuli, with sounds for cooperative work such as tugging, or with noises for making love.[2] Since guesswork such as this is no longer considered scholarly, we will not dwell on it.

It is impossible to show how man developed language out of a prior nonverbal communication system, or even whether he in fact did, but it is possible to compare the two means of communication as they exist today. For effective exchanges of information to any extensive degree, both verbal and nonverbal signals are indispensable. When either is missing, the loss is noticed. Even writing does not use verbal signals exclusively; it indicates some nonverbal actions by means of punctuation and varying types such as boldface and italics. Trying to decide which kinds of signals are the more im-

---

[2] An interesting discussion of these earlier theories can be found in Chapter 21 of Jespersen (1964).

portant may be like trying to determine which side of a coin is the more valuable. We would be severely restricted if we had to rely exclusively upon either verbal or nonverbal signals.

Suggested Reading

ARGYLE, MICHAEL, *Social Interaction*. London: Methuen & Co., Ltd., 1969.

BIRDWHISTELL, R. L., *Kinesics and Context*. Philadelphia: University of Pennsylvania Press, 1970.

BRUN, T., *The International Dictionary of Sign Language*. London: Wolfe Publishing Co., Ltd., 1969.

COOK, M., "Experiments on Orientation and Proxemics," *Human Relations* 23 (1970): 61–76.

EKMAN, P., "Non-verbal Leakage and Clues to Deception," *Psychiatry* 32 (1969): 88–106.

———, "Pan-cultural Elements in Facial Displays of Emotion," *Science* 164 (1969): 86–88.

FAST, JULIUS, *Body Language*. New York: M. Evans & Co., Inc., 1970.

GOFFMAN, ERVING, *Strategic Interaction*. Philadelphia: University of Pennsylvania Press, 1970.

HALL, EDWARD T., *The Hidden Dimension*. Garden City, N. Y.: Doubleday & Company, Inc., 1966.

———, *The Silent Language*. Garden City, N. Y.: Doubleday & Company, Inc., 1959.

HINDE, R. A., ed., *Non-verbal Communication*. Cambridge: Cambridge University Press, 1972.

VINE, I., "Communication by Facial-Visual Signals," in *Social Behaviour in Animals and Man*, ed. J. H. Crook. New York: Academic Press, Inc., 1971.

Features of
Verbal Communication

We have now taken an overview of nonverbal signals and seen how intimately related they are to language in acts of communication. When used in place of language, nonverbal signals are limited in the number of unambiguous ideas they can impart. Similarly, language without the nonverbal aspect is deficient in many ways. In this chapter we will be examining the more important features of verbal communication so that we can compare them with those of nonverbal acts and arrive at some notion of the nature of language and communication in general.

Language and Instinct

Linguists in the past have usually stated that language is not acquired instinctively but rather is culturally transmitted. Evidence for such a belief is not hard to find. Most instinctive actions are very much alike throughout the world and are not greatly affected by cultural differences: crying, yawning, sucking, kicking, and the like. If language were instinctive, there would be only one world language, not the twenty-five hundred or so which actually exist.

Language varies not only among cultures, but from one period of time to another, as we can easily see by comparing writing at periodic intervals in any language which has written documents extending back for several centuries. If the time machines of science fiction ever became a reality, we would expect the person sent back or ahead in time to see virtually no differences in the way people smile, cry, walk, and perform other instinctive actions. With language he would see considerable change. Any activity which varies radically with time and among different cultures is not instinctive.

Further evidence for the noninstinctive nature of language can be found among children who have not been exposed to human communication. Disregarding questionable accounts such as those of Romulus and Remus, the legendary founders of Rome, there are documented cases of children who have been discovered living alone in the forests or as extra cubs of wolves or other animals. Among these are the Hessian wolf boy (1349), the Lithuanian bear boy (1661), Wild Peter of Hanover (1724), Victor of Aveyron (1797), and Kamala and Amala of India (1920).[1] The story of Victor of Aveyron was made into the movie *L'enfant sauvage* (*The Wild Child*) by François Truffaut in 1969. None of these children had developed a language. Periodically another kind of isolated child comes to public notice—the one who is kept locked in an attic, cellar, or closet and given no attention other than feeding. Like the wild children, these have not developed a language. There are no verifiable accounts of children isolated from human communication who have learned to speak.

Two observations have led some people to suppose that learning a language is similar to learning other culturally transmitted skills. First, exposure to language is essential for its acquisition; and second, children will learn any language to which they are given sufficient exposure, regardless of the language spoken by their biological parents. Some educators have assumed that children upon experiencing a stimulus such as hunger imitate a word they have heard, *milk,* and are then rewarded with milk to drink. Through repetition the children reinforce what they have learned. Scholars writing with this assumption have generally presented conclusions that are indefensible when subjected to actual facts about language.

There are several ways in which learning to speak a language differs from acquiring other skills. Whereas a person can learn to play chess, to dance, or to make wood carvings at almost any age, his ability to learn a language natively deteriorates rapidly after he reaches puberty. After that time he must spend many hours of intensive study to gain any kind of facility, and except in the most rare cases he will speak the new language with a foreign accent. Second, in learning a language a person masters a body of material which is infinitely more complex than anything else he learns during the rest of his lifetime. One contribution of linguistic research of the past few years has been a demonstration of how complex language really is. By complexity linguists are not referring simply to vocabulary. Rather, they mean the system into which words fit. The greatest part of this learning is completed by the time the child is about six or eight years old. Third, if instruction or learning conditions are poor, a person will not learn to type, play the trumpet, or make pottery. Except in the most severe cases of mental retardation or emotional disturbance, however, a child who is exposed to a language learns it. No one is really "taught" his mother tongue; teaching is either nonexistent or very sketchy and poor. Similarly, learning conditions are never optimal, since poorly formed sentences are heard at least as often as those that are well constructed; yet the child in some way knows to ignore malformations when he is forming his theories about language. Fourth, all humans acquire a language, and there are discernible patterns in the ways

---

[1] A convenient discussion of children who have survived outside of human society can be found in Chapter 5 of Brown (1958).

in which they learn. There are no groups of people anywhere in the world without language. Fifth, motivation cannot have a major influence on the acquisition of a skill so uniformly distributed throughout the human race as language is. Some children are so neglected that it does not matter what they ask for or how they ask for it. Others are so pampered that they seem to obtain everything they want simply by yelling loudly.

Although language learning is not *instinctive* in the usual sense of the word, there is enough evidence to suggest that every child will learn the language or languages to which he is given sufficient exposure.[2]

Language and Voluntary Symbols

A related concept is that language is voluntarily produced. In this way it is not like a spontaneous blush, a gasp, or a giggle. These reactions and others like them communicate information about our emotional or physical state, but they are involuntary. Of course, a person who is not really hurt when he mashes his finger may think to say "Ouch!" or "Damn!" or even something more colorful. These are voluntarily produced words, unlike the sounds which come forth naturally and which are really impossible to represent with our spelling system.

The voluntarily produced utterances which constitute language are composed of **symbols.** In loose terms, we usually think of a symbol as something which stands for something else, as the color black does for mourning in most European countries. For another example, many public buildings have alarm systems which warn people to evacuate the building because of fire or some other danger. Traffic lights constitute another system of symbols, with three colors, flashing lights, and arrows signaling different kinds of information. A sports referee has various hand motions which signal his decisions. And a person when speaking represents ideas by characteristic combinations of sounds such as the words *bird, ground,* and *drink.* We are constantly encountering various kinds of symbols.

It is hard for some people to accept the statement that the words in a language are arbitrary. Especially to the person with limited contacts outside his own circle, it seems "natural" that an English speaking person should use *chair, shrub,* and *dog* to name certain objects. This kind of "logic" can be shown to be faulty when we compare words in various languages. What the Englishman calls a *dog* is a *chien* to a Frenchman, a *perro* to a Spaniard, a *Hund* to a German, a *sobaka* to a Russian, an *inu* to a Japanese, and a *kelb* to an Arab. There is nothing about the animal to make any of these terms more appropriate than the others.

We might try arguing that the etymologies of words often reveal reasons for names. For example, the English word for a writing instrument, *pen,* is ultimately derived from the Latin *penna,* "feather." Since pens were at one time made from feathers, the name *pen* seems natural. Similarly, in German the object is called a *Feder,* "feather," and in French a *plume,* "feather"

---

2 Lenneberg (1967) gives a full and interesting discussion of the ideas presented in this section.

(cf. *plumage*). Although such etymologizing goes back at least to the time of Plato, it actually proves nothing. We can link the name for a quill pen with that for a feather because the two were once the same thing. But what is logical about linking the word *feather, penna, Feder,* or *plume* with the object it names now? In reality, this kind of comparison provides evidence for the arbitrary nature of words. Once people stopped making writing instruments from feathers, there was no longer any logical reason to continue calling them by the name *pen,* or *Feder,* or *plume.* In fact, if names were based on logic, these should have been abandoned. Most languages have many words which show marked alterations from their earlier meanings. Since most paper is no longer made from papyrus and most spinsters have never been near a spinning wheel, such words as *paper* and *spinster* are now extremely arbitrary.

Another kind of possible argument for a logical connection between names and the objects they represent can be found in onomatopoeic words. When we say *pop, ring, crackle, splatter, swish,* or *drop,* we are attempting to reproduce the sound that we hear. Although words such as these normally show a recognizable relation to the sound, there is a certain amount of arbitrariness even in them. A rock falling into a body of water or wind whistling through trees probably sounds the same to everyone, yet people reproduce what they hear according to the conventions of their language. For example, the sound made by a dog is represented by *ouâ ouâ* in French, *hau hau* in Polish, *vau vau* in Latvian, *vov vov* in Norwegian, *hau hau* in Arabic, *wau wau* in German, *wang wang* in Chinese, *wan wan* in Japanese, *ho ho* in Persian, *waf waf* in Dutch, *amh amh* in Irish, *bhau bhau* in Hindi, *hau hau* in Gujarati, *hav hav* in Turkish, and *guau guau* in Spanish. A speaker of English calls the same sound *woof woof* or *bow wow,* the latter being an especially good example of arbitrariness. Dogs show much variation in the sounds they make, but it takes an especially vivid imagination to hear *bow wow* from any of them.

The Medium of Language

In most parts of the world, verbal communication can be found in various forms. Speech and writing are the most common, but there are others as well, such as Morse code, semaphore, sign language, and the like. To obtain a clear understanding of language, we need to determine whether these various manifestations of verbal communication are independent of one another or whether they are related in some way.

There are several reasons for saying that spoken language is primary and the others are derived from it, some of them indirectly. First of all, almost all children learn to speak before they learn to read and write. There are exceptional cases in which the child learns to read first because of physical handicaps, but these are rare. When a person is able to read and write, it can normally be assumed that he has command of the spoken language; the reverse is not necessarily true, since most children of pre-school age have a good command of the spoken language but limited or no knowledge of writing.

Second, children between the ages of about eighteen months and twelve years automatically learn any language to which they are given sufficient exposure. Except in the most severe cases of mental retardation or emotional disturbance, every child learns at least one spoken language. There is normally no tutoring, and the child encounters much variation in the ways words are pronounced as well as many errors such as stammers and poorly formed sentences. Yet he learns his language well in spite of these errors. With writing, the learning process is different. Children do not learn to read and write from exposure alone. Nor are all children predisposed to learn to read; a child has to have a certain kind of cultural environment before he shows any interest in reading. Even with highly intelligent, well motivated children, there must be a certain amount of teaching if they learn to read. It is doubtful if anyone would ever subject children to an experiment in which the writing they encountered made use of various type fonts, varying spellings for each word, words omitted or transposed, and interrupted sentences—analogous to the spoken language the child hears. If such an experiment were conducted, we could predict that the child would read poorly, if at all. We do know that the development of reading proficiency depends to a great degree upon the pedagogical skills of teachers.

A third reason for saying that speech is more basic than writing involves groups of people. The earliest written records that have been discovered in any language are not more than five thousand years old; some scholars feel that this figure is too generous, that the cuneiform tablets of the Tigris-Euphrates valleys and the Egyptian hieroglyphics are not quite this old. Whatever the exact date, in comparison to the time man has been on earth, these records are very recent. Languages which have written records over two thousand years old are exceptional; most, like English, date from the last fifteen hundred years. In fact, there are still a great many languages in the world which do not have written representations; yet all people of whom we have ever had any knowledge, including the Tasaday, a stone-age tribe of the Philippines, have a spoken language that is fully developed. The written form of any language is always much more recent than the spoken. Every language which has a written form also has a spoken form; the reverse is not true.

Fourth, writing is based on speech, not the other way around. Writing systems represent some level of the spoken language, such as entire words, syllables, or sounds which the speakers recognize as distinct. The linear ordering in which we arrange written representations is based on the time sequence of sounds and words in speech. In an alphabetic system, such as the one used for English, restrictions on combinations and orderings of letters are derived from spoken restrictions. For example there could be no word written *ptk* which followed English spelling conventions because the spoken equivalent would be impossible to pronounce. Furthermore, many of our punctuation conventions follow intonation patterns in speech, yet this correspondence is inexact in some ways, such as the capital letter, which has no spoken counterpart.

Further evidence that writing is based on speech can be found in the fact that changes in the written form of a language usually occur as reflections of earlier changes in the spoken form. The Old English words for *nut, ring, link* were pronounced and spelled with an initial [h]: *hnutu, hring, hlencu.* In the course of time the [h] ceased to be pronounced, and as a result it was dropped in spelling. The English spelling system is extremely conservative, and it is seldom changed in modern times. Such spellings as *nite, tho,* and *thru* have been suggested because of changes in the spoken forms of these words in which the *gh* no longer represents a consonant sound. At one time *blood, stood,* and *mood* were all pronounced with the same vowel, the one heard in Modern English *hope;* hence they are spelled with the same vowel letters. The change in pronunciation was not accompanied by one in spelling. Today if we were to try to make spelling and pronunciation closer, our solution would be to respell the words as *blud, stood,* and *mude.* We would not try to make people repronounce the words to conform with the spellings. That is, we feel that the spoken form of the language should dictate the written form, not the other way around.

The fifth major reason for claiming that speech is more basic than writing lies in frequency of usage. Even highly literate people use spoken language more often than writing; there are, of course, some scholars, writers, editors, and the like who are exceptions. We could add that there are many affairs which people prefer to conduct orally rather than in writing, but this is probably due largely to the nonverbal signals which accompany speech and give a great deal of information.

In the past, statements that speech is "primary" or "more basic" than writing have sometimes been misunderstood; we should, therefore, stress what these statements do *not* mean. The linguists' claim that spoken language is primary does not in any sense make it "better" than writing. Everyone agrees that the English written by Shakespeare and Milton is more aesthetic and worthy of preservation than is a verbal argument in a bar. Furthermore, writing serves a useful function in extending language beyond the space of the speaker's voice and the time in which he speaks. Most written language is more highly polished than speech. In some countries the spoken and written forms of the language may show great differences, such as classical Latin and the language actually spoken during the last centuries of the Roman Empire. With most modern languages, such as French, German, English, Italian, or Russian, the written language can be very close to the spoken, as is true of a note or a letter to an intimate friend. For more formal styles, however, there are usually major differences in vocabulary and sentence structure. In fact, teaching formal composition to native speakers is in many languages—especially English—like teaching a foreign language. Since even the most informal writing differs in some respects from speech, it would be a mistake to think that writing is nothing more than a recording of the spoken language. But it should also be obvious that the spoken language is primary and the written secondary.

We might ask why the primary medium of language is sound, specifically the sound produced by the vocal apparatus. One answer is that for most of the senses, the human body is poorly equipped to project a variety of controlled sensations. For any attempt to communicate by taste, for example, two people would have to be in direct contact, and no one can turn off one taste and turn on another at will. Even if there were a mechanical apparatus which one person could operate while another touched it with his tongue, the process would be cumbersome and its flexibility as an adequate communication system doubtful. Besides, many of the sensations which we think of as coming from taste are really from smell.

We might consider communicating by means of smells. Many living creatures signal sexual and other information by this means. Some of the odors which man projects, such as the one connected with fear, are noticeable only to other species, normally not to man himself. Others such as those of sexual arousal or unwashed feet are not symbolic or controlled but rather a part of the emotion or cleanliness of the body. Even if we had a machine which could emit a variety of controlled smells, communication would be a lengthy process since we would have to wait for each smell to vanish before projecting the next one.

The sense of touch offers greater possibilities for communication since there is no lingering effect, and parts of the body can learn to recognize many different patterns of pressure and vibrations. For example, the sender could shape his fingers in a number of ways which the receiver would feel with his hand. Helen Keller learned to "listen" to music by placing her hand on a radio. Other people "spoke" to her by means of hand signals which they made in her palm; she also learned to place her hands on a speaker's lips and throat and understand what he was saying. In spite of the possibilities of touch, people with normal hearing usually limit it to such tasks as classifying fabrics and determining temperature.

For communication, the sense of sight is more adaptable than is that of touch, as has been effectively shown by semaphore and the sign languages of the deaf and of the American Indians. A person can even learn to read lips with great skill, although this ability is always less perfect than is that of hearing a spoken message. One of the most impressive uses of sight for communication is found in writing. There are many possibilities for effective communication by appealing to the sense of sight. Does the use of sound have any advantages over it?

As with visual communication systems, those with sound do not require that sender and receiver be in physical contact, as those with taste and touch do. They can be anywhere within hearing range of each other. Unlike smells, sound fades rapidly, thereby permitting a rapid succession of audible symbols. Whereas most of the activities we engage in require the use of our hands and eyes, only a few make use of the mouth and ears. Hence, if we use speech for communication, we can free other parts of the body for driving a car, knitting, or carving wood. Although we usually watch a person speaking, at least part of the time, visual contact is not necessary. We can listen to people who are not within sight because of physical obstructions or darkness. A speaker can easily change and adjust his patterns to accommodate the receiver, something which is hardly possible with writing.

Some of the features of speech are not necessarily advantages, but they do influence communication. Because physical contact is not necessary, anyone within range of the speaker's voice can hear the message, not just the intended receiver. Also, the speaker can hear his own messages and correct some of his mistakes. This would not be possible with communication systems which depended upon taste or touch nor with some of those which depended upon sight.

At one time it was popular among linguists to say that there are really no speech organs. The lungs, oral and nasal passages, teeth, tongue, and so forth have the primary function of breathing and eating. Man could not survive without these activities, but he could without language. It was believed that language was purely a product of cultural transmission and that man had learned to make use of the organs of eating and breathing for the secondary, overlaid function of transmitting sound. The lungs and tongue were considered to be speech organs only to the degree that the feet are skating organs or the fingers typing organs.

In recent years researchers in biology, linguistics, and related disciplines have questioned these beliefs. We have already seen that all children except in rare cases learn the language or languages to which they are exposed from around the age of eighteen months to twelve years. There are many ways in which mastering a first language is different from other learning activities.

In addition, various anatomical features are of questionable value if the lungs, tongue, and related organs are intended solely for breathing and eating. For example, the tongue is far more flexible than is needed for directing food between the teeth, and the ear is much more sensitive than is necessary for distinguishing noises in nature. Also, speaking greatly affects breathing actions, increasing the speed of inhaling and decreasing that of exhaling. Whereas swimming, playing the trumpet, and performing similar activities require much practice and instruction in breath control, no one has to be taught how to breathe for normal conversational speaking. Furthermore, a person can speak for an indefinitely long time without noticing any breathing discomfort. Usually mental exhaustion stops a long-winded speaker before any actual physical fatigue does.[3]

If we compare speaking to activities which are unquestionably culturally transmitted—playing the piano or violin, dancing, typing, and the like —we see a great difference. So far no one has proved that man is biologically predestined to speak, in spite of the various observations which have been made. Yet it no longer seems accurate to say that man has organs of speech only to the degree that he has organs of skating, playing the flute, or knitting.

The Systematic Nature of Language

So far, we have had no occasion to comment on the organization of language. This is the topic which will concern us now, and we can illustrate it more clearly if we begin with another possible kind of communication system.

Literature is full of accounts of strange creatures that have been encountered on voyages of discovery. Ulysses came in contact with the one-eyed Cyclops; Othello told about "men whose heads do grow beneath their shoulders"; Raphael Hythloday described the Utopians; Lemuel Gulliver was intrigued by the Lilliputians, Brobdingnagians, and Houyhnhnms. Let

[3] See Lenneberg (1967:80).

us also imagine a mythical land in which everyone is mute and deaf. These people communicate exclusively by means of colors. Everyone carries with him a small machine which permits him to reveal any part of the color spectrum he chooses.

These people live in an environment which forces them to be concerned exclusively with self-protection, finding food, and reproduction. They have only a dozen or so ideas which they communicate to one another, and the system is something like this:

Concept	*Color*
Food	Red
Danger	Blue
I don't like you.	Green

With this system each concept has its unique color symbol to represent it. The relationship between concept and symbol is noninstinctive and arbitrary. Since these people have only a handful of ideas which they communicate, the system is adequate. Of course, the sender of the message must be reasonably near the receiver and in front of him for the colors to be seen. And the system breaks down when it is too dark to distinguish colors or when the intended receiver is not looking in the right direction. Yet it functions reasonably well, and it even allows the introduction of a few new ideas with their own symbols. Since the color spectrum is a continuum on which colors do not exist as discrete units but rather blend into one another, there is really no limit to the positions at which a person may stop and project a shade different from all others.

In another part of this land there is another tribe of people who have learned to control some of the hostilities in their environment, and they have a need for a more sophisticated communication system than that of their neighbors. In fact, they have around two hundred different messages which they send to one another. At first they had the same system as the first tribe, but when their conceptual universe began expanding, they divided the color spectrum more finely, and eventually the system reached the limits of effectiveness. There was no real problem with remembering which color corresponded to each idea, but with rapid communication there was a mechanical problem of the sender's hitting the exact spot on the spectrum. Also, the receiver had trouble distinguishing similar shades and frequently confused messages. For example, by mistaking puce for maroon, he could interpret "Stay away from my territory" as "Come share the feast."

By chance some weird nonconformist came up with a remedy. Instead of restricting the system to a one-to-one basis, he found it possible to use two colors in succession to signal one idea. Other members of the tribe noticed what he was doing and found him a rich source of amusement, as they did the walk of cripples. To add to their merriment, they began imitating him. Soon that which had started out as mockery became the usual practice as the novelty wore off and the advantages became apparent. Of course, everyone did not accept the innovation, and some older members were worried about the future of their tribe if such licentiousness continued.

According to this system, a color by itself symbolized nothing; only combinations had meaning:

Concept	*Colors*
Food	Red + Yellow
Danger	Blue + Green
I don't like you.	Red + Blue

The number of colors in use was limited to ten, a number which could be easily produced and recognized. In this way if the sender did not hit directly on the color but slightly to the left or right of it, no harm was done. The receiver recognized a color as red even if it was slightly purple. At first the ordering of the colors made no difference. *Red + Blue* meant the same thing as *Blue + Red*. However, as the need for more signals developed, someone discovered that the number of possible messages could be doubled if restrictions were placed on the ordering of colors. Since a color could not be combined with itself (e.g., *Red + Red*), ordering was always distinctive. This meant that *Yellow + Purple* did not mean the same thing as *Purple + Yellow*.

In still another part of the land there is a third tribe which has expanded its conceptual universe so far that a much larger number of messages is needed. To accommodate this expansion, they hit on the idea of treating each combination of colors such as *Orange + Blue* as a unit which can be added to other units such as *Pink + Blue* to form a message. Also, they discovered that by permitting more than two colors to come together in each unit, they could multiply the number of units by many times. Hence, a comparison of messages from the three tribes would look like this:

Tribe One: Blue
Tribe Two: Blue + Red
Tribe Three: (Blue + Red) (Orange + Green + Pink) (Green + Red)

The corresponding meanings might be something like the following:

Tribe One: There is danger.
Tribe Two: There is danger behind you.
Tribe Three: There is a dangerous snake behind you.

The system employed by Tribe Two permits the communication of more information than that of Tribe One. The system of Tribe Three permits the most.

There are various problems that the members of Tribe Three have encountered in the past and found solutions to. First of all, people became impatient with the time it took to transmit a message. As a solution they learned that it was not necessary to reveal each color as a separate act with pauses between colors. Rather, they could keep the color machine on throughout the message and let the colors merge into one another without pausing. Visitors from other tribes were unable to make sense of the rapidly changing, blending colors, but members of Tribe Three learned to concentrate on the central point of each color and to ignore the transitional effects. For example, in shifting from yellow to blue there would be a greenish tint, but everyone learned to ignore it and after a time did not even realize that it was there; all they "saw" were yellow and blue.

Another problem arose with the learning process. Members of Tribes One and Two learned their system through repetition. Whether danger was signaled by one color or two, people learned to react to the message and noticed that others who did not react suffered. For each message, if a person gave the correct response, he was rewarded or he avoided something unpleasant. If he gave an incorrect response or none at all, he missed the reward or suffered. With enough repetition he learned the system of communication; those who failed to learn it did not survive. Members of the third tribe probably learned each of their clusters such as *Red + Brown* in this way, but there were too many different messages for this to be possible for the entire system. Even with a limit of ten color units, three units to the cluster, and three clusters to the message, there would be several thousand possible messages. Learning this number of messages would be impossible if all elements were totally arbitrary. Besides, some of them would be encountered so seldom that they would soon be forgotten, and others would not make their initial appearance to a person until he was quite old. There is only one way this problem can be effectively solved. If units are not combined indiscriminately to form messages, but rather are combined by a few regulatory processes, that is, if they are combined systematically, a person will not have to learn each complete message. Instead, he will learn the clusters and a few processes for combining them. As a result he will be able to form or interpret any of the possible messages, whether he has seen them before or not. He will probably not realize the difference between new messages and those he has used in the past.

A third problem that arose involved the intensity with which a person had to concentrate on the process of sending and receiving messages. If equal care has to be given to each color, the process of communication can become quite fatiguing. Also, if the sender makes any mistakes or if the receiver is distracted at any point, the message will not be understood. On the other hand, if the system has a certain amount of repetition and predictability in it, a person can miss parts of the transmission and still understand the overall message. Hence a message such as "There's a snake behind you. It's poisonous. Look out" contains repeated warnings, and a person can miss any of the three components and still be warned. Furthermore, if all combinations of colors are not permitted, the possibilities for misunderstanding are lessened. Perhaps the combination of red and orange is not allowed, either because of custom or because of the difficulty in distinguishing two similar colors in juxtaposition. A person receiving a message may know that one unit within a cluster is red, but he is partially distracted and does not notice whether the other is yellow or orange. Since orange is not permitted with red, the other is obviously yellow. Thus mistakes and distractions will not necessarily lead to total confusion, nor will the receiver have to concentrate intently throughout the entire message.

Our purpose in inventing these three tribes with their communication systems is not to show that human languages are like any of them. Although the system of the third group comes very close to that of language, in some important respects it is less powerful as a means of communication. Nor is it our intention to show that human language evolved through stages like those of Tribes One, Two, and Three. A progression like this is possible, but it would be purely speculative. Since there has already been an abundance of guesswork about the origin of language, there is no point in adding to it. Linguists, anthropologists, and scholars in a great many other fields would be delighted if a tribe of people were discovered who had a language system as simple as that of our second tribe. Their system could furnish a missing link between the call systems of the great apes and human languages. At one time it was thought that languages developed along with the culture of a people, that primitive societies had primitive languages and sophisticated societies sophisticated languages. There were even attempts to show that languages evolved from a state of simplicity to one of complexity, or vice versa. These ideas have been suspect for a great many years. Whereas linguists of the past have been correct in recognizing a simplifying drift in some aspect of a language, they have erred in not recognizing a compensatory complication of another aspect. It has not been shown that an entire grammar becomes simplified or more complex. Furthermore, even the languages of people living in stone-age cultures are well developed and complex. We do not know enough about linguistic structure in general or the structures of particular languages for us to make a satisfactory comparison of the complexity of languages. If there are differences of this nature, they are probably not the kind envisioned by scholars of the past.

The communication systems of Tribes Two and Three made use of ten color units which were transmitted visually. Human languages use a slightly larger number of orally transmitted units called **phonemes.** We will give a precise definition for the phoneme in the section on phonology, but for now we can say that phonemes are generally the sounds which are represented by the letters in an alphabetical writing system. Phonemes refer to the spoken representation, letters to the written. To illustrate, we say that the word *pit* consists of three phonemes, as represented by the letters *p, i,* and *t.* Just as the tribesmen could produce more than ten colors, no language makes use of all the phonemes that are possible. There is practically an unlimited number of different sounds a person can produce with his vocal apparatus, but the number that can be easily distinguished in rapid speech is quite small, usually twenty to fifty. Some phonemes such as those represented by the consonants *p* and *t* in *pit* and by the *a* in *father* are found in almost all languages, but others such as the one represented by *th* in *those* are found in only certain ones. Each language has its own inventory. Phonemes are not produced separately, but rather merge into one another. Some, such as the first sound in *pit,* are not pronounced in isolation but need a vowel sound to accompany them. Although phonemes are altered by those which precede and follow, the speakers of a language ignore these predictable variations and think of them as if they were uttered separately and purely, like the letters on a printed page. In addition, if the speaker does not hit squarely on the vowel sound that is intended for *pit* but comes close enough that it does not sound like the vowel of *Pete, pate,* or *pet,* the listener ignores the variation.

Phonemes by themselves have no meaning, as we can see by the sounds represented by the letters *p, i,* and *t* taken in isolation. Phonemes are organized into units which may have reference, such as *pencil, apple,* and *Agnes.* Other units do not, but rather serve to indicate structure: *to, the, and,* and the like. All combinations of phonemes are not possible. Because of the design of the human vocal apparatus, no language has a word consisting of just the consonants *ktgb.* We speak of the system that governs the phonemes of a language as its **phonology.** This system includes an inventory of phonemes for the language under consideration and restrictions on their arrangement. The system of English, for example, permits *slid* and *snid* as possible words, but not *znid* or *snüd. Znid* violates a restriction against the combination *zn* at the beginning of a word, and *snüd* contains the non-English *ü.* These restrictions apply to English specifically rather than to languages in general, since Russian permits words to begin with *zn,* and both French and German have *ü* as in French *pur* and German *grün.* English permits both *slid* and *snid.* Although only the first is an actual word in the language, the other is possible as a future addition. A fluent speaker of English in some way knows these restrictions on which combinations of phonemes are possible words of the language and which ones are not, although he may not be able to say why, other than that some sound fine and others peculiar.

In addition to phonemes and words, a language has restrictions on the formation of sentences and parts of sentences such as phrases and clauses. These restrictions constitute the **syntax** of the language. Syntax may deal with the ordering of words, as we can see by these sentences:

3.1   The teacher spanked Tommy.
3.2   Tommy spanked the teacher.

This ordering is a characteristic of English, wherein the name of an agent who performs the act is placed before the verb and the object at the end. The concepts of agent and object are probably found in all languages, but the means used to express them vary.

One way of showing that sentences have structure is to examine such ambiguous sentences as

3.3a   He read the magazine you gave him last week.

If the magazine was given to him last week, we understand the structure to be organized like this:

3.3b   He read the magazine [you gave him last week].

That is, *last week* is part of the cluster to which *gave* belongs. For the meaning "Last week he read the magazine you gave him," this grouping is understood:

3.3c   He read the magazine [you gave him] last week.

For another example, we can examine this sentence:

3.4a   They gave preference to young men and women.

The sentence has two possible meanings, depending upon whether we interpret *young* as going with both *men* and *women*—

3.4b   They gave preference to young [men and women].

or just with *men*—

3.4c   They gave preference to [young men] and women.

Finally, consider this sentence:

3.5a   He turned in his grave.

For the usual meaning, *in his grave* constitutes a unit:

3.5b   He turned [in his grave].

There is also a rather farfetched meaning of a person who did not like his grave and turned it in:

3.5c   He [turned in] his grave.

In each of these sentences the person's understanding of the structure determines the meaning he will give to the sentence.

A large part of this book is devoted to an examination of linguistic structures. At this point all we are showing is that language has system. It is not just an unstructured collection of phonemes and words.

Creativity in Language

The existence of such stock phrases as *I'll see you later, Thanks for the ride,* and *I didn't know whether I was coming or going* may suggest that language is nothing more than a set of ready-made expressions. There are unquestionably a great many that everyone knows and uses. In fact, some students discover that much of their writing is composed of such sentences and phrases when they have papers returned with *trite* marked on almost every line. There are several reasons why language must consist of more than stock phrases. The fact that no one has attempted a compilation of English phrases or sentences similar to a dictionary of words suggests that such a project would be impractical. The number of sentences that each person would have to retain would be so large that even a genius could not manage them. Furthermore, if we had to rely upon previously constructed sentences, we would have no way to communicate new ideas. Conversations, lectures, and books which present new information would be impossible, as would many jokes and advertising gimmicks. It is easy to create an unusual sentence such as *The cross-eyed aardvark read poetry on the moon.* A person fluent in English has no trouble understanding the sentence although he has obviously not encountered it before. However, we do not have to use such an unusual sentence to illustrate the creative nature of language. Most people have never heard or seen the following sentence before: *John read eleven books last week.* A person with nothing better to do could waste many hours in the library or before the television set searching for the sentence. Since most of the ideas communicated to us each day are new, most of the sentences we hear are original creations.

One comparison that linguists have frequently made is between language and mathematical skills such as addition. A person who has learned the principles of addition can add any pair of numbers such as 54876 and 23045, whether or not he has ever added them previously. He knows the numbers one through nine and zero, he knows how to form numbers of more than one digit, and he knows a few rules such as the sum of five and six and the carrying principle. Since it is always possible to make a number larger by adding another digit, there is no limit to how many numbers may exist. Yet a person who has learned a few rules can add any of them, whether he has seen them before or not. Language is similar. A person learns a limited number of words and a limited system of rules for combining them into sentences. Because of this system he can create and understand an indefinite number of new sentences.

Each person, then, has acquired a system which permits him to produce and understand the sentences of his language. We can call this system a **grammar** of the language. The actual form of this grammar is still unknown. We can observe and comment on the sentences it produces, but we do not yet know enough about how people think to describe the grammar itself. Trying to understand how language operates, linguists have constructed artificial grammars on paper. The term *grammar* as we are using it means a system which accounts for the sentences of a language. We can use the term to refer to the internalized system that the speaker of a language possesses, a system which is poorly understood but which performs excellently in producing sentences; or we can use it to refer to the linguist's creation. We hope that this creation has much in common with the native speaker's internalized grammar; at present, however, it is incomplete.

Language and the Immediate Environment

Because language is creative, capable of expressing almost any new idea, it is not restricted to statements about the immediate concrete universe. It is not necessary to restrict ourselves to statements about unique objects and actions. Instead, we can group them into larger classes as when we say that Eunice Edwards is a woman, an adult, a human, a Democrat, a Methodist, a philatelist, and the like. We can compare objects and make allusions. We can even talk about quite abstract qualities which have no physical existence, such as truth and optimism. As we see from this book, we can also talk about language.

In addition, we do not have to limit ourselves to comments about nearby objects and events. A person in Tokyo can talk about happenings in Auckland, Vienna, Oslo, or Caracas. He can even talk about objects in outer space. Nor is he limited to statements about that which is currently happening. He can talk about the past, including events he witnessed and others he has been told about, and he can make predictions and statements of intent about the future.

Language handles imaginative statements as well as it does facts. A person can lie, exaggerate, or make understatements. He can daydream and produce fictional creations, and his language is capable of expressing anything he has to say about them. Language is by no means limited to the immediate environment.

Summary

One of the most often cited definitions of language was given by the linguist Edward Sapir (1921:8): "Language is a purely human and non-instinctive method of communicating ideas, emotions, and desires by means of a system of voluntarily produced symbols." A few years ago most linguists would have felt confident about dismissing animal communication with a few paragraphs, showing that it always consists of a closed inventory of a dozen or so signals which relate to fundamental emotions. Whereas some species may indeed have communication systems as primitive as that of our fictional Tribe One, recent research in animal communication has shown that it has been misunderstood and grossly underestimated. Although there has been a large amount of research concerning dolphins, apes, bees, and other species, none of it is far enough advanced yet to be very useful for comparative studies with human language. There are obviously fundamental differences between the communication systems of humans and other species, but no one is in a position to give a precise account of them. If we limit language to verbal communication, many people still agree with Sapir in saying that it is purely human, but they are less smug than some of Sapir's successors were in the evidence they provide for supporting this assertion.

Although over fifty years have passed since Sapir wrote his celebrated definition, we still agree with most of it. Like Sapir's writings in general, it has survived the radical fluctuations of twentieth-century linguistics. As we have seen, the term *noninstinctive* needs qualification, but otherwise the definition is sound. In this chapter we have discussed the features of language which Sapir gave and added to them others, such as creativity, which linguists of today feel are equally important.

Suggested Reading

BROWN, ROGER W., *Words and Things.* Glencoe, Ill.: Free Press, 1957.

CARROLL, JOHN B., *The Study of Language.* Cambridge, Mass.: Harvard University Press, 1953.

CHOMSKY, NOAM, *Language and Mind,* enlarged edition. New York: Harcourt Brace Jovanovich, Inc., 1972.

DE VITO, JOSEPH, *The Psychology of Speech and Language.* New York: Random House, Inc., 1970.

HOCKETT, CHARLES F., "The Origins of Speech," *Scientific American* 203 (1960): 89–96.

HOCKETT, CHARLES F., and R. ASCHER, "The Human Revolution," *Current Anthropology* 5 (1964): 135–68.

LENNEBERG, ERIC H., *Biological Foundations of Language.* New York: John Wiley & Sons, Inc., 1967.

————, "Understanding Language Without Ability to Speak: A Case Report," *Journal of Abnormal Social Psychology* 65 (1962): 419–25.

SINGH, J. A. L., and R. M. ZINGG, *Wolf Children and Feral Man.* New York: Harper & Row, Publishers, 1942.

part **2**

Syntax

chapter 4

Basic Sentence Structure

So far we have examined the uses of language and compared its features with those of nonverbal communication. One of the features of language that we noticed in Chapter 3 is its systematic nature. We will now focus on this topic and study the structure of sentences.

Syntactic Concepts

Many people believe that the ability to use a language involves nothing more than knowing a large number of words. This is certainly implied in some books designed for increasing the vocabulary. And if a person has trouble understanding a sentence, chances are he is more conscious of the unfamiliar words in it than he is of the complex sentence structure or ideas. It is not uncommon to hear such reactions as, "I can't understand him; he uses too many big words." Many people look upon mastering a foreign language as nothing more than learning which words correspond and replacing the words of one language with those of another. They cannot see why many linguists have abandoned for the near future the hope of successful machine translation.

Probably no one would deny that the ability to use and understand words is essential for most of the activities we engage in. The more complex our activities and ideas are, the more extensive our vocabularies need to be. At the same time, we should not assume that vocabulary is all there is to language. As an example, we can examine the words *old, kill, wolf,* and *man.* Although we understand the meanings of all the words, we do not know how they relate to one another. All we know is that there is an act of killing involving a man and a wolf, one of which is old. In English, to indicate which one killed the other, we arrange the words in a conventional order:

> man   kill   wolf

By placing *man* before *kill,* we are designating the agent who performed the act. By placing *wolf* after *kill,* we are indicating the object affected by the action. The relationships are changed if we reverse the order:

> wolf   kill   man

The meaning we wish to convey determines which word precedes *kill* and which one follows. We use the ordering of words also to show whether it is the man or the wolf that is old. By the use of word order, we can produce the following structures:

old man	kill	wolf
man	kill	old wolf
old wolf	kill	man
wolf	kill	old man

We produce different meanings with each of the changes in word order.

If we say, "Old man kill wolf," our basic idea is clear. Whether we pause after *man* or not determines whether we are telling an old man to kill a wolf or merely reporting an action. If a small child says, "Old man kill wolf," we accept the sentence as normal; on the other hand, if an adult says it, we are irritated. We want to know whether the old man is unidentified or some specific person whom we have identified in an earlier sentence or through shared knowledge. If he has not been identified in some way, we refer to him as *an old man;* but if he has been previously designated, we call him *the old man.* Similarly, we want the speaker to use *a wolf* or *the wolf,* depending upon whether or not we know which wolf is meant. By adding *the* or *a,* we can produce the following structures:

an old man	kill	the wolf
a wolf	kill	the old man
the man	kill	the old wolf

There are sixteen possible combinations.

"The old man kill the wolf" is better than "Old man kill wolf," but it still seems incomplete. A speaker of English wants to know certain information about the act. For example, is it an action that occurred in the past ("The old man killed the wolf"), or is it going on in the present ("The old man is killing the wolf")? If it occurred during the past, are we commenting on it in relation to some other past action?

4.1   The old man killed the wolf.
4.2   The old man had killed the wolf when I found him.
4.3   The old man was killing the wolf when I found him.

In sentence 4.1, the act of killing occurred prior to the time in which the sentence is stated, but in the others it is related to other past actions. In 4.1 and 4.2 the action is completed; they differ in that for 4.1 the act was completed before the present time and in 4.2 before an action in the past, "when I found him." According to 4.3, the act of killing was in progress at the time of discovery.

All the information that we have examined for a sentence such as "The old man killed the wolf" is just as essential to our understanding of meaning as is our knowledge of the individual words *old, kill, wolf,* and *man.* The sentence would be meaningless to us if we lacked either kind of information: the meanings of the individual words or the devices used to indicate such ideas as the agent who performed the action and whether he has been previously identified. We say that this second kind of information provides the **syntax** of the sentence.

Word Groups

Certain ideas in English are conveyed by the order of the words:

4.4   A man killed the old wolf.
4.5   The old wolf killed a man.
4.6   *Old killed man wolf the a.

Sentences 4.4 and 4.5 do not have the same meaning because of the difference in word ordering, and 4.6 is meaningless. The asterisk indicates that this is not a possible English sentence.

In addition to a linear, one-two-three order, words in a sentence may cluster together, as we indicate by pauses in speech and punctuation marks in writing:

4.7   When we looked inside the room became dark.

The sentence is meaningless if we take *when we looked inside the room* as one unit and *became dark* as another. The only possible clustering is *when we looked inside* and *the room became dark.* A sentence can be totally impossible to understand if we do not recognize how the words are grouped:

4.8   That that is is that that is not is not.[1]

Sentences like this have often been used by English teachers to stress the need for following standard punctuation practices. Another example is

4.9   Woman without her man is a savage.

With a different division of word groups, we can change the meaning:

4.10   Woman! Without her, man is a savage.

Sentences which permit such radical changes in meaning with varying divisions are rare, yet the speaker of English uses word clustering at least as much as linear ordering to determine the meaning of a sentence.

The sentence *The man sang loudly* contains four words which we could group in several ways:

the	man	sang	loudly
the	man sang loudly		
the	man sang	loudly	
the man	sang loudly		

[1] That that is, is; that that is not, is not.

Only the last grouping is satisfactory. We know that *the man* constitutes a unit since we can substitute a single word for it such as *he* or *Oliver*. If we ask, "Who sang loudly?" someone might answer, "Oliver did." *Sang loudly*, in other words, can be shown to be a unit since *did* substitutes for it. We can illustrate the arrangement of the sentence like this:

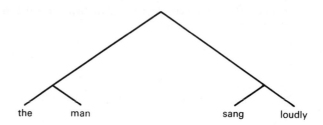

the   man   sang   loudly

Because the lines branch out, we call this representation a **tree;** we refer to the points at which lines meet as **nodes.** *The man* is shown to be a unit since both words are attached to lines which come from the same node. *Sang loudly* is also shown to be a unit, as is *the man sang loudly*. The tree shows that the sentence is not arranged into such units as *the* and *man sang loudly*.

The tree gives some of the information which the native speaker possesses about English, but it still leaves much unexpressed. At times we need to compare units in two or more sentences.

4.11   The man sang loudly.
4.12   The woman saw the goat.

We can show that *the man* and *the woman* are the same kind of structure since they can substitute for each other:

4.13   *The woman* sang loudly.
4.14   *The man* saw the goat.

On the other hand, *the woman* cannot substitute for *sang loudly*, which is another kind of structure:

4.15   *The man *the woman.*

One means of indicating that *the man* and *the woman* are the same kind of structure would be to refer to them as the first word group in the sentence. Such a proposal is objectionable for two reasons: It is clumsy and it does not accommodate all of the facts. It is true that *the man* and *the woman* are exchangeable in these sentences, but so is *the goat:*

4.16   *The goat* saw *the man.*

Labeling the unit by its position is inadequate.

We will follow traditional practices in calling *man, woman,* and *goat* **nouns.** Each of these nouns can be preceded by *the* and can be made plural:

the men, the women, the goats. The is not the only word which can function before these nouns: *a man, that man, this man, their man,* and so on.
We will call such words as *the, a, that,* and the like **determiners.** The unit
composed of a determiner and a noun could be logically called a noun
phrase, a noun cluster, or a noun unit. Since **noun phrase** is more widely
used than the other terms, we will use it. On the tree we can now add the
abbreviations **N, Det,** and **NP** for *noun, determiner,* and *noun phrase:*

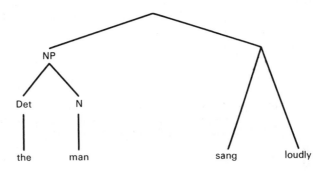

The unit *sang loudly* and its components now need labels. We will
call *sang* a **verb (V)** and *loudly* an adverb **(Adv).** The entire unit *sang
loudly* is called a **verb phrase (VP).** This last term has been used in traditional grammar to name the structure composed of a verb and its auxiliaries;
we are not using it in this sense. Some people use the term *predicate phrase*
instead of *verb phrase,* but we are using the latter term because it is the one
most often found in current linguistic writings. By adding these labels and
S for **sentence,** we have a tree like the following:

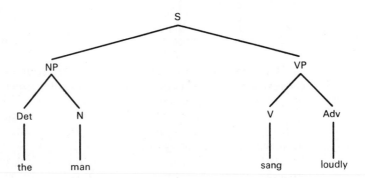

We are now showing the structure of the sentence and are naming its parts.
    Adverbs, of course, are not the only structure which may occur after
the verb:

4.17   Kate dropped her pencil.

Her pencil is a noun phrase, and it appears on the tree like this:

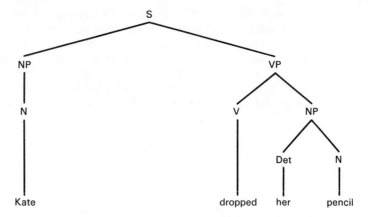

Since a tree does not mention structures which are not present in the given sentence, there is no adverb shown. In case both noun phrase and adverb follow the verb,[2] they are both given on the tree:

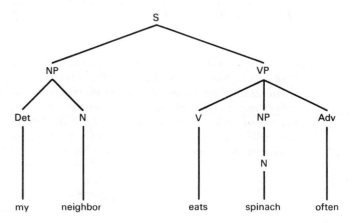

Our classifications so far have been in terms of **structure;** we can also classify sentence elements according to the **function** they perform. *My neighbor* is a noun phrase which functions as a **subject,** and *eats spinach often* is a verb phrase which functions as a **predicate.** The noun phrase *spinach* functions as the **direct object.** In the past, various definitions have been suggested for these functions, but all have been inexact. We will discuss these functions more fully in Chapter 8, but for now we will merely illustrate them. It is important to notice that we are making a distinction between a structure (noun phrase) and the way in which it functions (subject, direct object).

Not all elements within a noun phrase are determiners and nouns:

4.18   A suspicious inspector opened the big box.

Suspicious and *big* are called **adjectives (Adj).**

[2] In Chapter 5 we will see that adverbs may appear in other positions as well. Here we are merely illustrating one position in which they are found.

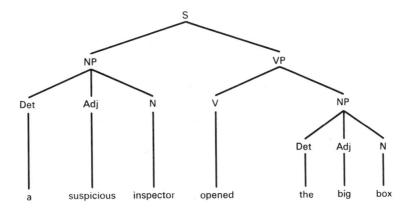

We have several reasons for distinguishing between determiners and adjectives:

1. Only one determiner may occur in a noun phrase (**the** box, *****his the** box**, *****a that** box), but adjectives are not so restricted (the **big black box**).
2. Many adjectives may be compared (*bigger, biggest; more suspicious, most suspicious*), but determiners may not be (*****thiser**, *****hisest**).
3. Some singular nouns must have a determiner preceding them (***Their** car is outside; *****Car** is outside); an adjective will not satisfy this requirement (*****New** car is outside).
4. Determiners precede adjectives (**the new** car, *****new the** car).

Although there are good reasons for distinguishing determiners from adjectives, it is far from clear that all of the words commonly called determiners actually constitute a unified, significant group. Providing evidence that a list of words should not be classified as adjectives does not prove that they are like one another. The determiner system has so far been subjected to very little investigation. Until linguistic research provides real insight into the determiner system, we will continue to classify such words as *a, some, that,* and *those* as determiners; at the same time we will remember that the reasoning which lists these words in one category is less than astounding.

Some adjectives may be modified by other words: *a **very** big elephant, some **rather** dull people, an **extremely** good movie.* Words such as *very, rather,* and *extremely* are often called adverbs, but this classification is not altogether satisfactory since most adverbs cannot function in this position: *****a **carefully** big elephant, *some **tomorrow** dull people.* Nor can words like *very* and *rather* function like adverbs: *****He ran **very**, *****They ate lunch **extremely**.* We will call the group of words which includes *very, extremely,* and a few others **intensifiers (Int)**. In addition to adjectives, they may modify certain adverbs: *He ran **very** fast. They ate **rather** slowly.* The unit consisting of an intensifier and an adverb is called an **adverb phrase (Adv P)**; an intensifier and an adjective is an **adjective phrase (Adj P)**. An adjective phrase is entered on a tree like this:

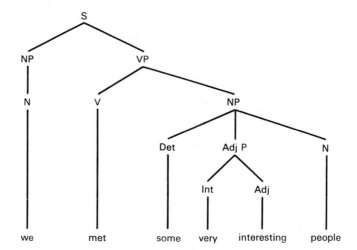

In this way we are showing that the noun phrase *some very interesting people* contains the unit *very interesting*. The tree shows that *very* goes with *interesting* rather than with some other element within the noun phrase.

Adjectives are not restricted to positions within the noun phrase. They may follow certain verbs such as *seem, look,* and *feel:*

4.19   The room seems *warm.*
4.20   You look *very tired.*
4.21   I felt *silly.*

Most verbs of the senses—*feel, taste, smell,* and the like—may be followed by adjectives. Sentence 4.20 looks like this on a tree:

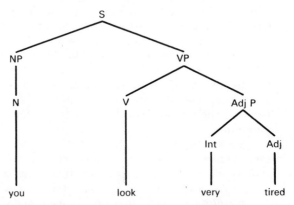

An adjective which follows the verb is said to function as **a predicate adjective** or a **subjective complement.**

The last structure which we will consider in this section is the **prepositional phrase (Prep P),** a structure which consists of a **preposition (Prep)** and a noun phrase: *in the yard, during the night, with a saw.* Prepositional phrases may be included within noun phrases, or they may occur in the same positions as adverbs:

4.22   The dog under the porch howled for an hour.

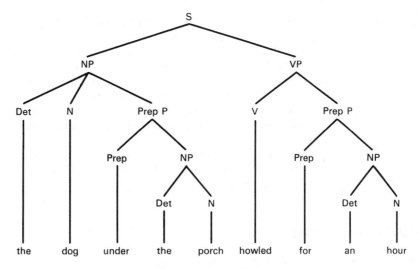

The tree shows the structure of the sentence, and it labels each of the units.

In a few cases, such as our separation of determiners from adjectives and intensifiers from adverbs, we are departing from traditional classifications, but for the most part our treatment of sentence structure differs little from that found in traditional accounts. Some texts have departed considerably from traditional analyses, but we have not chosen to do so. Much that is found in traditional grammars seems to be essentially correct, and many linguists today feel that we should not reject traditional grammar, but rather let it serve as a base for more exact analyses.

Our trees may look quite different from traditional diagrams, but a careful comparison of the two shows many similarities, as can be seen in the treatment of *The old man opened the door carefully*.

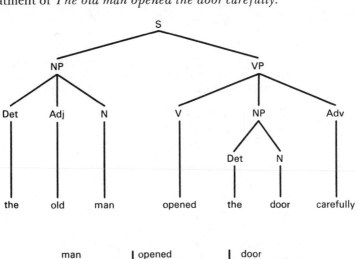

A traditional diagram designates functions rather than structures. The subject and predicate are divided by the long vertical line between *man* and *opened;* the direct object is indicated by the short vertical line between *opened* and *door*. Determiners, adjectives, and adverbs are placed on slanted lines beneath the main horizontal line. The tree, on the other hand, indicates structures such as noun phrases, determiners, and adverbs. We can derive the function of each structure by its position on the tree, just as we can name structures from their function in the traditional diagram. If we were going no farther with sentence analysis than we have in this chapter, it would not matter whether we used trees or traditional diagrams; for the matters we will discuss in the chapters which follow, trees are more informative than diagrams.

Plurality and Tense

One of the goals of linguistic research is to develop a grammar that performs the same functions as an internalized grammar. By drawing a tree of a sentence, we provide a description of its structure:

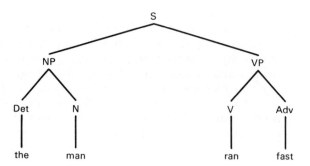

This analysis corresponds fairly closely to the organization understood by fluent speakers of English. Yet it leaves some information unexpressed, as we can see by comparing the following sentences:

4.23   The man ran fast.
4.24   The men ran fast.
4.25   The hen ran fast.

The noun phrases look like this on trees:

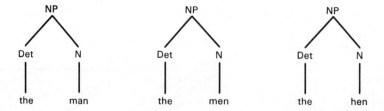

The speaker of English recognizes *man* and *men* as being essentially the same word; they differ only in that one is singular and the other is plural. *Hen,* on the other hand, is a different word entirely. If we use our internalized grammars, this kind of information is obvious, but from the trees alone it is not. *Man* and *men* differ by one letter or sound, depending upon whether we are speaking of the written or spoken form of the word. *Hen* and *men* differ by the same degree: one letter or sound.

We can express the idea that *man* and *men* are related forms by using the concept of the **morpheme,** a minimal syntactic unit.[3] *Man* consists of only one morpheme, but *men* consists of two: *man* and *plural*. In addition to the kinds of trees we have been drawing, we can use others which show morphemes rather than words:

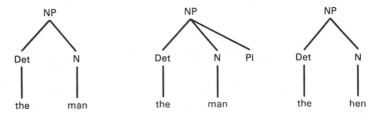

In this way we are indicating that *men* is *man* with the plural morpheme added. With this kind of representation, *men* and *hen* are shown to be different nouns.

There are additional generalizations that we can capture by discussing sentence elements in terms of morphemes rather than words:

4.26a   Mona talked fast.
   b   Mona talks fast.
4.27a   Mona walked fast.
   b   Mona walks fast.

The internalized grammar recognizes *talked* and *talks* as variants of the same word, as are *walked* and *walks*. The grammar we have developed so far does not reveal this information, since the trees we have been drawing merely list the words as verbs with no further analysis. *Walked* and *walks* differ by one sound, but *walked* and *talked* show no more difference. If we looked these words up in a dictionary, we would find only the forms *walk* and *talk*. The difference between *walked* and *walks* or *talked* and *talks* is one of **tense**. *Walked* and *talked* are forms that are in the **past tense;** *walks* and *talks* are **present tense**. If we speak in terms of morphemes rather than words, *walked* consists of the morphemes *past tense* (or just *past*) and *walk*. The tense morpheme is included within a structure called the **auxiliary**

---

[3] A number of years ago the morpheme was usually defined as "the smallest meaningful unit." According to this definition, the word *unfeelingly* can be shown to contain four morphemes: *un, feel, ing,* and *ly,* none of which can be broken down into smaller meaningful units. It was later noticed that some morphemes actually had very little meaning, and the definition was generally abandoned. In spite of its shortcomings, this earlier definition may be useful to a person for whom the concept of the morpheme is totally new.

(**Aux**). For the sentence *The girls walked fast,* we can represent this information on a tree as follows:

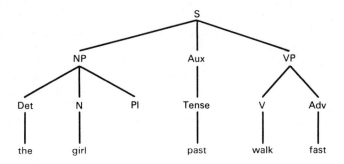

We will refer to a representation such as *the girl Pl past walk fast* as a **syntactic surface structure** or, more briefly, as a **surface structure.**[4] A representation which shows how the sentence is actually pronounced is a **phonetic structure:** *The girls walked fast.* In a more formal grammar, phonetic structures would be written in a special phonetic alphabet rather than in conventional spelling. Also, a complete grammar would contain **phonological rules** which convert syntactic surface structures into phonetic structures. These rules would tell how to pronounce such combinations as *girl Pl* and *past walk* and give other information about pronunciation. We will discuss phonological rules and phonetic structures in Part 3 of this book. For now we will use conventional spellings since our present concern is restricted to syntax.

We can now draw two kinds of trees for sentences. Here is one which gives the syntactic surface structure for *Some bees stung Ramona:*

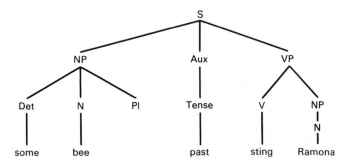

This kind of tree represents the structure of the sentence in terms of its morphemes. We can also draw a tree of the phonetic structure:

[4] Some works which are concerned solely with syntax give surface structures as finished sentences. This practice is defensible since it allows the reader to concentrate exclusively on the issues under discussion. But for a study which includes phonology as well as syntax, a distinction between syntactic surface structures and phonetic structures is necessary. The differences between the two will be made clear in Chapter 12, "Phonological Rules."

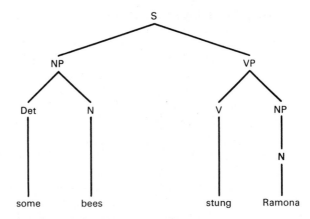

Since trees which separate morphemes are more useful in syntactic analysis than are those of phonetic structures, we will normally use only surface-structure trees. It is nevertheless important to understand each kind, because both are found in scholarly publications.

Exercises

A. Examine the following sentence: *A fat barber thanked the customer.*
   1. How do you know who thanked whom?
   2. How do you know who is fat?
   3. Has the barber or the customer been previously identified? How do you know?

B. Which of the following divisions best reveals the grouping of words understood by a fluent speaker of English?
   1. An ugly   woman stood in   the rain.
   2. An ugly woman   stood in the rain.
   3. An   ugly woman stood   in the rain.

   Provide reasons for your answer.

C. Which of the following units from the sentence below are noun phrases: *the woman, saw, the small child, behind the nurse, the nurse, the woman saw?*

   The woman saw the small child behind the nurse.

D. Illustrate the following in original sentences: NP, Det, Adj, Adv, Prep P, Adj P, VP, Prep.

E. Draw trees of the syntactic surface structures of the following sentences:
   1. This car started quickly.
   2. The tired applicant waited for a long time.
   3. You seem pretty industrious.
   4. A pedestrian noticed my flat tire.
   5. The tree in the yard provides shade.

F. If you speak or have studied a language other than English, translate the following sentences into that language and draw phonetic-structure trees of your translations and of their English counterparts:

1. Mary sees a horse.
2. My car is green.
3. The boy reads a book.
4. The glass is on the table.
5. George sings very well.

Comment on similarities and differences in word order and structure between English and the other language, limiting your observations to the five sentences above.

G. In each of the following sentences draw one line under the subject NP and two lines under the verb. Then classify the structure following the verb as a noun phrase, adjective phrase, adverb, or prepositional phrase. Provide evidence for your classifications.

1. The dog buried a bone.
2. She lives near me.
3. The ship sails today.
4. The band is outside.
5. That picture is crooked.
6. Her name is Mildred.
7. Bill left because of the noise. [Treat *because of* as a preposition.]
8. The apple was awfully good.
9. He left with reluctance.
10. She sews for a living.
11. Those children played in the yard.
12. They are twins.
13. It rained during the night.
14. The water ran very fast.
15. The chairs are similar.

chapter 5

Underlying Structures

We have seen that a sentence is composed of a noun phrase and a verb phrase, each of which may consist of only one word or of several. That is, a noun phrase may contain just a noun or a pronoun, or it may contain a determiner and an adjective. These sentences illustrate various possibilities:

5.1   *Fred* cried. (N)
5.2   *Some cars* passed us. (Det N)
5.3   *Friendly people* are welcome. (Adj N)
5.4   *A stupid clerk* gave me too much change. (Det Adj N)

Similarly, the verb phrase may consist of just the verb, or it may contain other elements as well:

5.5   The stars *twinkled.* (V)
5.6   A rather peculiar woman *giggled quietly.* (V Adv)
5.7   The horse *kicked the bucktoothed sergeant.* (V NP)
5.8   The conductor *seemed rather awkward.* (V Adj P)
5.9   We *found the lizard under a rock.* (V NP Prep P)

By using trees with several levels of branches, we are able to describe the structures of sentences such as 5.1–5.9 in a way that agrees with the fluent speaker's knowledge of English.

So long as we work with languages which have structures similar to those of English, the framework within which we have been analyzing English will accommodate sentences in those languages as well. For example, the tree for the English sentence *The man sings well* can be used for the corresponding Spanish sentence:

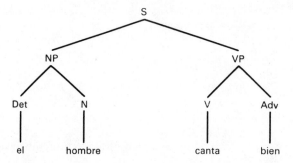

We could easily replace the Spanish words with those in French, Italian, German, Dutch, or a number of other languages. In some instances there are slight differences, such as in Russian, Latin, and other languages which do not have the full range of determiners found in English, such as *a* and *the*. However, the system easily accommodates the Russian counterpart of *The man sings well:*

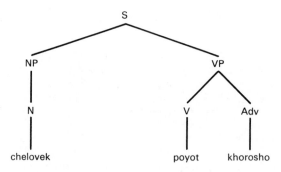

So long as we limit ourselves to certain types of simple structures, we have no major difficulties.

Classes of Verbs

In some instances we are free to select or reject various structures in the NP and VP. That certainly appears to be true for the following groups of sentences:

5.10   The woman wrote.
5.11   The tall woman wrote.
5.12   The tall woman wrote a letter.
5.13   The tall woman wrote a funny letter.
5.14   The tall woman wrote a funny letter to her sister.

Each of these is a complete, grammatical sentence. Assuming they all describe the same event, we can say that they differ only in the amount of detail they express. The overall context determines how much of this detail we want to give. If there is only one woman about whom we have been talking or if we are looking at a group of people containing only one woman, it is enough to identify her as *the woman.* If there are more than one, however, we need to identify her by some characteristic trait. We can call her *the tall woman* if the others are of average height or shorter; or we may need to say *the tall woman in the green dress,* or give other details to identify her. In like manner, we select as much information to follow the verb as is needed to convey the speaker's message. The more information about the situation the speaker and listener share, the less detail that needs to be expressed.

Meaning and shared information, however, are not the only features that determine which elements are present in a sentence, even though they may be the most important. The first sentence of each of the following pairs is not grammatical, regardless of what the speaker wants to say or how much the listener already knows about the topic:

5.15a   *Walter sent.
   b   Walter sent a dozen roses to the hostess.
5.16a   *We found.
   b   We found mud on our shoes.
5.17a   *My grandmother likes.
   b   My grandmother likes licorice.

Whereas some sentences do not have noun phrases following the verb, others must have them. This restriction is caused by the verb, not by the subject noun phrase:

5.18   Walter laughed.
5.19   We tittered.
5.20   My grandmother winked.

Each of the noun phrases in 5.15–17 can be the subject in a sentence without an object noun phrase. Regardless of which noun phrase we give as the subject for *send, find,* or *like,* the resulting sentence is ungrammatical without an object. Grammarians recognized this restriction many centuries ago, and they gave the name **transitive** to those verbs which are followed by direct objects.

They also recognized another class of verbs, which they called **intransitive.** These verbs are not followed by noun phrases:

5.21a   The tires screeched.
5.22a   The old witch stinks.
5.23a   My foot itched.

If we try placing objects after intransitive verbs such as *screech, stink,* and *itch,* the result is not grammatical:

5.21b   *The tires screeched *rubber.*
5.22b   *The old witch stinks *dead fish.*
5.23b   *My foot itched *a rash.*

Intransitive verbs may be followed by nothing, as in the *a* versions of these sentences, or they may take adverbs or prepositional phrases:

5.21c   The tires screeched *loudly.*
5.22c   The old witch stinks *in spite of the perfume.*
5.23c   My foot itched *because of the rash.*

Noun phrases may be present within prepositional phrases after intransitive verbs, but such verbs are not followed by object noun phrases, as the *b* versions show.

   Logically all verbs which are not transitive should be included in the category intransitive, as the negative prefix *in-* suggests. However, there is a third group which is composed of those few verbs which may be followed by adjective phrases:

5.24   The cake smelled *fresh.*
5.25   Some people are *extremely jealous.*

These verbs are often called **linking** or **copulative** verbs. The most conspicuous members of this group are the verbs of the senses (*smell, taste, feel,* and the like) and forms of *be* (*am, is, are, was, were, be, been, being*). The addition of *become, remain, seem,* and *appear* practically exhausts the list of English linking verbs. Some of these verbs can also have noun phrases following them:

5.26   That ugly child is *her daughter.*
5.27   They remained *enemies.*
5.28   Smith and Atkins became *copartners.*

Unlike the direct object, which follows a transitive verb, the noun phrase which follows a linking verb has the same referent as the subject. The structure following a linking verb is called a **predicate adjective** or a **predicate noun** (or **predicate nominative**); the two may be grouped together as **subjective complements.**

   There is nothing in the pronunciation or spelling of a verb to indicate whether it is transitive, intransitive, or linking. We can illustrate this by examining a few potential verbs: *squelp, plish, fram, keem.* Whereas we know how their past-tense forms should be pronounced, we do not know whether they are to be followed by objects, subjective complements, or nothing. Part of the meaning of each verb is its classification, and most dictionaries label each one with such abbreviations as *vt* or *vi* for "verb transitive" or "verb intransitive."

   That these classifications are not unique with English can be shown by the following German examples:

5.29a   *Meine Schwester öffnete. "*My sister opened."
   b   Meine Schwester öffnete die Tür. "My sister opened the door."
5.30a   *Johann starb sein Leben. "*John died his life."
   b   Johann starb. "John died."
5.31a   *Sie war. "*She was."
   b   Sie war freundlich. "She was friendly."

Sentence 5.29 illustrates a transitive verb, 5.30 one that is intransitive, and 5.31 one that is linking. With a slightly different use of *open,* as found in some card games, 5.29a would be a grammatical sentence meaning, "My sister opened the bidding." For the meaning of *open* in 5.29b, an object must follow.

Understood Information

So long as we restrict ourselves to such transitive verbs as *send, find,* and *like,* such intransitives as *screech, stink,* and *itch,* and the linking verbs *smell, seem,* and *appear,* we can form classifications which are neat and exclusive. If we examine additional verbs, we eventually find some which fit into two categories: both transitive and intransitive, transitive and linking, or even intransitive and linking. One objection that has been raised about some earlier grammars is that they do not accommodate sentences other than the carefully selected few contained within the examples and exercises. Ideally, a grammar should handle not only a few illustrative sentences but also all others in the language, including those which have not yet been created. With our current state of knowledge about language, it is impossible for any grammar to achieve this ideal, yet this does not excuse us from coming as close to it as possible.

Some verbs, such as *write* in 5.10–14, may or may not be followed by noun-phrase objects. Here are a few other examples of the many verbs like this:

5.32a Darrell ate early today.
 b Darrell ate lunch early today.
5.33a Louise waved.
 b Louise waved her hand.
5.34a Joe read all night.
 b Joe read comic books all night.
5.35a Emily helped.
 b Emily helped us.

For both sentences in each pair the verb has the same meaning, the only difference being whether the object is stated or not. Labeling the verbs in the *a* sentences intransitive and those in the *b* versions transitive is, therefore, unsatisfactory, especially since a speaker of English *understands* the verbs in the *a* sentences as having objects even though they are not stated explicitly.

Because we are trying to make our grammar account for the fluent speaker's knowledge of his language, it should take into account what this speaker understands about sentences as well as their actual form. There is no satisfactory way we can do this if we restrict ourselves to the way sentences actually appear in speech and writing; however, we can accommodate both kinds of information if we give each sentence two representations:

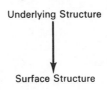

Underlying Structure

Surface Structure

The surface structure is the arrangement of morphemes as they occur in actual sentences of the language. The underlying structure contains all the information that the speaker understands about the sentence. In sentence 5.33a, for example, we understand *her hand* after waved; hence both 5.33a and 5.33b have the same underlying structure:

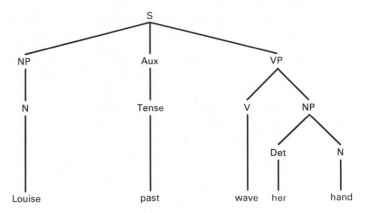

There are other conceivable objects of *waved: her foot, a red flag, the sign,* and so on. Each of these is usually considered less normal than *her hand* and must be expressed if intended. However, if there is no possibility for confusion and the object is *her hand,* this object noun phrase is normally deleted, giving the following surface structure:

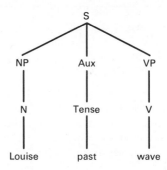

The first tree, which contains all the understood information, represents the **underlying structure** of *Louise waved;* the second tree gives the **surface structure.**

There are a great many verbs that are like *wave* in having one object that is considered normal and is usually deleted. Other possible objects are less normal and must be expressed if intended. Here are a few examples:

		Normal	*Less normal*
5.36	Emily saves _____.	(money)	(old newspapers)
5.37	David teaches _____.	(students)	(dogs)
5.38	Donna draws _____.	(pictures)	(swastikas)

So long as there is no reason for confusion, normal objects are deleted.

For some verbs the normal object is a reflexive (*himself, themselves,* etc.) or a reciprocal (*each other, one another*) pronoun:

		Normal	*Less normal*
5.39	Patricia bathes ——— often.	(herself)	(the baby)
5.40	Peter shaved ——— this morning.	(himself)	(the patient)
5.41	They met ——— in Dublin.	(each other)	(me)

There are, of course, other possibilities for less normal objects. Since a person fluent in English understands each of these verbs as having an object even if none is given, as in *Patricia bathes often,* we will always express the object in the underlying structure:

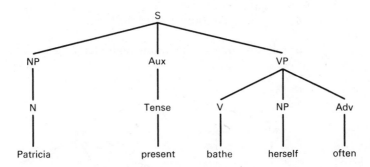

Except in rare cases the normal object is deleted; hence, for this sentence we will derive the following surface structure:

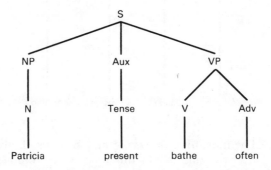

The underlying structure gives all understood information, and the surface structure gives only those elements which are actually expressed.

When we restrict ourselves to surface structures, verbs and sentences may show much variation that a native speaker does not feel is really significant. The same thing is true of certain structures of one language when we compare them with those of another. This is especially true of the reflexive verbs in German and French, which appear so strange to the beginning student:

5.42   Ich muss mich waschen. "I must wash myself."
5.43   Er hat sich schon rasiert. "He has already shaved himself."

5.44   Elle se lave. "She is washing herself."
5.45   Je me lève toujours de bonne heure. "I always get (myself) up early."

At the underlying level, these verbs have reflexive objects in English as well as in French and German. The difference is that English deletes this object on the surface, whereas the other two languages do not. The underlying structures show similarities which are not obvious on the surface.

Sometimes the speaker does not want to be specific about the object, even though he recognizes that the verb is acting on something. In cases such as this the underlying object is vague. Such verbs as *eat, read,* and *write* are of this type:

5.46   I ate after the concert.
5.47   I ate a hamburger after the concert.

For 5.46 we can give the following underlying structure:

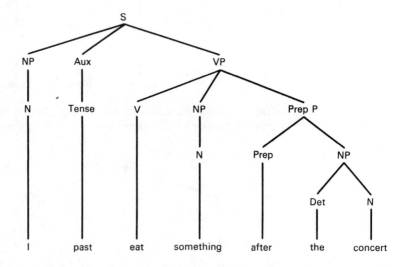

The indefinite *something* may be deleted, giving the surface structure *I ate after the concert.* In this way we are commenting on the act of eating; we are not concerned with the kind of food.

Noun phrases are not the only elements that may be deleted, as we can see in an anecdote attributed to Samuel Johnson. A woman is reported to have said to him, "Sir, you smell!" Dr. Johnson, who freely admitted that he had little concern for personal cleanliness, immediately retorted, "Madame, you smell; I stink." The woman's sentence had the understood adjective *bad:* "You smell bad." Johnson was objecting to this usage, insisting upon using *smell* as a transitive verb: "You smell odors," in which the noun phrase may be deleted. Today there is no controversy over the uses of *smell,* and either of the following sentences is possible:

5.48   Her breath smelled.
5.49   Her breath smelled sweet.

The underlying structure of 5.48, like that of 5.49, has an adjective following the verb; it is only on the surface that it is missing.

The two uses of *smell* bring us to another issue involving certain verbs of senses: *smell, taste, feel,* and *sound.* Each of these may be action verbs, in which case they are transitive and are followed by noun phrases and optional adverbs:

5.50   The cat smelled the food cautiously.
5.51   She tasted the soup eagerly.
5.52   I felt the jolt suddenly.
5.53   He sounded the horn loudly.

Each of these verbs can also name a state rather than an action, in which case they are linking and are, therefore, followed by adjectives:

5.54   The soup smelled scorched.
5.55   The pudding tasted salty.
5.56   I felt sick.
5.57   He sounded peculiar.

Although there is a clear relationship in meaning between the two uses of each verb, we will treat them separately, calling those in 5.50–53 transitive and those in 5.54–57 linking. If we consider the two uses of *smell* as two different verbs, there is no problem with our system of classification. Verbs which appear to be both transitive and linking are treated as two distinct verbs, depending upon whether they denote actions or states.

Another problem concerns verbs which appear to be intransitive in some sentences and transitive in others, as seen in the *a* and *b* versions below:

5.58a   We waited for an hour.
   b   We waited an hour.
5.59a   Henry stopped for the night in Phoenix.
   b   Henry stopped the night in Phoenix.

If we restricted ourselves to surface structures, there would be no way to show that not only the verbs but the entire sentences mean the same thing in the *a* and *b* versions. If we incorporate a concept of underlying structures into our grammar, we can account for this synonymy. The underlying structure for each sentence will have a preposition following the verb; it is deleted in the *b* sentences but not in those marked *a*. Hence, *wait* and *stop* are clearly intransitive verbs at the underlying level. This analysis will also classify most verbs of distance and measurement as intransitive:

5.60   The old woman walked a mile.
5.61   He swam four hundred meters.
5.62   The room measures ten feet across.
5.63   The box weighs eight pounds.

According to this proposal, each of these verbs is followed by a prepositional phrase at the underlying level. Unlike the prepositions after *wait* and *stop*, which may or may not be deleted, those after *measure* and *weigh* are obligatorily deleted, and those after *walk* and *swim* usually are, although *for* sometimes occurs in surface structures.

By using underlying as well as surface structures, we are able to account for part of the fluent speaker's knowledge of his language, such as understood object noun phrases, adjectives, and prepositions. At the underlying level verb classification is regular and coincides with the speaker's understanding of meaning. If we confined ourselves to surface manifestations, on the other hand, the classification would be haphazard. Verbs could have a given classification in one sentence and a different one in another and yet show no change in meaning. A process such as deletion which converts one structure into another is called a **transformation.**

Deletion of Repeated Structures

When information is obvious, we normally do not wish to insult the people we are addressing by stating it overtly; hence, certain prepositions and objects of verbs are normally deleted. Conversations often seem full of choppy, fragmented structures because obvious information has not been stated overtly. Consider the following examples:

"Do you want to play poker?"
"No."
"Why not?"
"Headache."
"Really?"
"Yes."
"Too bad."

There is much information which is understood but which is not given because it seems unnecessary. We can understand the nature of this information if we repeat the conversation with it included in parentheses:

"Do you want to play poker?"
"No, (I don't want to play poker)."
"Why (do you) not (want to play poker)?"
"(I don't want to play poker because I have a) headache."
"(Do you) really (have a headache)?"
"Yes, (I really have a headache)."
"(It's) too bad (that you have a headache)."

In spite of some well-meaning people who advise others always to speak in complete sentences, few people do. The highly elliptical expressions in the first rendering of the conversation are much more functional and less irritating than their expanded versions.

Certain verbs have characteristic noun phrases which are so frequent in following them that they are understood if not expressed overtly, but other kinds of unexpressed information are also easily understood. As the conversation in the preceding paragraph shows, information that is repetitious is often deleted. Since the current state of grammatical theory does not provide a satisfactory framework for dealing with relations among sentences in a paragraph or a conversation, we will be limiting ourselves to systems which are found within individual sentences. Probably much of what we will say about the sentence will also be applicable to the entire discourse, but we will leave this topic to future investigations.

Let us turn to the following sentence:

5.64a   Mae can't help you, but I can.

We feel that something is understood after *I can,* and if we draw a tree of the sentence we can see that all elements normally found in a sentence are not present in this one, at least not overtly.

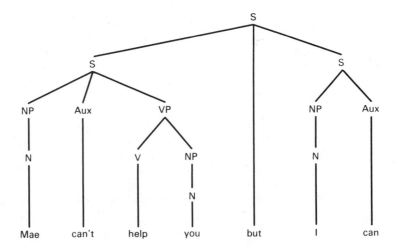

All that we see in the second sentence are NP and Aux, no VP. Either the underlying structure contains elements that are later deleted, or this is a very strange sentence. We next can try to determine whether there is information which all fluent speakers of English understand to be present in the second sentence. If there is no basis for assigning an underlying VP, then there should be no consistency among people as to which of the following parenthesized continuations they would select:

5.64b   Mae can't help you, but I can (pickled beets every summer).
   c   Mae can't help you, but I can (be running along).
   d   Mae can't help you, but I can (wash my hair).
   e   Mae can't help you, but I can (help you).

The *b* version uses *can* as a main verb, not an auxiliary, and 5.64c seems very strange with another auxiliary following *can.* The *d* version seems better structurally, but it still does not give the desired information. It is 5.64e which agrees with our real understanding of the sentence:

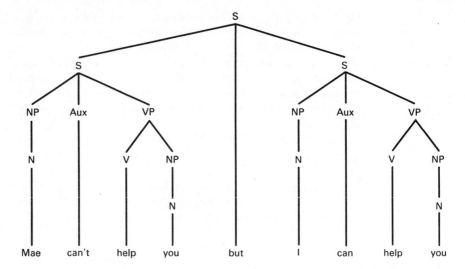

If we accept an underlying structure such as this, we find that the second sentence contains all the expected structures within the verb phrase, not just the auxiliary and noun phrase. The VP is deleted because it is identical to the VP in the first sentence.

If we do not have to restrict ourselves to structures which can be analyzed according to the information given in the preceding chapter, we can illustrate the process of deletion of identical material more satisfactorily. In fact, we have already done this with the negative *n't* (*not*) in the various versions of 5.64. Since these structures do not affect the process of deletion, there is no reason why we should avoid them. Each of the following sentences is normally found with the repeated structure deleted from the surface manifestation:

5.65　The car rolled through the fence and (the car) crashed into the house. [identical subject NPs]
5.66　Tommy (appeared rude to Becky) and Elizabeth appeared rude to Becky. [identical VPs]
5.67　I am taller than you are (tall). [identical adjectives]
5.68　I am taller than you (are tall). [identical VPs]
5.69　I read the editorials, and Maude (reads) the sports page. [identical verbs]

Since a fluent speaker of English understands the parenthesized structures to be present in each of these sentences, they are present at the underlying level.

For several years pairs of sentences such as the following have been popular in discussions of grammar:

5.70a　Perry is hard to deceive.
5.71a　Perry is eager to deceive.

In 5.70 we understand someone else to be deceiving Perry, but in 5.71 Perry is doing the deceiving. We can account for this knowledge about the meanings of the sentences if we set up underlying structures like these:

5.70b   [Someone deceives Perry] is hard
5.71b   Perry is eager [Perry deceives someone]

Processes that will be discussed in Chapter 7 delete the tense of *deceive* and add *to*. The indefinite *someone* and the repeated *Perry* are then deleted, giving the surface structures 5.70a and 5.71a.

    This kind of analysis will also permit us to explain why certain sentences are ambiguous, that is, with two or more possible meanings.

5.72a   Laurie is too little to tease.

Depending upon the overall situation and context, we can understand this sentence to mean that Laurie is too little for us to tease her or that she is too little for her to tease us. Each of these meanings has its unique underlying structure, on the order of the following:

5.72b   Laurie is too little [People tease Laurie]
    c   Laurie is too little [Laurie teases people]

The underlying structure of each sentence is much closer to being a representation of the meaning than the surface structure is.

    It becomes obvious with sentences such as 5.72a and the corresponding underlying structures that it is incorrect to speak of one sentence as being transformed into another. From some pairs this is not obvious. Indeed some early works in transformational grammar, especially textbooks, suggest this process. Sentences like 5.72a, however, do not always have alternate surface versions which include all of the understood information: *Laurie is too little for her to tease people.* Research of the past few years has shown that the deepest underlying structures for each sentence are much more abstract than had been previously thought. It seems safe to say that there are always differences between the underlying and surface structures of a sentence. For this reason we say that two synonymous sentences have identical underlying structures, not that one surface structure is derived from the other.

Verbs and Particles

    In addition to recognizing deleted material, a speaker of English understands a great deal about sentences which is not obvious on the surface. For example, the following sentences are ambiguous, each having two possible meanings:

5.73   I ran into an old friend today.
5.74   We stared at the man with red pants a block behind.

The internalized grammar provides two possible meanings for each of these sentences.

    In addition, it rejects certain sentences as not possible for English:

5.75a   *Was crying a certain girl.

It is interesting that when a person encounters a sentence such as 5.75a, he does not merely say that it is meaningless; he corrects it in his mind to try to give it meaning:

5.75b   A certain girl was crying.

Although there are some sentences which people disagree over, all reject those that are as deviant as 5.75a.

A person's internalized grammar also enables him to recognize certain pairs of sentences as synonymous:

5.76a   He turned in his brother.
   b   He turned his brother in.

Although 5.76a is ambiguous, we will ignore the grotesque meaning and consider only the usual one. Since we would like the grammar that we are writing to be as much like an internalized grammar as possible, we should try to account for the synonymy of the two sentences.

If these sentences are the only synonymous pairs that differ in this way, then our task is simple: We can merely write both sentences and say that they mean the same thing. However, there are other pairs that differ in the same way:

5.77a   She bawled out her mother.
   b   She bawled her mother out.
5.78a   They closed up the office.
   b   They closed the office up.
5.79a   We put off the job.
   b   We put the job off.

Since there are a number of sentences which are like 5.76a and 5.76b, we should try to discover the system that relates them.

Obviously we cannot just say that words may be rearranged in a structure, although that is how the above pairs differ. If we did not specify which words may be rearranged, we could derive a sentence like 5.80:

5.80   His brother turned him in.

This sentence differs from 5.76b only in ordering, but it is not synonymous with the pair 5.76a and 5.76b. We must specify which elements may be rearranged without affecting meaning.

We might say that *in* may be moved from between the verb and noun phrase to the position immediately following the noun phrase. Such a statement would account for the synonymy of 5.76a and 5.76b and for that of the following pairs of sentences:

5.81a   We carried in the groceries.
   b   We carried the groceries in.
5.82a   She wrote in her name on the form.
   b   She wrote her name in on the form.

It looks as though we have formed a valid generalization, but when we examine other sentences, we discover problems.

5.83a   We ate in the kitchen.
   b   *We ate the kitchen in.

5.84a He turned in his grave.
  b *He turned his grave in.

Sentence 5.83b is impossible. Sentence 5.84b is possible only for the far-fetched meaning of 5.84a; for the usual meaning it is not.

Not all structures consisting of verb, *in,* and noun phrase are alike although they may appear to be. Let us examine two illustrative sentences:

5.85a The boys swam in the lake.
5.86a The boys pulled in the rope.

In may be moved in 5.86a but not in 5.85a:

5.85b *The boys swam the lake in.
5.86b The boys pulled the rope in.

There are other differences as well. An adverb such as *often* may come between the verb and *in* in 5.85 but not in 5.86:

5.85c The boys swam often in the lake.
5.86c *The boys pulled often in the rope.

By substituting *there,* we can show that *in the lake* is a syntactic unit, but *in the rope* is not:

5.85d The boys swam there.
5.86d The boys pulled there.

Sentence 5.85d has the same structure as 5.85a. It has the same general meaning, but it is less specific about the place of swimming. We cannot say the same thing for 5.86d. Sentence 5.85a has a prepositional phrase following the verb:

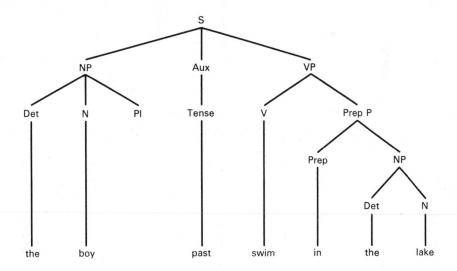

Although 5.86a at first may appear to have the same structure, we have seen that it does not. In this case, *in* is not a preposition but rather a **particle (Prt),** as shown in the tree on page 70. Differences such as that between preposition and particle are often not revealed by an examination of word order alone. The trees show that sentences 5.85a and 5.86a have different structures.

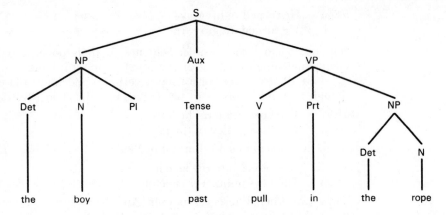

Sometimes we find different structures that have the same words and ordering:

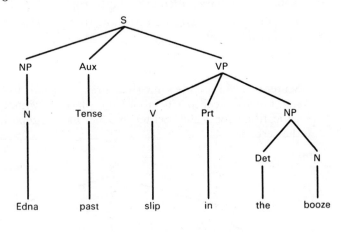

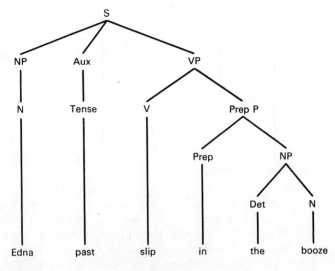

Both structures appear as the following sentence:

5.87   Edna slipped in the booze.

The sentence is ambiguous, but our grammar accounts for the two possible meanings. For many people there are slight differences in intonation between the spoken forms for the two meanings. These differences are provided for by phonological rules, which depend upon the syntactic structure for their application.

We have not yet accounted for the synonymy of sentences such as these:

5.88a   Mike turned off the light.
   b   Mike turned the light off.

We say that underlying both sentences is the following structure:

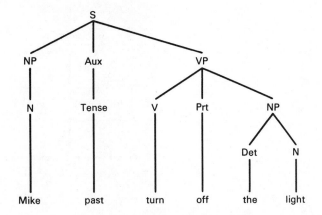

To derive 5.88a, we apply phonological rules such as the one which tells us how to pronounce the past of *turn*. To derive 5.88b, we rearrange the structure by a process called the **particle-movement transformation:**

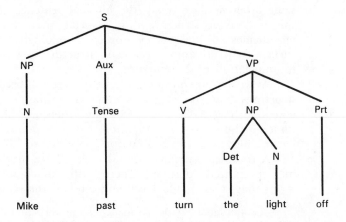

This tree represents the **surface structure** for *Mike turned the light off.* Before the application of the particle-movement transformation, we represented the sentence with the **underlying structure** *Mike past turn off the light*. At first it may appear that we have done nothing more than rearrange words, but the trees show that the structure has been affected as well.

We have now progressed far enough to make some comments about the grammar we are developing. In Figure 5.1 we see that the sentence is repre-

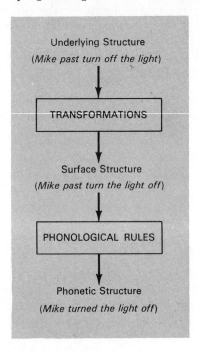

Figure 5.1

sented by an underlying structure which is quite different from the surface form. In the sentence we are illustrating, the morphemes are not in the same order as they are in the finished sentence. Transformations convert this underlying structure into a surface structure, which has all of the morphemes in their proper order. Phonological rules next convert the surface structure into a phonetic structure, a representation of the ideal pronunciation of the sentence.

As we develop our grammar further, it will become clear that all surface structures have undergone some transformations. Two synonymous sentences such as 5.88a and 5.88b have identical underlying structures and undergo the same transformations up to a point. They differ in that the particle-movement transformation is applied to 5.88b but not to 5.88a.

A complete grammar would have all transformational rules expressed in a specialized notation.[1] There is still much uncertainty over the exact forms that rules should have, and most of the scholarly literature that has

---

[1] For illustrations of the notations used in syntactic rules, see Bach (1964), Roberts (1964), Koutsoudas (1966), Roberts (1968), and Liles (1971). For a more thorough discussion of rules in grammar, see Chomsky (1964).

been published during the last few years has not expressed rules in formal notation. In this book, therefore, we will state rules in an informal manner. Our rule for the particle-movement transformation can be stated like this: "Move a particle from between the verb and noun phrase to the position immediately following the noun phrase. (Optional)" The transformation is optional. If it is performed, the ultimate result will be a sentence such as *Mike turned the light off;* if it is not performed, a sentence such as *Mike turned off the light* will be derived.

This rule accounts for a large number of sentences, but it still needs refinement, as the following examples show:

5.89a   We looked up the number.
  b   We looked the number up.
  c   *We looked up it.
  d   We looked it up.
5.90a   I let out the cat.
  b   I let the cat out.
  c   *I let out her.
  d   I let her out.

Whereas the rule is optional if the noun phrase contains a noun, it is obligatory if it contains a pronoun. Sentences 5.89a and 5.90a are possible even though the transformation has not been performed, but 5.89c and 5.90c are not. The difference is that the *a* sentences contain nouns, whereas the *c* sentences contain pronouns. We, therefore, must revise the rule:

> **Particle Movement:** Move a particle from between the verb and noun phrase to the position immediately following the noun phrase. (Optional if the noun phrase contains a noun; obligatory if it contains a pronoun)

In any grammar, most rules have a few exceptions. For some verb-particle combinations the transformation must be performed even when the noun phrase contains a noun:

5.91a   *He saw through the project.[2]
  b   He saw the project through.
  c   *He saw through it.
  d   He saw it through.
5.92a   *She yelled down her daughter.
  b   She yelled her daughter down.
  c   *She yelled down her.
  d   She yelled her down.

There are also a few combinations which do not permit the transformation even when the particle is followed by a pronoun:

5.93a   We agreed on the contract.
  b   *We agreed the contract on.
  c   We agreed on it.
  d   *We agreed it on.

[2] Sentences 5.91a and 5.91c are ungrammatical only in the sense "carry out to the end"; for the meaning "understand the true meaning," *see through* is not exceptional.

5.94a   She stood by her guilty husband.
   b   *She stood her guilty husband by.
   c   She stood by him.
   d   *She stood him by.

A dictionary, or **lexicon,** will be part of a complete grammar. In many ways this lexicon will be similar to the dictionaries which currently exist. As part of the entries for such words as *man, foot,* and *tooth,* dictionaries indicate that their plurals are formed irregularly. The lexicon for a transformational grammar will follow the same practices, and it will also list some entries as behaving irregularly in regard to certain transformations. The entries for such combinations as *see through, yell down, agree on,* and *stand by* will contain information about their exceptional status regarding the particle-movement transformation.

Indirect Objects

A rearrangement of structures usually results in an alteration of meaning or in an impossible sentence; but in some specifically defined structures such as those with particles, it produces stylistic variations but no major change in meaning. To describe these cases, we provided underlying structures and transformational rules which converted them into surface structures.

The following pairs of sentences have different structures, yet they are synonymous:

5.95a   The parking attendant gave the stub to you.
   b   The parking attendant gave you the stub.
5.96a   The architect showed the plans to me.
   b   The architect showed me the plans.

We could easily multiply the number of sentences such as these, especially with the use of such verbs as *tell, send, throw, hand, give, show,* and the like. The relationship between the pairs of sentences must be systematic rather than idiosyncratic and is, therefore, worthy of investigation.

The structure underlying 5.96a can be illustrated as follows:

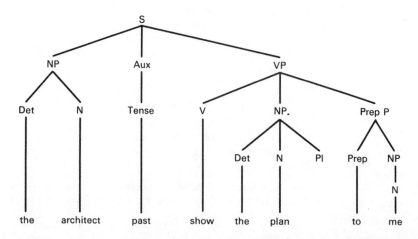

This is also the underlying structure for 5.96b, but 5.96b has undergone a transformation that 5.96a has not. This transformation deletes the preposition *to* and erases the nodes *Prep* and *Prep P;* it also moves the noun phrase *me* between the verb and the other noun phrase. This transformation converts the underlying structure into the following surface structure:

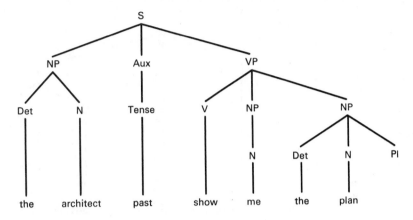

The noun phrase *me* is said to function as an **indirect object,** and it is positioned by the **indirect-object transformation.**

The indirect-object transformation cannot be performed on all structures containing prepositional phrases with *to:*

5.97a   He sent the letters to that man.
   b   He sent that man the letters.
5.98a   He sent the letters to that address.
   b   *He sent that address the letters.

The major distinction between 5.97 and 5.98 is whether or not *to* is followed by an animate noun. The transformation can be performed only if the second noun phrase contains an animate noun. In addition, for most dialects of American English the transformation is blocked if the first noun phrase contains a pronoun:

5.99a   He gave it to Tom.
   b   *He gave Tom it.

Many Englishmen have a different restriction and will accept

5.99c   He gave it Tom.

If a verb such as *send, give, tell,* and the like is followed by a noun phrase and a prepositional phrase containing *to* or *for* and an animate noun phrase, the indirect object transformation may be performed.[3] As with most rules, there are a few exceptions.

The indirect-object and particle-movement transformations permit us to rearrange certain carefully defined structures and not alter the meaning.

---

[3] In Chapter 8 we will introduce a slightly different grammatical framework which will permit a more satisfactory treatment of indirect objects.

Adverbs and Prepositional Phrases

In addition to particles and indirect objects, it is possible to move some adverbs and prepositional phrases without materially affecting the meaning. Usually these structures follow the verb:

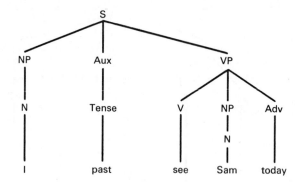

By a transformation we may move the adverb to the beginning of the sentence:

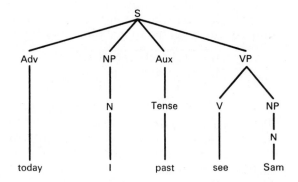

Depending upon whether or not we perform this transformation, we eventually derive the following synonymous sentences:

5.100a   I saw Sam today.
     b   Today I saw Sam.

Other examples can be readily found:

5.101a   We will be ready in a few minutes.
     b   In a few minutes we will be ready.
5.102a   There was an old troll under the bridge.
     b   Under the bridge there was an old troll.
5.103a   We read comic books sometimes.
     b   Sometimes we read comic books.

The notion of synonymy is not so clear as it might appear. Some people have argued convincingly that in two sentences such as 5.100a and 5.100b there is a difference in emphasis and hence a difference in meaning. One linguist, Wallace L. Chafe (1971), has claimed that sentences which are really synonymous are extremely rare. Others have expressed similar views. A person might use either 5.100a or 5.100b, but not in the same situations; if they are not equally desirable in all circumstances, there must be a difference of some kind in meaning. One source of confusion in much current linguistic literature is that the terms *meaning* and *synonymous* have not been defined precisely, and linguists vary in their use of them. Some linguists use a narrow interpretation of the terms and say that sentences which differ in any respect, including emphasis, are not synonymous. Others use a broader interpretation and accept sentences which describe the same event or state and have the same truth value as having the same meaning. For example, 5.100a and 5.100b do not differ in the event they describe, and if one is true the other is also. Conversely, if one is false, the other is false for the same reason: it was yesterday, not today; it was someone else, not Sam; I heard him but did not actually see him; and so on. There seems to be a need for a system which indicates that 5.104a and 5.104b are closer in meaning than either is to 5.105:

5.104a Bob wrote to Lucy last week.
    b Last week Bob wrote to Lucy.
5.105 Lucy wrote to Bob last week.

We will follow the broader interpretation of meaning and say that 5.104a and 5.104b are synonymous, whereas 5.105 has a different meaning.

Using this broader interpretation of meaning, we have seen that some sentences may have different structures but still be synonymous. To account for this relationship, we give the sentences the same underlying structure. Highly restrictive transformational rules, such as particle movement, indirect object, and adverb movement, permit us to rearrange the structure to produce a surface structure. One of the functions an internalized grammar can perform is to relate certain sentences to each other. The grammar we are developing makes use of underlying structures and transformations to perform this function.

Exercises

A. At the underlying level which of the following verbs are transitive and which ones intransitive: *wander, carry, peel, steal, watch, pour, injure, decay, bring, smoke*? Which transitive verbs from this list may have their objects deleted?

B. What objects or subjective complements do you understand in the following sentences?

1. The enlisted man saluted.
2. The waiter was so rude I didn't tip.
3. She clapped after the performance.

4. Does the water smell?
5. Do you want to wash before you eat?

C. Write the dialogue for a casual conversation between two close friends. Then submit it to several people and ask them to give all understood information. You should probably start with an example such as the one in this chapter so that your readers will have a clear understanding of what you are asking them to do. How closely do their answers agree? Try to account for any differences in responses which you receive.

D. Account for the synonymy of the following pairs of sentences:

1a. He read through the report.
 b. He read the report through.
2a. We hurried up the typist.
 b. We hurried the typist up.

E. Each of the following sentences is ambiguous because of two possible interpretations of the structure. Illustrate these structural differences by drawing two trees of each sentence, one for each meaning.

1. Weldon might have decided on the boat.
2. We looked over the chair.

F. Provide evidence to show whether the following sentences have the same structure or not:

1. He ran up the bill.
2. He ran up the hill.

G. From the following sentences determine the conditions under which particle movement is optional and those under which it is obligatory:

1. The clerk read out the names.
2. The clerk read the names out.
3. *The clerk read out them.
4. The clerk read them out.
5. He turned down the offer.
6. He turned the offer down.
7. *He turned down it.
8. He turned it down.

H. Ignoring possible differences in emphasis, are the following pairs of sentences synonymous?

1a. We found some bread crumbs under the rug.
 b. Under the rug we found some bread crumbs.
2a. We will fly to Calcutta next week.
 b. Next week we will fly to Calcutta.

Explain how we can account for the synonymous (or near synonymy) of these sentences.

I. Draw two trees of the following sentence, one for the underlying structure and the other for the surface structure: *Yesterday the girls found some mice.*

J. Use the following sentences to determine whether it is always possible to move the adverb or prepositional phrase:

1. He walked to the window carefully.
2. He walked carefully.
3. Judy turned on the air conditioner because of the heat.
4. We slept in the front bedroom.
5. We slept well in the front bedroom.
6. Anita ate slowly.
7. Anita ate the sandwich slowly.

K. Do the following pairs of sentences differ in truth value? Are there any differences in meaning?

1a. I like this.
  b. This I like.
2a. I saw Carl, but I didn't see Trudy.
  b. I saw Carl, but Trudy I didn't see.
3a. I already know Robert.
  b. Robert I already know.

Describe the transformation which relates these pairs of sentences.

Suggested Reading

CHOMSKY, NOAM, *Aspects of the Theory of Syntax*. Cambridge, Mass.: The M.I.T. Press, 1965.

ELGIN, SUZETTE HADEN, *What Is Linguistics?* Englewood Cliffs, N. J.: Prentice-Hall, Inc., 1973.

GRINDER, JOHN T., and SUZETTE HADEN ELGIN, *Guide to Transformational Grammar*. New York: Holt, Rinehart & Winston, Inc., 1973.

HALLE, MORRIS, "Questions of Linguistics," in *Modern Studies in English,* ed. David A. Reibel and Sanford A. Schane. Englewood Cliffs, N. J.: Prentice-Hall, Inc., 1969.

JACOBS, RODERICK A., and PETER S. ROSENBAUM, *English Transformational Grammar*. Waltham, Mass.: Blaisdell Publishing Company, 1968.

LANGACKER, RONALD W., *Language and Its Structure,* 2nd ed. New York: Harcourt Brace Jovanovich, Inc., 1973.

LANGENDOEN, D. TERENCE, *Essentials of English Grammar*. New York: Holt, Rinehart & Winston, Inc., 1970.

————, *The Study of Syntax*. New York: Holt, Rinehart & Winston, Inc., 1969.

LESTER, MARK, *Introductory Transformational Grammar of English*. New York: Holt, Rinehart & Winston, Inc., 1971.

LILES, BRUCE L., *An Introductory Transformational Grammar*. Englewood Cliffs, N. J.: Prentice-Hall, Inc., 1971.

————, *Linguistics and the English Language*. Pacific Palisades, Calif.: Goodyear Publishing Co., Inc., 1972.

LYONS, JOHN, *Introduction to Theoretical Linguistics*. Cambridge: Cambridge University Press, 1969.

POSTAL, PAUL, "Underlying and Superficial Linguistic Structure," in *Modern Studies in English,* ed. David A. Reibel and Sanford A. Schane. Englewood Cliffs, N. J.: Prentice-Hall, Inc., 1969.

chapter 6

Relative Constructions

In investigating the grammatical knowledge which a fluent speaker of English possesses, we have seen that there is an understanding of the structure of sentences. Words are not strung together in a random fashion, or 6.1a would be as acceptable as 6.1b, both of which contain the same words:

6.1a   *Table the on lay rag dirty a.
  b   A dirty rag lay on the table.

Certain sequences of words are recognized as meaningful, whereas others are nonsensical. Also, some alterations in word ordering produce no major changes in meaning:

6.2a   We turned off the faucet.
  b   We turned the faucet off.

Other rearrangements do affect meaning:

6.3   We threw the man on top of the bed.
6.4   We threw the bed on top of the man.

Word order is only one part of the fluent speaker's syntactic knowledge. He also recognizes that certain words in a given sentence cluster together as constituents, such as the noun phrase *a dirty rag* or the prepositional phrase *on the table* in 6.1b. These constituents are often arranged hierarchically; for example, the noun phrase *the table* is part of the larger construction *on the table,* a prepositional phrase. This structure is part of the verb phrase *lay on the table,* which in turn is part of the sentence *A dirty rag lay on the table.* We can list the elements of this hierarchy as follows, from largest to smallest:

> *Sentence:* A dirty rag lay on the table.
> *Verb phrase:* lay on the table
> *Prepositional phrase:* on the table
> *Noun phrase:* the table

Or we can represent this information on a tree:

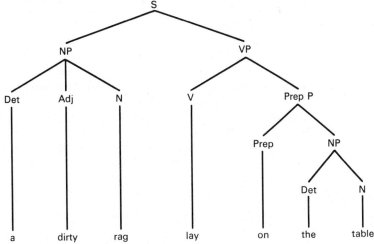

This is a representation of the phonetic structure of the sentence. We could as easily have represented the surface syntactic structure, in which morphemes are given independently, such as *past* and *lie* instead of *lay*.

If we restrict our investigation to the order in which morphemes actually occur in surface structures, we are unable to account for much of the knowledge that a speaker of the language possesses. Why do some changes in word order result in only stylistic variations, whereas others produce radical changes in meaning? Why do we recognize some sentences as ambiguous and some pairs as synonymous? How are we able to understand pronoun reference? How are speakers of English with different backgrounds able to agree on what is understood in sentences such as the following?

6.5   Andy cooks better than Sally.
6.6   I won't be here tomorrow, but Karen will.

Without knowing anything about who Andy, Sally, or Karen is, speakers of English agree on which of Sally's activities we are commenting on or where Karen will be tomorrow. To account for this information in the grammar which we are writing, we give both underlying and surface structures. The deepest underlying structure provides full and unambiguous information about a sentence. Transformations then convert this structure into a syntactic surface structure, which includes only the morphemes, in proper order, that are actually heard or written. Phonological rules then convert this surface syntactic structure into a phonetic structure, which is a representation of the pronunciation of the sentence under ideal conditions.

We are using the word *grammar* in two senses. With one use it means the knowledge that a fluent speaker of a language possesses which permits him to speak, understand, and comment on sentences. The other meaning is that of the written creation of students of language. It is important to keep these two meanings of *grammar* separate and to realize that one is not an exact reproduction of the other. For a comparison, we can look at the drawing an anatomist makes of the human circulatory system and his description of the circulation of the blood. This is a highly accurate representation of a system which has a physical existence. A written grammar, on the other hand, is not a model of how spoken utterances are produced from ideas. During the last few years, neurologists have learned a great deal about the brain and its operations, but they are still a long way from telling us how various kinds of linguistic information are stored and how they are combined. Therefore, it would be a mistake to think of a person subjecting a fully formed idea to a series of transformations as we have stated them to produce a surface structure, which in turn is operated upon by phonological rules to produce a phonetic structure. All we are saying is that there must be something in the thinking process which corresponds to the various components of our written grammar.

Relative Clauses

A sentence such as 6.7 contains information which the native speaker of English understands but which is not accounted for by the grammar we have developed so far:

6.7   The woman slapped the man who insulted her.

Her, of course, means "the woman" or some other girl or woman mentioned in an earlier sentence. We understand this because *her* is a feminine singular pronoun, and the only possible antecedent which is both feminine and singular is *the woman.* We also understand *who* as referring to *the man,* but we cannot use the same reasoning as we did for *her* to explain this. *Who* can refer to persons of either sex, individually or in groups:

6.8   The woman slapped the girl *who* insulted her.
6.9   The woman slapped all the people *who* insulted her.

The pronoun *who* when used in structures like those seen in 6.7–6.9 has the same referent as the noun phrase which precedes it.

After all phonological rules have been applied, the tree for 6.7 looks like this:

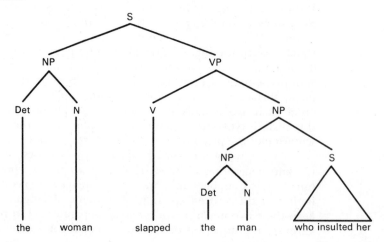

As is usual in publications in linguistics, we use a triangle to abbreviate part of a tree. That is, *who insulted her* is marked as a sentence by the *S* node. Since the exact structure of this sentence is not important for the purposes of our discussion, we have not given all the details. For very complicated sentences, the triangle serves a useful function in that it permits the reader to concentrate directly on the issue under discussion without being distracted by irrelevant details. An underlying structure for *The woman slapped the man who insulted her* has nouns in place of pronouns:

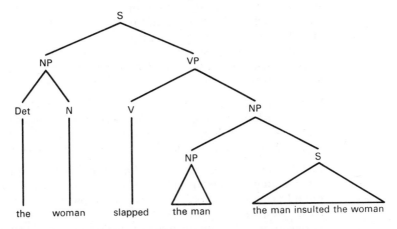

A **pronominalization** transformation substitutes the pronouns *who* and *her* for *the man* and *the woman* to derive the surface structure. A sentence embedded in a noun phrase in the manner of *who insulted her* is called a **relative clause** (or an **adjective clause**). The pronoun *who* is called a **relative pronoun.**

Let us examine another underlying structure to see what kind of relative clause we can derive:

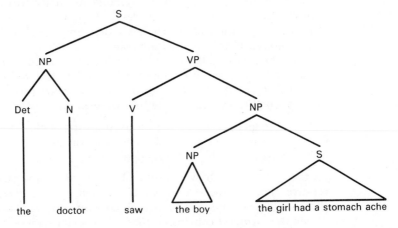

For some reason this structure does not make sense. Although there is a possible semantic relationship between a doctor seeing a patient and someone having a stomach ache, it is not one involving a relative clause. For example, 6.10 is a possible sentence:

6.10   Although the girl had a stomach ache, the doctor saw the boy.

If the subject of the embedded sentence had been *the boy,* however, we could have derived

6.11   The doctor saw the boy [who had a stomach ache].

A relative clause must contain an instance of the same noun phrase as the one to which it is adjoined; that is, the embedded sentence of 6.11 must contain the noun phrase *the boy,* just as the one in 6.7 must contain *the man.*

We may ask just what is achieved by embedding one sentence inside another that could not be accomplished by conjoining them. For example, what difference is there between the following pairs of sentences?

6.12   The stewardess pinched the child [who kicked her].
6.13   The child kicked the stewardess, and she pinched him.
6.14   The child kicked the stewardess [who pinched him].
6.15   The stewardess pinched the child, and he kicked her.

In 6.12 and 6.13 the act of kicking preceded that of pinching, and the reverse sequence holds in 6.14 and 6.15. The embedded sentence and the compound are about equally effective for showing the sequence of events and for suggesting that there is a cause and effect relationship. The difference is one of relative importance of ideas. In the compounds both acts are equally important, but in sentences 6.12 and 6.14 the main idea is expressed by the higher sentence, not by the one embedded in it. In other words, we have *subordinated* one idea to another. In 6.12 we are primarily concerned with the fact that the stewardess pinched the child; *who kicked her* is used to designate which child she pinched. In 6.14 we have the reverse situation. The kind of relative clause with which we are concerned in these sentences serves an identifying function. Usually it consists of information which has been given earlier or which is available mutually to the speaker and the listener. In the compound sentences 6.13 and 6.15, all that is assumed is that the listener is aware of which stewardess and which child are being mentioned; both acts are equally important.

All the relative clauses which have been examined so far have modified object noun phrases. We should ask whether this reflects a restriction on this kind of structure or whether it is an accidental property of the sentences we happened to examine. The following provide additional evidence:

6.16   The girl [who giggled] received a dirty look.
6.17   The librarian gave a dirty look to the girl [who giggled].
6.18   Susan is the girl [who giggled].

As these sentences show, a noun phrase used in any function may have a relative clause embedded in it. If we had restricted our investigation to those sentences among 6.7–15 which contain relative clauses, we would have drawn the incorrect conclusion that relative clauses modify only object noun phrases. Furthermore, we could have added thousands of sentences that would support this conclusion. The same problem exists with investigations which limit the data to a number of printed pages of a book or a newspaper or to tape-recorded conversations. The data may be skewed so that only certain structures appear, whereas others which are perfectly grammatical are by chance not included. There are advantages in beginning an investigation with a limited number of sentences, but it should not end with them. In the case of relative clauses, we have easily shown that our initial observation was inaccurate. In linguistic research it is always easier to refute a claim than it is to prove it. To refute the claim that only object noun phrases may be modified by relative clauses, all we had to do was find sentences such as 6.16–18 in which other noun phrases are modified. On the other hand, if we had been unable to think of any counterexamples, that in itself would not have proved that the claim was true. We could say that it is probably true, realizing that within an hour, a day, a month, or a year we might come up with examples which refute it.

Another idea which we may investigate is whether it is just the subject noun phrase within the relative clause which is replaced by a relative pronoun. This is the case in all of the sentences which we have examined so far, but our examples may not be representative of the full range of English relatives. Here is the underlying structure for an embedded sentence in which the object noun phrase is the one that will need to be pronominalized:

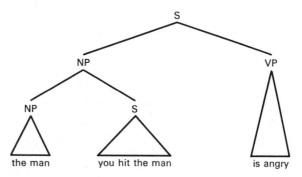

If we substitute *whom* for the repeated noun phrase *the man,* we derive

6.19a   The man [you hit **whom**] is angry.

This, of course, is ungrammatical, but if we perform another operation and move *whom* to the beginning of the embedded sentence, the result is grammatical:

6.19b   The man [**whom** you hit] is angry.

As we observed earlier, we have subordinated the statement about the act of hitting. Our main concern is that the man is angry, and this is the new information we are transmitting. We assume that the listener already knows that he hit someone, and so we are using this information to identify the person about whom we are speaking.

Relative clauses, then, require two transformations for their formation: fronting of the repeated noun phrase and pronominalization. The embedded sentence of the structure underlying 6.19b looks like this:

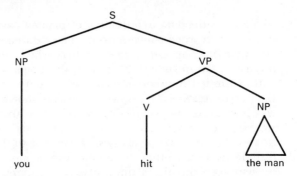

We call the process which fronts the noun phrase the **relative transforma-tion.** After its application the tree looks like this:

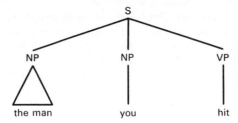

The pronominalization transformation then applies to give the surface structure:

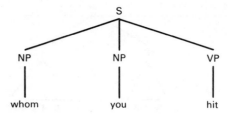

This is the process for forming relative clauses that has been accepted in much of the professional literature.

Working with relative clauses in various historical periods of the English language, Bever and Langendoen (1972) have suggested a slight revision. They interpret the relative transformation as *copying* the noun phrase instead of *moving* it. Hence, the effect of the transformation is as follows:

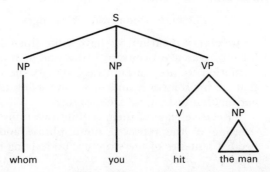

The copy is placed at the front of the sentence in the form of a relative pronoun. A second transformation deletes the original noun phrase, leaving *whom you hit*.

Linguistic theory is not far enough advanced to provide a satisfactory framework for comparing the two methods so that one is clearly preferable to the other. At issue is not just the nature of relativization, but the entire process of transformation. All of the transformations which we have encountered involving movements of particles, adverbs, or noun phrases in relative clauses can as easily be explained by transformations which copy the structure in the desired place and then delete the original. Instead of four processes of transformation—addition, deletion, rearrangement, and substitution—there may be only two: addition and deletion. Eventually we hope that linguistic theory will be able to evaluate competing analyses and show which one is preferable. It will also specify the way in which grammars should be written and define precisely the ways in which transformations may operate. Although impressive beginnings have been made in this direction, it is still impossible to make any very convincing statements about which competing analyses are the best. For this book we will accept the relative transformation as one which moves constituents, realizing that developments in future years may show that this analysis should be abandoned for the one which copies and deletes or for some other analysis still. Until theoretical work is much farther advanced than it is now, it would be foolish to accept any grammatical analysis as The Truth and not subject to revision.

We have seen two relative pronouns, *who* and *whom*, in sentences 6.7 and 6.19b, repeated here for convenience:

6.7   The woman slapped the man [*who* insulted her].
6.19b   The man [*whom* you hit] is angry.

If we use our internalized grammars to tell us which pronoun is normal in each sentence, we find that only *who* is possible in 6.7, as shown by the ungrammatical

6.20   *The woman slapped the man [*whom* insulted her].

The substitution of *who* in 6.19b, however, does far less damage. In fact, many speakers find it perfectly acceptable:

6.19c   The man [*who* you hit] is angry.

Our grammar can handle the choice of *who* and *whom* fairly easily. At some stage of the derivation of a sentence, all pronouns which are used as objects are assigned a feature, which we will arbitrarily call **OBJ**, that is, **objective.** Before this transformation applies, all pronouns are in their subject forms (*I, he, she, we, they, who*). Later rules in the phonological component will give the proper pronunciation for each pronoun. Derivations like the following will be found:

Underlying:	I saw **he**	The man **who** you hit is angry.
Objective:	I saw **he + OBJ**	The man **who + OBJ** you hit is angry.
Phonological:	I saw **him**	The man **whom** you hit is angry.

All pronouns used as subjects or subjective complements (*We are* **they**) remain unchanged, but those assigned OBJ are converted to their object forms. Although there is some dialectal variation with compound pronouns (*Tom and me did it* vs. *Tom and I did it*), the rule is fairly rigorous for personal pronouns. For the relative, however, there is much variation. Some speakers never use *whom* under any circumstances; for them the rule which adds OBJ applies only to personal pronouns, never to relatives. Others use *whom* in object positions for formal situations but *who* for others, such as conversation and informal writing. For these speakers the rule is optional for relative pronouns, depending upon the formality of the situation. There are still other speakers who consistently use *whom* for objects and *who* for subjects in all situations.

In addition to *who* and *whom*, we find other pronouns used as relatives:

6.21   The money [*that* you lost] was found by a salesman.
6.22   We found the coat [*which* you had lost].

That and *which* can be used as objects as in 6.21 and 6.22 or as subjects:

6.23a   The car [*that* is outside] belongs to Harry.
   b   The car [*which* is outside] belongs to Harry.

Our first reaction might be that *who/whom, which,* and *that* can be freely interchanged, and to a degree this is possible:

6.24a   The woman [*whom* you ridiculed] is Gertrude's mother.
   b   The woman [*that* you ridiculed] is Gertrude's mother.
6.25a   The house [*which* they bought] is in the next block.
   b   The house [*that* they bought] is in the next block.

There are restrictions in some cases:

6.24c   *The woman [*which* you ridiculed] is Gertrude's mother.
6.25c   *The house [*whom* they bought] is in the next block.

The restriction is based upon whether the referent is human or not. Noun phrases with human referents may be realized as the pronoun *who* but not *which;* those with nonhuman referents may be realized as *which* but not *who. That* may be used for either. This generalization can be easily tested by constructing various sentences with relative clauses and seeing which of the three pronouns are possible. These patterns were not always found in English, as can be seen in the writings of the sixteenth and seventeenth centuries, in which the pronoun *which* is used to refer to humans, as in "Our father, *which* art in heaven."

There is one structure in which *that* may not be used for any noun phrase, human or nonhuman. If the noun phrase is the object of a preposition, the relative transformation may move just the noun phrase or the entire prepositional phrase:

Underlying: the man [you were talking *with the man*] left early
Relative: the man [*with the man* you were talking] left early
Pro: the man [with *whom* you were talking] left early

Whereas 6.26a is grammatical, neither of the other versions is:

6.26a   The man [with *whom* you were talking] left early.
   b   *The man [with *who* you were talking] left early.
   c   *The man [with *that* you were talking] left early.

That may not be used, nor is there any choice between *who* and *whom*. A less formal sentence would have moved just the noun phrase in the relative transformation:

Underlying: the man [you were talking with *the man*] left early
Relative: the man [*the man* you were talking with] left early
Pro: the man [*that* you were talking with] left early

Here all three options are possible:

6.26d   The man [*that* you were talking with] left early.
   e   The man [*who* you were talking with] left early.
   f   The man [*whom* you were talking with] left early.

A fourth possibility without any pronoun will be discussed in the next section:

6.26g   The man [you were talking with] left early.

Although all of these are possible, some people find 6.26f objectionable because it mixes styles: *whom* from formal and the non-shifted preposition from informal.

There are similar restrictions for noun phrases with nonhuman referents:

Underlying: the horse [she was sitting *on the horse*] bucked
Relative: the horse [*on the horse* she was sitting] bucked
Pro: the horse [on *which* she was sitting] bucked

As with human noun phrases, *that* is not possible if the preposition has been fronted along with the noun phrase:

6.27a   The horse [on *which* she was sitting] bucked.
   b   *The horse [on *that* she was sitting] bucked.

If the preposition is not fronted, both *which* and *that* are possible:

6.27c   The horse [*which* she was sitting on] bucked.
   d   The horse [*that* she was sitting on] bucked.

Although there are personal stylistic preferences regarding the selection of *which* or *that* and *who* or *that* in sentences which permit choices, there are no rules that make a general restriction for the language as a whole.

Perceptual Restrictions on Relativization

As we saw in the last chapter, certain pairs of sentences can be recognized as synonymous by a fluent speaker of a language. In some cases we are able to account for this understanding by giving both sentences the same underlying structure and deriving the surface structures by differences in the transformations which are applied. For example, these sentences are synonymous:

6.28a Last week I handed out the assignments.
 b I handed the assignments out last week.

The sentences have identical underlying structures; therefore, they have the same meaning. They have different surface forms because different transformations have been applied: adverbial fronting in 6.28a and particle movement in 6.28b.

There are also relative clauses which differ in surface representation but which are synonymous:

6.29a The fish [that you caught] were too small to eat.
 b The fish [you caught] were too small to eat.

The difference between these structures is not one of surface ordering, as it is in 6.28a and 6.28b. Rather, it is one of understood information which is not overtly expressed in 6.29b. We can derive this sentence by giving all understood information overt expression at the underlying level and then deleting it by a transformation. Thus both 6.29a and 6.29b have the following derivation:

Underlying: the fish [you caught *the fish*] were too small to eat
Relative: the fish [*the fish* you caught] were too small to eat
Pro: the fish [*that* you caught] were too small to eat

If we do nothing more, we have sentence 6.29a. However, we may perform deletion:

Deletion: the fish [you caught] were too small to eat

This gives us sentence 6.29b. The differences in surface structures are accounted for by the **deletion transformation.**

With some structures deletion of relative pronouns is not possible. To determine the conditions under which it is or is not possible, let us examine several sentences:

6.30a The story [*which* I read last night] gave me nightmares.
 b The story [I read last night] gave me nightmares.
6.31a The cake [*that* you baked for us] was too sweet.
 b The cake [you baked for us] was too sweet.
6.32a I gave it to the woman [*whom* you designated].
 b I gave it to the woman [you designated].
6.33a The novelist [*who* died last year] was quite famous.
 b *The novelist [died last year] was quite famous.
6.34a Those shirts [*which* lay in the drawer] weren't cheap.
 b *Those shirts [lay in the drawer] weren't cheap.
6.35a The rock [*that* hit me] was sharp.
 b *The rock [hit me] was sharp.

Whereas the pronoun may be deleted in 6.30–32, it may not be in 6.33–35. Since both groups of sentences contain all three relative pronouns, referring both to human and nonhuman referents, the difference must not be in the choice of pronouns. Close examination will show that the relative pronouns in 6.30–32 are all objects within their clauses, whereas those in 6.33–35 are subjects. We can form a generalization that object relative pronouns may optionally be deleted but that subjects may not be. However, the generalization can be extended to include subjective complements:

6.36a   He is no longer the man [**that** he once was].
   b   He is no longer the man [he once was].

A better statement is that relative pronouns may be optionally deleted unless they are subjects.

We can list thousands of sentences which support our generalization, yet this alone is not enough to confirm it. We must also find no counterexamples, such as the following:

6.37a   The woman [who I was talking with] was rude.
   b   The woman [I was talking with] was rude.
   c   The woman [with whom I was talking] was rude.
   d *The woman [with I was talking] was rude.

Objects of prepositions may be deleted like other nonsubject noun phrases, so long as the preposition has not been fronted. A revision of our generalization which is more adequate is "A relative pronoun may be optionally deleted unless it is a subject or immediately preceded by a preposition."

Many patterns and restrictions exist in languages for no reason that we can recognize other than convention. There are others which have explainable sources. The shape of the human mouth precludes the presence of certain conceivable sounds, such as one produced while the lower lip is touching the soft palate or while the tongue tip is touching the uvula. Some structures do not exist because there are universal constraints against them, although they would be physically possible to produce. For example, it would be logically possible for a language to form questions from statements by placing *duh* after each word: "*The duh gloves duh are duh in duh this duh drawer duh?" For some unexplained reason no language forms questions in any manner like this. Still other restrictions exist because of perceptual reasons. The prohibition against deleting subject relative pronouns seems to stem from such a reason.

Let us see how a person hearing 6.35b, repeated here, would react:

6.35b   *The rock hit me was sharp.

There is nothing to indicate that *hit me* is an embedded sentence. In fact, the listener will begin interpreting *the rock* as subject of *hit me* as he would if the entire sentence were *The rock hit me.* Then he hears *was sharp,* which has no apparent subject. *Was sharp* cannot be treated as an adverbial such as *yesterday* or *on the head.* The listener is stymied because there is nothing to tell him that *hit me* is a modifier and that *the rock* is the subject of *was sharp.* We can easily show that there are only a few kinds of structures which a person expects to find after a sentence beginning with a noun phrase:

6.38   The man saw you. . . .
6.39   The man who saw you. . . .
6.40   The rock hit me. . . .
6.41   The rock that hit me. . . .
6.42   The man you saw. . . .

As 6.38 and 6.40 show, we interpret a noun phrase and an immediately following verb as subject and predicate. Only certain structures such as adverbials or a conjunction and a noun phrase or a verb phrase are expected
to follow:

6.43   The man saw you (on the hill).
6.44   The man saw you (and liked you).
6.45   The man saw you (and me).

If a person hears something like

6.46   The man saw you liked you.

he probably corrects it to

6.47   The man saw you *and* liked you.

If, as in 6.39 and 6.41, the first noun phrase is followed by *that* or *who*—
words that are known relative pronouns—the listener expects a modifying
clause which will be followed by the predicate verb of the first noun phrase.
He mentally does something equivalent to placing brackets around the relative clause. If some noun or pronoun other than a relative follows the first
noun phrase, as in 6.42, a relative clause is still recognized as a possibility;
however, a compound structure is also possible:

6.48a   The man the woman. . . .
    b   The man the woman saw looked amused.
    c   The man, the woman, and the child ran.

It is obviously because of strategies we have as listeners for recognizing syntactic structures that there is a restriction against deleting relative pronouns
used as subjects.[1]

Other restrictions resulting from perceptual problems can be found in
structures with multiple embedding. Since a noun phrase used in any way
can have a sentence embedded in it, there is nothing to prevent a noun
phrase within an embedded sentence from having a sentence embedded
within it, producing a very long sentence. The following, for example, is
grammatical and perfectly understandable even if it is not a model of stylistic elegance:

6.49   The man chased the boy who hit the dog that frightened the cat
        which killed the mouse that ate the cheese which was moldy.

Multiple embeddings that pile up at the end are usually easy to understand.

Embedded sentences in other positions, however, sometimes cause trouble, especially when they involve certain types of structures and have deleted

---

[1] A fuller discussion of the subject can be found in Bever and Langendoen (1972).

relative pronouns. With the relative pronoun expressed, 6.50 is fairly easy to understand:

6.50a   The boy that the man hit cried.

Without the pronoun, the sentence becomes fuzzy:

6.50b   The boy the man hit cried.

Most people if presented with 6.50b in writing do not at first understand it unless they have been given a sentence such as 6.50a first. Some find it incomprehensible even after several minutes. If a person reads the sentence aloud, concentrating on the intended meaning and reading slowly, the listener has no problems understanding it. On the other hand, if the person reading aloud uses a normal intonation pattern, the sentence is as baffling as when it is read silently. We can make the sentence even more complicated by further embedding. If we embed *whom the girl loved* as a relative clause modifying *the man,* we derive the noun phrase *the man whom the girl loved,* or without the relative pronoun, *the man the girl loved.* Now let us place the additional clause within the sentence:

6.51a   The boy the man the girl loved hit cried.

Even after having the sentence explained, most people find it very difficult, if not totally incomprehensible. The problem is that the usual perceptual clues which help us assign structural descriptions are missing. Nor is 6.51 much more understandable if we add relative pronouns:

6.51b   The boy whom the man whom the girl loved hit cried.

Multiple embedding of this nature is usually found unacceptable because the surface structures are difficult or impossible to interpret.

It has been customary in the transformational literature of the past to say that perceptual difficulties are matters of performance which do not affect the grammaticalness of a structure. Hence, sentences with multiple embedding between the subject noun phrase and the verb of the highest sentence are considered grammatical even though they never actually appear. There is something suspicious about a grammar which accepts sentences that a fluent speaker finds impossible. This is a different matter from finding sentences improbable, as we can see from the following examples:

6.52   Bill drank the shoe polish.
6.53   Loretta defrosted the refrigerator last week.
6.54   The student the teacher the parent praised spanked cheated.

The first two are unquestionably grammatical, yet their occurrence is improbable, as is that of most sentences. Most people will never hear 6.52, yet they would agree that it is a possible sentence should the occasion ever occur in which it is needed. Similarly, most people will never hear 6.53, even though the need for it seems much more probable than that for 6.52. If we evaluate sentences according to their probability of occurrence, then all three are equally unlikely to be heard by most people. Except for a few stock phrases, this is true of every sentence.

Reduced Relative Clauses

In Chapter 4 we saw that on the surface a noun phrase may have a prepositional phrase embedded within it:

6.55a   *The lion [in the cage]* looks hungry.

The prepositional phrase *in the cage* can be derived in two possible ways: (1) It is already in the most remote underlying structure in this form, just as *lion* is. (2) It is derived transformationally. Our choice of sources should be based upon a decision as to which one provides greater insight into the structures of the English language.

So far we have seen two main reasons for having underlying structures which differ from those on the surface. They account for material which is understood, and they account for syntactic similarities and differences which are not explainable from just surface manifestations. These two may overlap. Let us compare 6.55a with 6.55b:

6.55b   The lion [that is in the cage] looks hungry.

Sentences 6.55a and 6.55b mean the same thing, yet if we derive them differently, there is no way to account for this synonymy. Let us see if there is some way to derive them from the same underlying structure, namely

6.55c   the lion [the lion is in the cage] looks hungry

The relative transformation does not affect the ordering. The pronominalization transformation gives 6.55b. Since the relative pronoun is a subject, deletion is impossible:

6.55d   *the lion [is in the cage] looks hungry

On the other hand, if we permit a transformation to delete not just the relative pronoun but the form of *be* as well, we will have 6.55a, repeated here:

6.55a   The lion [in the cage] looks hungry.

This solution accounts for the synonymy of 6.55a and 6.55b.

But transformations are supposed to express significant generalizations about the language. If we limited ourselves to one or two sentences or phrases, we could come up with a great many observations. For example, we could examine the words *radar* and *Serutan,* the noun phrase *mad dog,* and the sentence *Able was I ere I saw Elba* and make a generalization about reading words and structures backward. The conclusion would be trivial, since the process is rare and does not lend itself to any classification scheme. The examples we can think of are either accidental or deliberate concoctions, not representations of regular processes that exist in the language. We should likewise guard against ad hoc transformations that apply to only one or two sentences. Transformations should apply to entire classes of structures, and they should reflect in some way the internalized grammar. Under no circumstance should they be just games invented by the linguist, regardless of how ingenious they may be.

Let us examine a tentative rule called **relative reduction**, which deletes the relative pronoun and an immediately following form of *be,* along with tense. This transformation will account for the synonymy of 6.55a and 6.55b, repeated here:

6.55a   The lion [in the cage] looks hungry.
   b   The lion [that is in the cage] looks hungry.

We could argue that we understand *that is* before *in the cage* in the *a* version, but we would probably have trouble convincing someone who disagreed and said that nothing is understood. However, there is nothing to prevent *that is* from being in the embedded structure, and we can think of several other elements that are implausible: *that growled in the cage, that chased me in the cage,* and the like, all of which are possible structures but are not understood in 6.55a.

Let us try another sentence:

6.56a   I shot the lion [in the cage].

This sentence is ambiguous, since *in the cage* can designate which lion I shot or where I shot it. One method people use to disambiguate a sentence about which they are questioned is to paraphrase it. A fairly typical paraphrase for one of the meanings of 6.56a is

6.56b   I shot the lion [that was in the cage].

If this analysis does not prove that the fluent speaker of English understands a relative pronoun and a form of *be* before *in the cage* in 6.55a and 6.56a, it at least shows that such an analysis is not incompatible with the workings of the internalized grammar.

Will relative reduction account for other sentences with prepositional phrases and their synonymous counterparts with relative clauses? Here are some examples:

6.57a   The balloon [on the roof] burst.
   b   The balloon [that was on the roof] burst.
6.58a   I knew the woman [in the car].
   b   I knew the woman [who was in the car].

We could easily add thousands of sentences like these if we had the time and desire. We can also think of prepositional phrases embedded within noun phrases which have no relative clause counterparts:

6.59a   The answer [to the question] is simple.
   b   *The answer [which is to the question] is simple.
6.60a   The Danes held control [of the battlefield].
   b   *The Danes held control [that was of the battlefield].
6.61a   His fear [of strangers] is appalling.
   b   *His fear [that is of strangers] is appalling.
6.62a   The father [of his second wife] makes jigs.
   b   *The father [who is of his second wife] makes jigs.

Obviously all prepositional phrases are not derived from relative clauses, yet a large number are.

Sometimes a surface noun phrase has an adverb embedded in it, as in this sentence:

6.63a   The people [downstairs] are noisy.

This is synonymous with

6.63b   The people [who are downstairs] are noisy.

The relative reduction transformation can show that these sentences are related and does not conflict with the knowledge of a fluent speaker of English. Furthermore, there are other such pairs:

6.64a   The people [here] are obnoxious.
   b   The people [who are here] are obnoxious.
6.65a   The dog [outside] is mad.
   b   The dog [that is outside] is mad.

The proposed transformation thus accounts for other surface structures as well as prepositional phrases.

Next we can examine present participial phrases to see whether there is anything understood but not expressed in them:

6.66a   The person [ringing the doorbell] finally went away.

We understand this to be equivalent to

6.66b   The person [who was ringing the doorbell] finally went away.

There are also other pairs of sentences like these:

6.67a   Do you know the woman [eating her pudding with a fork]?
   b   Do you know the woman [who is eating her pudding with a fork]?
6.68a   The snow [falling outside] looks clean.
   b   The snow [which is falling outside] looks clean.

The same transformation will also handle past participial phrases:

6.69a   The cheese [eaten by the rat] was poisoned.
   b   The cheese [that was eaten by the rat] was poisoned.
6.70a   Were you the person [trapped in the elevator]?
   b   Were you the person [who was trapped in the elevator]?

Relative reduction provides us with a device for relating a number of surface structures with synonymous relative clauses.

Let us now see whether relative reduction is applicable to all relative clauses in which the pronoun is immediately followed by a form of *be:*

6.71a   Here is some fruit [which is ripe].

If we apply relative reduction, we produce

6.71b   *Here is some fruit [ripe].

This is ungrammatical, yet there is a possible sentence with different word order:

6.71c   Here is some [ripe] fruit.

It is possible to use this process to derive most adjectives which precede nouns on the surface. Since 6.71a and 6.71c mean the same thing, we would like to give them the same underlying structure. This is possible if we derive 6.71c through relative reduction and a transformation called **adjective preposing,** which moves an adjective in front of the noun.

In case the pronoun *something* or *someone* is the noun phrase modified by the relative clause, adjective preposing is inapplicable:

Underlying:	I found something [something was good]
Relative:	I found something [something was good]
Pro:	I found something [that was good]
Reduction:	I found something [good]
Preposing:	*I found [good] something

Similarly, *Someone fat sat in front of me* is a grammatical sentence, whereas *Fat someone sat in front of me* is not. However, if we substitute a noun phrase such as *a book* for *something* and *a woman* for *someone,* then adjective preposing must be performed.

We find similar transformations in other languages. For example, here is the derivation for the adjective *new* in English, German, and French.

English

Underlying:	my book [my book is new] is very interesting
Relative:	my book [my book is new] is very interesting
Pro:	my book [that is new] is very interesting
Reduction:	my book [new] is very interesting
Preposing:	My [new] book is very interesting.

German

Underlying:	mein Buch [mein Buch ist neu] ist sehr interessant
Relative:	mein Buch [mein Buch ist neu] ist sehr interessant
Pro:	mein Buch [das ist neu] ist sehr interessant
Reduction:	mein Buch [neu] ist sehr interessant
Preposing:	Mein [neues] Buch ist sehr interessant.

German has rules which assign certain endings to adjectives which precede the nouns they modify; hence, there is an *-es* on *neues* when it precedes *Buch,* but no ending when it follows *ist.* For the transformations which are actually involved in deriving the adjective and positioning it properly, the rules are identical to those for English.

With French we see a difference:

French

Underlying:	mon livre [mon livre est nouveau] est très intéressant
Relative:	mon livre [mon livre est nouveau] est très intéressant
Pro:	mon livre [qui est nouveau] est très intéressant
Reduction:	Mon livre [nouveau] est très intéressant.

Since most adjectives in French follow the nouns they modify, the adjective preposing transformation is normally inapplicable. Yet there are a few common adjectives which do precede nouns: *beau, jeune, joli, petit, vieux,* and the like. Hence, the derivation of *The little boy was studying* is as follows:

Underlying: le garçon [le garçon était petit] étudiait
Relative: le garçon [le garçon était petit] étudiait
Pro: le garçon [qui était petit] étudiait
Reduction: le garçon [petit] étudiait
Preposing: Le [petit] garçon étudiait.

It appears that all languages have relative clauses, or at least structures corresponding to them. The fact that those in English, German, and French are almost identical in derivation is a coincidence of their common descent from Indo-European. We find more variation outside of this language family. For example, Japanese has no relative pronoun, and relative clauses precede the nouns they modify. In spite of these surface differences, the underlying structures are obviously the same as those for English and other Western languages.

Even within the Indo-European languages there is much variation among the types of relative pronouns used. English *who* and *which* are identical in form to the interrogative pronouns (*Who left? Which one did you see?*), and *that* is identical to the demonstrative (*That is mine*). In German the relatives are like the definite articles *die, der, das* and their inflected forms. In Old English there was a relative particle (not pronoun) ðe, which introduced many relative clauses. If we choose to emphasize differences among languages, we will find a rich area for investigation; we will also find that the differences are limited to a well-defined range of possible forms. On the other hand, if we decide to look for similarities among languages, these are also abundant. Whether we find differences or similarities depends primarily upon whether we study surface or underlying structures.

Before leaving the subject of relative reduction, we should make one observation about synonymy, as shown in the following sentences:

6.72a   My car that is new is outside.
   b   My new car is outside.

With our use of the term *synonymous,* these two sentences do mean the same thing. That is, if one is true, the other is also; if one is false, the other is for the same reason. There is another sense, however, in which the sentences differ. Sentence 6.72a carries the presupposition that the speaker has more than one car. Whereas the *b* version may include this presupposition, it does not necessarily do so. At present we have no idea how, where, or whether presupposition should be incorporated into a grammar. This is a topic that will reappear now and again in the chapters which follow, but no solution will be offered.

Possessives

One type of prenominal modifier which is interestingly complex is the possessive noun or pronoun, as illustrated in the following sentences:

6.73   I found [Bill's] coat.
6.74   I found [his] coat.

Traditional grammarians generally did not question the appropriateness of calling *Bill's* a noun in the possessive (or genitive) case; after all, it is similar in form to the noun *Bill,* and it can have the pronoun *his* substituted for it. With *his,* however, they were not so firmly in agreement. Although students of Old and Middle English for centuries had been accepting *his* as a pronoun, some writers of textbooks for use in secondary schools noticed a problem which resulted from their definitions for the various parts of speech. If a noun is the name of a person, place, or thing, then *his* must be a noun or a word which substitutes for a noun—a pronoun. On the other hand, if an adjective is a word which modifies a noun or a pronoun, then *his* also fits this definition. Rather than question the accuracy of their definitions, these pedants presented arguments to show that *his* and similar pronouns were "really" pronouns or that they were "really" adjectives. Some coined new terms to permit them to be both pronoun and adjective: *pronominal adjective* or *adjectival pronoun.* Later the American structuralists of the 1940s used examples like this as evidence for the weaknesses of traditional definitions.

During the 1950s, various attempts were made to classify the various structures in a noun phrase which may precede the noun.[2] It was noticed, for example, that determiners are mutually exclusive, but that they may coexist with other modifiers:

6.75   He lost [all the green] marbles.
6.76   *He lost [all the those] marbles.

The articles *the* and *a,* along with the demonstratives *this, that, these,* and *those* constitute a class of modifier of which only one may be selected for each noun phrase. Possessives are also in this class:

6.77   [Tom's] apples are rotten.
6.78   *[These Tom's] apples are rotten.
6.79   *[The Tom's] apples are rotten.

Sometimes a determiner does precede a possessive noun:

6.80   Have you seen [that man's] shoes?
6.81   *Have you seen those [man's] shoes?

As these sentences clearly show, the determiner belongs with the possessive, not with the noun which it modifies. (There is another structure, *men's shoes,* meaning "shoes for men," which may be preceded by a determiner, but it is different from that found in 6.81.)

As with the discussions of whether possessives are primarily names or modifiers, those who observed that they fill the same position as articles and demonstratives provided interesting information. But now that we have a more powerful grammatical framework to work with, we can see that studies which limit themselves to surface structures are missing a great deal.

Our grammar makes it clear, first of all, that such possessives as *Tom's* and *his* have as much semantic content as *Tom* and *he* do. *The* and *a,* on the other hand, do little more than indicate whether the following noun

---

[2] One of the best examples can be found in Chapter 11 of Hill (1958).

has been specified or not. The demonstratives merely point out the noun they modify. One could easily give a noun at the underlying level certain features such as definite and demonstrative and be able to predict which article or demonstrative would be needed to spell out these features. It would not be possible to distinguish *Tom's* from *Doug's* in this way.

Second, possessive nouns may be modified by determiners and adjectives:

6.82a   [The sick man's] daughters visited him.

Obviously *the* and *sick* modify *man's*, not *daughters*. The fluent speaker of English understands that the man is sick and that nothing has been said about the health of the daughters. He can contrast *the sick man's daughters* with *the man's sick daughters*. Also, he can substitute *a, this,* or *that* for *the* and still have a grammatical sentence; these determiners are all singular and cannot modify the plural noun *daughters*. *Possessives,* then, are not simply nouns or pronouns but complete noun phrases.

Third, noun phrases used as possessives are often synonymous with prepositional phrases:

6.82b   The daughters [of the sick man] visited him.

The fluent speaker of English certainly understands this sentence to mean the same thing as 6.82a, but if he must rely solely upon surface structures, there is no way for him to account for this synonymy. It also seems reasonable that *sick* should be derived from a relative clause, whatever the surface form may be:

6.82a   [The sick man's] daughters visited him.
   b   The daughters [of the sick man] visited him.
   c   The daughters [of the man [who was sick]] visited him.

Through relative reduction and adjective preposing, we can already show the relationship between the *b* and *c* versions. It seems that there should also be some way to relate these structures to the one in 6.82a.

Finally, the relationship which is understood between a possessive and the noun it modifies shows much variation among sentences, although on the surface they all appear to be alike. To give some idea of the differences, we can provide the following examples:

6.83   *The sun's rays* are bright. (origin)
6.84   *The woman's purse* was stolen. (possession)
6.85   *Their love* for each other was surprising. (subjective)
6.86   She barely escaped from *her pursuers*. (objective)
6.87   It's *a day's walk* from here. (measure)

Such distinguished traditionalists as Curme and Jespersen[3] noticed differences of this nature and commented on their meaning. These differences are made evident by the ambiguity of

6.88   Have you seen *my picture?*

---

[3] Curme (1935:133), Jespersen (1949:VII, 311ff.; 1924:180–82). For the use of these ideas by an American structuralist, see Fries (1940:72ff.).

Is the picture one which I painted (or took with my camera), one which was painted of me by someone else, or merely one which I own? All of these are alike on the surface.

Although relatively little research has been performed by transformationalists upon possessives, the following steps, adapted from Smith (1964: 44), have been suggested:

1. the book [Kathy has a book] is missing
2. the book [the book is Kathy's] is missing
3. the book [which is Kathy's] is missing
4. the book [of Kathy's] is missing
5. [Kathy's] book is missing

There is much that is ad hoc about most of this derivation, but no satisfactory alternative has been advanced.[4]

Restrictive and Nonrestrictive Modifiers

Traditional grammars usually contained discussions of different kinds of relative clauses, as illustrated in the following sentences:

6.89   The woman [who lives next door] sent us some brownies.
6.90   Maude Adams, [who lives next door], sent us some brownies.

The clause *who lives next door* is related to the noun phrase it modifies in a different way in each of the sentences. In 6.89 the clause identifies the woman about whom we are speaking. Without it the listener does not know which woman is indicated:

6.91   The woman sent us some brownies.

In 6.90, however, *Maude Adams* is identified by her name, and *who lives next door* merely gives additional information about her. The relative clause is not needed for identification:

6.92   Maude Adams sent us some brownies.

A clause which is needed for identification is said to *restrict* the noun phrase it modifies; in 6.89 we are restricting the class of women to a specific one. Clauses with this function are said to be **restrictive clauses.** Those like 6.90, which give added information but which do not serve a limiting function, are called **nonrestrictive clauses;** in some books they are referred to as **appositive clauses.**

There are differences in form between the two kinds of relative clauses. Nonrestrictives are set off in speech by a slight pause and a characteristic change in pitch both before and after. These features are indicated in writing by commas. Restrictives are not set off by such features. We repeat 6.89 and 6.90 here for convenience:

---

4 Langacker (1968) studies French possessives within this general framework.

6.89   The woman [who lives next door] sent us some brownies.
6.90   Maude Adams, [who lives next door], sent us some brownies.

There may be a pause after a long subject, such as after *the woman who lives next door* in 6.89, but this is not caused by the nature of the clause; there is no pause between *woman* and *who*. The intonation patterns are clearly different for the two kinds of clauses.

Another difference is in the choice of relative pronouns. Restrictive clauses may contain *who* to refer to humans and *which* to nonhumans; they may contain *that* for either:

6.93a   My daughter [who graduated last night] is spoiled.
    b   My daughter [that graduated last night] is spoiled.
6.94a   The car [which is outside] isn't mine.
    b   The car [that is outside] isn't mine.

With nonrestrictive clauses *that* may not be used:

6.95a   Frances, [who graduated last night], is spoiled.
    b   *Frances, [that graduated last night], is spoiled.
6.96a   My new car, [which is parked outside], is green.
    b   *My new car, [that is parked outside], is green.[5]

To a degree, the nature of the modified noun phrase determines whether the relative clause is to be restrictive or nonrestrictive. Since proper nouns usually refer to unique objects or persons, they are normally followed by nonrestrictive clauses since the clause is not needed for identification:

6.97   Martha, [who waited until last], received the biggest prize.
6.98   Bloomington, [which is only thirty miles from here], has a good library.

If the speaker is talking about more than one person named Martha or more than one city named Bloomington, he may use relative clauses to differentiate them. In this case the clauses serve a restrictive function, not one of merely giving additional information:

6.99   The Martha [who waited until last] wasn't the one who received the biggest prize.
6.100   The Bloomington [which is only thirty miles from here] doesn't have as good a library as the one in Indiana.

It should be noted that when there are several people or objects with the same name, as in 6.99 and 6.100, the name is preceded by a determiner as well as followed by a restrictive clause. When the name is considered unique, as in 6.97 and 6.98, neither a determiner nor a restrictive clause is possible.

Sometimes other modifiers serve to limit a noun so that only nonrestrictive modifiers are possible:

---

[5] Sentence 6.96b is ungrammatical only with the nonrestrictive reading. For the restrictive reading (i.e., if a person has more than one new car), it is possible. This example shows that the possibility of the relative pronoun *that* is definitely determined by whether the clause is restrictive or nonrestrictive.

6.101   My grandfather [who lives in Commerce] is interested in transfor-
        mational grammar. (restrictive)
6.102   My maternal grandfather, [who lives in Commerce], is interested in
        transformational grammar. (nonrestrictive)
6.103   Her daughter [who is in kindergarten] is smarter than her older
        children. (restrictive)
6.104   Her youngest daughter, [who is in kindergarten], is smarter than
        her older children. (nonrestrictive)

The phrases *my maternal grandfather* and *her youngest daughter* refer to
unique individuals, whereas *my grandfather* and *her daughter* may have
more than one possible referent.

Often it is the knowledge which the speaker and listener share that
determines whether clauses are to be restrictive or nonrestrictive:

6.105   My brother [who lives next door] is on vacation.
6.106   My brother, [who lives next door], is on vacation.

If the speaker has several brothers, *who lives next door* is needed to indicate
which brother is meant, as opposed to the one who lives across town or the
one who lives in Nashville. If the speaker has only one brother, the noun
phrase *my brother* is enough to designate him. Knowledge such as this is
necessary in determining whether such noun phrases as the following have
unique referents: *our car, Lucille's cat, Valerie's house, my book,* and the
like. Even such a noun phrase as *Bessie's husband* by itself may or may not
designate a unique individual, depending upon whether Bessie is monoga-
mous (or has had several marriages in succession). It is easy to think of con-
texts in which *the devil, the moon,* and *the sun* have unique reference, and
any modifying clause is nonrestrictive; yet we may wish to speak of a region
which has several devils, of a planet such as Saturn with several moons, or
various galaxies, each with its own sun. In cases such as these, relative
clauses may be restrictive.

Earlier in this chapter we derived restrictive clauses from structures
like this:

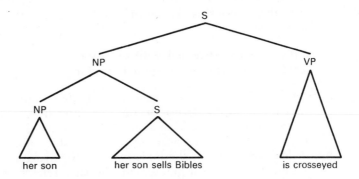

After application of the relative and pronominalization transformations, we
derive

6.107   Her son who sells Bibles is crosseyed.

It would be undesirable to have the same underlying structure for non-restrictive clauses. Since they give added information, it has been suggested that they be derived from underlying conjoined sentences:

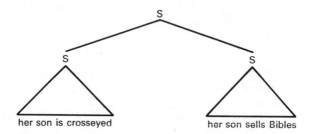

In this way the following sentences have the same underlying structure:

6.108a   Her son is crosseyed, and he sells Bibles.
     b   Her son, who sells Bibles, is crosseyed.

The surface forms differ because of the selection of transformations.

The structures from which relative clauses are derived have received considerable discussion in transformational literature, but so far no very convincing evidence has been produced for any of them. The earliest studies merely listed two sentences for restrictive clauses:

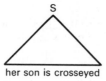 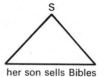

At that time it was stated that either sentence could be embedded within the other, since this version of transformational theory was not concerned with meaning:

6.107   Her son who sells Bibles is crosseyed.
6.109   Her son who is crosseyed sells Bibles.

By the mid-1960s, it was generally felt that meaning should in some way play a role in the derivation of a sentence; it was further decided that all elements of meaning should be present at the deepest underlying level of representation.[6] One means of providing this information is to permit embedded structures at the underlying level—structures that must contain an instance of the noun phrase with the same referent as the one modified. If we follow such a grammar, then, sentences 6.107 and 6.109 differ in meaning according to which sentence is embedded within the other.

---

[6] See Katz and Postal (1964) and Chomsky (1965).

Conclusion

Within a noun phrase there may be various kinds of modifiers:

6.110   The car *which he bought* has been stolen. (relative clause)
6.111   I caught the ball *dropped from the window*. (past participial phrase)
6.112   The man *opening the door* is the manager. (present participial phrase)
6.113   The trees *on this street* are dying. (prepositional phrase)
6.114   I found a *valuable* coin. (adjective)
6.115   The people *inside* are restless. (adverb)
6.116   Did you speak to *the child's* teacher? (possessive)

All these structures fulfill the same function of limiting the noun they modify, yet they are radically different from one another in form. By deriving all of them from embedded sentences which are adjoined to the noun they modify, we are recognizing their likeness in function. With a handful of transformations we are able to account for their differences in form. Their similarities are shown at the underlying level, their differences on the surface.

Exercises

A. Perform the relative and pronominalization transformations:

1. do you know the name of the poem [Ann is reading the poem]
2. .the girl [the girl spoke] is a senior
3. he told the story to the people [he was riding with the people]

B. What evidence can you provide to show that *the men at work* is a noun phrase in the following sentence: *The men at work heard the announcement*?

C. Explain why the following sentences are not grammatical:

1. *I don't know the girl which opened the door.
2. *The people with that she lives are out of town.
3. *The pen with whom I am writing cost less than a dollar.
4. *The pen with I am writing cost less than a dollar.
5. *The boy sneezed has a bad cold.

Now use your imagination to provide a situation in which sentences 1 and 3 would be possible. To do this, do you actually violate the rules for selection of relative pronouns, or do you alter the classification of *girl* and *pen*?

D. In the following sentences locate the noun modifiers and label them as to their surface-structure forms (relative clause, prepositional phrase, etc.); then give their underlying structures and perform all transformations needed to derive the given surface structures:

1. The woman who asked the question was rude.
2. The ugly duckling waddled away.
3. The fish we ate were good.
4. I opened the package lying on the floor.
5. She gave the keys to the tall man by the door.
6. The rumor started by Fred shocked the man who heard it.
7. The letter he wrote went astray.
8. The girl sitting in the chair hid the pink dress.

E. Sentence 4 in the preceding exercise is ambiguous. What underlying structure would you suggest for the meaning in which the participial phrase does not modify *package?*

F. Explain why our grammar does not permit adjectives inside the noun phrase at the underlying level. Wouldn't it be simpler to start out with *the lovely rose* rather than to derive *lovely* from a relative clause?

G. Use underlying structures and transformations to account for the synonymy of the following sentences:

1a. The man that she is dancing with is her husband.
 b. The man with whom she is dancing is her husband.
 c. The man she is dancing with is her husband.
2a. The man who was waiting in line didn't see the laughing woman.
 b. The man waiting in line didn't see the woman who was laughing.

H. Account for the ambiguity of this sentence: *He opened the package in the kitchen.*

I. Explain how a person who has not studied formal grammar can recognize synonymous, ambiguous, and ungrammatical sentences. What can you say about these sentences that a person who has not studied formal grammar cannot?

J. Consider the following noun phrases in Spanish, for which an English translation is given preserving the Spanish word order:

1. un sombrero grande "a hat large"
2. dos muchachos malos "two boys bad"
3. su hermana bonita "your sister pretty"
4. mi abuela gorda "my grandmother fat"

Spanish adjectives within the noun phrase are derived from relative clauses, as are those in English, except for one transformation. What is it? For this aspect of the grammar, which of the two languages is the more systematic? Which is the more logical?

K. Some people have referred to *the girl* in the following sentence as being simultaneously the subject of *sings* and the object of *met: The girl you met sings in the choir.* Why is this analysis inaccurate?

Suggested Reading

BEVER, T. G., and D. T. LANGENDOEN, "The Interaction of Speech Perception and Grammatical Structure in the Evolution of Language," in *Linguistic Change and Generative Theory,* ed. Robert P. Stockwell and Ronald K. S. Macaulay. Bloomington: Indiana University Press, 1972.

JESPERSEN, OTTO, *A Modern English Grammar on Historical Principles,* Vol. III. Copenhagen: Ejnar Munksgaard, 1927.

LANGACKER, RONALD W., "Observations on French Possessives," *Language* 44 (1968): 51–75.

REIBEL, DAVID, and SANFORD SCHANE, eds., *Modern Studies in English.* Englewood Cliffs, N. J.: Prentice-Hall, Inc., 1969.

STOCKWELL, ROBERT P., PAUL SCHACHTER, and BARBARA HALL PARTEE. *The Major Syntactic Structures of English.* New York: Holt, Rinehart & Winston, Inc., 1973.

THOMPSON, SANDRA ANNEAR, "The Deep Structure of Relative Clauses," in *Studies in Linguistic Semantics,* ed. Charles J. Fillmore and D. Terence Langendoen. New York: Holt, Rinehart & Winston, Inc., 1971.

chapter 7

Noun Clauses, Infinitives, and Gerunds

A grammar which includes underlying as well as surface structures is potentially able to account for much of the knowledge that a fluent speaker of a language possesses. We have seen how such a grammar can provide identical underlying structures for two sentences which differ on the surface and predict that they will be recognized as synonymous; or it can provide two or more underlying structures for sentences which are superficially identical and predict that more than one meaning will be recognized. In other instances, people with quite different backgrounds are able to agree that certain elements are understood in a surface structure although they are not actually spoken or written. The grammar is able to account for this knowledge by including all meaningful elements at an underlying level and later deleting some of them if well-defined conditions exist.

Although transformational grammars are by far the most powerful means yet developed for accounting for the native speaker's understanding of his language, they are far from perfect. We have already begun seeing certain areas of sentence structure, such as possessives, which are at present very poorly understood. In spite of the enormous amount of linguistic scholarship that appears every year, much of it contributing substantially to our understanding of language, it would be foolish to assume that at some date in the near future we will have a complete understanding of English or any other language. It would be even more foolish to suppose that we will have a comprehensive knowledge of language in general. In this respect linguistics is like most other scholarly disciplines. Whatever the field —astronomy, bacteriology, psychology, Shakespearean studies, or linguistics —there will still be many unanswered questions in the year 2000, and no doubt in 2500 and 3000.

All written grammars are artificial to a degree. No one knows very much about how the brain stores knowledge such as the vocabulary and grammar of a language or how it uses this knowledge in producing, understanding, and evaluating sentences. In dealing with such matters as synonymy, ambiguity, deletion, pronominalization, and the like, transformational grammars have accomplished a great deal and show promise as a means for future research. Leading scholars in the field, however, have frequently given warnings that their grammars are not reproductions of internalized grammars. In fact, it is most unlikely that a person who wants to say something first produces an underlying structure in his mind which contains the concepts he wishes to communicate, then submits this structure to a series of transformations, one at a time, until he derives a surface structure. Yet there must be something similar to underlying structures and transformations in an internalized grammar. The transformational grammar and the one which is internalized probably have much in common, but no one seriously claims that one is a faithful representation of the other.

Noun Clauses

In the last chapter we saw that a noun phrase may contain an embedded sentence which appears on the surface as a relative clause, a phrase, or an adjective. Such transformations as pronominalization, relative reduction, and modifier preposing enable us to relate a large array of surface structures. One of these is the relative clause:

7.1   The suggestion [that we heard at the dinner table] was repulsive.

We recognize the embedded clause as being derived from the same structure that underlies

7.2   We heard the suggestion at the dinner table.

At first the following sentence appears to contain a relative clause similar to the one in 7.1:

7.3   The suggestion [that we should brush our teeth at the dinner table] was repulsive.

If we consider the semantic relation of the embedded clause to *suggestion,* however, we see a major difference. In 7.1, the relative clause tells which suggestion we are talking about, but it does not indicate what the suggestion was. The embedded sentence in 7.3, on the other hand, does state the suggestion. If a grammar is successful in relating meaning to surface manifestations, it should distinguish in some way between these kinds of embedded structures.

Some traditional grammars classified structures like the embedded sentence in 7.3 as restrictive appositives. They relate to noun phrases in the same way as single-word appositives do:

7.4   My brother *Tim* answered the phone.
7.5   The word *puny* offended me.
7.6   The belief *that we were invited to the party* was erroneous.

Unlike adjectival modifiers, appositives rename the noun they follow. The structure normally given for sentences such as 7.6 is as follows:

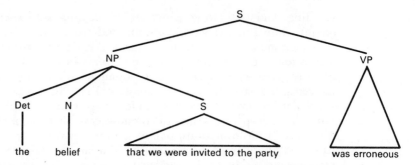

Following Rosenbaum (1967), most transformational analyses of structures like this have called *that we were invited to the party* a **noun phrase complement.** In such works as Kiparsky and Kiparsky (1970) and Stockwell et al. (1973), much of this analysis has been refuted. We, therefore, are returning to the traditional interpretation of saying that the structure functions as an appositive. Since it functions as a noun and contains a subject and verb with tense, by structure it is classified as a **noun clause.** In this way we are continuing to classify nominals in two ways: (1) By *structure* they are nouns, pronouns, noun clauses, and the like. (2) But they *function* as subjects, objects, appositives, and so on.

We can contrast diagrams which have been given for relative clauses with those for noun-clause appositives by the use of skeleton trees:

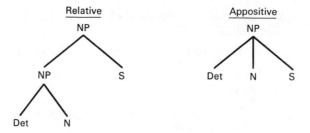

In recent years it has become obvious that this difference in trees is arbitrary. It really says nothing significant about the differences between relative clauses and noun clauses used as appositives. All it really illustrates is two different ways of adjoining one structure to another. The one for the appositive, frequently called **sister adjunction,** adds *S* as a co-constituent of *Det* and *N.* This type of relationship is suspicious since it claims that *the* and *that we were invited to the party* relate to *belief* in the same way. By contrast, the analysis given for the relative clause is known as **Chomsky adjunction.** According to this interpretation, the *S* is added as a co-constituent of the entire noun phrase taken as a unit. At present transformational theory is not adequate to provide criteria for judging the relative merits of sister and Chomsky adjunction. From a purely intuitive standpoint, both the noun-clause appositive and the relative clause seem to relate to the noun phrase *the belief* as a unit, thereby suggesting that the tree given for relative clauses should be used for appositives as well. It is even more likely that we have not yet discovered the ultimate underlying structures for appositive clauses. Treatments of them currently in print have barely gone beneath the surface structures. Since no better proposals have been suggested, we will continue to use sister adjunction for appositive clauses and Chomsky adjunction for relatives, realizing that much research is needed on the subject. None of the analyses which we will present in the remainder of the chapter will be affected by this choice.

Usually semantic differences are accompanied by differences in syntax. Since relative and noun clauses differ semantically in their relationship to the noun which they follow, we should see if their structural similarity is real or merely a superficial appearance. Here are two examples:

7.7   The fact [that he is wrong] bothers me.
7.8   The fact [that he suggested] bothers me.

In 7.8 we may substitute *which* for *that,* since *fact* is nonhuman:

7.9   The fact [*which* he suggested] bothers me.

For 7.7, however, such a substitution is not possible:

7.10   *The fact [*which* he is wrong] bothers me.

Whereas relative clauses freely admit *who* or *which,* and under certain conditions *that,* noun clauses permit only *that.*

In 7.8 the word *that* is clearly a pronoun, meaning *the fact,* and it functions as the direct object of *suggested:*

7.11   [he suggested *the fact*]

The relative transformation moves *the fact* to the beginning:

7.12   [*the fact* he suggested]

Pronominalization then replaces *the fact* with the pronoun *that:*

7.13   [*that* he suggested]

The word *that* in *that he is wrong* is different, in spite of the fact that it is pronounced and spelled the same as the relative pronoun. The *that* found in a noun clause is not a pronoun since it does not have reference. Also, it is merely placed at the front of the clause to indicate its embedded status; as such, it does not function as a subject, object, or other noun phrase. Without it we still have a complete sentence:

7.14   He is wrong.

Without the relative pronoun in *that he suggested,* however, the structure is incomplete:

7.15   *He suggested.

We clearly have two distinct words with identical spellings.

Instead of relativization and pronominalization, we derive *that* in a noun clause by the **that-insertion transformation.** We can illustrate it in additional noun phrases:

7.16	Underlying:	the fact [she is stupid]
	That-insertion:	the fact [*that* she is stupid]
7.17	Underlying:	the belief [we were right]
	That-insertion:	the belief [*that* we were right]

Since this use of *that* does not have referential meaning, it does not occur at the deepest underlying level.

So far we have seen two syntactic differences between relative and noun clauses: (1) the introductory words which they permit and (2) the way these introductory words function within the embedded sentence. We can discover others as well.

A third difference is found in the noun phrases that are contained within the embedded sentence. A relative clause must contain an instance of the same noun phrase as the one which the clause modifies:

7.18   the assumption [he held *the assumption*] was ridiculous

If the embedded sentence does not contain such a noun phrase, relativization is impossible. Noun clauses have no such restriction:

7.19   the assumption [he would win] was ridiculous

In fact, noun clauses containing such noun phrases are rare or perhaps even impossible.

The kind of noun phrase which can have an embedded clause adjoined to it provides a fourth difference between noun clauses and relatives. Most nouns permit adjoined relative clauses:

7.20   The man [who whistled] thought you were cute.
7.21   The birds [that flew away] were robins.
7.22   The water [which you drank] was contaminated.
7.23   The joy [that I have known this week] has been unbelievable.
7.24   We laughed at the suggestion [which she wrote on the card].

Of these noun phrases, only *the suggestion* permits a following noun clause:

7.25   *The man [that we were laughing] thought you were cute.
7.26   *The birds [that they opened the door] were robins.
7.27   *The water [that the sugar dissolved] was contaminated.
7.28   *The joy [that she was elected queen] has been unbelievable.
7.29   We laughed at the suggestion [that she was elected queen].

Noun clauses may not function as appositives to concrete nouns such as *man, bird, water,* or *building,* which exist in space and can be touched. Many abstract nouns, such as *joy,* do not permit them either. In fact, there is only a small class of nouns which do permit noun-clause appositives: *fact, idea, suggestion, proposition, belief,* and the like.

A fifth distinction can be seen in the determiners which the noun permits. Relative clauses may modify nouns with any determiner, and the nouns may be singular or plural:

7.30   We forgot *a* fact [that was important].
7.31   We forgot *some* facts [that were important].
7.32   *Those* ideas [that he initiated] were ludicrous.

Noun-clause appositives follow only singular nouns which have the determiner *the:*[1]

7.33   *We forgot *a* fact [that she was blind].
7.34   *We forget *some* facts [that she was blind and crippled].
7.35   We forgot *the* fact [that she was blind].

This is a very narrow restriction on nouns which precede appositive clauses that is not shared by those which precede relatives.

As we encounter additional kinds of structures, we will see that there are other differences between the two kinds of embedded clauses. For now, these five are certainly sufficient for showing that there are syntactic differences accompanying those in meaning.

Extraposition and Factivity

Some sentences with noun-clause appositives are synonymous with other sentences in which there is no noun before the clause:

7.38   We realized the fact that he was lame.
7.39   We realized that he was lame.

Because of the syntactic structure, the noun phrase *the fact* seems almost redundant in 7.38, and it is understood in 7.39. We, therefore, give both sentences identical underlying structures and apply the **fact-deletion transformation** to 7.39 but not to 7.38.

Noun clauses may occur as subjects as well as objects:

7.40   The fact [that you are dishonest] disturbs me.

A tree for this structure looks like this:

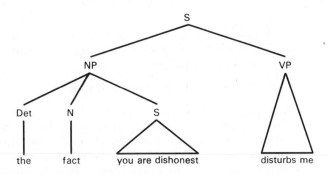

---

[1] It may appear that noun phrases with the determiner *a* may also take appositive clauses, as in this sentence:

7.36   It's a fact that she is blind.

Later in this chapter we will see that this sentence at an underlying level has the structure [*she is blind*] *is a fact*. It is only on the surface that noun-clause appositives follow nouns with the determiner *a*. Another structure which may raise a question is this one:

7.37   Bill's suggestion that we stay here was agreeable.

This is derived from an underlying structure something like [*Bill suggested [we stay*

It is possible to perform *fact*-deletion on 7.40, giving the following structure:

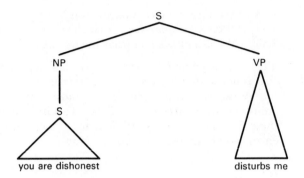

After *that*-insertion, we have the following sentence:

7.41   [That you are dishonest] disturbs me.

We may leave the structure like this, or we may perform the **extraposition transformation,** which moves the embedded sentence to the end of the higher sentence:

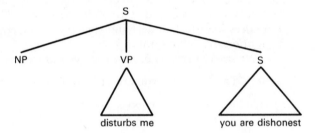

It should be noted that extraposition moves sentences, not noun phrases; therefore, the NP node remains at the beginning of the sentence. Performing *that*-insertion, we derive

7.42   *Disturbs me [that you are dishonest].

Although the sentence is perfectly clear, it is irritating to most people. In Modern English we insist upon having subjects for all sentences except imperatives such as *Open the window.* To conform to practices of current English, we fill the vacant NP position with *it.* After the application of *that*-insertion and the **it-insertion transformation,** the structure looks like this:

---

here]] *was agreeable.* Sentences like these do not serve as counterexamples to the statement that *the* is the only determiner permitted in a noun phrase which takes an appositive. Because of space limitations and the problems involved in the derivation of structures like that found in 7.37, they are not discussed in this book. Discussions of the structures can be found in Lees (1960), Lakoff (1970), and Chomsky (1970).

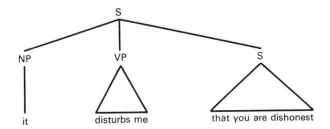

7.43   It disturbs me that you are dishonest.

This use of *it* is different from that of the pronoun in

7.44   *It* is outside.

The *it* in 7.44 has reference, but *it* in 7.43 does not. A word such as *it* in 7.43 which has no referential meaning and which serves as a filler is called an **expletive**. *It* in this function is not a pronoun, even though it may look like one. The expletive *it* can be found also in such sentences as *It is snowing, It is hot in here,* and the like.

Once we have proposed an analysis of a structure, we need to test it to determine whether it accounts for all structures of the same kind. The following sentences provide additional examples of extraposition:

7.45   It amuses me [that Karen missed her flight].
7.46   It appears [that Karen missed her flight].

Sentence 7.45 has a counterpart which has not undergone extraposition, but 7.46 does not:

7.47   [That Karen missed her flight] amuses me.
7.48   *[That Karen missed her flight] appears.

Obviously extraposition is obligatory with *appear* but optional with *amuse*. Listing other verbs which permit noun-clause subjects, we discover that with some extraposition is obligatory but with others it is optional:

Optional	*Obligatory*
amuse	appear
bother	seem
matter	happen

We could easily extend this list, but it is long enough to show us that there is nothing in the pronunciation or form (such as a suffix or prefix) to distinguish the two classes of verbs.

One possibility for determining whether extraposition is optional or obligatory would be to mark the dictionary entry of each verb which permits subject noun clauses. This solution is acceptable only if there really is no property which is found in one class but not in the other. If there is such a property, we would prefer stating it as a generalization about the language. We will later see that these classes of verbs differ in ways in addition to extraposition.

There is a semantic difference in sentences containing these two classes of verbs.[2] Let us reconsider 7.45 and 7.46, repeated here for convenience:

7.45   It amuses me [that Karen missed her flight].
7.46   It appears [that Karen missed her flight].

In 7.45 the speaker has accepted Karen's missing her flight as a fact, and he is commenting on his reaction to it. We say that he **presupposes** the truth of the embedded sentence. It does not matter that he may be misinformed and that it is really Lucy who missed the flight, not Karen, or that Karen may have lied to him and he believed her. The important thing is that he has accepted Karen's missing her flight as a fact and is using it as a presupposition in 7.45. In 7.46, on the other hand, there is no such presupposition. The speaker is asserting what appears to be the case, but he has not accepted it as a fact.

It should be noted that negating the verb in the higher sentence does not affect the presupposition contained in the embedded sentence. We have accepted Karen's missing her flight as a fact whether we say *It amuses me that Karen missed her flight* or *It doesn't amuse me that Karen missed her flight.* For 7.46, however, there is a difference: *It appears that Karen missed her flight* vs. *It doesn't appear that Karen missed her flight.*

If we substitute other verbs for which extraposition is optional for *amuse,* we see that they all presuppose that the noun clause is a fact, whereas the verbs for which extraposition is obligatory do not. We will call those verbs like *amuse* and *bother,* which carry this presupposition, **factive verbs.** Those like *appear* and *seem* are **non-factive verbs.**

The division of verbs into factive and non-factive categories extends to those which take noun-clause objects:

Factive	*Non-factive*
regret	think
resent	suppose
hate	claim

Again, the listing is illustrative rather than exhaustive.

There are several ways in which this semantic difference is matched syntactically. In addition to that which we have already noticed about extraposition of subject noun clauses, there is a difference with deletion. For non-factive objects *that* may be optionally deleted:

7.49a   He thinks *that* you are younger than your sister.
   b   He thinks you are younger than your sister.
7.50a   They claim *that* they are twins.
   b   They claim they are twins.

Deletion of *that* is normally not possible with objects of factive verbs:

7.51a   I would prefer *that* you leave.
   b   *I would prefer you leave.

---

[2] The analysis which follows is based largely upon Kiparsky and Kiparsky (1970).

7.52a   I hate that you will miss the concert.
    b   *I hate you will miss the concert.

For some verbs there is variation among dialects. Some people will accept 7.52b as grammatical; for them, *hate* is an exception to the restriction of *that*-deletion to objects of non-factives. For those people who find 7.52b ungrammatical, *hate* is not an exceptional verb. Generally, extraposed subjects may undergo *that*-deletion regardless of the class of the governing verb:

7.53a   It is unfortunate *that* you missed the concert.
    b   It is unfortunate you missed the concert.
7.54a   It appears *that* you missed the concert.
    b   It appears you missed the concert.

A third difference between factive and non-factive verbs can be seen in whether they permit the word *fact* to precede the noun clause. Factive verbs allow *fact,* but non-factives do not:

7.55   We resent the fact that you are always late.
7.56   I soon grasped the fact that she didn't know the answer.
7.57   The fact that you have the mumps irritates me.
7.58   *She supposed the fact that it was snowing.
7.59   *They maintain the fact that they are lost.
7.60   *The fact is possible that we are lost.

This distinction follows logically from the meaning of the word *fact* and the presupposition, or lack of presupposition, associated with the verb and its noun clause.

All subject or object noun clauses of factive verbs have the word *fact* before them at the underlying level:

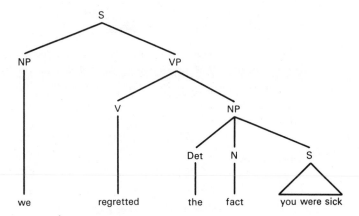

Non-factives differ in that there is no noun such as *fact* preceding the noun clause:[3]

---

[3] Such non-factive noun phrases as *the assumption that he is a genius* appear to be counterexamples. Structures such as this are derived from more abstract underlying forms like *Someone assumes that he is a genius.*

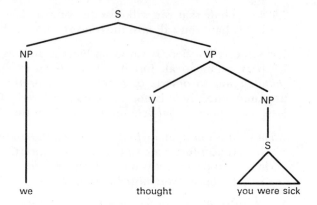

This means that at the underlying level we find distinct structures:

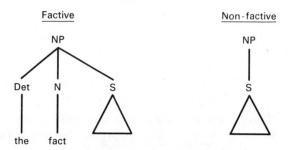

If *fact*-deletion is performed, the two kinds of structures will appear alike on the surface, as illustrated by these sentences:

7.61   We regretted [that you were sick].
7.62   We thought [that you were sick].

Although the surface trees for these sentences are identical except for the choice of *regretted* or *thought,* they differ at the underlying level. As we have seen, there are good reasons for distinguishing sentences such as these.

Infinitives

In most languages there are structures like those bracketed in the following sentences:

7.63   We expected [Bill to leave early].
7.64   We expected [Bill to have left early].
7.65   We expected [Bill to be leaving early].

In each sentence *Bill* is the subject of the embedded structure, yet the verb in that structure does not agree in person or number with its subject, as it does in the following:

7.66a   We think [that Bill *leaves* early every day].
   b   We think [that they *leave* early every day].
7.67a   We think [that Bill *has* left early].
   b   We think [that they *have* left early].
7.68a   We think [that Bill *is* leaving early].
   b   We think [that they *are* leaving early].

Although some texts have referred to the tense of the embedded structure of 7.63 as present and that of 7.64 as past, there is really no tense expressed in either. Notice that we cannot alter tense forms in any of them:

7.69   *We expected [Bill to *left* early].
7.70   *We expected [Bill to *had* left early].
7.71   *We expected [Bill to *was* leaving early].

Verb forms that are not marked for person, number, or tense are said to be without limits; they are, therefore, called **infinitives.** Verbs which carry tense and which agree with their subjects in person and number are called **finite verbs.**

    The infinitive is the most neutral form of the verb since it does not contain any markers for tense, person, or number. We can see this by comparing various forms of the verb *sing:*

Form	Tense	Person	Number
sings	Present	3	Singular
sang	Past	——	——
sing	——	——	——

Sing, of course, is also the form for present-tense plurals and singulars of first and second person. The verb *be* provides a less ambiguous example:

Form	Tense	Person	Number
am	Present	1	Singular
is	Present	3	Singular
are	Present	——	Plural
was	Past	1, 3	Singular
were	Past	——	Plural
be	——	——	——

As we saw in Chapter 4, each of the finite forms can be classified as infinitive plus one or more additional morphemes of tense and number.

    In English most infinitives are preceded by *to: to go, to eat, to sleep,* and the like. In certain constructions *to* does not appear on the surface:

7.72   We let Fred *do* the work.
7.73   We should *go.*
7.74   You had better *go.*
7.75   I would rather *stay* here.
7.76   She did nothing but *sleep.*

Among other languages it is somewhat rare to find infinitives marked with a preceding particle such as *to.* More common, at least among European languages, is a characteristic ending:

Old English	*-an:*	singan, helpan, ridan
German	*-en:*	singen, helfen, reiten
French	*-er:*	chanter, aider, aller
Spanish	*-ar:*	trabajar, preguntar, bailar

French and Spanish, of course, have various infinitival endings, depending upon the conjugation of the verb. The fact that Modern English lacks a characteristic ending for the infinitive makes it sometimes difficult to recognize, especially when *to* is missing as in 7.72–76. Uses like these are further complicated by the fact that the infinitive form is identical with that of the present tense for all persons in the plural and for first and second persons in the singular:

to stay

I stay	we stay
you stay	you stay
	they stay

Although there may be no difference in surface form between infinitives and finite verbs, in some instances (such as past tense and third person singular of the present tense) there is.

A second difference between infinitives and other verbs has frequently been noticed: that infinitives, but not finite verbs, may function as nouns:

Subject: To err is human.
Direct Object: He wanted *to help.*
Object of a Preposition: He did everything except *cry.*
Subjective Complement: Your job is *to drive.*

If we consider larger structures with infinitives, we soon see that it is the entire construction that functions as the noun, not the infinitive itself:

Subject: To steal peaches is dangerous.
Direct Object: He wanted *Lucian to help us.*
Object of a Preposition: He did nothing except *open the door.*
Subjective Complement: Your job is *to drive the car.*

Later in this chapter we will see that all infinitives such as *to err* in *To err is human* are derived from larger constructions (*For a person to err is human*); there is, therefore, no underlying difference between the two types of constructions we illustrated earlier in this paragraph. If we compare the infinitive construction with the noun clause, we see a similarity in function within the sentence:

7.77   We wanted [you to help us].
7.78   We thought [that you would help us].

It does not make sense to say that *to help* is the object of *wanted* in 7.77 any more than it does to call *would help* the object of *thought* in 7.78. In each sentence it is the entire embedded construction which is the object of the verb, not some part of it. This so-called difference between infinitives and finite verbs does not hold up under even a cursory examination. Infinitives do not function as nouns; they occur within structures that do. These structures are usually called **infinitive phrases** (or **infinitive clauses** in some books).

As for similarities between infinitives and other verbs, it has long been noticed that both may have subjects:

7.79   We expected [*Nancy* to marry Ed].
7.80   We thought [that *Nancy* would marry Ed].

At times the subject may be deleted on the surface. For finite verbs subject deletion is highly restricted, occurring only in imperatives, compound constructions, and certain positions in very informal usage:

7.81   (You) stop here.
7.82   He helped me change the tire and then (he) left.
7.83   (I) can't see.

Infinitives, on the other hand, frequently have their subjects deleted:

7.84   It is hard [(for anyone) to climb a flagpole].
7.85   Audrey wanted [(Audrey) to go with us].

Whatever the surface manifestations may be, infinitives are like other verbs in having underlying subjects.

Both infinitives and finite verbs may be transitive—

7.86a   He expected [the police to stop Emma].
    b   He thought [that the police would stop Emma].

or intransitive—

7.87a   He expected [Emily to smile].
    b   He thought [that Emily would smile].

If the infinitive or finite verb is transitive, it may be active, as in 7.86, or passive:

7.88a   He expected [Emma to be stopped by the police].
    b   He thought [that Emma would be stopped by the police].

Both may be linking, taking subjective complements:

7.89a   He expected [Emily to be the loser].
    b   He thought [that Emily would be the loser].

They may take the same range of complements and adverbial modifiers:

7.90a   He expected [Emma to give her purse to him promptly].
    b   He thought [that Emma would give her purse to him promptly].

Finally, both have the same selectional restrictions:

7.91a   He wanted [Karen to drive the car].
    b   He said [that Karen would drive the car].
7.92a   *He wanted [the rock to drive the car].
    b   *He said [that the rock would drive the car].
7.93a   *He wanted [Fay to read the hepatitis].
    b   *He believed [that Fay read the hepatitis].

7.94a   He wanted [Fay to read the note].
  b   He believed [that Fay read the note].

In most ways infinitives and finite verbs are alike.

How should our grammar show the similarities between infinitives and finite verbs and also their surface differences? If we derive infinitive phrases from underlying sentences, infinitives will be no different from finite verbs; this treatment will account for such similarities as identical selectional restrictions, transitivity, and presence of subjects and objects. We can have an underlying structure like this:

7.95a   I would like [Andy sits there]

The **infinitive transformation** deletes tense and adds *for* and *to* before the subject NP and the verb, respectively:

7.95b   I would like [for Andy to sit there].

In this way we are giving both infinitive phrases and noun clauses full sentences as their underlying structures.

Like noun clauses, infinitive phrases used as subjects may undergo extraposition:

Underlying: [Tom sees the room] would be a disaster
Infinitive: [for Tom to see the room] would be a disaster
Extraposition: would be a disaster [for Tom to see the room]
It-insertion: It would be a disaster [for Tom to see the room].

Depending upon whether we perform extraposition, we can derive synonymous sentences with infinitive phrases:

7.96a   [For Tom to see the room] would be a disaster.
  b   It would be a disaster [for Tom to see the room].

Since we already need the extraposition and *it*-insertion transformations for noun clauses, we do not have to add rules to account for the surface form of a sentence such as 7.96b.

In our comparison of infinitives with finite verbs, we said that the subjects of infinitives are often deleted. Let us now examine the conditions under which this deletion takes place. We may have an underlying structure like this:

7.97a   Fred wanted [Bill helps us]

We then perform the infinitive transformation:

7.97b   Fred wanted [Bill to help us].

Now let us change the subject of the embedded sentence so that it is identical with the noun phrase in the higher sentence:

7.98a   Fred wanted [Fred helps us] (*underlying structure*)

The infinitive transformation gives

7.98b   Fred wanted [Fred to help us]

This is not a possible surface structure if both instances of *Fred* refer to the same person. If they are coreferential, we must perform the **Equi-NP deletion** transformation:

7.98c   Fred wanted [to help us].

Because of this transformation, infinitive phrases sometimes have their subjects deleted.

The identical NP in the higher sentence does not have to be the subject, as we can see in this example:

7.99a.   Ann told Betty [Betty stops the car]

The infinitive transformation applies to give

7.99b   Ann told Betty [for Betty to stop the car]

Equi-NP deletion then deletes the subject of the embedded sentence (and a later transformation deletes *for*):

7.99c   Ann told Betty [to stop the car].

The speaker of English understands *Betty* as the subject of *stop,* yet the only instance of *Betty* on the surface is outside the embedded sentence. The underlying structure, as given in 7.99a, gives the information as the fluent speaker understands it.

Another kind of deletion in embedded sentences involves indefinite pronouns:

7.100   *Underlying:*   [anyone lifts this box] is hard
          Infinitive: [for anyone to lift this box] is hard
          Extraposition: is hard [for anyone to lift this box]
          It-insertion: It is hard [for anyone to lift this box]
          Indef. del.:   It is hard [to lift this box]

We call this transformation **indefinite deletion.**

On the surface, then, infinitive phrases may appear with or without subjects:

7.101   Everyone believes [Sandra to be innocent].
7.102   We hope [to be in Honolulu next week].
7.103   It would be advisable [to lock the door].

Sandra is not deleted in 7.101 because it is not coreferential with a noun phrase in the higher sentence, nor is it an indefinite pronoun. In 7.102, the underlying subject in the embedded sentence, *we,* is deleted because it is coreferential with the noun phrase *we* in the higher sentence. The indefinite *one* (or *someone, anyone, you, they,* and the like) is deleted in 7.103 by the indefinite deletion transformation. In each sentence the speaker understands a subject even though none is present on the surface in 7.102 and 7.103. The deletion transformations relate the understood information given in the underlying structures with the forms of the surface structures.

Gerunds

An embedded sentence at the underlying level may appear on the surface in various forms. Sentence 7.104, for example, may contain a noun clause (7.104b) or an infinitive phrase (7.104c):

7.104a   [Ray answered the door] was a surprise (*underlying*)
     b   It was a surprise [that Ray answered the door].
     c   It was a surprise [for Ray to answer the door].

There is still another possible surface structure:

7.104d   [Ray's answering the door] was a surprise.

A structure such as *Ray's answering the door* is called a **gerund phrase,** and *answering* is a **gerund.**

Gerunds have much in common with infinitives in that they do not agree with their subjects in person or number:

7.105a   [My guessing the answer] shocked everyone.
     b   [Your guessing the answer] shocked everyone.
     c   [Her guessing the answer] shocked everyone.
     d   [Our guessing the answer] shocked everyone.
     e   [Their guessing the answer] shocked everyone.

Regardless of the number or person of the subject, the gerund stays the same: *guessing.* Furthermore, gerunds are not marked for tense.

As is the case with infinitives, gerunds have the same classifications and selectional restrictions as finite verbs:

Transitivity

7.106   [Anne's finding the present] was unfortunate. (*transitive*)
7.107   [Anne's leaving] was unfortunate. (*intransitive*)

Active and Passive Voice

7.108   He is afraid of [killing someone]. (*active*)
7.109   He is afraid of [being killed]. (*passive*)

Subject Restrictions

7.110a   *[Marie's evaporating] shocked us.
     b   *Marie evaporated.
7.111a   *[Enthusiasm's falling to the floor] shocked us.
     b   *Enthusiasm fell to the floor.

Object Restrictions

7.112a   *[Sandra's scattering the door] was a surprise.
     b   *Sandra scattered the door.
7.113a   *[Lon's throwing the age] confused everyone.
     b   *Lon threw the age.

Other illustrations could be easily provided, but these are enough to show that the similarities between gerunds and finite verbs are great, whereas their differences are minor and purely of a surface nature.

If we derive gerund phrases from underlying sentences, we can do so with a simple transformation similar to the one which forms infinitives:

7.114a   [Frank wrote the letter] was a mistake (*underlying*)

If we delete tense, *Frank wrote* will become *Frank write*. Next, if we add *possessive* to the subject NP *Frank* and *ing* to the verb, we derive *Frank's writing:*

7.114b   [Frank's writing the letter] was a mistake.

As with infinitive phrases, the subject of a gerund is deleted if it is identical to a noun phrase in the higher sentence or if it is an indefinite pronoun:

Underlying: Emma disliked [Emma got her feet wet]
Gerund: Emma disliked [Emma's getting her feet wet]
Equi-NP del.:   Emma disliked [getting her feet wet].

It should be noticed that noun clauses do not permit such deletion, as we can see in the following derivation:

Underlying: Emma said [Emma got her feet wet]
That-insertion: Emma said [that Emma got her feet wet]

The NP *Emma* within the embedded sentence may be replaced by a pronoun:

Pronominalization: Emma said [that she got her feet wet].

But deletion is not possible:

Equi-NP del.:   *Emma said [that got her feet wet].

This difference between structures containing finite and nonfinite verbs is, of course, superficial, and not at the underlying level.

Since gerunds and present participles both end in *-ing*, some people have trouble distinguishing them. Actually there is no reason for confusion if we look at the entire sentence in which they are embedded. For example, if we look just at the word *wearing*, we have no way of knowing whether it is a gerund or a participle. We can see which it is only by looking at its function in a sentence:

7.115   [Wearing that silly hat] made her look foolish.
7.116   The woman [wearing that silly hat] looks foolish.

From the surface alone, we can see that *wearing that silly hat* functions as the subject NP of *made* in 7.115, whereas it functions as a modifier of *the woman* in 7.116. The structure is, therefore, a gerund phrase in the first sentence, a participial phrase in the second. If we look at the underlying structures, we see additional differences:

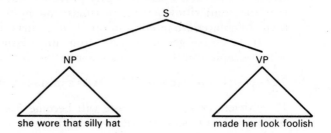

The gerund transformation will convert *she wore that silly hat* into *her wearing that silly hat,* and Equi-NP deletion will produce *wearing that silly hat.* Sentence 7.116, on the other hand, is derived from this underlying structure:

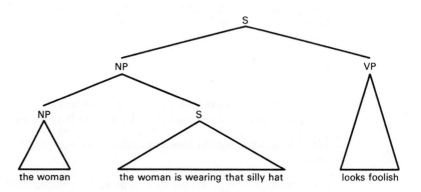

The subject NP undergoes the following transformations:

Underlying:	the woman [the woman is wearing that silly hat]
Relative:	the woman [the woman is wearing that silly hat]
Pronominalization:	the woman [who is wearing that silly hat]
Reduction:	the woman [wearing that silly hat]

Although both 7.115 and 7.116 contain the structure *wearing that silly hat,* there are good reasons for saying that there are syntactic differences in function and derivation in the two sentences.

During the 1950s the following sentence was frequently used as an example of syntactic ambiguity:

7.117   Flying planes can be dangerous.

With one meaning *flying* is a gerund, with the other a participle. A grammar which contains underlying structures can easily explain the ambiguity. For the participial structure, this is the underlying form:

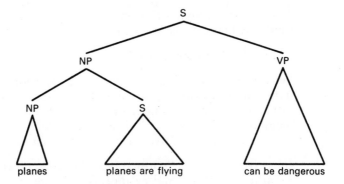

The subject noun phrase undergoes these transformations:

Underlying: planes [planes are flying]
Relative: planes [planes are flying]
Pronominalization: planes [that are flying]
Reduction: planes [flying]
Preposing: [flying] planes

The gerund, on the other hand, has this underlying structure:

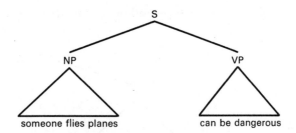

Underlying: someone flies planes
Gerund: someone's flying planes
Indef. del.: flying planes

Although both structures appear as *flying planes* on the surface, the native speaker understands a major syntactic difference, which our grammar is able to explain.

Subject Raising

One use of the infinitive which we have not yet examined is illustrated in the following sentence:

7.118   Audrey appears [to be spying on us].

Some traditional grammars classified *to be spying on us* as an adjectival functioning as a subjective complement (e.g., House and Harman 1950:327).

This interpretation has seemed forced to many people, who see no real similarity between the infinitive phrase and an adjective:

7.119   Audrey appears *sad.*

Yet within surface structures there is no solution which is more convincing unless we try classifying the infinitive phrase as an adverbial. Does a grammar which contains underlying structures offer an analysis that is more plausible?

We could try to give 7.118 the following derivation:

Underlying: Audrey appears [Audrey is spying on us]
Infinitive: Audrey appears [for Audrey to be spying on us]
Equi-NP deletion: Audrey appears [to be spying on us].

We would certainly obtain the required surface structure in this manner, but there is something disturbing about the underlying structure. Is it Audrey that appears or the proposition expressed by the embedded sentence? Also, this derivation does not show why 7.118 is synonymous with 7.120:

7.120   It appears [that Audrey is spying on us].

This sentence has the following underlying structure:

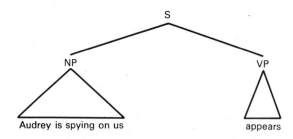

Underlying: [Audrey is spying on us] appears
Extraposition: appears [Audrey is spying on us]
It-*insertion:*   It appears [Audrey is spying on us]
That-*insertion:*   It appears [that Audrey is spying on us].

This deep structure is plausible, since it places the entire proposition *Audrey is spying on us* as the subject of *appears,* not just *Audrey.* Since *appears* is a non-factive verb, extraposition is obligatory.

If we derived 7.118 from the same underlying structure as 7.120, we could account for the synonymy of the sentences and also have an intuitively satisfying underlying structure. This proposal appears to be thwarted by the fact that *appears* does not freely take infinitive subjects:

7.121   *It appears [for Audrey to be spying on us].

However, let us see what the structure looks like after extraposition but before any other transformations are performed:

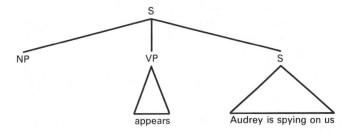

Instead of performing *it*-insertion, what will happen if we raise the subject of the embedded sentence, *Audrey,* into the vacant NP position? We can call this the **subject-raising transformation:**

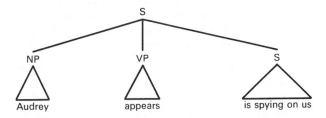

The infinitive transformation then applies to the embedded sentence:

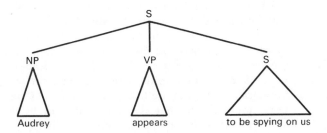

If this derivation applies to more sentences than just this one, it will certainly be worth exploring.

There are, in fact, other sentences which permit this series of transformations. In the following groups, the *a* version is the underlying structure, *b* results from extraposition, *it*-insertion, and *that*-insertion, and *c* from extraposition and subject raising:

7.122a   [the clock is broken] seems to me
   b   It seems to me [that the clock is broken].
   c   The clock seems to me [to be broken].
7.123a   [the phone was off the hook] happened
   b   It happened [that the phone was off the hook].
   c   The phone happened [to be off the hook].
7.124a   [she will be late] is likely
   b   It is likely [that she will be late].
   c   She is likely [to be late].

We could easily expand the list, but this is sufficient to show that the subject-raising transformation is applicable to more than one sentence. This derivation accounts for the synonymy of the *b* and *c* versions, and it allows a plausible interpretation for the *c* sentences. If *appear* is hard to accept as a linking verb, *happen* and *be likely* are doubly so.

Subject raising is not always possible, as we can see from the following examples:

7.125a   [you forgot the combination] was funny
   b   It was funny [that you forgot the combination].
   c   *You were funny [to forget the combination].
7.126a   [they were together] startled me
   b   It startled me [that they were together].
   c   *They startled me [to be together].
7.127a   [we are out of gas] is no laughing matter
   b   It is no laughing matter [that we are out of gas].
   c   *We are no laughing matter [to be out of gas].

It is the verb or adjective in the higher sentence which permits or prohibits subject raising, as we can easily see by taking such verbs as *seem* and *startle* and varying the composition of the embedded sentence. Similarly, we can substitute the embedded sentences in 7.125–27 for those in 7.122–24 and see that if the higher verb or adjective permits it, subject raising is possible.

It may be that there is no way to predict whether a given verb or adjective will permit subject raising or not; if so, each word will have to be marked individually in the lexicon. But there is something suspicious about features which apply idiosyncratically to a large number of words. Most aspects of language are more systematic than that. Let us, therefore, see if the verbs and adjectives in 7.122–24 share some property not found in those in 7.125–27. It takes only a brief inspection to notice that the former are non-factive, whereas the latter are factive. As we add other verbs and adjectives, we discover that the generalization holds. A few non-factive verbs and adjectives do not permit subject raising: *possible, false,* and the like. Also, some factive verbs and adjectives appear to permit the transformation:

7.128a   It was stupid [for Tom to give Ellen the money].
   b   Tom was stupid [to give Ellen the money].

Similarly, *crazy, goofy, smart,* and so on. These adjectives may indeed be exceptional, but there is another structure which casts doubt on subject raising as the source for 7.128b:

7.128c   It was stupid of Tom [to give Ellen the money].

The subject of *give* has been deleted because it is coreferential with *Tom* in the higher sentence. There appears to be some other transformation which then moves *Tom* into subject position. If so, these factive adjectives are not exceptions to the statement that only non-factives permit subject raising.

Whatever future research tells us about this handful of apparent exceptions, we have further support for distinguishing between factives and non-factives. Earlier in this chapter we noticed the following differences:

1. With factive verbs and adjectives the speaker presupposes the truth of the embedded sentence, whereas with non-factives he does not:

   Factive: Hal regretted [that he was delayed].
   Non-factive: Hal said [that he was delayed].

   Negating the higher verb does not affect the presupposition:

   Factive: Hal didn't regret [that he was delayed].
   Non-factive: Hal didn't say [that he was delayed].

2. Extraposition of subject noun phrases is optional with factive verbs but obligatory with non-factives:

   Factive: [That he was busy] surprised me.
   Non-factive: *[That he was busy] appeared to me.

3. Factives may be preceded by *the fact,* but non-factives may not be:

   Factive: Andy hated the fact [that he was short].
   Non-factive: *Andy said the fact [that he was short].

4. We can now add a fourth difference: Non-factives permit subject raising but factives do not:

   Factive: *Sue is tragic [to miss the train].
   Non-factive: Sue is likely [to miss the train].

There are several ways in which the semantic notion of factivity is reflected in the syntax.

Object Raising

The subject-raising transformation permits us to explain the synonymy of pairs of sentences such as

7.129a   It is certain that Judy will accept the offer.
   b   Judy is certain to accept the offer.

The derivation we have given also accounts for our understanding that it is not *Judy* which is the logical subject of *is certain,* but rather the entire proposition *Judy will accept the offer.*

The following pair of sentences seem to be similar:

7.130a   It is hard to catch a lion.
   b   A lion is hard to catch.

The underlying structure for both surface versions must be something like this:

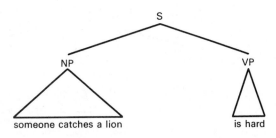

Extraposition gives

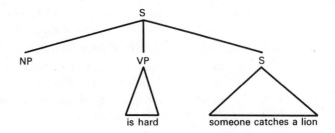

After *it*-insertion and the infinitive transformation, we derive

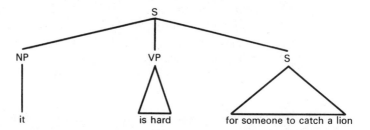

Deletion of the indefinite *someone* in the embedded sentence gives 7.130a:

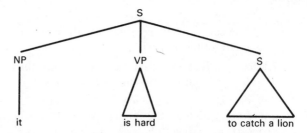

The transformations we have already encountered thus provide for the derivation of the *a* version of the sentence.

Subject raising cannot account for 7.130b since it is not the subject of the embedded sentence which has been raised. Rather, it is the object. If we apply extraposition to our underlying structure, we derive

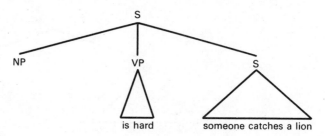

Instead of *it*-insertion, if we raise the object of the embedded sentence into the first NP position of the higher sentence, we will have

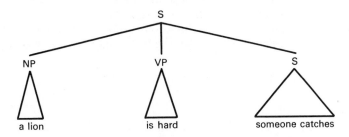

After the infinitive transformation, the embedded sentence is *for someone to catch*. Deletion of the indefinite subject gives

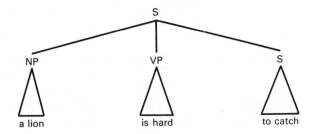

We can call the transformation which raises *a lion* into the higher sentence **object raising,** a term parallel to *subject raising.*

Object raising can be seen in additional sentences:

7.131a   It is fun to work crossword puzzles.
    b   Crossword puzzles are fun to work.
7.132a   It is easy for me to distinguish them.
    b   They are easy for me to distinguish.
7.133a   It will be a breeze for Tom to pass this test.
    b   This test will be a breeze for Tom to pass.
7.134a   It will be tough for Ed to remember the number.
    b   The number will be tough for Ed to remember.

Some linguists (e.g., Postal, 1971:27–31) call this transformation *tough-movement* since it is usually restricted to adjectives and other structures designating difficulty or ease, one of which is *tough* as in 7.134. We have chosen to call it object raising since it is similar to subject raising.

Object raising is needed if we are to explain the fluent speaker's understanding of sentences such as the following, originally introduced by Noam Chomsky and since then used by many other linguists:

7.135   John is easy to please.
7.136   John is eager to please.

On the surface it appears that the only difference in the two sentences is word choice. The structures look the same, just as the structure of 7.135

would be the same if we selected *Bill* instead of *John, hard* instead of *easy,* or *disappoint* instead of *please.* Closer inspection, however, shows that there are differences of structure in addition to those of word choice between 7.135 and 7.136. In the first sentence, we understand *John* as the object of *please,* whereas in the second *John* is the understood subject.

For 7.135 we have the following underlying structure:

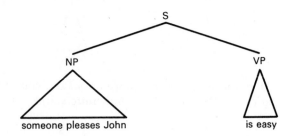

We use these transformations:

Underlying:	[someone pleases John] is easy
Extraposition:	is easy [someone pleases John]
Object raising:	John is easy [someone pleases]
Infinitive:	John is easy [for someone to please]
Indefinite deletion:	John is easy [to please]

If we had not performed object raising, we could have used *it*-insertion and obtained the surface structure *It is easy to please John.*

Suppose we said that the following was the underlying structure for 7.136:

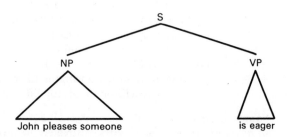

The underlying structure would account for our understanding that *John* is the subject in this embedded sentence but the object in 7.135: *John pleases someone* vs. *Someone pleases John.* We could apply the following transformations:

Underlying:	[John pleases someone] is eager
Extraposition:	is eager [John pleases someone]
Subject raising:	John is eager [pleases someone]
Infinitive:	John is eager [to please someone]
Indefinite deletion:	John is eager [to please]

Unlike 7.135, which has the alternate *It is easy to please John,* there is no corresponding *it* version for 7.136: **It is eager to please John.* A closer inspection of our proposed underlying structure (*John pleases someone is eager*) shows a logical problem. It is *John,* not the entire proposition, that is eager. We can contrast this with 7.135, in which it is the entire proposition, rather than John, that is logically the subject of *is easy.* A more plausible underlying structure for 7.136 should have *John* as the subject of *is eager*:

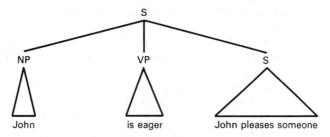

The exact location of the embedded sentence has not been satisfactorily explained in current transformational literature; we are arbitrarily sister-adjoining it to NP and VP, realizing that future research may show that it belongs within the VP or that it has some other relationship to other elements in the sentence. Whatever the exact structure may be, it is different from that which underlies 7.135. After deletion of the coreferential *John* and the indefinite *someone* and application of the infinitive transformation, the surface structure is as follows:

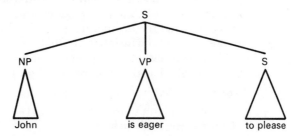

This, of course, is the same surface structure as that for 7.135:

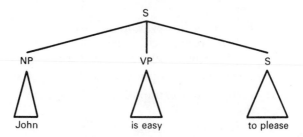

The surface structure alone cannot show the differences which a fluent speaker of English recognizes between the two sentences. Only a grammar which incorporates underlying structures can do this.

Conclusion

In this chapter, as in those which precede it, we have seen that much of the knowledge which fluent speakers of a language share cannot be satisfactorily explained from surface structures alone Similarities such as those between finite verbs and infinitives may be obscured by superficial differences in form. Similarly, different structures may look alike on the surface (e.g., relative and noun clauses, or *John is eager to please* and *John is easy to please*), yet fluent speakers of the language understand them differently. At an underlying level this information can be easily accommodated; the surface manifestations are effected by transformations.

Another principle which is emerging is that the form and meaning of a structure are closely related. In the past, matters of form have often been delegated to a syntactic component of the grammar and those of meaning to a dark, uncharted semantic component. A semantic property such as factivity and its syntactic consequences show that neither syntax nor semantics can be studied in isolation. In the chapters which follow we will be finding further instances of this relationship.

Exercises

A. What reasons can you give to show that the embedded clauses in the following pairs of sentences are or are not the same kinds of structures?

   1a. The table [that he was painting] collapsed.
    b. The car [that he bought] was a lemon.
   2a. We resented the insinuation [that she fled].
    b. We resented the insinuation [that she made].
   3a. Many people hold the belief [that accidents can't happen to them].
    b. We laughed at the proposal [that we eat no meat except liver].

B. Perform the *that*-insertion transformation:

   1. he dreamed [you were leaving for Germany]
   2. I gather [she is disturbed]
   3. Janice thinks [she is pretty]

C. Perform the extraposition, *it*-insertion, and *that*-insertion transformations:

   1. [Tony is sneaky] worries Carl
   2. [you are engaged] seems odd
   3. [the house needs painting] is true

   Is extraposition optional or obligatory in these sentences?

D. Perform the extraposition, *it*-insertion, and *that*-insertion transformations:

   1. [we are late] seems
   2. [she is his wife] happens

   Is extraposition optional or obligatory? Why?

E. For the following sentences give the deepest underlying structure and perform all transformations needed to derive the given surface structure. Illustrate each step with a tree.

1. It amuses Helen that you are a failure.
2. Tony likes to meet people.

F. Are the italicized verbs or phrases in the following sentences factive or non-factive? Justify your answers.

1. It *saddens* me that you are so gullible.
2. It *is unlikely* that he will find it.
3. I *suspect* that she lied.
4. It *knocked me for a loop* that he resigned.
5. It *is lucky* for you that I found your passport.

G. What reasons are there for deriving gerund and infinitive phrases from underlying sentences rather than dealing exclusively with their surface forms? Which of these reasons are valid for participial phrases as well? Illustrate your reasons with original sentences.

H. Trace the derivation of each of the following sentences from the deepest underlying structures through each transformation to the surface. You may write them out in linear form as in the examples in this chapter or draw trees, depending upon which is the more useful for you.

1. It is hard for us to be careful all the time.
2. Audrey's serving champagne in paper cups was weird.
3. We would like to help you.
4. They seemed to know you.
5. The egg was hard to break.
6. Pansy regretted telling the truth.
7. It amused Helen to see you in trouble.
8. They are prone to be cautious.

Suggested Reading

Jacobs, Roderick A., and Peter S. Rosenbaum, eds., *Readings in English Transformational Grammar.* Waltham, Mass.: Ginn and Co., 1970.

Jespersen, Otto, *A Modern English Grammar,* Vol. V. Copenhagen: Ejnar Munksgaard, 1940.

Kiparsky, Paul, and Carol Kiparsky, "Fact," in *Progress in Linguistics,* ed. Manfred Bierwisch and Karl Erich Heidolph. The Hague: Mouton, 1970.

Lakoff, Robin T., *Abstract Syntax and Latin Complementation.* Cambridge, Mass.: The M.I.T. Press, 1968.

Postal, Paul M., "On Coreferential Complement Subject Deletion," *Linguistic Inquiry* 1 (1970): 439–500.

———, *On Raising.* Cambridge, Mass.: The M.I.T. Press, 1974.

Rosenbaum, Peter S., *The Grammar of English Predicate Complement Constructions.* Cambridge, Mass.: The M.I.T. Press, 1967.

Stockwell, Robert P., Paul Schachter, and Barbara Hall Partee, *The Major Syntactic Structures of English.* New York: Holt, Rinehart and Winston, Inc., 1973.

chapter 8

Functions and Meanings of Nominals

For at least twenty-five hundred years, grammars written in the Western world have included constituents of the sentence corresponding to subjects and predicates. Plato called the two basic sentence elements *onoma* and *rhēma,* which can be respectively equated with nouns and verbs or subjects and predicates. Other grammars of classical Greek and of Latin continued to recognize these two basic constituents of the sentence, and they were incorporated into the later grammars of English and other European languages. During this century we have seen practically every other grammatical concept challenged, but not that of subject and predicate. Although there has been some variation in terminology, the concept has remained firm.

Subject-verb Agreement

Perhaps the most obvious reasons for recognizing subjects and predicates are found in agreement, or concord. In many languages certain properties of the subject determine the form of the predicate verb. In English this principle is found more extensively with *be* than with any other verb. A conjugation of the simple present and past tense illustrates the process of subject-verb agreement:

Present		*Past*	
I am	we are	I was	we were
you are	you are	you were	you were
he is	they are	he was	they were

The verb *be* agrees with its subject in number. For both present- and past-tense forms, there are differences between singulars and plurals (*I am* vs. *we are, I was* vs. *we were*). The second-person *you are, you were* is exceptional since in Modern English there is no distinction between singular and plural for this person. For present-tense singulars there is also agreement governed by the person of the subject: *I am* (first person) vs. *he is* (third person).

With verbs other than *be* the only form which is affected by properties of the subject is the third person singular, present indicative, as illustrated by *climb:*

Present		*Past*	
I climb	we climb	I climbed	we climbed
you climb	you climb	you climbed	you climbed
he **climbs**	they climb	he climbed	they climbed

For some dialects, in particular some varieties of Black English, there is no third-person ending. Since these dialects normally delete *be* or else use it in its infinitival form, they do not have surface manifestations of subject-verb agreement. For those dialects which retain a subjunctive, there is no agreement (*if I be, if he be,* or *if I were, if he were,* and the like), nor is there agreement with infinitives and participles. Nevertheless, there are still enough vestiges of subject-verb agreement in some varieties of English to reinforce the concepts of subject and predicate.

For some languages the property of agreement is found much more extensively than it is in English. Classical Latin, for example, had a characteristic ending for each person in both numbers, as we can see from the present-tense conjugation of *cantō,* "sing."

Singular	*Plural*
cantō	cantāmus
cantās	cantātis
cantat	cantant

Agreement is expressed much more fully than in English.

The form of the verb may be affected by other features of the noun than person and number. The Russian verb in the present tense indicative has three distinct singular endings and three different plural endings, each determined by the person of the subject. Here are the present-tense forms of *chitat',* "to read":

Singular	*Plural*
chitayu	chitaem
chitaesh'	chitaete
chitaet	chitayut

In the past tense there is no agreement for person, but there is for number:

Singular	*Plural*
chital	chitali
chital	chitali
chital	chitali

In addition, for singulars in the past tense there is agreement with the gender[1] of the subject. *Chital* is the form used if the subject is masculine, but it changes to *chitala* for a feminine subject or *chitalo* for one that is neuter.

In some languages gender concord between subject and verb is much more extensive than it is in Russian. The Bantu languages of Africa, of which Swahili is the most well-known member, consistently use a prefix on the verb which is predictable by the gender of the subject. Unlike European languages, those in the Bantu family usually have more than three genders, ranging from six in Swahili up to twelve in some of the other languages.

There are a number of ways in which verbs agree with their subjects, and this property of agreement is found in a wide variety of languages throughout the world. The concepts of subject and predicate are essential to a grammar.

Definitions for the Subject

For concepts which are so widely recognized as subject and predicate, it seems that good definitions should be readily available. Ironically, there is no really satisfactory definition for either subject or predicate. Let us examine several that have been proposed to see where their inadequacies lie.

We could define the subject as the one who performs an action. Such a definition would be fine for many sentences:

8.1 *Shelby* wrote the letter.
8.2 *The dog* chased its tail.
8.3 *The baby* cried.

But if there is no action indicated by the verb, there can hardly be an actor:

8.4 *The room* seems stuffy.
8.5 *We* sat there for thirty minutes.
8.6 *That bird* is pretty.
8.7 *She* resembles her mother.

Defining the subject as the one who performs an action is inadequate even in many sentences which contain action verbs:

8.8 *This dress* was ironed by Kathy.
8.9 *This dress* irons easily.

---

[1] In Modern English we usually classify animate nouns as masculine or feminine, according to sex. Inanimate nouns are said to be neuter gender. Many languages have a different system of classification, which is not based exclusively on sex. In French and Spanish, for example, all nouns are either masculine or feminine, even those which name such inanimate objects as *door, chair, house,* and *shoe.* In German and Russian there are three genders, but an inanimate noun is often masculine or feminine, rather than neuter. Although there is some relationship between sex and gender in these languages, the reader may find the comments in this paragraph and the one that follows less confusing if he thinks of gender in terms of noun classes, rather than sex.

8.10   *The dress* tore.
8.11   *The garden* is swarming with bees.
8.12   *He* suffered a thump on the ear.
8.13   *John* broke his hip.

In each of these sentences something happens to the subject; it does not *perform* an action. Defining the subject as the performer of an action may be acceptable for some sentences, but for others such a definition is untenable.

Since most rules and definitions in grammar have exceptions, we might try to retain the definition which equates subject with performer and label all other instances as exceptions. This would be similar to saying that noun plurals are formed by adding the sound [s], [z], or vowel plus [z] to the singular form or by adding the letter *s* or *es* in writing. Such nouns as *mouse, child, deer, cherub,* and *alumnus* are exceptions. This procedure is good if the rule accounts for all but a handful of cases. On the other hand, if the number of exceptions is large, say a third or a half of the cases, the rule is inadequate. Since the number of possible sentences in any language is unlimited, there is no means of determining the number for which a definition of subject as performer of action would be inadequate. We do know that the number is far too large merely to list them as exceptions.

One definition which has appeared in countless grammars is "The subject is that of which something is said or asserted." Some books use *predicated* instead of *said.* This definition is somewhat vague, but it avoids many of the pitfalls of the definition which links the subject to a performer of action. It relates the *subject* of a sentence to other uses of the word: *subject* of a conversation, *subject* of a debate, and the like. It is the main topic which is being discussed, the "subject matter." Such a definition will handle most of those sentences in which an action is performed:

8.14   *The dog* howled.
8.15   *The deer* ran.

It will also designate subjects which do not perform action:

8.16   *This gas tank* holds eighteen gallons.
8.17   *The sandwich* smelled good.
8.18   *The desk* measured six feet across.
8.19   *The house* has been painted.

In these sentences we are saying something about the gas tank, sandwich, desk, or house.

But if we look at additional sentences, we discover problems:

8.20   A car ran over my cat.

In 8.20 we could as easily say that we are talking about the cat as the car, and the speaker is probably more concerned about the cat than the car. Further problems can be seen in these sentences:

8.21   Bob is my roommate.
8.22   My roommate is Bob.

Since Bob and my roommate are the same person, how can we say that we are talking about one and not the other? We could perhaps establish a distinction between the roommate and Bob along the line of specificity, but it would be largely artificial. In answer to the question "Who is your roommate?" a person will normally say just "Bob." If he answers with a complete sentence, he might use either 8.21 or 8.22.

There are still more complicated examples:

8.23   It is in the closet.
8.24   It is snowing.

In 8.23, *it* refers to something nonhuman, such as *the coat* or *the bad smell*, and is what we are talking about, the subject. In 8.24, however, *it* has no meaning. We are talking about the action of snowing, yet the meaningless *it* functions as the grammatical subject of the sentence.

Another attempt to explain the meaning of the subject says that it is the expression of known material in the sentence, whereas the predicate is the new information. For many sentences this observation is true:

8.25   The floor is dirty.
8.26   Your son broke my window with his football.

In 8.25, the listener already knows that a floor exists and which one is being mentioned. It is the predicate *is dirty* which imparts new information. Similarly, in 8.26 the listener already knows that he has a son; he is being told what his son did. Although evidence such as this is easily provided, counterexamples can be found almost as easily. For example, there may be no new information in 8.25 or 8.26, since the speaker may be stating information which the listener already knows. Sentence 8.25 may be a suggestion to the listener to mop the floor, 8.26 that the listener owes the speaker the cost of replacing the window. In some instances neither the subject nor the predicate contains known material, as we can see from the answer to the question "What happened to you?"

8.27   A wasp stung me.

The known material is that an action occurred in the past to the speaker. An even more revealing example can be seen in the answer to the question "Who helped you?"

8.28a   Mike helped me.
    b   Mike did.
    c   Mike.

Whether the complete predicate is expressed on the surface, replaced by *did,* or deleted, the new information is contained in the subject. The concept of new versus known information is useful in determining which elements in a sentence may be deleted or pronominalized. That is, known information may be deleted or replaced with a pronoun or with words such as *do, there,* and *then,* whereas new information cannot be deleted or replaced. But as a definition for subject and predicate, the distinction between new and old information is useless. Since predicates can sometimes be deleted, as in 8.28c, the new information is obviously not always in the predicate.

The Danish linguist Otto Jespersen (1924:150–54) suggested that the subject is the more specific, or more definite element in the sentence. In the following examples, the idea of definiteness can be seen in *my brother* and *Gertrude,* as opposed to *a salesman* and *a dollar:*

8.29   My brother is a salesman.
8.30   Gertrude found a dollar.

But counterexamples are easily found:

8.31   A man shoved me.
8.32   Someone bought the red tie.
8.33   A cat killed a bird.

Obviously *me* and *the red tie* are more definite than *a man* and *someone,* and *a cat* and *a bird* are equally indefinite. Definiteness is not a reliable definition for the subject of a sentence, although many subjects do have this property.

As a pedagogical device some teachers have used the procedure of asking "Who?" or "What?" before the predicate to locate the subject. Of course, for sentences such as 8.24 (repeated here) this device is not very helpful:

8.24   It is snowing.

"What is snowing?" cannot be given a sensible answer. But for most sentences, such as 8.31, it is applicable: "Who shoved you?" "A man." There is nevertheless considerable question as to the real value of such a device. To follow it, a person must be able to recognize the predicate; hence, he is able to recognize the subject as well, since it is everything in the sentence which is not part of the predicate. An alternative way of wording the procedure is to say that *who* or *what* is substituted for the subject. Actually, it is even more ineffective than we have shown. If a person is able to choose between *who* and *what* in asking his question, he has not only already located the subject; he has classified it as to whether it is human or not. Whatever the pedagogical value of this line of questioning may be, if any, it is obviously not a definition of the subject.

Surface Manifestations of Subjects and Other Nouns

No satisfactory statement has been made about the meaning of the subject, but the form it takes in surface structures is reasonably clear. Let us now see how subjects and other nouns appear on the surface.

One of the most widespread devices for representing nominal functions is word order, as we can see from the following sentences:

8.34   The dog bit the cat.
8.35   The cat bit the dog.

Although there are other possible orderings, such as found in questions and some emphatic sentences, the most normal order for English is subject before and object after the verb. For a grammar which recognizes both underlying and surface structures, there is one level of representation for which subjects appear in a constant position in relation to the verb; differences in surface ordering are accounted for by specific transformational rules. Violations of the conventions of ordering can be seen in the following deviant sentences:

8.36 *The dog the cat bit.
8.37 *The cat the dog bit.
8.38 *Bit the cat the dog.
8.39 *Bit the dog the cat.

Although most people will try to give these sentences the meaning of 8.34 or of 8.35, they have no way of choosing one over the other unless they read 8.36–39 with special stress on *the dog* or *the cat*. Word order is essential for telling who bit whom.

Most languages of Western Europe employ the basic word order of subject + verb + object (SVO) the same as English, yet this is only one of several surface orderings found among the languages of the world. Greenberg (1966:77) gives the three most common types as VSO, SVO, and SOV. The last of these, SOV, is the one normally found in Japanese:

	(the) dog	*(the) cat*	*bit*
8.40	Inu wa	neko o	kamimasita

At present there is no reason for us to believe that any one of these three surface orderings is more "basic" or "natural" than the others.

A second way of indicating syntactic relations is through the use of **prepositions.** In English there are alternate means of designating some sentence elements: by word order and by prepositions. For example, the agent that performs an action may be a surface subject, as shown by the ordering:

8.41 *The fool* broke the window.

Or it may be marked by the preposition *by:*

8.42 The window was broken *by the fool.*

Another example involves the indirect object. This noun may be indicated by a preposition:

8.43 Colleen handed the orange *to Joseph.*

In other surface structures it may be designated by word order:

8.44 Colleen handed *Joseph* the orange.

After certain verbs such as *hand, give,* and *send,* if there are two noun phrases not introduced by prepositions, the first is the indirect object. Other uses of prepositions can be seen in the following sentences:

8.45   She wrote *with her left hand.*
8.46   He left the party *with his neighbor.*
8.47   They fought *against the enemy.*
8.48   I walked *to the door.*

In English, prepositions and word order are the most common means for designating syntactic relations.

Although many languages make wide use of prepositions, they are not found universally. It is true that most European languages do have prepositions, but this is because of their common ancestry,[2] not any universal linguistic features. Japanese has no prepositions, but it does have **postpositions.** That is, the syntactic particle does not precede the noun it accompanies, but rather follows it. Let us return to sentence 8.40, repeated here:

	(the) dog	*(the) cat*	*bit*
8.40	Inu wa	neko o	kamimasita

Wa is a particle which follows subjects, *o* one which follows objects. Hence, the sentence means, "The dog bit the cat." Normally, each noun in a Japanese sentence is followed by a postpositional particle to designate its function. There are a few situations in which this particle is deleted, but it is probably present at some underlying level for all nouns. We say that English makes use of word order and prepositions to indicate syntactic relations in surface structures. Similarly, Japanese uses word order and postpositions. There are differences in degree of usage, since Japanese uses postpositions much more extensively than English does prepositions.

The last major device for signaling syntactic functions of nouns is **inflection.** This can be seen to a degree in the English pronouns *I, he, she, we,* and *they,* which are subject forms, contrasting with the object forms *me, him, her, us,* and *them.* We can illustrate their use:

8.49   I see him.
8.50   He sees me.

Distinct subject and object forms for pronouns are not unique with English, as we can see in the German and Russian equivalents for 8.49 and 8.50:

English: I see him.   He sees me.
German: Ich sehe ihn.   Er sieht mich.
Russian: Ya vizhu yego.   On videt menya.

As these sentences show, just as English has *I* and *he* as subject forms, German has *ich, er* and Russian *ya, on,* respectively.

In English the noun does not change form to indicate syntactic function:

8.51   The woman sees the girl.
8.52   The girl sees the woman.

---

2 Basque, Hungarian, Finnish, Estonian, Turkish, and a few others are not part of the family to which most of the European languages belong.

Word order is used to designate the subject and the object. In many languages there are characteristic endings which signal these functions, as in the Latin versions of these sentences:

8.53   Femina puellam videt. "The woman sees the girl."
8.54   Puella feminam videt. "The girl sees the woman."

The *-a* ending on *femina* (8.53) and *puella* (8.54) is used for subjects; the *-am* on *feminam* (8.54) and *puellam* (8.53) is used for objects. Although the word order given is the most usual one, others are possible for special emphasis:

8.53a   Femina puellam videt.
   b   Puellam femina videt.
   c   Videt puellam femina.

All mean the same thing, as indicated by the endings on the nouns. The only such noun ending that English has today is the possessive *'s*.

In addition to noun endings which designate subject and object, some languages have a great many more to designate other functions, such as indirect object, location, and instrument. Anyone who has studied Latin or Greek is familiar with such cases as accusative, dative, and genitive, each with distinctive endings. The student of Russian can add instrumental and locative, and the student of Finnish can add several others such as inessive, adessive, illative, and allative.

Semantic Roles

Such surface devices as word order, prepositions, postpositions, and inflections are used to indicate the syntactic functions of subject, direct object, and the like. As we saw earlier in this chapter, these functions are not easily defined according to meaning. A subject, for example, can be the agent that performs an action, a person or thing that is described, an instrument that is used in an action, or even the receiver of the action.

If we take a popular definition, such as the one which names the direct object as the receiver of the action, we find an array of problems as great as those for defining the subject. Each of the italicized noun phrases in the following sentences seems to be the receiver of the action, yet not all of them are direct objcts:

8.55   A rock hit *Sue*.
8.56   *Sue* was hit by a rock.
8.57   *His foot* got caught in the door.
8.58   *Tom* felt a thump on his ear.
8.59   *The glass* broke.

Earlier transformational grammars derived passive sentences such as 8.56 from active structures such as the one underlying 8.55. At the underlying level both of these sentences have an object that is the receiver of the action. A similar treatment may be possible for 8.57, but it is not for the remaining sentences.

It has been suggested that much of our difficulty in assigning meaning to functions such as subject and object is that we are relying too heavily upon surface manifestations. Let us try another procedure. First, we will examine some of the semantic roles a noun phrase can play; next we will see how they are realized in surface structures. Our problem will then be to determine how we should relate them.

An **agent (Agt)** performs an action by means of its own energy, as illustrated in the following sentences:

8.60   *The zebra* ran.
8.61   *The children* hit each other.
8.62   *Trudy* wrote the letter.

Agents are not associated with non-action verbs such as *resemble, appear, know,* and the like. One test that has been suggested for agentivity is the use of *do* in questions such as "What did the zebra do?" Since "The zebra ran" is a sensible answer, *the zebra* is an agent. Contrast this with "What did Ann do?" "She resembled her mother" is an unsatisfactory answer. Or we may use the structure "What the zebra did was run." *Resemble* hardly fits this structure: *"What Ann did was resemble her mother." The test with *do* is not foolproof. Such verbs as *stay, sit,* and *stink* do not express action and, therefore, do not permit agents; yet the following sentences are not impossible:

8.63   What he did was stay there and say nothing.
8.64   All she did was sit there.

Test sentences involving *do* at times provide undesired results, yet they can be helpful if used with caution.

By saying that an agent performs an action by means of its own energy, we are excluding subjects of sentences such as the following, which do not contain verbs of action:

8.65   John owns a new motorcycle.
8.66   The baby weighs seven pounds.

The definition also excludes the subjects of some sentences with action verbs:

8.67   Brenda was shoved.
8.68   The door opened easily.

Brenda in 8.67 did not perform any action, nor did the door in 8.68 open by its own force.

A second semantic role is that of **instrument (Ins),** as seen in these sentences:

8.69   We cut the string with *a razor blade.*
8.70   Vera scratched her back with *a stiff brush.*

8.71   Vera scratched her back with *her fingernails.*
8.72   Gwendolyn used *dental floss* to clean her teeth.
8.73   *The nail* punctured his right front tire.

Just as the agent is almost always animate, the instrument is typically inanimate. There may be some question as to whether parts of the body, as
in 8.71, should be classified as inanimate; yet they do function as instruments the same as inanimate objects, as we can see by comparing 8.71 with
8.70. A more revealing test is that they take the pronoun *it* in the singular.
Speaking of one fingernail, we would say, "Vera broke it," not "Vera broke
her" or "Vera broke him." It should be noted that an inanimate object
cannot perform an action by means of its own energy; hence, *the nail* in 8.73
is an instrument, not an agent.

   Also related to verbs of action is a third semantic role, that of **patient**
(Pat). This is the one directly affected by the action, as illustrated by the
following sentences:

	Agt	**Pat**	**Ins**
8.74	*Eva* trimmed *her eyebrows* with *scissors.*		

	Agt	**Ins**	**Pat**
8.75	*Thomas* used *his teeth* to open *the bottle.*		

	Agt	**Pat**
8.76	*My cat* drank *the milk.*	

	Ins	**Pat**
8.77	*A rock* hit *the car.*	

	Ins	**Pat**
8.78	*His voice* cracked *the glass.*	

	Agt	**Pat**	**Ins**
8.79	*He* cracked *the glass* with *his voice.*		

	Pat
8.80	*The glass* cracked.

As we can see from the last three sentences, any of the roles may function
as subject. We can identify the patient by asking "What happened to X?"
Only if X is the patient will the question yield a sensible answer. For 8.80,
we can say, "What happened to the glass?" and receive the answer, "It
cracked." If we compare this to 8.78, we see that we cannot say, "What happened to his voice?" and have "It cracked the glass" as a sensible answer.
Nor in 8.79 can we say, "What happened to him?" and expect to be answered
with "He cracked the glass."

   The semantic role most frequently associated with nonaction verbs is
that of **experiencer (Exp):**

8.81   *Nathan* felt miserable.
8.82   Karen *knew* the answer.
8.83   It seemed to *Perry* that the picture was crooked.

Some nonaction verbs have action counterparts: *see* vs. *look at, hear* vs. *listen to,* and so on. We can illustrate the roles of agent and experiencer in the following sentences:

        Exp   **Pat**
8.84   *We* saw *the wild duck.*

        Agt   **Pat**   **Agt**   **Pat**
8.85   *We* looked at *the wild duck. We* watched *the wild duck.*

        Exp   **Pat**
8.86   *Larry* heard *the music.*

        Agt   **Pat**
8.87   *Larry* listened to *the music.*

Patient may not be the best classification for that which is experienced, as in 8.84 and 8.86, but we will not investigate this problem further; our main concern is the distinction between agent and experiencer. Similarly, a better term than *experiencer* would be desirable since this category includes such purely descriptive functions as "Olivia appeared bored."

There are additional semantic roles, possibly as many as a dozen. The four which we have given will be sufficient for our discussion of how these roles are realized on the surface.

Surface Manifestations
of Semantic Roles

With the kinds of underlying structures we have encountered in previous chapters, there is no satisfactory way to link a particular semantic role with the array of surface positions in which it can occur. We can illustrate this difficulty with the instrument role:

8.88   Edwin cut the rope with *a knife.*
8.89   Edwin used *a knife* to cut the rope.
8.90   *A knife* cut the rope.

True, we could probably devise transformations which would provide a common underlying source for *a knife* in the above sentences, but they would be extremely ad hoc. One principle we try to observe in forming rules is that they have wider applicability than just to a narrow class of structures.

In the late 1960s a new approach to transformational grammar emerged: **case grammar.** This new development and others of a similar nature showed that the underlying structures which had previously been provided for sentences were too close to the surface and that there should be something underlying them.

Instead of looking for such functions as subject and object in underlying structures, we may be better served to specify only the semantic roles:

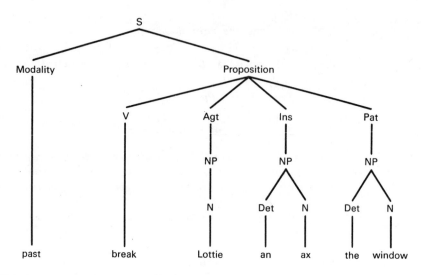

This is the structure which underlies

8.91   Lottie broke the window with an ax.

As before, we are separating tense from the verb. Under modality we place
tense, time adverbials, and a few other elements such as the modal auxiliaries (*should, can, would,* and the like). Under the proposition are the verb
and all noun phrases which are associated with it in the given sentence.
Whether these noun phrases should be in some particular order at this stage
or whether they should be unordered has not been satisfactorily answered.
We will assume that they are unordered. That is, we could have given patient first instead of agent, or patient between agent and instrument.

For languages which use prepositions, there is a transformation which
adds a preposition to each noun phrase. We can tell that the preposition
usually found with instrument is *with,* but the sentences we have examined
so far do not provide evidence for any preposition with the other roles.
From passive sentences such as "The window was broken by Lottie," we
see that agent may be accompanied by the preposition *by.* Linguists are
not in agreement as to the preposition which accompanies patient. Since
there is usually no preposition on the surface with this role, a zero preposition has been suggested for the underlying level.

Now using **M** as the abbreviation for **modality** and **Prop** for **proposition,** we can draw a tree for our structure after the prepositions have been
assigned:

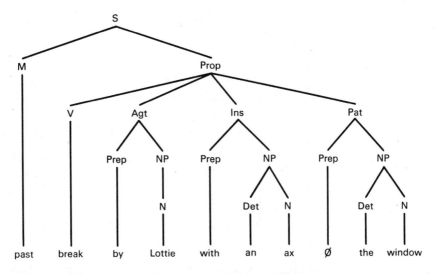

A transformation which we call **subjectivalization** moves agent to subject position:

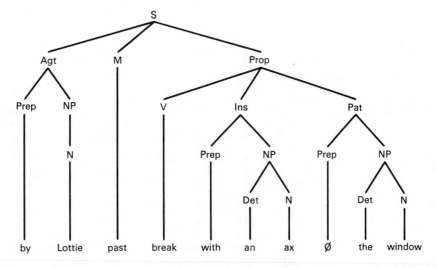

In English, subjects are not preceded by prepositions. We, therefore, apply the **subject-preposition deletion** transformation. At the same time we delete the agent node. We will be following a convention which deletes the node naming the semantic role whenever the preposition has been deleted.

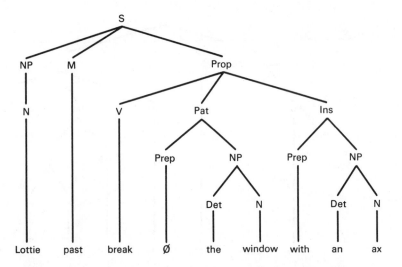

We have now applied three transformations: preposition insertion, sub-jectivalization, and subject-preposition deletion. Next we apply **objectivalization.**

If our original ordering had placed patient before instrument—as it could have since we gave no ordering restrictions for the original tree—we would still perform objectivalization even though it applied vacuously, with no change in ordering.

Next we delete the object preposition and with it the Pat node:

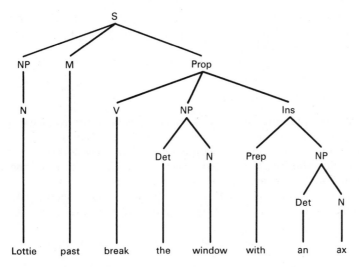

We have now completed the series of transformations which are basic to our sentences:

1. Preposition insertion
2. Subjectivalization
3. Deletion of subject preposition
4. Objectivalization
5. Deletion of object preposition

These transformations will be the only ones needed for the discussion which follows.

The trees may at first look strange and totally unlike anything we have encountered previously in this book. On closer inspection, we see that it is possible to replace three terms in the last tree: *auxiliary* for *modality, verb phrase* for *proposition,* and *prepositional phrase* for *instrument.*

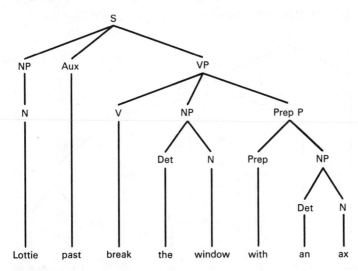

This, of course, is the kind of tree we have been seeing all along in previous chapters. What we are now saying is that there is a deeper analysis underlying this structure.

All sentences do not contain instrument. For example, instead of 8.91 we could have had

8.92   Lottie broke the window.

To derive this sentence, we would follow the same steps as we did with the preceding trees. The only difference would be that there is no instrument node on any of them. It would be a good exercise for the reader to test his understanding of the discussion so far by performing the needed transformations and drawing the trees in the derivation of 8.92.

There is still another possibility. Instead of having agent, patient, and instrument, we could have only instrument and patient:

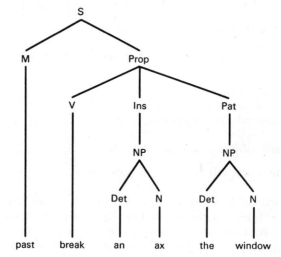

Preposition insertion now applies:

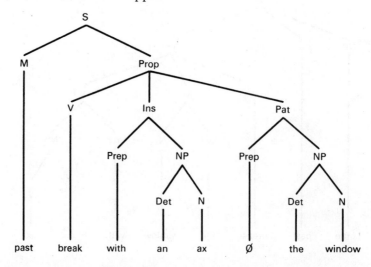

Next we move instrument to subject position:

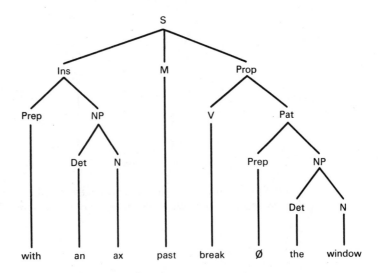

We then apply deletion of subject preposition:

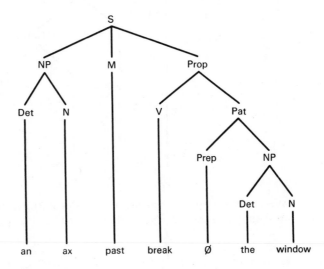

Objectivalization does not effect any changes in word order, but we apply it anyway for consistency. Otherwise we would have to complicate our rule by stating when it is applicable and when not. After deletion of object preposition, we have the following structure:

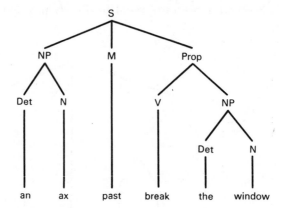

Our rules also provide for sentences in which only one noun phrase exists, as seen in the following after preposition insertion has been applied:

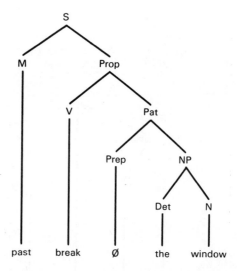

We apply the subjectivalization transformation, which moves Ø *the window* into subject position. Next, deletion of subject preposition yields

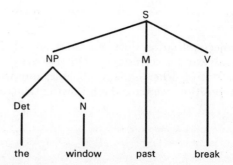

Just as we delete case nodes which do not have prepositions, we delete the Prop node whenever the verb is the only constituent left.

By using an underlying structure which does not include such concepts as subject or object, we are able to link semantic roles with their varied surface manifestations. The following sentences have been examined:

8.91   Lottie broke the window with an ax.
8.92   Lottie broke the window.
9.93   An ax broke the window.
8.94   The window broke.

Regardless of where the noun phrases appear on the surface, *Lottie* is understood as agent, *the window* as patient, and an *ax* as instrument.

It should not be assumed that we are claiming sentences 8.91–94 to be synonymous. They obviously are not. Yet they are very close in meaning, the chief difference being in how much information is supplied. Our treatment allows us to show the semantic roles of agent, instrument, and patient. It also permits us to consider *break* as one verb, not two as earlier grammars would demand, with a transitive meaning in 8.91–93 and intransitive in 8.94.

Traditional grammarians long ago recognized that the class of the verb determines the number and kinds of noun phrases that may appear with it. Any student of school grammars is familiar with such verb classifications as transitive and intransitive; these classifications are also found in most dictionaries as part of the entries for verbs. Verbs in a case grammar are likewise classified, but in a more precise manner. We list *break*, for example, as a verb which tolerates agent, patient, and instrument. As we have seen from the preceding examples, however, only patient has to be selected. We can represent this information as follows:

[*break:* Pat, Agt, Ins]
[*break:* Pat, Agt]
[*break:* Pat, Ins]
[*break:* Pat]

By using parentheses to enclose optional material, we can condense these four statements as follows:

[*break:* Pat (Agt) (Ins)]

We may select either parenthesized element, neither, or both.

There are two classes of action verbs, distinguished according to whether they take patient. Such verbs as *open, close, lock, smash, split,* and *crash* have the same description as *break.* Others like *giggle, laugh, cry, frown,* and *creep* do not readily permit patient or instrument. Hence, *giggle* is represented as [*giggle:* Agt].

One may ask why we give every noun phrase a preposition by one transformation and then in some cases delete it by another. This may seem like digging holes just to fill them back up. Our treatment allows us to show certain regularities in the language which would otherwise be impossible. The most obvious of these is that regardless of which case category is subjectivalized, it will have no preposition on the surface. We can explain why *an ax* is preceded by the preposition *with* in 8.91 but not in 8.93. Our treatment also assumes that many prepositions are predictable from a knowledge of the semantic role of the noun phrase.

Although the ordering of underlying case categories may be free, their selection for subjectivalization and objectivalization is not. For example, if we have agent, instrument, and patient, we select agent as the subject and patient as the object:

8.95a   Homer brushed his teeth with shaving cream.

Other choices would have resulted in ungrammatical sentences:

8.95b   *Shaving cream brushed his teeth by Homer.
   c   *His teeth brushed Homer with shaving cream.
   d   *Homer brushed shaving cream his teeth.

Similarly, if only instrument and patient are present, instrument is the normal choice for subject, patient for object:

8.96a   A sharp rock cut his foot.
   b   *His foot cut with a sharp rock.

A few verbs are exceptional in that they do permit subjectivalization of patient:

8.97a   This key opened the door.
   b   The door opened with this key.

As we can see from 8.96b, however, this degree of freedom is not found with all verbs.

Although agent is the normal choice for subject in a sentence containing agent and patient, patient is sometimes subjectivalized; hence, we can have both of the following sentences, one with an agent subject, the other with patient:

8.98a   Madeleine ate the cucumber.
   b   The cucumber was eaten by Madeleine.

When patient is made the subject, objectivalization does not take place; hence, the agent preposition *by* remains. Let us see how 8.98b is derived. First, we start with an underlying structure:

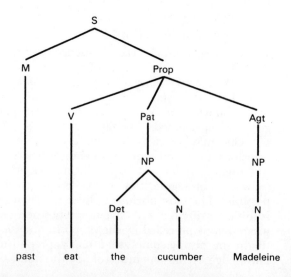

We now apply preposition insertion:

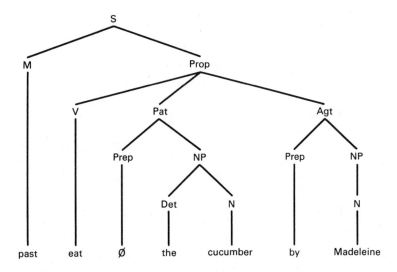

Placing agent as subject and patient as object gives us 8.98a after we delete subject and object prepositions:

8.98a   Madeleine ate the cucumber.

However, let us see what happens if we subjectivalize patient:

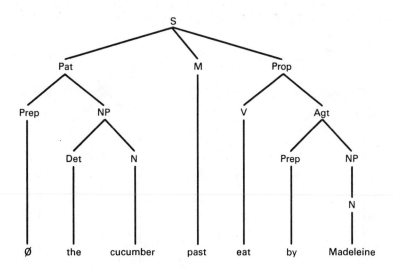

Deletion of subject preposition then gives

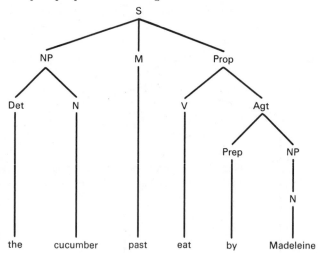

We now need some way to show that we have not selected the normal choice for subject. To do this, we add to the modality element the morphemes *be* and the past participial *en*. We will use *en* as an abbreviation for "past participle of." In some cases the past participle of a verb is spelled with the suffix *-en: eaten, given, written, taken,* and a few others. Most of the time it is the same in form as the past tense: *opened, closed, dropped, chased, begged, judged, cheated, added, gagged,* and the like. The past participle is the form that regularly occurs after *have: have seen, have opened, have drunk, have combed,* and so on. Now if we add *be* and *en* to the modality node, we have the following structure:

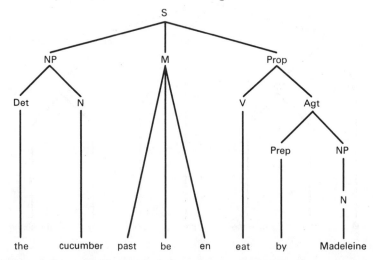

We can read the modality and verb constituents as follows: "the past form of *be* and the past participle of *eat.*" When the subject is third person singular, the past of *be* is *was;* the past participle of *eat* is always *eaten.* Hence, the sentence is

8.98b   The cucumber was eaten by Madeleine.

Earlier grammars usually derived passive sentences from underlying actives. Since our deepest underlying structures do not contain subjects and objects, we do not have to follow this procedure. We are saying that the two kinds of sentences are related and that the active sentence with agent as subject is the more normal; at the same time, we are not deriving one from the other.

Verbs and Nouns of Location

According to the grammatical model which we are now presenting, all nouns are derived from underlying semantic roles, regardless of their surface realization. Hence, *Albert* is an agent in both of these sentences:

8.99a   Albert found the shoe.
  b   The shoe was found by Albert.

The preposition *by* has been deleted in the *a* version since agent has been subjectivalized. It remains in the *b* version because agent has been neither subjectivalized nor objectivalized. We are treating noun phrases which appear on the surface as objects of prepositions within the same framework as those which appear as subjects and objects.

Following this procedure, we should assign underlying semantic roles to both *the bird* and *the tree* in the following sentence:

8.100   The bird sang in the tree.

The bird is an agent since it names an animate being which performs an act by means of its own energy. We can ask, "What did the bird do?" *The tree* is obviously not a patient or it would be objectivalized. Also, if we asked, "What happened to the tree?" the answer "The bird sang in it" would be an unsatisfactory reply. Nor is *the tree* an instrument or experiencer.

We need to add a new semantic role: that of place or location. Following the practice of grammars of Sanskrit and Russian, we will call this a **Locative (Loc).** An underlying structure for 8.100 looks like this:

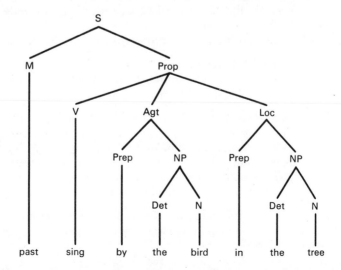

Agent is subjectivalized, and the preposition *by* is deleted, giving the surface ordering.

We have no difficulty finding other examples of locatives:

8.101   We played cards *in the den.*
8.102   The hawk hovered *over the chickens.*
8.103   Suddenly we saw a deer *in front of our car.*
8.104   There is an incinerator *behind the building.*
8.105   The dog sat *on the burning deck.*
8.106   The pen is *under your chair.*
8.107   They stood *beside the building.*

Unlike the prepositions which accompany agent and instrument, those with locatives are not predictable from syntactic information alone. We can illustrate this with two sentences in which prepositions have been omitted:

8.108   He hit me _____ a bat.
8.109   They played _____ the house.

If we know that *a bat* in sentence 8.108 is instrument, *with* is the only likely preposition which we can use. Knowing that *the house* is a locative in 8.109, however, does not permit us to select any single preposition as the most likely. A few such as *with* and *of* are impossible, but any of the locative prepositions (*near, in, under,* and so on) are possible.

Since the earliest times, English has created new prepositions from a compound of two already existing prepositions or from phrasal units. The origins of such forms as *upon* and *within* are fairly obvious, but *behind, before, beside, between,* and several others were also originally more than one word. Today we see the process continued in such units as *in front of, in back of, on top of,* and others. Some people have wondered about how these units should be treated. Such pairs as *behind* and *in back of* are, in fact, quite similar. Both are formed from earlier phrases, but *behind* has undergone changes in spelling and pronunciation which *in back of* has not experienced. Whatever the ultimate derivation of *in front of* and similar forms should be, we will be treating them as single prepositional units, the same as *before* and *in.*

Prepositions, like other words, may have more than one meaning:

8.110a   He fought *with* his brother. ("against")
     b   He fought *with* his brother. ("accompanied by")
     c   He found the nail *with* a magnet. ("by means of")

Since these three uses of *with* are etymologically related, it might be possible to group them together in the lexicon; however, studies in semantics do not yet indicate how or whether this should be done. We are, therefore, treating these uses of *with* as three separate prepositions which happen to have the same pronunciation and spelling.

The same situation exists with *by:*

8.111a   Agatha found the package *by* the door.
     b   The package was found *by* Agatha.

In the *a* sentence, *by* means "beside" and is clearly a locative. The *b* sentence is ambiguous, depending upon whether *Agatha* is agent or locative. This information is, of course, provided at an underlying level.

With most verbs, locatives are optional:

8.112   I read the book (at home).
8.113   He explained the situation to Tom (at the office).

Some intransitive verbs, however, require them:

8.114   *He lurked.
8.115   *They lay.

With *lie, stand, glance, go, look, sneak,* and a few others, locative or directional adverbs are usually required. A verb like *lurk* can be described as [*lurk:* Agt, Loc].

Sometimes a locative is the only role found in a sentence:

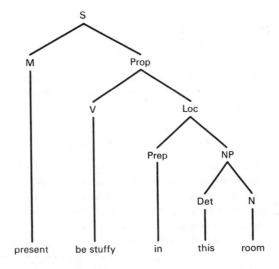

If locative is subjectivalized, the final sentence is

8.116a   This room is stuffy.

Subjectivalization of locative is usually possible only when it is the only semantic role present in the sentence. On the other hand, subjectivalization of locative is optional. If it does not occur in this sentence, there will be no noun phrase in subject position. *It*-insertion will then be applicable, giving

8.116b   It is stuffy in this room.

Other examples are easily found:

8.117a   Her office was gloomy.
    b   It was gloomy in her office.
8.118a   The party was pleasant.
    b   It was pleasant at the party.

Although these pairs are not exactly synonymous, the semantic roles of the noun phrases are constant.

Locatives may appear in surface structures not only as subjects, but also as objects:

8.119a   We loaded junk onto *the cart.*
    b   We loaded *the cart* with junk.
8.120a   We painted daisies on *the wall.*
    b   We painted *the wall* with daisies.

The semantic roles are the same for both versions of each sentence, but the pairs are clearly not synonymous. In 8.119a the cart may or may not be full after our action, but in 8.119b it is fully loaded. Similarly, in 8.120a we may have painted daisies on only part of the wall, but they are more uniformly spread in the *b* version. This difference exists for all sentences of the same structure as 8.119 and 8.120.

Semantic Roles with Verbs of Direction

In English there is rarely any difference in form between expressions involving direction and those with location. One of the few instances in which a distinction is made is with *in* and *into:*

8.121   The dog ran *in* the yard.
8.122   The dog ran *into* the yard.

Either may be an answer to "Where did the dog run?" *Where* does not distinguish between location and direction. Earlier English used *whither, whence,* and *where* as well as *thither, thence,* and *there,* but today, except in such rare cases as *in* and *into,* this distinction must be inferred from the meaning of the verb.

There are other languages that give surface expression to these features much more overtly than English does. German, for example, uses the three interrogative adverbs *wo, wohin,* and *woher* to correspond to the earlier English *where, whither,* and *whence.* In addition, a number of directional adverbs differ in form from the corresponding locatives by the presence of a prefix: *hinunter, herunter* vs. *unter; hinaus, heraus* vs. *aussen;* and the like. As in many other languages, objects of directional prepositions are in a different case from objects of locatives. In German these cases are dative with locatives and accusative with directionals:

8.123   Ich spielte hinter der Kirche. "I played behind the church." (dative)
8.124   Ich ging hinter die Kirche. "I went behind the church." (accusative)

The definite article accompanying the feminine noun *Kirche* is *der* when dative as in 8.123, but *die* when accusative as in 8.124. Latin makes a similar distinction with the dative case for locatives, accusative for direction toward, and ablative for direction from.

Russian has even more elaborate surface manifestations of these features. In addition to distinct prepositions and cases, there are verbal prefixes which designate the nature of the direction: to arrive at, to enter, to come up to, and to go through, around, off of, out of, and the like. Finnish is even richer in making distinctions of this sort on the surface.

With such diversity among languages, it is far from clear how many semantic roles should be recognized. Rather arbitrarily, we are recognizing only two for direction: **source** and **goal**:

8.125   The apple fell from *the tree.* (source)
8.126   The apple fell to *the ground.* (goal)
8.127   The apple lay on *the ground.* (location)

At present, listing any additional categories would be guesswork. Both source and goal may occur within the same sentence:

8.128   We drove from Memphis to Little Rock.

Locative is incompatible with source and goal.

The indirect object is a typical example of goal:

8.129a   Homer gave a banana to Irma.
    b   Homer gave Irma a banana.

Whereas traditionalists usually recognized the relationship between the two sentences, some of them debated whether *to Irma* in the *a* version should be classified as an indirect object or not. Transformationalists generally agreed that the sentences should be derived from the same underlying structures, since they are synonymous. As with active and passive pairs, however, one sentence had to be more basic and closer to the underlying structure than the other. The usual explanation was that 8.129b had undergone a transformation which had not been performed on 8.129a.

With case grammar it is not necessary to say that either surface structure is more basic than the other. For these sentences we have the following underlying structure after preposition insertion has been performed:

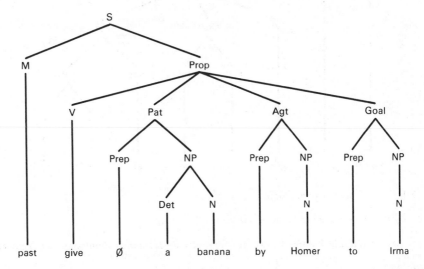

Subjectivalization of agent[3] and deletion of subject preposition give:

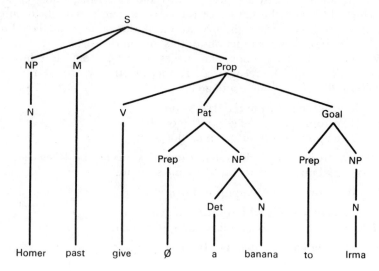

If patient is objectivalized, sentence 8.129a (repeated here) results after the deletion of the object preposition:

8.129a   Homer gave a banana to Irma.

Instead of objectivalizing patient, we could move Irma:

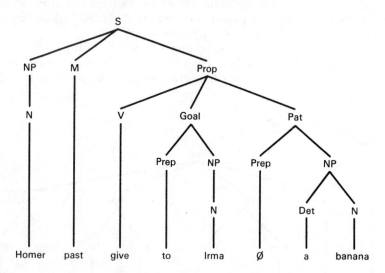

Deletion of object preposition then gives

8.129b   Homer gave Irma a banana.

---

[3] Some published works in case grammar classify *Homer* as simultaneously agent and source.

Both versions of 8.129 have the same underlying structure. They differ according to which role is made the object. In this way we are showing their relationship without claiming priority for either.

Earlier in this chapter, we saw difficulties with various definitions of the subject. We now can see the reason why some of these are faulty, particularly those that try to provide definitions using semantic criteria. Any of the semantic roles may function as a surface subject:

8.130   Agent: *The horse* kicked me.
8.131   Patient: *The window* cracked.
8.132   Patient: *I* was shoved.
8.133   Instrument: *The key* opened the door.
8.134   Experiencer: *John* heard us.
8.135   Locative: *The room* is crowded.
8.136   Goal: *Sharon* was given the message.

It is pointless to try to define the subject of a sentence by semantic terms, since any of the roles may be subjectivalized. In fact, the subject does not necessarily have referential meaning:

8.137   Expletive: *It* is raining.

The subject is a purely syntactic function, not one of semantics. It is the noun phrase that is moved to a particular position by a syntactic transformation.

Syntax and Semantics

Since language is a device for conveying meaning from one nervous system to another, it is unavoidable that any discussion of the subject should comment on how it interacts with meaning. To the ancient Greeks, the study of language and meaning were not separate, since both were part of their larger field of philosophy. Generally speaking, there was no major effort until recently to separate the two.

During the first half of the twentieth century, some linguists—particularly those identified with the American structuralist school—raised objections to the way meaning had been used in previous discussions of language. In some cases it seemed that earlier linguists had been making such circular statements as, "X belongs to class A because it means Y, and X means Y because it belongs to class A." Linguists making these objections attempted to separate their study of language structure from the study of meaning, not because they considered meaning unimportant, but because they had no framework within which to study it objectively and because they believed that their grammatical analyses would be more valid if linguistic structure were studied by itself. These views, while widespread during the 1930s, 1940s, and 1950s, were not held universally. Notable exceptions were Hjelmslev and other linguists of the Copenhagen circle.

In the early 1960s, it became obvious that it was impossible to study language structure apart from meaning. By the middle of this decade, the transformationalists had developed a model of grammar which made syntax the central component, the one which specified which structures were possible in a language. According to this model, the deepest underlying structure was known as a deep structure; it was subjected to various transformations to produce a surface structure. This is basically the model which has been presented in this book, with one exception: We have not been using the term *deep structure,* since recent developments have raised questions as to which levels of underlying structure are valid. As we have seen, the trend has been to keep pushing underlying structures back in degree of abstraction. Within the model of the mid-1960s (illustrated in Figure 8.1), there

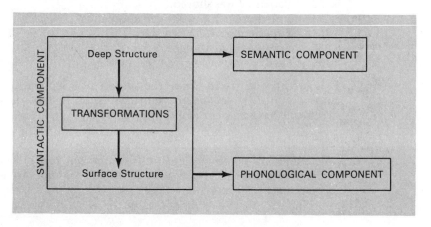

Figure 8.1

was a phonological component which operated on the surface structure to produce a phonetic representation. There was also a semantic component which interpreted the deep structure to provide the meaning of the sentence. Since transformations were looked upon as meaning-preserving, the deep structure contained all the information needed to say what the sentence meant. Except for a few pioneering studies such as Katz and Fodor (1963), most linguists were so involved with matters of syntax that they gave little attention to the actual form or operation of the semantic component. As such, it remained a mystery. According to this model, the semantic component *interpreted* the meaning of the structure produced by the syntactic component, assigning meanings to some structures and labeling others as impossible or meaningless. The semantic component in this model has, therefore, been referred to as **interpretive semantics.**

By the late 1960s, linguists had begun asking questions about the semantic component: what it looked like, how its rules operated, and how its representations compared with those of the syntactic component. Eventually, a slightly different model emerged, in which the semantic component did not *interpret* the deep structure, but rather *provided* it. This model belongs to a theory known as **generative semantics.** Proponents of this theory have denied the relevance of a syntactic deep structure which is different from a semantic structure. Instead, they have developed the model illustrated in Figure 8.2. According to this type of grammar, a **conceptual struc-**

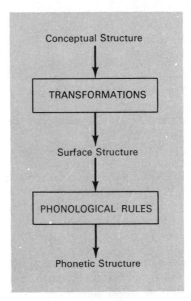

Figure 8.2

ture, or semantic representation, can be represented by means of a tree similar to those used for syntax. Transformations convert this conceptual structure to a syntactic surface structure without recourse to a separate level known as deep structure. With this model, semantic and syntactic rules are not separated.[4]

Although case grammar is close to the generative semantic model, it is not totally incompatible with the notion of interpretive semantics. At this time it is not possible to know which theory is the better. Instead of arguing between them, we will look at some of the problems of meaning which an adequate semantic component of a grammar will have to accommodate, regardless of which model is accepted.

Such notions as subject, object, and modifier are both syntactic and semantic; any study of semantics, therefore, must recognize syntactic structures as indicated by trees. In addition, all underlying structures can be looked upon as attempts to account for some aspect of meaning: why certain pairs of sentences are recognized as synonymous, why a given sentence is ambiguous, why a person understands two sentences as having the same or different structures even though the surface form does not reveal this information. It is doubtful that a person can really study syntax and semantics separately.

It is generally recognized that a grammar should account for synonymous sentences such as these:

8.138a   She gave the cake to the bachelor.
   b   She gave the bachelor the cake.

4 For a fuller discussion of the differences between interpretive and generative semantics, see Maclay (1971), Lakoff (1971), Chomsky (1971, 1972), McCawley (1968a, 1968b), Jackendoff (1972), and the references cited in these works.

But what about 8.139? Should the semantic component show that it is synonymous with 8.138a?

8.139   She presented the cake to the unmarried man.

Such a prospect seems reasonable, but how should the semantic component handle such information?

Similarly, certain undertones, implied meanings, and presuppositions are realized syntactically or phonologically, as we saw with factive verbs in the last chapter. Here are some more:

8.140   Your child is an underachiever.
8.141   Your grandmother certainly looks girlish.
8.142   He was ostensibly asking about the assignment.
8.143   The captain was sober all day.
8.144   You are cute.

A dictionary entry could easily indicate that *underachiever* is a euphemism often used by educators to mean "dumb" or possibly "lazy." The entry for the suffix *-ish* could state that it is normally pejorative in meaning, as in *girlish, womanish, mannish, teacherish, big brotherish,* and the like. Similarly, *ostensibly* suggests that the act mentioned is not the main concern, that a person ostensibly asking about the assignment is in reality asking about something else. When we come to 8.143, we find no way the dictionary can provide the suggested meaning, namely that the captain is normally not sober. The speaker of 8.144 may indicate by intonation whether he is being flattering or sarcastic, but often the answer lies in his normal use of *cute*. Some people never refer to an adult as *cute*. Should the semantic component of a grammar be able to interpret individual uses?

The semantic roles introduced by proponents of case grammar are not just semantic notions, since their syntactic relations to other elements in the sentence are predictable. Some linguists have suggested that the deepest underlying structures of a case grammar are in fact conceptual structures. They may be right, but there is not yet enough evidence to answer one way or the other. Judging from past developments in linguistics, a person would be wise to be skeptical of such a statement and to assume that real conceptual structures contain more information and are probably even more abstract than those presented in a case grammar.

Since language is so closely merged with our other activities, it may be impossible to distinguish between a person's linguistic knowledge and his knowledge of the world in general. We saw in our discussion of restrictive and nonrestrictive clauses that the difference may be signaled by syntactic means, but it may also depend upon the speaker's extralinguistic knowledge. A person's understanding of what a sentence means is dependent only partly upon his knowledge of the language; also included are his past experiences, his present environment, and his beliefs and biases. It is no wonder that students of semantics have found some areas of study in which they can make advances but others in which they are still floundering. Philosophers have been doing the same for two millennia.

Exercises

A. Are the surface functions of the noun phrases in the following sentences indicated by word order, prepositions, or inflections?

1. The elephant walked to me.
2. Judy's husband threw her a can of soup.

B. Classify each of the noun phrases in the following sentences as to its semantic role (agent, instrument, patient, or experiencer):

1. Beth hit Gladys with a rock.
2. The window was broken by Fred.
3. A sharp object cut my hand.
4. The soup tasted too salty to Nancy.
5. Nancy tasted the soup to see if it had been heated.

C. For each of the following sentences draw a tree which shows the underlying semantic roles and perform all transformations needed to derive the given surface structure:

1. The needle scratched the record.
2. Bobbie slapped Trudy.

D. Explain how the following sentences differ in meaning:

1. The mirror cracked.
2. A rock cracked the mirror.
3. Ted cracked the mirror with a rock.
4. Ted cracked the mirror.

In what ways are the sentences alike? How do the trees of their underlying semantic roles show their differences and similarities?

E. Which semantic roles do the following verbs permit: *kick, tickle, scream, run, thump, cough, remove, turn, please, sweat, sleep, build*?

F. All of the following verbs take the same semantic roles; name them: *bend, rip, slap, stroke, melt, cut, rub.* Divide these verbs into two classes according to the roles which must appear in a surface structure. What semantic differences do you find in the two classes?

G. Explain how a case grammar accounts for the synonymy of the following sentences:

1. Sue broke the chair.
2. The chair was broken by Sue.

H. How do the locative prepositions differ from those with agent or instrument?

I. Give the semantic role for each noun phrase in the following sentences:

1. I used a nail to open the bottle.
2. Larry heard the men in the yard.
3. The diary was found under the bed.
4. The cat ran to the kitchen.
5. The child jumped from the table.

Suggested Reading

ANDERSON, JOHN M., *The Grammar of Case*. Cambridge: Cambridge University Press, 1971.

CHAFE, WALLACE L., *Meaning and the Structure of Language*. Chicago: University of Chicago Press, 1970.

CRUSE, D. A., "Some Thoughts on Agentivity," *Journal of Linguistics* 9 (1973): 11–23.

DOUGHERTY, RAY, "Recent Studies on Language Universals," *Foundations of Language* 6 (1970): 505–61.

FILLMORE, CHARLES J., "The Case for Case," in *Universals in Linguistic Theory*, ed. Emmon Bach and Robert T. Harms. New York: Holt, Rinehart and Winston, Inc., 1968.

———, "The Grammar of *Hitting* and *Breaking*," in *Readings in English Transformational Grammar*, ed. Roderick A. Jacobs and Peter S. Rosenbaum. Waltham, Mass.: Ginn and Company, 1970.

FLETCHER, PAUL, "Case Grammar: Its Viability as an Alternative Grammatical Model," *Lingua* 28 (1971): 237–50.

HALLIDAY, M. A. K., "Notes on Transitivity and Theme in English," *Journal of Linguistics* 3 (1967): 37–81; 199–244; 4 (1968): 179–215.

HUDDLESTON, RODNEY, "Some Remarks on Case Grammar," *Linguistic Inquiry* 1 (1970): 501–11.

LANGENDOEN, D. TERENCE, *Essentials of English Grammar*. New York: Holt, Rinehart and Winston, Inc., 1970.

LYONS, JOHN, *Introduction to Theoretical Linguistics*. Cambridge: Cambridge University Press, 1969.

STOCKWELL, ROBERT P., PAUL SCHACHTER, and BARBARA HALL PARTEE, *The Major Syntactic Structures of English*. New York: Holt, Rinehart and Winston, Inc., 1973.

TRAUGOTT, ELIZABETH CLOSS, *A History of English Syntax*. New York: Holt, Rinehart and Winston, Inc., 1972.

chapter 9

The Influence of Higher Sentences

Our study of syntax, like that of language in general, has the goal of understanding what language is, how it is organized, and how it functions. Because of the complexity of the subject and the highly imperfect state of our knowledge about it, there are many problems which are left unsolved in this book and many more which are not even touched upon. A book not limited by length and written for professional linguists with considerable background in the subject could certainly provide a much fuller account of syntax, yet even such a book could explain only a fraction of the problems. In spite of the profusion of linguistic scholarship appearing each year, there is no reason to believe that within the foreseeable future we will have a reasonably complete account of syntax. We are, therefore, exploring a few selected topics which are illustrative rather than exhaustive.

We began our study of syntax with surface structures. Next we noticed that much of what a fluent speaker of a language understands is not obvious from surface realizations alone; we proposed underlying representations to accommodate this information. Through studying various kinds of embedded sentences, we have gradually pushed these underlying structures farther and farther back from the surface. With case grammar we made our ultimate underlying structures still more abstract. In this chapter, we will first look at the possibility of higher sentences which have been deleted and then use this analysis to study imperatives and questions.

Performatives

Traditional grammarians customarily classified sentences as declarative, interrogative, imperative, or exclamatory. Working within a broader and slightly different framework, the Oxford philosopher J. L. Austin analyzed sentences in a way that has been seminal for linguistic research on sentence types.

Among other things, Austin differentiated between two classes of sentences which he called **constative** and **performative.** The first group can be illustrated as follows:

9.1   They are man and wife.
9.2   I fed your fish while you were away.
9.3   Alex will pay the bill.

Any of these sentences may be true or false. If false, the speaker may be deliberately lying or merely misled. These sentences contrast with performatives, such as the following:

9.4   I pronounce you man and wife.
9.5   I promise to feed your fish while you are away.
9.6   I order you to pay the bill.

Although these may be uttered inappropriately (insincerely, on the wrong occasion, to the wrong person, and the like), they cannot be true or false. Also, a sentence such as 9.5 constitutes an act of promising, whereas one like 9.2 does not constitute an act of feeding.

Following this line of distinguishing sentences, Ross (1970) has argued that all sentences at an underlying level have higher performative verbs which are later deleted. Hence, a structure like this should be given to underlie 9.1:

(I tell you) they are man and wife.

Although we are giving the verb in the higher sentence as *tell,* a more technical grammar would not give it a surface spelling, but rather would merely treat it as an abstract entity with the features *performative* and *present tense.* The important elements of the higher sentence are that the subject is *I,* the verb is performative and present tense, and the indirect object is *you.* Something like "I say to you" meets these requirements as well as "I tell you" does. Whereas other performative verbs (*vow, pronounce, command, request, warn, empower, counsel,* and the like) remain in surface structures, the abstract performative verb is always deleted along with its subject and indirect object.

If any of the conditions are missing, the sentence is not a performative. Hence, only 9.7 is performative, not 9.8 or 9.9:

9.7   I caution you not to eat the fish.
9.8   I cautioned you not to eat the fish.
9.9   I cautioned him not to eat the fish.

Sentences 9.8 and 9.9 are reports, not actual acts of cautioning in themselves.

There have been various kinds of evidence suggested to support the claim that all sentences contain a performative verb at some underlying level. The following are adapted from Ross (1970).

We can freely comment on our own feelings and on those of others:

9.10   I feel silly.
9.11   I felt tired.
9.12   Harry feels bored.
9.13   Jacob felt uncomfortable.

With second-person subjects, however, restrictions occur:

9.14   *You feel silly.[1]
9.15   *You feel energetic.
9.16   ?You felt hopeful.

With past tense, as in 9.16, some people find the structure acceptable, but with present tense it is clearly impossible. The restriction is confined to declarative sentences, since questions are unobjectionable:

9.17   Do you feel silly?
9.18   You feel silly, don't you?

Also, with certain modals (*should feel* and others) there is no problem.
    It would be too strong a restriction to say that *you* cannot be the subject of *feel* in present-tense, declarative, indicative sentences, for the following embedded structures are perfectly grammatical:

9.19   Carrie says that you feel guilty.
9.20   I am writing them that you feel better.

But some embedded sentences have restrictions:

9.21   *I am telling you that you feel silly.
9.22   *I told Harry that he felt lousy.
9.23   I told Harry that she felt lousy.

Sentence 9.22 is ungrammatical only if *he* refers to *Harry*.
    The restriction on the embedded sentences is that the subject of *feel* cannot have the same referent as the indirect object in the next higher sentence. Sentence 9.22 illustrates this clearly. If sentences 9.14–16 have underlying structures in which there is a higher sentence with the indirect object *you*—as the performative analysis claims—then only this one statement is needed to explain all of the sentences with the verb *feel* followed by an adjective. It seems plausible that all the ungrammatical sentences in 9.10–23 are violating the same rule.
    For another restriction which favors the performative analysis, let us examine sentences beginning with the phrase *according to*:

9.24   According to Maxine, the keys are in this drawer.
9.25   According to them, we shouldn't be here.
9.26   According to you, I'm the biggest fool in town.
9.27   *According to me, she's awfully tight.

[1] As is the case with illustrative sentences in almost all linguistics publications, there is variation among dialects as to the grammaticalness of individual sentences. For those people who find 9.14 and 9.15 acceptable in the same sense as 9.10 and 9.12 but not 9.18, there is apparently no restriction on the subject of *feel*. Speakers of these dialects should turn to Ross (1970) for additional evidence for the performative analysis.

At first we may think that the restriction is simply one which prohibits *me* from being the object of *according to,* but there are counterexamples:

9.28   That lying Kathy said that according to me, you won't need a ticket.

There must be some syntactic explanation why 9.28 is possible but 9.27 is not.

There are also sentences in which noun phrases other than *me* are not permitted with *according to:*

9.29   *Adam says that according to him, it won't rain.
9.30   Adam says that according to Tom, it won't rain.
9.31   *Beverly asserts that according to her, we'll be too early.
9.32   Beverly asserts that according to Ann, we'll be too early.

The restriction illustrated by these four sentences is that the object of *according to* cannot have the same referent as the subject in the next higher sentence. If *him* does not refer to *Adam* in 9.29 or *her* to *Beverly* in 9.31, then both sentences are grammatical. This is also the reason that *according to me* is possible in 9.28: The subject in the next higher sentence is not *I,* but *Kathy.* With *I* the sentence is ungrammatical:

9.33   *I said that according to me, you won't need a ticket.

If sentences 9.24–27 also have higher sentences with performative verbs at an underlying level, they are accounted for by the same restriction. A higher sentence like "I say to you . . ." with *I* as the subject causes no problems for any object of *according to* other than *me.* Hence, 9.24–26 with *Maxine, them,* and *you* are grammatical, but 9.27 with *me* is not.

We could provide several other types of restrictions which seem to support an underlying higher sentence with a performative verb, but these examples are sufficient for our purposes. We have shown that elements which are found at an underlying level may not be overtly expressed on the surface.

Imperatives

One kind of performative sentence is the command:

9.34   I order you to stop whistling.
9.35   I command you to obey my order.

These sentences constitute orders or commands, not mere reports of them as would be the case if we changed the tense or one of the pronouns.

There is also another kind of command, in which the higher verb has been deleted:

9.36   Stop whistling.
9.37   Obey my order.

These are understood as being orders or commands just as 9.34 and 9.35 are. Our problem is to relate the two and account for this understanding.

Traditional grammarians said that imperative sentences like 9.36 and 9.37 had an understood subject *you,* which they mentioned in parsing and which they enclosed in parentheses in their diagrams. This analysis agrees with our intuition about these sentences. When we say, "Stop whistling," to a person, he either stops or becomes indignant, saying that he wasn't whistling or that he can whistle if he chooses. The fact that people respond linguistically and nonlinguistically to our imperative sentences indicates that they understand them as directed to them (i.e., with the subject *you*) rather than to someone else or to the speaker. In a transformational grammar this means that the sentence should have the subject *you* at an underlying level.

We can provide syntactic evidence for assigning the underlying subject *you* to imperatives. The first of these involves certain verb phrases which describe actions a person performs with parts of his body: batting his eyes, clearing his throat, stubbing his toe, barking his shin, thumbing his nose, looking down his nose, opening his heart, holding his breath, and the like. These actions are those which are not performed on someone else. Hence, the sentences under 9.38 are grammatical, but those under 9.39 are not:

9.38a   I batted my eyes.
   b   We batted our eyes.
   c   Bill batted his eyes.
   d   They batted their eyes.
   e   You batted your eyes.
9.39a   *I batted Sue's eyes.
   b   *We batted your eyes.
   c   *Bill didn't bat my eyes.
   d   *They batted her eyes.
   e   *You didn't bat our eyes.

The possessive which precedes *eyes* must be coreferential with the subject of *bat.*

In imperative sentences we also find restrictions:

9.40a   Bat your eyes.
   b   *Bat their eyes.
   c   *Bat my eyes.
9.41a   Don't bat your eyes.
   b   *Don't bat her eyes.
   c   *Don't bat Hiram's eyes.

If we restrict ourselves to surface structures, we need two rules to account for sentences 9.38–41:

1. In the expression "bat _____ eyes," the possessive which precedes *eyes* must be coreferential with the subject of *bat.*
2. In imperative sentences *your* must be the possessive with *eyes* in the structure "bat _____ eyes."

With a separate statement for imperatives, we are denying that this restriction is in any way related to the first one. On the other hand, if we recognize an underlying structure which gives *you* as the subject of all imperatives, then we can account for the sentences under 9.40 and 9.41 by restriction one above. That is, the same rule applies for imperatives as for other sentences.

A second grammatical structure which supports an underlying subject *you* in imperatives is the reflexive:

9.42a   I hurt myself.
   b   *I hurt yourself.
9.43a   Ellen cut herself.
   b   *Ellen cut himself.
9.44a   The twins saw themselves in the mirror.
   b   *The twins saw myself in the mirror.

The reflexive pronoun must be coreferential with the subject. It is not enough that it agree in person, number, and gender; in 9.43a, *herself* must refer specifically to Ellen.

Imperative sentences also permit reflexives, but not without restriction:

9.45a   Control yourself.
   b   *Control myself.
9.46a   Don't pinch yourself.
   b   *Don't pinch themselves.
9.47a   Behave yourselves.
   b   *Behave herself.

Only *yourself* or the plural *yourselves* may serve as the object reflexive in an imperative sentence. As with phrases such as "bat _____ eyes," we could draw up two statements for the restrictions, one applying to imperatives and the second to other sentences. This procedure would be fine if the two restrictions were unrelated, but they seem to be very close or even identical. If we allow an underlying subject *you* in imperatives, only one rule is needed for all sentences. *Yourself* and *yourselves* are the only possible reflexives which are coreferential with the subject *you*.

The traditional explanation that imperative sentences have an understood subject *you* is valid. Traditional grammarians also stated that the tense of the verb in imperatives is present. Hence,

9.48   Hold your breath.

would be interpreted as having the understood subject *you*, present tense, and the verb phrase *hold your breath*. *Hold* is the form we find for the present tense with *you*, as we can see in sentences which unquestionably have present tense:

9.49a   You hold your breath more often than I do.
9.50a   If you hold your breath long enough, you'll turn blue.

We can compare these sentences with those with third-person singular subjects, where we have the clearly marked *-s* for present tense:

9.49b   He holds his breath more often than I do.
9.50b   If he holds his breath long enough, he'll turn blue.

Unfortunately, this is not proof that *hold* is present tense in *Hold your breath,* for this is also the form of the infinitive:

9.51a   I made you hold your breath.
   b   I made him hold his breath.

If we turn to the verb *be,* we find an unambiguous form, since the infinitive *be* is different from the second-person, present-tense form *are:*

9.52a   You are good.
   b   He is good.
9.53a   I'll make you be good.
   b   I'll make him be good.

The imperative is not **Are good,* as we would expect if imperative sentences contained present-tense verbs, but rather

9.54   Be good.

This, of course, is the infinitive, or form unmarked for tense. Imperatives do not contain tense.
   Yet we have assigned tense to every underlying sentence. For 9.55a there should be an underlying structure like 9.55b:

9.55a   Close your eyes.
   b   you ———— close your eyes

The underline indicates an unstated tense and possibly other elements. With only two tenses—present and past—we could select present by meaning, since we do not command people to do things in past time; but the relationship between time and tense in English is complicated, and arguments based solely on this relationship are unconvincing.
   However, there is a syntactic structure which may help:

9.56   I should be on the list, shouldn't I?
9.57   She can sing, can't she?
9.58   They are friendly, aren't they?
9.59   You have been crying, haven't you?
9.60   You will help us, won't you?

To form the tag question, we repeat tense and the first auxiliary, add *not,* and repeat the subject NP. Let us see what imperatives with tag questions look like:

9.61   Read this paper, won't you?
9.62   Come here, won't you?
9.63   *Walk the dog, wouldn't you?
9.64   *Help me, haven't you?
9.65   *Do me a favor, won't he?

These sentences lend additional support to the underlying subject *you* in imperatives, as we see from 9.65 or from any of the other sentences 9.61–64 if we substitute any other NP for *you*. They also seem to indicate that the underlying structure for imperatives should be *you will* X, where X is the material which remains on the surface. Hence, 9.61 has an underlying structure something like the one underlying

9.66   You will read this paper.

But the structure that underlies this sentence cannot be the same as the one underlying *Read this paper,* or we would have no way of accounting for the imperative meaning.

To distinguish between surface structures like *Read this paper* and *You will read this paper,* Katz and Postal (1964) introduced the symbol *imp* for the deep structures of imperatives. This symbol was later used in Liles (1971). With the performative analysis we are able to replace *imp* with a more satisfactory underlying structure, one which preserves the original meaning of *imp* but which states it more specifically:

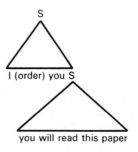

For imperatives we delete not only the higher sentence, but also *you* and *will* in the lower sentence. *Read this paper* and *You will read this paper* differ at the underlying level in the nature of the verbs in the higher sentence.

In the section of this chapter on performatives, we said that the only performative verbs to be deleted are those which are abstract; hence, these two sentences should have different underlying verbs in the higher sentence:

9.67   I promise you that I will love you forever.
9.68   I will love you forever.

Whereas 9.67 has the specific word *promise,* 9.68 has an abstract performative verb which is then deleted. Similarly, for imperatives there needs to be some distinction to separate sentences like these:

9.69   I order you to go home now.
9.70   Go home now.

The higher verb in 9.70 should not have a specific spelling such as *order* or *command;* rather, it should be an abstract verb with the features present tense, performative, and command.

The analysis we are proposing for imperatives continues to give an underlying subject *you*, agreeing with our intuitions about the structure and with the traditional treatment. It furthermore allows us to distinguish between imperatives and nonimperatives as well as between sentences with surface verbs of commanding and those without them. We have by no means covered all aspects of imperatives such as the military command "You *will* report at 0500 hours tomorrow" or the relationship between questions and commands. However, we have discussed the most common aspects of imperative sentences and provided a means for accounting for much of the knowledge a native speaker possesses about them.

Questions

Although it has long been customary to distinguish questions from imperatives, their differences are often more of surface form than actual meaning. As we saw in Chapter 1, questions in reality are often polite commands, as we can see from these sentences:

9.71a   Pass the salt.
    b   Would you pass the salt?

We can easily think of a great many examples of sentences which are questions in form but which are in actuality commands stated politely:

9.72   Do you know what time it is?
9.73   Can you help me lift this table?
9.74   Would you move down one seat?

If any of these "questions" is answered merely with "Yes" and no action, the speaker is surprised. He wonders whether the other person understood him correctly or is being rude, stupid, or cute. These sentences are interpreted differently from the following:

9.75   Is this the end of the line?
9.76   Have you been waiting long?
9.77   Are you planning to go somewhere this summer?

These can be properly answered with "Yes" or "No" and no additional action. The difference between 9.72–74 and 9.75–77 seems not to be grammatical but merely an element of social behavior. We will, therefore, have nothing further to say about it.

There is another sense in which all questions are commands or requests. That is, we could paraphrase 9.75–77 as follows:

9.78   Tell me whether this is the end of the line.
9.79   Tell me whether you have been waiting long.
9.80   Tell me whether you are planning to go somewhere this summer.

If we use a performative analysis for sentence 9.78, an underlying structure will look like this:

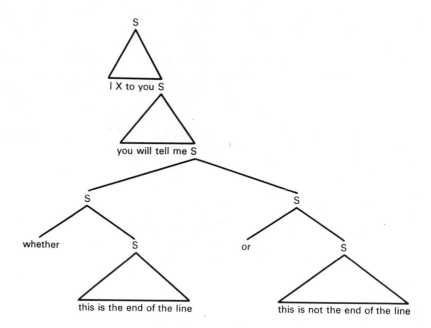

We are using X as the abstract performative verb of command. Since *whether* indicates a choice, the tree contains two sentences, one positive and one negative. The highest S will be deleted because it contains an abstract performative verb; since this verb is one of commanding, *you* and *will* in the next sentence down will also be deleted, leaving

9.81a   Tell me whether this is the end of the line or this is not the end of the line.

With repeated material deleted:

9.81b   Tell me whether this is the end of the line or not.

Sometimes we let *whether* carry the meaning of *not:*

9.81c   Tell me whether this is the end of the line.

The person answering may select "Yes" and the positive sentence ("Yes, this is the end of the line") or "No" and the negative ("No, this is not the end of the line"); or he may delete the repeated material, saying just "Yes" or "No."

Now let us return to the direct question:

9.75   Is this the end of the line?

Since this is close in meaning, if not identical to 9.81c, it should have a similar structure. In fact, if we use Y as an abstract verb in place of *tell,* we can produce this tree:

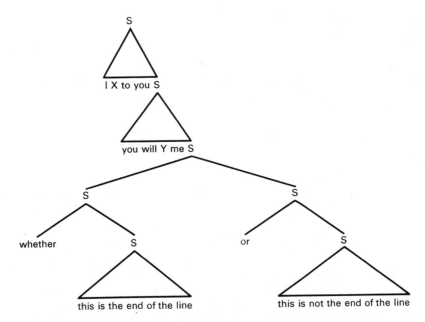

Since abstract performative verbs do not appear on the surface, both of the higher sentences in the tree are deleted. With imperatives, to indicate the meaning of the higher sentence, we deleted *you* and *will*. Similarly, here to indicate the deleted material, we rearrange the word order and delete *whether* and the negative sentence to give

9.75   Is this the end of the line?

Let us look at the exact nature of this rearrangement.
    The following are typical questions on the surface:

9.82a   Have you seen my comb?
9.83a   Was Tony sitting here?
9.84a   Had they been smoking?
9.85a   Could you have been wrong?
9.86a   Are the guests here?
9.87a   Were you at home?

These questions are related to the following declaratives:

9.82b   You have seen my comb.
9.83b   Tony was sitting here.
9.84b   They had been smoking.
9.85b   You could have been wrong.
9.86b   The guests are here.
9.87b   You were at home.

One way of determining that the declaratives and interrogatives are related is to provide possible answers for the questions. If a person asks, "Are the guests here?" he may be answered with, "Yes, the guests are here." For the sentences with second-person subjects, there is a shift to first person for the reply. Hence, "Were you at home?" will be answered with, "Yes, I was at home."

If we restricted our observations to 9.86a and 9.87a, we might decide that questions differ from declaratives in that for the former the verb precedes the subject. Looking at the other sentences in the group, we see that this first observation is incorrect. It is not the entire verb unit which precedes the subject, but rather just the verb which contains tense, whether it is a form of *be* or the first auxiliary. A verb unit may consist of up to four words in English, as in

$$\begin{array}{cccc} 1 & 2 & 3 & 4 \end{array}$$
9.88a   They should have been practicing.

We never move more than one of these in a question; hence, the related interrogative is

$$\begin{array}{cccc} 1 & 2 & 3 & 4 \end{array}$$
9.88b   Should they have been practicing?

Question formation provides a good example of the difference between a native speaker's knowledge of his language and the statements he may make about it. Native speakers never make mistakes in forming questions, apart from occasional slips of the tongue; texts devoted to correcting the speech of native speakers never even mention the subject. Yet when asked to tell someone else how to form questions, their statements normally have very little resemblance to their actual practice. If people were aware of the exact processes involved in forming the various grammatical structures which they manipulate freely, there would be no need to study linguistics. Our purpose in studying language, as we have been stressing throughout this book, is to learn how it functions.

We can derive "Are you going?" in the following way. First, our overall structure with higher sentences looks like this:

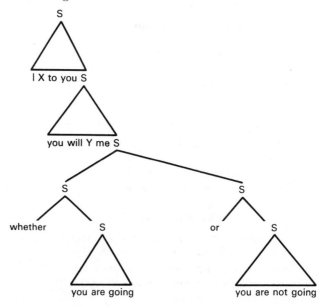

After deletion of the two higher sentences and the negative, along with *whether* and *or,* we have the following structure:

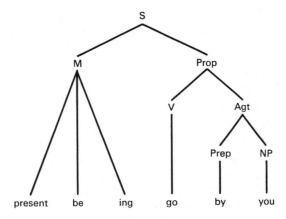

We subjectivalize agent and delete the preposition. Our structure then looks like this:

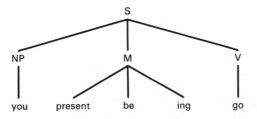

The **question transformation** now moves tense and *be* before the subject noun phrase:

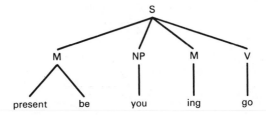

The present form of *be* is *are* when *you* is the subject, and the *ing* form (present participle) of *go* is *going.* This is the surface ordering for *Are you going?*

The statement that questions in English have the verb which carries tense placed before the subject holds true for a large number of sentences:

9.89   Must you sit there?
9.90   Are you listening to me?
9.91   Have they seen us?

9.92   Was she in the car?
9.93   *Saw you their new house?
9.94   *Knows he the way to school?

We could say that 9.93 and 9.94 are exceptions and keep our observation about word order for English questions. However, as we add other sentences, we find that any time *see* or *know* is the verb and there is no auxiliary preceding it, our rule does not hold. It does not matter whether the tense is present or past or what the subject is. Still other sentences show that the exceptions fall into a definite pattern:

9.95a   *Live they here?
9.96a   *Went you to town?
9.97a   *Remembered Harriet your name?

Each of the exceptions is a verb other than *be* which does not have an auxiliary. Depending upon the dialect, *have* may or may not be classified with *be*. Some people find "Have you any money?" acceptable, but others find it poetic and quaint.

    Below are the declarative sentences which are related to 9.95a–97a and the questions which are accepted for Modern English:

9.95b   They live here.
    c   Do they live here?
9.96b   You went to town.
    c   Did you go to town?
9.97b   Harriet remembered your name.
    c   Did Harriet remember your name?

Only tense has been moved before the subject, not the verb itself. Since tense cannot occur alone, we insert the semantically empty *do* to carry it. The derivation of 9.96c follows these steps:

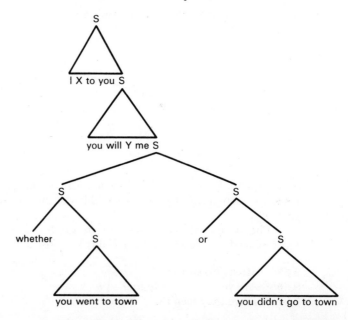

Let us concentrate just on the sentence *you went to town* since all other sentences are deleted:

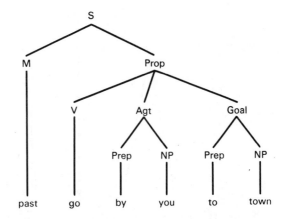

Subjectivalization and deletion of subject preposition give

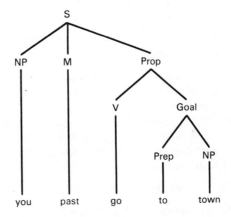

The question transformation moves tense before the subject:

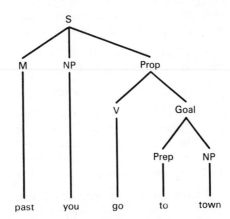

Now *do*-**insertion** occurs to provide a prop for tense:

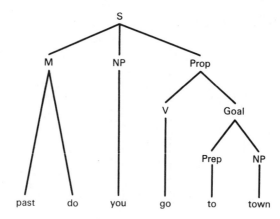

The inversion of subject and tense is similar to the transformation which inverts subject with tense and first auxiliary or *be*.

We have seen two kinds of questions: those which are embedded on the surface as 9.98a, and those which are not, such as 9.98b:

9.98a   Tell me whether you are having a good time (or not).
   b   Are you having a good time?

Those which are embedded on the surface are often called "indirect questions." Since the next higher sentence is present on the surface, there is no need to invert subject and part of the verb to indicate that it is a question. In 9.98b, however, the inverted word order is used to mark the sentence as a question. Actually, the word order is somewhat redundant since it is accompanied by a characteristic rising pitch at the end which does not fall. We also find questions without inversion:

9.98c   You are having a good time?

But it is the inverted ones which are our concern here.

Our rules for rearranging the word order for questions apply only to Modern English. At an earlier period of the language, all verbs which carried tense were placed before the subject to indicate questions; if this rule had not changed, these would be grammatical today:

9.99   Wrote you the letter?
9.100   Went they to the museum?

This is, in fact, the rule for forming questions in German:

9.101   Möchten Sie mich küssen? "Would you like to kiss me?"
9.102   Haben sie es gesehen? "Have they seen it?"
9.103   Ist er zu hause? "Is he at home?"
9.104   Singt er gut? "Does he sing well?"
9.105   Wohnen Sie hier? "Do you live here?"

Rearrangement is only one means of indicating that a sentence is a question. The pitch pattern in "You are having a good time?" is also indicative of an interrogative sentence. Most languages which use rearrangements of morphemes to signal questions also have characteristic pitch patterns for this kind of sentence; furthermore, it is usually possible to indicate a question solely by means of pitch, without rearrangement. Instead of word order, some languages use a special particle to mark a sentence as a question. Classical Arabic, for example, uses *hal* before the sentence, and Japanese uses *ka* at the end without rearrangement of word order.

All languages have means for forming questions, but they do not all use the same devices. Those that use word order do not necessarily employ the same arrangements, and those which use particles do not always position them in the same places. Yet it would be a mistake to assume that languages can vary in limitless ways in the formation of questions. The following have not been found for any language, and we are reasonably safe in predicting that they will not be found in any natural human language which is studied in the future:

> *Declarative:* I smell the blood of an Englishman.
> *Mirror image:* Englishman an of blood the smell I?
> *Repetition of entire sentence:* I smell the blood of an Englishman; I smell the blood of an Englishman?
> *Positioning of a particle after every word:* I yuk smell yuk the yuk blood yuk of yuk a yuk Englishman yuk?

There are, in fact, only a limited number of ways in which languages form questions, and they are severely restricted in how they operate within these ways. This observation is true not only for questions, but apparently for all aspects of language.

So far we have examined questions of this type:

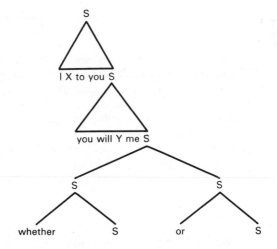

Although certain answers such as "I don't know" are possible, the most usual are "Yes" or "No." This kind of question is, therefore, called the **yes/no question**. There are also questions which prompt different kinds of answers, as illustrated by the following:

9.106   Tell me where you are going.
9.107   Tell me when you plan to leave.
9.108   Tell me what you saw.
9.109   Tell me how you will choose the winner.
9.110   Tell me why you love me.

The answers which are expected for these sentences are place, time, noun phrase, manner, and reason, respectively. Since each of these sentences except 9.109 contains a question word beginning with the letters *wh-* (*where, when, what, why*), they are often called **WH questions.** We include *how* in this group even though it does not begin with *wh*. We can also think of others which belong here: *who, whom, whose,* and *which.*

The underlying structures for these sentences differ from those for yes/no questions. Taking "Tell me what you saw" as an example, we have an underlying structure like this:

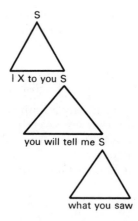

What you saw, of course, is not in its ultimate underlying form. Since a WH question does not present a choice, there is only one sentence given at the lowest level. We can contrast the WH question "Tell me what you saw" with the yes/no "Tell me whether you saw the giraffe." Both are requests for information, but of a different kind.

If we compare *what you saw* with *you saw the giraffe,* it becomes obvious that *what* and *the giraffe* correspond as objects in their respective sentences and that they appear in different positions on the surface. Rearranging *what you saw* to the word order of *you saw the giraffe,* we obtain

    you   saw   the giraffe
    you   saw   what

On the surface, *what* is moved to the beginning of the sentence. At the underlying level we do not want to give full spellings to predictable morphemes. If we know that the object of *saw* is an inanimate noun phrase, we know that it will appear on the surface as *what.* Similarly, human noun phrases appear as *who,* adverbials of place as *where,* those of time as *when,* and so on. We can abbreviate these as NP-WH, Place-WH, Time-WH, and the like. The indirect questions from 9.106–110 have underlying forms like the following:

	Underlying	*Surface*
9.106a	you are going Place-WH	where you are going
9.107a	you plan to leave Time-WH	when you plan to leave
9.108a	you saw NP-WH	what you saw
9.109a	you will choose the winner Manner-WH	how you will choose the winner
9.110a	you love me Reason-WH	why you love me

We call this the **WH transformation.** It moves the WH structure to the beginning and substitutes the appropriate question word for it.

Just as there are differences in form between embedded and nonembedded yes/no questions, so there are between WH questions:

9.111a   Tell me what you are reading.
9.112a   What are you reading?

The WH transformation is applied the same way in both sentences. Underlying structures are

9.111b   I X to you [you will tell me [you are reading NP-WH]]
9.112b   I X to you [you will Y me [you are reading NP-WH]]

Or without the material which does not appear on the surface:

9.111c   Tell me [you are reading NP-WH]
9.112c   [you are reading NP-WH]

For 9.111 the question transformation is not applicable since the question sentence remains embedded on the surface. The WH transformation shifts NP-WH to the beginning:

9.111d   Tell me [NP-WH you are reading]

and also substitutes *what* for NP-WH:

9.111a   Tell me [what you are reading].

For 9.112, however, the question transformation is applicable; this is not an embedded question. Hence, [you are reading NP-WH] becomes

9.112d   [are you reading NP-WH]

Then the WH transformation is applied:

9.112a   What are you reading?

By applying the question transformation first, we can state it and the WH transformation simply. With this ordering, each transformation moves material to the beginning of the sentence.

Let us review the kinds of questions we have been discussing. We have seen both yes/no and WH questions, either of which may be embedded or not. An underlying structure for a typical embedded yes/no question looks like this:

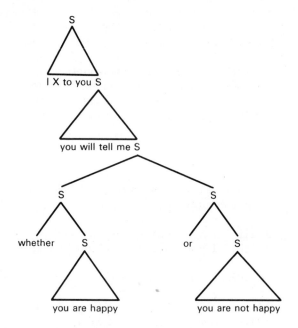

If the verb in the highest sentence had been fully specified, such as *command,* the surface structure could have been

9.113   I command you to tell me whether you are happy or not.

Whatever the higher sentences may contain, we delete all of the negative sentence or all except *not.* Since the highest verb is an abstract performative, we delete the entire sentence and perform the imperative transformation on the next one down, giving

9.114   Tell me whether you are happy or not.

Since we have spelled out *tell,* rather than giving an abstract verb, it remains on the surface. The interrogative sentence is embedded on the surface, and the question transformation is inapplicable.

For a nonembedded yes/no question we might have an underlying structure like this:

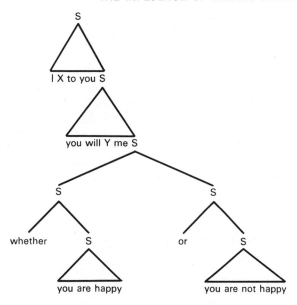

The top two sentences are deleted since both contain abstract verbs; the negative sentence and *whether/or* are also deleted. To retain the information that this is a question, we arrange the morphemes in a characteristic order. Tense and *be* are moved before the subject *you* to give

9.115   Are you happy?

By this analysis, we are giving the same basic structure for 9.115 as we did for 9.113 and 9.114. The sentences differ according to the nature of the verbs in the higher sentences. If higher verbs are present on the surface to express overtly all information about the nature of the sentence, there is no need for rearranging the word order of the lowest sentence. On the other hand, if the higher sentences are deleted, we need something to tell the listener or reader that the sentence is a question; the question transformation rearranges the ordering.

The same principles hold with WH questions. A typical structure at the underlying level is

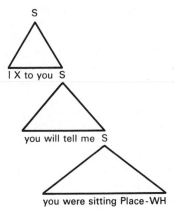

With the specific verb *tell* in the second sentence from the top, we retain all but the top sentence and perform the imperative transformation:

9.116a   Tell me [you were sitting Place-WH]

Since the question is embedded on the surface, the question transformation is inapplicable. The WH transformation moves *Place-WH* to the beginning of the sentence and replaces it with *where:*

9.116b   Tell me [where you were sitting].

If we had had an abstract verb instead of *tell* in the second highest sentence, we would have deleted both higher sentences, leaving only

9.117a   you were sitting Place-WH

The question transformation must be performed to preserve all information from the underlying structure:

9.117b   were you sitting Place-WH

Finally we perform the WH transformation:

9.117c   Where were you sitting?

We are thus able to account for the near synonymy of various surface structures and account for their differences in a systematic way.

The Study of Syntax

Now that we have examined a number of illustrative syntactic structures, let us try to draw together the conclusions we have reached in each chapter. We have defined our purpose in studying language, whether it be syntax or some other aspect, as an attempt to understand the native speaker's linguistic knowledge. This is not an unusual goal, even though we may later wish to apply this understanding to some specific use such as deciding what is good English, comparing literary styles of different authors, preparing teaching materials, or devising codes. All too often in the past, historians, sociologists, psychologists, and other scholars have shown that if they concentrate on too limited an area of a study, their conclusions become myopic and skewed. A larger exposure frequently provides insight that is missing from a more narrow investigation. A broader view also helps one to avoid many of the built-in biases fostered by a highly restricted approach to a subject. This is especially true of language study.

Syntactic information can be expressed in various ways, of which word order, particles (prepositions and postpositions), and inflections are the most common. To a degree, English makes use of all three: inflections for such concepts as tense and number, prepositions and word order for semantic roles of agent, patient, instrument, and the like. Most languages, like English, make use of all three devices, but with different orders of priority. In Classical Latin, for example, inflection was of primary importance, prepositions and word order secondary. One of the most noticeable differences between Classical Latin and the varieties of the language spoken during the last centuries of the Empire (Vulgar Latin) is that the latter began using word order and prepositions with more frequency, rather than inflections, to indicate syntactic relationships. Today the Romance languages, which evolved from Latin, are like English in their rigid systems of word order. There is probably no language which has completely free word order. In spite of suggestions to the contrary in some books, all languages apparently make some systematic use of this device, although it may be secondary in importance. On the other hand, all languages do not have particles and inflections. However, the usual case is for a language to use these as well as word order.

In an earlier chapter we noticed that unorthodox orderings of words can make a sentence ungrammatical:

9.118a *Jumped the over cow moon the.

This is not a possible sentence of English. Although anyone fluent in the language understands the meanings of all the words, together they form no recognizable structure. If a person tries to make out of it a meaning greater than the meanings of the words as isolated entities, he works at unscrambling the order and perhaps comes out with something like

9.118b The cow jumped over the moon.

For certain structures there are alternate orderings:

9.119a Yesterday I got a letter from him.
    b   I got a letter from him yesterday.
    c   *I got a letter from yesterday him.

These alternate orderings are strictly limited, as we can see from the *c* version. It is only in well-defined structures that we can rearrange the words and preserve the original meaning and the grammaticalness of the sentence.

Word order and prepositions indicate the semantic roles of the various noun phrases in a sentence. Agent, for example, appears before the verb in subject position or else after the preposition *by* when the verbal unit contains *be* and a past participle:

9.120a Janice scratched the floor.
    b   The floor was scratched by Janice.

Instrument is signaled by the preposition *with* or else by word order, since it is subjectivalized if there is no agent:

9.121a He opened the door with *this key*.
    b   *This key* opened the door.

Goal can likewise be designated by a preposition or word order:

9.122a I gave the keys to *Patsy*.
    b   I gave *Patsy* the keys.

As we saw in Chapter 8, there are characteristic positions and prepositions for each of the semantic roles.

Within a noun phrase, determiners precede the noun:

9.123a   *The boy* caught *a fish.*
   b   **Boy the* caught *fish a.*

If there are adjectives, they come between the determiner and the noun:

9.124a   *A tall woman* was dancing with *a short man.*
   b   **Tall a woman* was dancing with *a man short.*

Each language has its own rules, of course. Adjectives appear prenominally in English only if they are not part of a phrase; otherwise, they follow the noun:

9.125   The man, *purple with rage,* yelled at me.

This postnominal position is characteristic for all phrasal and clausal noun modifiers:

9.126   The suit *in the window* has been sold.
9.127   I like the dress *that you are wearing today.*

We could write a very lengthy discussion on the conventions of word order, but in so doing we would merely be repeating much of what we have discussed already.

If we are to write a grammar of a language like English, we will need to give a precise account of the ordering of morphemes, words, and other units. Word order is one of the basic devices which permit one person to understand what another is trying to say. If our purpose in writing a grammar is to describe the fluent speaker's knowledge, then we must certainly devote considerable attention to word order.

But that is not enough. Part of a person's understanding of sentences involves the organization of words, not just their sequential ordering. The following ambiguous sentences have two or more possible structural patterns, yet for each meaning the linear ordering is the same:

9.128   We rolled up the rug.
9.129   He kissed the old woman in the car.

To understand a sentence, a person must recognize the entire syntactic structure as well as the linear ordering of the words. For example,

9.130   The bold man who was ostentatiously reading aloud from the book declared to be obscene attracted no attention from the bored people walking past him.

We will not insult the reader by pointing out the various structures contained in this sentence, many of them embedded within others. After working through the chapters of this book to the present point, he is able to do that for himself. Anyone who understands 9.130 recognizes the overall structure of the sentence, whether he is able to comment on it in technical terms or not.

So a grammar of English which represents the knowledge of a fluent speaker of the language must describe the word order and the clusterings and hierarchies of structures. A tree of a surface structure performs both of these tasks.

Even with a means of describing linear arrangements and higher structures in a language, we have not given a complete picture of the fluent speaker's knowledge of his language. Often there is information that is understood but not directly expressed:

9.131   Show me the way to go home.
9.132   Fred wanted to help.
9.133   He couldn't hear you, but I could.

A grammar which explains nothing more than word order and structural hierarchies cannot show why all speakers of English understand *you* as the subject of *show* in 9.131, *Fred* as the subject of *help* in 9.132, and *hear you* as the verb phrase in the second part of 9.133.

A grammar which contains underlying structures, however, can accommodate this kind of information. It can furthermore show structural differences which are obscured on the surface:

9.134   We wanted the janitor to open the door.
9.135   We told the janitor to open the door.
9.136   Abner is slow to yield.
9.137   Abner is hard to find.

As we saw in Chapter 7, 9.134 and 9.135 appear to have the same structure, as do 9.136 and 9.137; yet it takes only a few minutes to discover that they do not. A grammar which contains both underlying and surface structures can easily show these differences.

Other kinds of information about syntax can likewise be explained by means of underlying structures. We find synonymous sentences:

9.138a   The girl waiting at the door read the letter to the woman who was sitting beside her.
b   The girl who was waiting at the door read the woman sitting beside her the letter.

Or ambiguity:

9.139   The horse is too hot to eat.

The following sentences are about as different on the surface as they could be and yet contain the same words and essentially the same meaning:

9.140a   Martha opened the box.
b   The box was opened by Martha.

Yet we understand *Martha* as agent and *the box* as patient in both sentences.

The grammar that we are developing aims at accommodating the information shared by fluent speakers of the language. It contains both underlying and surface structures and has transformations to relate the two. Since the number of possible sentences in any language is unlimited, it does not merely classify sentences that have been produced. It aims at the more general and comprehensive task of describing the processes by which sentences are formed. What we are trying to do is the same thing a mathematician analyzing division would do. He would not list all the possible numbers that can be divided and give the results in a table. Even if he restricted himself to numbers of one and two digits, his table would be prohibitively long. Since any number can be made larger by adding a digit, it would never be possible to give a complete listing of all the numbers that may exist. More seriously, a table of this kind would imply that division is unsystematic and unpredictable, each pair of numbers functioning in its own way. On the other hand, if he attempts to describe the *principles* of division, he can do this in a fairly short space and give precise, complete directions. Another person can follow these principles in dividing any numbers he encounters, whether he has ever seen them before or not. In the same way, a linguist who succeeds in describing the principles by which sentences are constructed can enable another person to follow these principles and construct, understand, and comment on sentences, many of which are new to him. Since language is considerably more complex than division, no one has given a complete description of its principles. Yet we do have a reasonably clear understanding of how part of the system functions.

Exercises

A. Which of the following sentences are used as performative utterances?
1. I hereby warn you to fulfill the contract.
2. Ben vows to love Connie forever.
3. I cautioned you to drive carefully.
4. I empower you to take my place.
5. I counsel them to find an attorney.

B. Examine these sentences:
1. Drivers like Helen are usually careful.
2. Drivers like her are usually careful.
3. *Drivers like herself are usually careful.
4. Helen told me that drivers like herself are usually careful.
5. Bill thinks that tennis players like himself should be given special favors.
6. *I think that tennis players like himself should be given special favors.
7. *Tennis players like himself should be given special favors.

What restrictions do you find on reflexive pronouns after *like* in structures such as these? In what way are the following sentences exceptional?
8. Drivers like myself are usually careful.
9. Tennis players like myself should be given special favors.

C. What restrictions exist for *own*?
1. I washed my own hands.
2. Rae scratched her own back.
3. Tony and Nancy painted their own home.
4. *Ralph saw my own sister.
5. *I shampooed her own hair.

At the underlying level do these sentences share the same restrictions?

6. Drive your own car.
7. Clean your own room.
8. *Open my own can of soup.
9. *Do his own work.
10. Albert wants to write his own report.
11. *Albert wants to write their own report.
12. Fran told me to iron my own shirt.
13. *Fran told me to iron her own shirt.
14. We objected to having to mend our own clothes.
15. *We objected to having to mend his own clothes.

D. Draw trees for the underlying structures of the following:

1. Grab the rope.
2. Were you restless?
3. What are they cooking?
4. Tell me who will meet us.
5. I order you to tell me whether you found the message.

E. Assume someone has said to you that the study of syntax should be confined to surface structures. What arguments would you give to show that only a grammar which contains underlying as well as surface structures can hope to account for the knowledge a fluent speaker possesses?

Suggested Reading

CHOMSKY, NOAM, *Language and Mind,* enlarged edition. New York: Harcourt Brace Jovanovich, Inc., 1972.

PETERS, STANLEY, ed., *Goals of Linguistic Theory.* Englewood Cliffs, N. J.: Prentice-Hall, Inc., 1972.

ROSS, JOHN R., "On Declarative Sentences," in *Readings in English Transformational Grammar,* ed. R. A. Jacobs and P. S. Rosenbaum. Waltham, Mass.: Ginn and Company, 1970.

STEINBERG, DANNY D., and LEON A. JAKOBOVITS, eds., *Semantics.* Cambridge: Cambridge University Press, 1971.

THORNE, J. P., "English Imperative Sentences," *Journal of Linguistics* 2 (1966): 69–78.

TRAUGOTT, ELIZABETH CLOSS, *A History of English Syntax.* New York: Holt, Rinehart & Winston, Inc., 1972.

part **3**

Phonology

chapter 10

The Sounds of Speech

It has become commonplace in recent linguistic literature to say that language is a device which links meaning with sound. Although it is possible to transfer a great deal of information from one nervous system to another by means of nonverbal communication, the more sophisticated type of communication known as language is indispensable for most of the activities humans engage in.

We can perhaps gain a better idea of how powerful language is if we compare it with a few simpler devices which also could link meaning with sound. It would be possible to signal information by means of a tone at different pitches. With this device, we could transmit one message with the tone at a high pitch, another at medium pitch, and a third at low pitch. Or we could repeat sounds, with one beep giving one message, two beeps another, and so on. The simplest systems all have one signal for each message.

The kind of system in which messages and signals are in a one-to-one relationship is inadequate if a great many messages are to be sent or if there is a need for creating new ones. Especially for human communication, a more complex system is needed. Languages have a limited number of sounds which their speakers recognize as distinct; but instead of linking them directly with meanings, the speakers of these languages combine the sounds into morphemes, which in turn are combined into syntactic structures. With this kind of system there is no limit to the number of messages that may be sent.

Most literate people feel that when they speak, they are using discrete sounds which roughly correspond to the individual letters on the printed page. Machines which analyze the speech signal show that the actual physical properties of speech are somewhat different, that a person speaking is producing a continuous flow of sound, not a sequence of individual, discrete sounds. Sounds merge with one another so that the onset of one sound is affected by the preceding one and the end by the one that follows. Similarly, there are pauses which are predictable by syntactic boundaries, but otherwise words are blended together, not uttered separately. A person listening to a language which he does not speak is unable to find the divisions between words. Experienced phoneticians have found that they make many mistakes in transcribing utterances from a totally unfamiliar language into phonetic notation.

Yet after a person begins to learn something about a language, his proficiency in recognizing individual words increases tremendously, as does that of the phonetician after he has begun learning the basic principles of the morphology and syntax of the language with which he is working. At one time linguists thought they were making an objective record of the physical speech signal when they wrote down an utterance in phonetic notation. We now know that they were doing no such thing, but were depending in part upon their knowledge of other features in the language.

Much of what a person "hears" in an utterance is the result of his ability to analyze syntactic and morphological patterns of the language. Just because much of this is not actually present in the physical acoustical signal does not make it any less real. The vowel in *men* may be acoustically very different from that in *pet,* but the speaker of English recognizes them as being the same because they contrast with those of *man* and *pat* as well as *mean* and *peat.* Sounds are not distinct entities. They merge with one another, yet a person can change his pronunciation from *tam* to *tan* or *pit* to *bit* as easily as he makes alterations in writing. If people did not think of the speech signal as composed of separate segments, spoonerisms such as "It is kistomary to cuss the bride" would not occur. It is the way people accept or recognize sounds that is our main concern as students of linguistics, not the actual acoustical signal itself.

Speech Sounds and Voicing

All sounds that a person produces with his mouth are not necessarily speech sounds. Hiccuping, giggling, sneezing, snoring, coughing, and clearing the throat usually have no communicative function, although the last two may be used for nonverbal communication. There are additional sounds which we make to signal various ideas but which are not combined with others to form words. The clicking of the tongue tip against the upper gum ridge, often spelled *tut tut,* is a sound which in English is used exclusively for nonverbal purposes. We make other sounds to spur on horses and to express such emotions as disgust, incredulity, surprise, pleasure, relief, and the like. We make characteristic non-speech sounds to indicate that we smell something good or foul. Although we may have difficulty repeating even a short utterance from a language we do not know, we easily recognize many sounds such as hiccuping and coughing as not possible speech sounds for any language. If our main concern were nonverbal communication, we would be spending a great deal of time on sounds such as these; since we are studying language, we will concentrate exclusively on speech sounds, those which cause a speaker of English to recognize *lamb* as a different word from *ram* or *bid* as different from *did*.

At one time it was popular to say that there are really no "organs of speech" any more than there are organs of throwing or skating or typing, that speech is a secondary function which has been assigned to organs primarily intended for breathing and chewing. The belief that language is an entirely man-made invention is no longer acceptable by everyone, as we saw in Chapter 3. In many ways it seems that man was intended to speak, whereas playing football, washing dishes, and knitting are activities which he developed on his own. Whatever the case may be, there is no other part of the human body as capable of making a large variety of controlled sounds as the vocal apparatus.

Speech sounds are made by altering the flow of air as we breathe. It would be conceivable for the air flow to be modified as we are inhaling or exhaling, or for us to modify it in both directions. Except for a few clicks which are found in some languages in the southern half of Africa, all speech sounds are made while exhaling. Occasionally, we may gasp out a "Stop!" or "No!" on ingoing air, but these are clearly exceptional.

When we are breathing normally and not speaking, our time for inhaling is about the same as that for exhaling. When speaking, we change this so that exhaling takes at least twice the time as inhaling does. Under normal circumstances we do not notice a speaker's breathing patterns; but sometimes we do, as when he expresses fear, excitement, or fatigue by breathing more rapidly than normal. Since this kind of information accompanies language but is not actually a part of it, it is not included in linguistic investigation.

We are familiar with the natural sounds made by wind as it whistles through trees or a canyon. It may set venetian blinds in motion and cause a noise if a window is open and the blinds are turned so that the slats are close together. Or a car window that is not closed securely allows some wind to enter and make a noise. A person can blow into various musical instruments and produce sound. In each of these cases the air flow is directed through a constricted opening, causing vibration of the bodies which the air touches. This vibration in turn sets sound waves in motion, and the ear may receive them.

Humans are capable of producing sounds in this manner within the **larynx,** which contains elastic bands of cartilage and muscle known as the **vocal cords.** In some men the larynx is very prominent and is called the "Adam's apple." Whether it is physically obvious or not, the larynx is an essential part of the speech-making process. The vocal cords are also used for other purposes, such as trapping air in the chest cavity, thereby allowing a person to exert pressure while lifting a heavy load or straining for some other reason. When a person is breathing normally, the vocal cords are wide open in a V shape. When they are brought firmly together, the air passage is shut off. For many speech sounds they are brought closely together without actually stopping the flow of air, but they vibrate as air is forced past them. In humming we allow the vocal cords to vibrate as we alter pitch.

There are several ways we can become conscious of vocal-cord vibration, or **voicing.** We can produce a protracted [s], the first sound in *sip,* and then a protracted [z], the first sound in *zip.* (We will enclose sounds in square brackets to distinguish them from ordinary letters of the alphabet, which are italicized.) By holding our hand over the larynx, we can feel a vibration for [z] but not for [s]. Or we can hold our hands over our ears and hear the difference. Actually, it is not necessary for us to do anything more than listen and concentrate on the two sounds to hear the difference in voicing. We say that [z] is a **voiced sound** and that [s] is **voiceless,** the difference being whether or not there is vocal-cord vibration.

Fricatives

The vocal cords are the first point at which outgoing air can be altered to produce speech sounds, but if there is no further modification no recognizable sounds are produced. With the mouth closed, the difference between humming and quiet breathing is effected by the vocal cords, which vibrate for the former but not for the latter. Similarly, if we leave the mouth open without causing our vocal cords to vibrate or forming any other obstruction, we are merely breathing through the mouth. With mouth open, vocal cords vibrating, and no further modification, we sound like an idiot, or at best like a patient saying "ah" for the doctor.

With [s] and [z] we see an obstruction made by the front part of the tongue at the **alveolum,** or upper gum ridge. The air is not completely blocked, but is forced through the opening between the tongue and alveolum and onto the teeth.

An obstruction such as that of the tongue at the alveolum alters the shape of the mouth, thereby affecting the nature of the sound. A person does not have to know much about physics to know that the size and shape of any air-filled object contributes to the sound that results when it is struck. There are only a limited number of ways in which the size and shape of the oral cavity can be changed. With a cavity surrounded by a highly flexible substance such as modeling clay, there are many ways to alter the shape of the cavity, but the human mouth is not so malleable. Whereas the tongue is marvelously flexible, the hard palate in the roof of the mouth is immovable. In fact, this is true of the entire upper surface from lip all the way back, except for one movement of the soft palate which we will mention presently. With modeling clay we could bring any two sides together— horizontally, vertically, or diagonally—to form an obstruction, but the mouth does not enjoy these possibilities. Because of the construction of the mouth, obstructions for speech sounds are limited to those in which the lower lip or tongue comes in contact with an upper surface.

The lower lip may touch the upper lip or the upper teeth. Although it may come in contact with the alveolum, such a movement is clumsy and relatively slow, making it unsatisfactory for the production of speech sounds. If the lower lip lightly touches the upper teeth so that the air is not blocked but is forced through a constricted space, the sounds [f] and [v] result. As might be expected, [f] is the voiceless sound at the beginning of *fan,* [v] the voiced sound at the beginning of *van.*

We will gradually be introducing a system of notation known as the **phonetic alphabet,** which is used to represent sounds. The morpheme *phone,* meaning "sound," is already familiar to the reader in such words as *telephone* and *phonograph.* Symbols in this alphabet, as we said earlier, are enclosed in square brackets, in contrast to letters of the written alphabet, which are italicized. Hence, [f] represents a sound, *f* one of the ways this sound is written on paper. A sound may be spelled in various ways, such as *f, ph, gh,* and *ff* in *full, phone, enough,* and *puff.* Since the sound is the same in all of these words, it is represented consistently as [f]. This phonetic alphabet will enable us to speak unambiguously about sounds, something we could not do if we had to rely upon traditional spelling. Also, it will allow us to compare sounds in various languages. The alphabet we are using is based on the **International Phonetic Alphabet (IPA),** which had its origins in the last half of the nineteenth century and received its final form in the early part of the twentieth. During the last two decades there have been a few departures from the symbols used in the **IPA.** Unfortunately, all linguists have not departed in the same directions, and for some sounds—in particular the vowels—there are two or three widely used systems of notation. We will be using the ones most common in recent American publications.

Now let us return to obstructions that we may form with the lower lip against an upper surface. In addition to [f] and [v], the lower lip may come in contact with the upper lip, as is the position for rest when we are not speaking. The speaker of English may find this a strange position for constricting air while still allowing it to pass through. He is used to closing the lips completely or opening them, not merely obstructing air which continues through them. Yet he may do just this to blow out a match or to express relief with a sound which is often written *phew.* There are languages which have speech sounds produced in this manner. The symbols for them are [ɸ] when voiceless and [β] when voiced—the Greek letters *phi* and *beta,* respectively. As might be expected, [ɸ] sounds very much like [f] and [β] like [v]. The voiced [β] is the usual pronunciation of *b* and *v* between vowels in many dialects of Spanish, as in *lobo, abuelo, caballo, nuevo,* and *noventa.* Some speakers of Spanish use this sound for *b* and *v* in all positions, including initially.

We will refer to the four sounds [f, v, ɸ, β] as **labials,** i.e., "lip" sounds. It is possible to classify those in which the two lips touch as **bilabial** (*bi-* as in *bicycle,* meaning "two") and those in which the lower lip touches the upper teeth as **labiodentals** (*labio-,* "lip," + *dental,* "teeth," as in *dentist, dentures,* etc.). However, there seem to be no languages in which two words differ only in that one has a bilabial sound and the other a labiodental. This observation may be proved faulty as we investigate more languages of the world, particularly those not spoken natively in the Western world. (In fact, Ewe, a language of Africa, has been said to have a contrast between [ɸ] and [f].)

There are a number of positions at which the lower lip can come in contact with the upper lip and teeth: slightly in front of the upper lip, squarely in the center, or slightly behind it. It takes only a little imagination to think of even finer differentiations for points of contact, and similar ones can be extended to labiodental positions. In speech, such minute distinctions are not feasible. A person speaking at a normal rate would have trouble hitting exactly on the right spot and would make many mistakes. Even when he was precise, it is doubtful that anyone could train his ear to distinguish a *pre-bilabial* from a *medio-bilabial* or a *post-bilabial*. Although there are many potentially different labial sounds, only two are normally distinguished: a voiced and a voiceless. A person is allowed a great deal of freedom in his actual execution of these sounds; so long as he distinguishes voicing according to the conventions of his language, the rest is fairly free. In fact, a speaker of English may use the voiceless bilabial [ɸ] in rapid speech in such words as *cupful* and *camphor,* where a bilabial consonant precedes. The articulation of [v] in *obvious* is normally farther forward than is that for [v] in *vent,* yet we hear them as the same.

If there are several positions at which the lower lip may come in contact with the upper lip and teeth, there are an indefinite number at which the tongue may touch the upper surface of the mouth. There are no speech sounds formed by the tongue touching the upper lip, but starting with the teeth and alveolum, some part of the tongue can come in contact with the entire upper surface. Actually only three of these positions are significant in distinguishing one sound from another.

The first of these is at the upper teeth. If the tongue is allowed to rest lightly under the upper teeth and (for some speakers) to protrude slightly past them, not blocking the flow of air but permitting it to flow through the obstruction, the sounds spelled *th* in English result: *those, them, thimble, thick,* and the like. Since literate people are strongly influenced by their spelling conventions, the person who has not studied phonology usually assumes that the spelling *th* corresponds to only one sound. Yet, he hears a clear difference between *mouth* (noun) and *mouth* (verb). The same difference is heard in *loath* and *loathe* as well as *thigh* and *thy.* The first vowel may or may not be the same in *either* and *ether,* depending on the speaker, but everyone uses different *th* sounds in these words. The difference is one of voicing. The sound heard in *thigh, ether, mouth* (noun), and *loath* is voiceless, represented by a Greek *theta*: [θ]. The voiced consonant heard in *thy, either, mouth* (verb), and *loathe* is represented by a symbol which was originally a *d* with a line crossed through it; the symbol is tilted slightly to the left: [ð].

Because of spelling conventions, some people have trouble at first deciding when they are using [θ] and [ð], although they have no trouble when speaking. Here are a few words with the voiceless [θ]: *thumb, thimble, thick, myth, ethics, catharsis, lethal, path.* The following have voiced [ð]: *they, then, seethe, soothe, dither, leather, father.* A person can listen for the voice hum or hold his hand over his throat while prolonging [θ] or [ð] in these words. Another device is to interchange the sounds, pronouncing *thumb, thimble, think* with [ð] and *they, them* with [θ]. Still another approach is to substitute [d], the initial sound of *date,* for [ð] and [t], the initial sound of *top,* for [θ]. In this way we will be saying what fiction writers spell as *dem guys, dose punks, tanks a lot, a tousand bucks.*

With the tongue tip forming an obstruction at the alveolum, we can produce [s] and [z], as we saw earlier in the discussion. Whereas [s] is found in most of the languages of the world, [θ] and [ð] are found only in certain ones. English is one of the few European languages to have [θ] and [ð]. Foreigners learning English, therefore, tend to substitute a sound that is familiar to them from their own language for the unfamiliar [θ] and [ð]. A common substitution is [s] for [θ] (*sank* for *thank, sink* for *think,* etc.) and probably [z] for [ð], but this is less frequent. Also, [θ] and [ð] are among the last sounds children acquire. Until they have attained them, they may substitute the labials [f] and [v], maintaining the voicing contrasts. That is, [v] is always substituted for [ð] and [f] for [θ], never the other way around.

Linguists working with a large number of languages and considering more features than those we have examined at this point have decided not to consider dentals and alveolars as radically different. We will follow this decision and classify both as **dentals,** in the same way as we called both bilabials and labiodentals merely labials. We have seen two main points of obstruction, each of which can be subdivided when necessary:

Labials		Dentals	
(Bilabials)	(Labiodentals)	(Dentals)	(Alveolars)
[φ, β]	[f, v]	[θ, ð]	[s, z]

For the sake of consistency we are placing the voiceless member of each pair first, but this ordering has no significance beyond the immediate presentation.

The dental sounds are formed by raising the **blade** of the tongue: the front part including the tip. When a person is not speaking, his tongue lies at rest on the floor of the mouth, the blade beneath the alveolum. If an obstruction is made with the blade slightly farther back on the alveolum than for [s, z] and with the center of the tongue, or **body,** raised to the front part of the hard palate, while allowing the air to flow through the constricted opening, the first sound in *ship* is produced. Although English usually spells this sound with two letters, it should be noticed that only one sound is involved. If a person positions his tongue for [s] and then for the sound in *ship,* he will see that they are different and that the latter is made farther back than [s]. To represent this sound, we use the letter *s* with a wedge on top: [š]. It is found initially in such words as *shout, she, shoe,* and *sugar;* medially in *worship, pressure,* and *action;* finally in *wish* and *blush.* With a little observation, one will notice that [š] is voiceless.

The voiced counterpart of [š] is written [ž], the sound found medially in such words as *pleasure, azure,* and *leisure.* The IPA symbols for [š] and [ž] are [ʃ] and [ʒ], respectively, but we will be using the first two symbols since they are the ones most frequently found in current linguistics publications. Many speakers of English have [ž] finally in several words which have been borrowed from French: *mirage, garage, camouflage, rouge, beige, loge,* and the like. French has this sound initially in such words as *jus, jour, Jacques,* and *jeune.* Russian also has it initially in such words as *zhito, zheltyj,* and *zharko,* but in English it never occurs at the beginning of a word. Since the position of the obstruction for [š] and [ž] is the back part of the alveolum and the front part of the palate, they are often called **alveolo-palatals** or **palato-alveolars**. Alveolo-palatals function with other sounds articulated at the palate, not with alveolars and dentals; we, therefore, place them in a third main grouping after labials and dentals, the **palatals.**

Most dialects of Modern English have no consonant sounds in the same series as [f, v, θ, ð, s, z, š, ž] which are produced with an obstruction farther back, but since some languages do it will give us a better perspective on the English system if we look briefly at the other possibilities. Slightly farther back than the alveolo-palatals but still articulated at the hard palate are the palatals [ç] and [ʝ], the first voiceless and the second voiced. The voiceless [ç] is heard in such German words as *ich* and *Knecht*. It occurred in earlier periods of English, but does not now. The voiced [ʝ] is very rare in the languages of the world, although it is easily formed by raising the body of the tongue to the hard palate but not forming a complete closure.

Finally, there are the **velars.** The voiceless [x] occurs in some dialects of English spoken in Scotland in *loch* and a few other words. It occurs commonly in German in such words as *machen, doch,* and *durch.* The voiced [γ] is found in Spanish, spelled *g* between vowels as *preguntar, agua,* and *cigarro.*

A summary of the sounds we have examined so far can be found in Table 10.1. No language has all of these sounds, yet all occur in some lan-

Table 10.1. FRICATIVES

Labials	Dentals	Palatals	Velars
[ɸ] [f]	[θ] [s]	[š] [ç]	[x]
[β] [v]	[ð] [z]	[ž] [ʝ]	[γ]

guages of the world. Of these, certain ones such as [s] are found in practically all languages; others, such as [ð], are much more rare.

The sounds in Table 10.1 are often call **fricatives** because of the large amount of friction which is found in their production. This noisiness is called **stridency.** Some of the consonants are more strident than others, as we notice when listening to people whisper. In particular, [s] and [š] stand out as especially noisy. The voiceless fricatives are more strident than their voiced counterparts. Stridency is a feature which exists in degrees, unlike voicing, which is either present or not. Using just the voiceless fricatives in English, we can rank them according to their degree of stridency: [š, s, f, θ]. The last is so much quieter than the others, that some recent works on phonology have gone so far as to call it nonstrident. Nevertheless, there is a slight degree of stridency present even with [θ]. There are also differences among languages in degree of stridency. Even within the speech of a given individual, there may be varying degrees. We can see an example of this in the prolonged [š] used to tell someone to be quiet. If the person who makes the sound is especially irate, he will say it much louder than normally, with an accompanying increase in stridency.

Stops

The sounds we have examined so far obstruct the flow of air without actually stopping it. There are other sounds which are formed by completely blocking the air and then releasing it. If we hold the lips firmly together and let air pressure build up behind them, when we release the air we produce the first sound in *pick,* written [p]. If we add voicing, we produce the consonant sounds in *Bob,* written [b]. Sounds produced by blocking the flow of air are called **stops, explosives,** or **plosives.** We will be using the first of these terms.

Because of the abruptness of articulation for a stop, it is not possible to prolong it as we did [s] and [z] to test for voicing. When we say the letters of the alphabet *p* and *b,* we are adding a vowel after the consonant. Since this vowel is voiced, we naturally hear voicing for both. It takes concentration to notice that the onset of voicing starts later for *p* than it does for *b.*

The dental stops are [t] and [d], the sounds found initially in *to* and *do,* respectively; [t] is voiceless, [d] voiced. In many languages these sounds are pure dentals, produced with the tongue tip touching the upper teeth; but for English they are alveolars, with the tongue tip at the gum ridge.

Since palatal stops are usually considered variants of velars rather than distinctive sounds in themselves, we have no special symbols for them. We therefore pass on to the velars with the voiceless [k] and the voiced [g], as in *come* and *gum,* respectively. When we need to designate the palatal stops, we usually do so with a diacritic: [k̂] and [ĝ]. A fairly good idea of the distinction between [k̂] and [k] can be obtained by saying *kit* and *caught.* The obstruction is farther forward for *kit* than it is for *caught.* The speaker of English can feel this with his tongue, but he will probably not hear it. It should be repeated that phonetic representation is more consistent than regular spelling, as we can see from [k], which may be spelled variously as in *come, keep, back,* and *sacque.*

Arabic, Hebrew, and several other languages have postvelar stops as well as the ones found in English. These are produced with an obstruction farther back than for [k] and [g]. The postvelar stops are written [q] (voiceless) and [G] (voiced).

In addition, a great many languages have a sound known as the **glottal stop,** represented [ʔ]. It may or may not function as a distinctive sound. For example, it exists in English but does not differentiate one morpheme from another. It often occurs before a vowel at the beginning of a word: *apple, upon, easy,* and the like. The impression that one receives when the glottal stop is present in these words is a slight catch in the throat. It is heard also in the negative *uh uh* and the positive *uh huh.* Some New Yorkers and speakers of several British dialects use it instead of [t] between vowels: *glottal, bottle, battle, little,* and so forth. In some languages the glottal stop functions as a distinctive consonant and is used to distinguish one morpheme from another.

The most common stops are summarized in Table 10.2.

Table 10.2.   STOPS

Labials	Dentals	Palatals	Velars	Glottal
[p]	[t]	[k̬]	[k] [q]	[ʔ]
[b]	[d]	[g̬]	[g] [G]	

Affricates

So far we have examined two classes of consonants: the stops, for which there is complete closure, and the fricatives, for which an obstruction is made but the air is not actually blocked. It is possible to combine the two, beginning as a stop and releasing as a fricative, and produce a sound known as an **affricate**.

In English there are only two affricates: [t͡s] and [d͡z], found initially in *chump* and *jump,* respectively. The voiceless [t͡s] is heard both at the beginning and at the ending of *church,* [d͡z] in both places in *judge.* Since these affricates function in English as single sounds, not as two in succession, they are usually written as single symbols: the voiceless [t͡s] as [č] and the voiced [d͡z] as [j]. In the discussion which immediately follows, we will use the double-symbol representation to show their position with other affricates, but after that we will use [č] and [j].

Affricates are not composed of just any combination of stop and fricative, but only of those which agree in voicing and point of obstruction. Hence, there is no [t͡z] because [t] in voiceless and [z] voiced. Nor is there a [p͡x], although both [p] and [x] are voiceless; they are too far apart in point of obstruction. Since the symbols give a reasonably clear indication of the pronunciation of each affricate, we will merely list them in Table 10.3 and not give a detailed description.

Table 10.3.   AFFRICATES

Labials	Dentals	Palatals	Velars
[p͡f]	[t͡s]	[t͡š]	[k͡x]
[b͡v]	[d͡z]	[d͡ž]	[g͡γ]

One problem in the description of affricates is determining whether two successive sounds such as [t] and [s] constitute separate segments or only one. This was a lively topic of discussion during the 1940s, but the solutions which were arrived at then are not altogether satisfactory today. We can say that the difference between an affricate and a sequence of two consonants is whether they function as one sound or two, but what does this mean? Machines which analyze the speech signal do not provide an answer. It is generally assumed that two sounds which make up an affricate must be in the same syllable and morpheme. Hence, [ts] in English is a sequence of two consonants, not an affricate. In such words as *eats, debts,* and *fatso,* the [t] and [s] belong to separate morphemes. In Italian, however, there is an affricate [t^s], spelled *z* in such words as *pizza, piazza, scherzo, mezzo,* and the like. German and Russian also have this affricate.

The voiceless affricates, with the exception of [k^x], are fairly common. The voiceless velar affricate, though rare, does occur in some dialects of German and in a few other languages. But of the voiced ones, only the dentals and palatals are found with any frequency among the languages of the world. The voiced labial and velar affricates are extremely rare, if they exist at all.

Liquids and Nasals

[r] and [l], the first consonant sounds in *red* and *led,* are often called **liquids.** [l] is also known as a **lateral** because in its production the tongue tip makes a complete closure at the alveolum or teeth and air is released on both sides. Many languages have only one liquid, either [l] or [r]; a few have neither.

The actual pronunciation of [r] varies widely among languages and even within a given language; there are several symbols given in the IPA to represent part of these. The two most common types in English are heard at the beginning of *red* and in the middle of *corn.* The [r] in *red* is a **retroflex** sound, made with the tongue tip raised and turned slightly backward. In *corn* it is not the tip, but the body of the tongue that is raised. (For some dialects this [r] is deleted.) In neither case does the tongue actually touch the palate, nor does it come as close as would be needed for a fricative. With the trilled [r] of Spanish, Italian, and Russian, the tongue tip does touch the alveolum intermittently. There is also a variety of [r] in which the **uvula,** the fleshy appendage at the back of the velum, is trilled. This [r] is common in many dialects of French and German. Still another variety is the "flap" found in *very* and a few other words by some speakers of British English. The flap is regularly found in Spanish in such words as *caro, pero,* as opposed to the trilled [r] in *carro, perro.* For an adult learning a foreign language, the [r] is frequently the most difficult sound to execute. Both [r] and [l] are voiced.

Another group of consonants are classified as **nasals.** For all of the sounds discussed so far, the flow of air is exhaled through the mouth, and the velum is raised to shut off the nasal cavity. When a person is breathing normally through the nose, the velum is lowered, and there is a direct passage from the nostrils to the lungs. There are a few speech sounds which are produced by lowering the velum and permitting the air to pass through the nasal cavity: [m] as in *me,* [n] as in *no,* and [ŋ] as at the end of *song.*

Because of the spelling, the last looks as though it should be [ng], but careful attention to the tongue position in forming [n] and then [g] shows that we do not say [ng] at the end of *song,* but rather a single nasal consonant. [m] is labial, [n] is alveolar (or, in many languages, dental), and [ŋ] is velar. There is also a palatal nasal, written [ñ], found in such Spanish words as *señor, año, baño,* and *español,* spelled with ñ. It is spelled *gn* in Italian in such words as *incognito, signorina, legna, cagna,* and the like. The palatal nasal does not exist in English. All nasals are voiced.

Features of Consonants

Speech sounds are said to *contrast* with one another. By this we mean that a given sound is heard to be different from the others in the system. We could describe these differences in several ways, such as in terms of their acoustic properties; but the means that is most amenable to direct observation without laboratory equipment is the one we have been using in the preceding discussion: the physiological actions of the speaker.

The symbols we have been using in our phonetic alphabet should not be thought of as basic units which cannot be further subdivided or analyzed, but rather as abbreviations for bundles of features. That is, [m] is an abbreviation for a sound that is nasal, voiced, nonstrident, and labial. Since we will often find it convenient to discuss all labials or nasals or some other group, we will summarize the features which we gave in discussing the production of each group of sounds in the preceding discussion. We will be drawing our examples exclusively from the consonants found in English, but the reader should have no difficulty in using the same materials for the other sounds as well.

As we have seen, consonants are either nasal or oral. We will refer to nasals as having the feature [+nasal]. All oral sounds are [−nasal]. We are thus using only one term but giving it plus and minus values. In English only three consonants are [+nasal], all others [−nasal].

A second feature describes the action of the vocal cords. A voiced sound has the feature [+voice]; one that is voiceless has [−voice]. Most consonants in English are voiced, the only voiceless ones being [p, t, k, f, θ, s, š, č]. The stops, fricatives, and affricates come in voiced and voiceless pairs, but the liquids and nasals do not.

The feature of stridency is found primarily with fricatives. Since [θ] and [ð] have such a low degree of stridency, we will classify them as [−strident]; all other fricatives in English—[f, v, s, z, š, ž]—are [+strident]. Since the affricates are released as fricatives, [č] and [j] are also [+strident]. The stops, liquids, and nasals are [−strident].

For the point of obstruction we could continue to use the terms *labial, dental, palatal,* and *velar;* we obviously need to know what they mean since they are found frequently in linguistic literature. The use of four features would have certain disadvantages in that we could not show that palatals are in many ways more like velars than they are like labials or dentals. Also, there are times when we want to group labials and velars together as opposed to dentals and palatals. To provide this kind of information in the feature system, we follow Chomsky and Halle (1968) in introducing the features anterior and coronal.

Anterior sounds, as the name implies, are those which are produced with an obstruction toward the front of the mouth. The dividing point for front versus back sounds is at the alveolum. Hence, labials and dentals (including alveolars) are [+anterior], and palatals and velars are [−anterior].

Coronal is the feature which is used to link labials and velars together as opposed to dentals and palatals. If there is an obstruction produced by raising the blade of the tongue, the sound is said to be [+coronal]. Otherwise, it is [−coronal]. Dentals are produced by forming an obstruction with the tongue tip at the teeth or at the alveolum; hence, [t, d, θ, ð, s, z, n, l] are all [+coronal]. Since the obstruction is at the alveolum or farther forward, they are also [+anterior]. Similarly, the palatals [š, ž, č, ǰ, r] are formed with the blade of the tongue raised and are, therefore, [+coronal]. Unlike the dentals, the obstruction is back of the alveolum, and they are [−anterior]. Since labials are formed with the lower lip rather than the tongue, they are necessarily [−coronal]. They are, however, [+anterior] since the obstruction is in the front part of the mouth. Velars are [−coronal] and [−anterior]. The obstruction is in the back of the mouth, and the blade of the tongue is not used to form them. The back of the tongue, not the blade, forms the obstruction in [k, g, ŋ]. The features anterior and coronal are illustrated in Table 10.4.

Table 10.4. THE FEATURES ANTERIOR AND CORONAL

Labials $\begin{bmatrix} +anterior \\ -coronal \end{bmatrix}$	Dentals $\begin{bmatrix} +anterior \\ +coronal \end{bmatrix}$	Palatals $\begin{bmatrix} -anterior \\ +coronal \end{bmatrix}$	Velars $\begin{bmatrix} -anterior \\ -coronal \end{bmatrix}$
[p, b]	[t, d]	[č, ǰ]	[k, g]
[f, v]	[θ, ð, s, z]	[š, ž]	
[m]	[n, l]	[r]	[ŋ]

We can list the features of a given sound as follows:

$$
[p] \begin{bmatrix} +\text{anterior} \\ -\text{coronal} \\ -\text{voice} \\ -\text{nasal} \\ -\text{strident} \end{bmatrix}
\quad
[d] \begin{bmatrix} +\text{anterior} \\ +\text{coronal} \\ +\text{voice} \\ -\text{nasal} \\ -\text{strident} \end{bmatrix}
\quad
[š] \begin{bmatrix} -\text{anterior} \\ +\text{coronal} \\ -\text{voice} \\ -\text{nasal} \\ +\text{strident} \end{bmatrix}
\quad
[ŋ] \begin{bmatrix} -\text{anterior} \\ -\text{coronal} \\ +\text{voice} \\ +\text{nasal} \\ -\text{strident} \end{bmatrix}
$$

The combination of features uniquely describes each sound. That is, no two sounds which might be used to distinguish one word from another in a given language have exactly the same combination of plus and minus values.

A few examples will be useful to illustrate this notion of uniqueness:

$$
[k] \qquad\qquad [g]
$$

$$
\begin{bmatrix} -\text{anterior} \\ -\text{coronal} \\ -\text{voice} \\ -\text{nasal} \\ -\text{strident} \end{bmatrix}
\qquad
\begin{bmatrix} -\text{anterior} \\ -\text{coronal} \\ +\text{voice} \\ -\text{nasal} \\ -\text{strident} \end{bmatrix}
$$

The consonants [k] and [g] are alike in many respects. For both there is an obstruction farther back than the alveolum ([−anterior]), and the blade of the tongue is not raised to form the obstruction ([−coronal]); this combination specifies the velar area. Neither sound is a nasal; the velum is raised so that the air flows through the oral cavity ([−nasal]). There is no friction accompanying either sound ([−strident]). They differ in that [k] is [−voice] and [g] is [+voice]. The list of features shows that the two consonants are very similar, but that they are not identical.

Let us now look at two sounds that have very little in common:

$$
[m] \qquad\qquad [s]
$$

$$
\begin{bmatrix} +\text{anterior} \\ -\text{coronal} \\ +\text{voice} \\ +\text{nasal} \\ -\text{strident} \end{bmatrix}
\qquad
\begin{bmatrix} +\text{anterior} \\ +\text{coronal} \\ -\text{voice} \\ -\text{nasal} \\ +\text{strident} \end{bmatrix}
$$

All that [m] and [s] agree in is that both are front sounds: [+anterior]. For [m] the obstruction is in the labial region ([+anterior, −coronal]), but [s] is dental ([+anterior, +coronal]). The difference between labials and dentals is indicated by the feature coronal, which is determined by whether the blade of the tongue is raised or not. All of the other features given above differ for [m] and [s].

In addition to giving a unique description of each sound, the features also provide a means of grouping sounds which share some quality such as nasality or stridency. Hence, we can give features like those in the left column below and show what the sounds in the right column share:

[+nasal]	[m, n, ŋ]
[+strident]	[f, v, s, z, š, ž, č, ǰ]
[+anterior, −coronal]	[p, b, f, v, m]

Before going on to the vowels, we need to list another feature to distinguish [f] from [p], [z] from [d], and the like. Normally, stridency will do this, but it is also useful to group all stops together as opposed to fricatives. The feature we use is **continuant.** If the air is allowed to flow through the oral cavity without stopping, the sounds are [+continuant]. Hence, all of the fricatives and liquids share this feature, and the stops are [−continuant]. Since there is stoppage of air in part of the production of affricates, they are also [−continuant]. The name of this feature is not altogether a happy one, since nasals are produced without interruption of the flow of air. Yet they are [−continuant] since the air does not flow through the *oral cavity* without interruption. Table 10.5 summarizes the features which we have given

Table 10.5. FEATURES OF ENGLISH CONSONANTS

	p	b	t	d	č	ǰ	k	g	f	v	θ	ð	s	z	š	ž	r	l	m	n	ŋ
Consonantal	+	+	+	+	+	+	+	+	+	+	+	+	+	+	+	+	+	+	+	+	+
Vocalic	−	−	−	−	−	−	−	−	−	−	−	−	−	−	−	−	+	+	−	−	−
Anterior	+	+	+	+	−	−	−	−	+	+	+	+	+	+	−	−	−	+	+	+	−
Coronal	−	−	+	+	+	+	−	−	−	−	+	+	+	+	+	+	+	+	−	+	−
Voice	−	+	−	+	−	+	−	+	−	+	−	+	−	+	−	+	+	+	+	+	+
Nasal	−	−	−	−	−	−	−	−	−	−	−	−	−	−	−	−	−	−	+	+	+
Strident	−	−	−	−	+	+	−	−	+	+	−	−	+	+	+	+	−	−	−	−	−
Continuant	−	−	−	−	−	−	−	−	+	+	+	+	+	+	+	+	+	+	−	−	−

so far and lists two more which will be introduced presently. These are the features which are the most important for discussing consonants. Table 10.6

Table 10.6. ENGLISH CONSONANTS

	$\begin{bmatrix} +anterior \\ -coronal \end{bmatrix}$	$\begin{bmatrix} +anterior \\ +coronal \end{bmatrix}$	$\begin{bmatrix} -anterior \\ +coronal \end{bmatrix}$	$\begin{bmatrix} -anterior \\ -coronal \end{bmatrix}$
$\begin{bmatrix} -continuant \\ -nasal \end{bmatrix}$ Stops, Affricates	p b	t d	č̠ ǰ̠	k g
$\begin{bmatrix} +continuant \\ -nasal \end{bmatrix}$ Fricatives	f̠ v̠	θ s̠ ð z̠	š̠ ž̠	
$\begin{bmatrix} +continuant \\ -nasal \end{bmatrix}$ Liquids		l	r	
$\begin{bmatrix} -continuant \\ +nasal \end{bmatrix}$ Nasals	m	n		ŋ

Strident consonants are underscored.

provides the same information in a less direct way, but it has advantages for the person who is receiving his first exposure to features.

Vowels

The vowels, as every child in the primary grades knows, are *a, e, i, o, u,* and sometimes *w* and *y.* It takes only a brief inspection to conclude that this statement applies to written representation, not to spoken language. Since our investigation of language involves much more than an analysis of the twenty-six letters of the alphabet, we need to study the vowels with more precision.

There are two ways for stating the members of a group such as vowels or consonants. One of these is simply to list them; the other is to state the principles by which they are distinguished. Whereas a listing was impossible with syntactic structures, which have no limits, it is not a prohibitive task for consonants, as we saw in Tables 10.5 and 10.6. Since there are fewer vowels than consonants, a similar listing would be possible for them. Listings like this, however, provide us with only the most superficial account of the material involved. If we are able to state briefly and precisely *how* consonants and vowels differ, we will be able to provide the same information as the listing does, but we will also be able to do more. We will be providing the information in a more concise manner, and we will be explaining *why* we classify a given sound as a consonant or a vowel. We will be saying that the grouping is not arbitrary, but rather that it follows a system.

No single feature that we have given so far is sufficient for defining consonants. If all consonants were voiceless and all vowels voiced, this would be a way to distinguish them; but we saw that many consonants are voiced. To say that a consonant is a sound that is or is not nasal or strident is worthless as a definition. Yet there is one aspect of production that we did take into account for all consonants: the point of obstruction. **A consonant is a sound produced with an obstruction in the oral cavity; a vowel is a sound produced without obstruction.** The consonantal obstruction may be complete closure as for the stops [p, b, t, d, k, g], or it may be a severe restriction, as with the fricatives [f, v, θ, ð, s, z, š, ž]. Affricates obviously have a major obstruction since they are like stops at the beginning and fricatives at the end. It takes only a little experimentation to notice that the production of liquids and nasals also involves a major obstruction. If we contrast these with the vowels, we see a basic difference. Since we have not yet introduced the phonetic symbols for the vowels, we can say the letters of the alphabet *a, e, i, o, u* and see that there is no obstruction in their production.

If there is no obstruction in the production of vowels, one may ask how we can have more than one vowel. The answer is that we can change the shape of the mouth, thereby affecting the quality of the sound initiated at the vocal cords. As we saw earlier, the human mouth is not designed to be twisted in just any way. There are only two alterations which function for speech: movements of the jaw and of the tongue. If the jaw is lowered as far as it will go, the oral cavity is at its largest; the jaw may be raised by degrees, gradually reducing the size of the oral cavity. Often this movement is spoken of as height of the tongue instead of the jaw, but the two move together and the jaw is more readily observable than the tongue. In addition to an up-and-down movement, the tongue can be moved toward the front or back of the mouth, thereby altering the shape of the oral cavity and hence affecting the quality of the sounds produced. We will, therefore, be considering two dimensions in the discussion which follows: (1) high versus low, referring to relative jaw height, and (2) front versus back, referring to relative tongue position.

If the jaw is in a low position and the back of the tongue slightly raised, with vocal cord vibration we get the vowel which appears as *a* in *father.* But this is a fairly rare spelling in English; the sound is usually spelled *o* as in *bother, hot, pod, sock,* and so on. Since the symbols for the IPA were based on the spelling systems of European languages other than English, they normally do not correspond to typical English spellings. The vowel in *hot, pod, sock* is written [a].

By raising the jaw as high as we can without actually making an obstruction, spreading the lips, and raising the tongue slightly in the front of the mouth, we produce the vowel sound heard in *heat, leap, seed,* and *me.* It is represented phonetically as [i], as one might expect from such European spellings as French *machine, signe, dispenser;* or Italian *nido, libro.*

With the jaw still raised but the tongue in a back position and the lips rounded, we produce the vowel heard in *rude, loon,* and *food:* [u]. The letter of the alphabet *u* is pronounced with a [y], the initial sound in *yet* and *you.* When we say *u,* we are not giving just a vowel, but [yu]. Hence, *ooze* is [uz], but *use* is [yuz]. The symbol [u] does not include the [y] sound; as an exclamation the vowel is sometimes spelled *ooh.*

If we alternate between [i] and [u] several times, we notice a distinction in addition to tongue position. For [u] the lips are rounded, but for [i] they are not. Nor are they rounded for [a]. The three vowel sounds presented to this point provide examples of contrasts in the dimensions of height, backness, and rounding:

	Front unrounded	Back unrounded	Back rounded
High	[i]		[u]
Low		[a]	

Some texts recognize a central position, halfway between front and back; however, the feature of lip rounding permits us to recognize only two positions. The reader can establish the difference between front and back by repeating [i] and [u] in succession several times. Similarly, the dimension of height can be demonstrated by alternating these two vowels with [a]. Lip rounding is readily observable.

Some languages have only the three vowels [i, a, u], and these are the three most commonly found in the languages of the world. If we admit a height between high and low, we can easily accommodate two more vowels, one front and the other back. This position is often called *mid*, but with the feature system it is more economical to call it [−high, −low]; that is, it is neither high nor low. The front mid [e] is the sound heard in *ache, gape,* and *hate*. For a few non-English examples, we can include Spanish *beber, delante,* and *mesa*. The back mid [o] is heard in *hope, roast,* and *code*. Adding [e] and [o] to our chart, we see the following arrangement:

	$\begin{bmatrix} -\text{back} \\ -\text{round} \end{bmatrix}$	$\begin{bmatrix} +\text{back} \\ -\text{round} \end{bmatrix}$	$\begin{bmatrix} +\text{back} \\ +\text{round} \end{bmatrix}$
$\begin{bmatrix} +\text{high} \\ -\text{low} \end{bmatrix}$	[i]		[u]
$\begin{bmatrix} -\text{high} \\ -\text{low} \end{bmatrix}$	[e]		[o]
$\begin{bmatrix} -\text{high} \\ +\text{low} \end{bmatrix}$		[a]	

Since this was the vowel system of Classical Latin, it is no accident that the Latin alphabet contains five letters for vowels.

In some languages there is a low front vowel, [æ], as in *bat, hand,* and *rack*. Whereas [i, e, a, o, u] are fairly common among languages, [æ] is found in only certain ones. In addition to the low front [æ] and the low back unrounded [a], some phonetic alphabets recognize two or three other *a*-like sounds. We will restrict ourselves to two, since there are apparently only two different vowels of this type which distinguish one morpheme from another. Another vowel found in some languages is the low back rounded [ɔ] as in *caught, fought,* and *Maude*.[1] We can now add [æ] and [ɔ] to our chart:

---

[1] In some dialects of English these words are all pronounced with [a]; speakers of these dialects may not have [ɔ].

	$\begin{bmatrix} -\text{back} \\ -\text{round} \end{bmatrix}$	$\begin{bmatrix} +\text{back} \\ -\text{round} \end{bmatrix}$	$\begin{bmatrix} +\text{back} \\ +\text{round} \end{bmatrix}$
$\begin{bmatrix} +\text{high} \\ -\text{low} \end{bmatrix}$	[i]		[u]
$\begin{bmatrix} -\text{high} \\ -\text{low} \end{bmatrix}$	[e]		[o]
$\begin{bmatrix} -\text{high} \\ +\text{low} \end{bmatrix}$	[æ]	[a]	[ɔ]

Utilizing three dimensions of height, front versus back, and lip rounding, we have seven vowels. There are additional modifications which can be made to provide further possible distinctions. One of these is duration. In English we may say, "That was sweet," with a normal [i] in *sweet,* or we may prolong the sound for emphasis, usually adding other features as well: "That was *sweet!*" We can indicate this increase in duration by a colon: [i:]. We still recognize *sweet* as the same word, whether we pronounce it with [i] or [i:]. That is, the increase in duration does not serve to distinguish one morpheme from another in English, although it gives added information such as surprise, anger, and the like. It is also found regularly in certain phonetic environments, especially before voiced consonants. *Beat,* with the vowel followed by a voiceless stop, has a shorter [i] than *bead,* with a voiced stop. The vowel in *bees,* with a following voiced fricative, is longer still. Also, a vowel is held longer in final position than it is when followed by a voiceless stop: *bee* vs. *beet.*[2]

In some languages duration does serve to distinguish one morpheme from another. This was the case in Classical Greek, where separate letters of the alphabet were used to distinguish some pairs of short and long vowels, such as *omicron* ("small o") and *omega* ("big o"). In Latin and Old English, vocalic length was significant in distinguishing morphemes, although both long and short vowels were written with the same letters. Sometimes modern editors place a macron (e.g., $\bar{a}$) over the long vowels, but this was not a common practice in the original manuscripts.

In Modern English the issue of vocalic length, or duration, is complicated because it is related to other features. As we saw earlier, length is used for emphasis, but there are also differences depending upon the phonetic environment of the vowel. In addition, it is related to tenseness.

Some sounds are produced with more tenseness of the vocal apparatus than others. The vowel in *beet,* for example, is **tense** in comparison to the one in *bit,* which is **lax.** As we saw earlier, we represent the vowel in *beet* as [i]. The one in *bit, dig,* and *kick* is written as [ɪ].

Another tense/lax pair is [u] as in *true, prune, fool* and [ʊ], the lax vowel in *full, put, wood.* These two vowels can be contrasted in pairs of words which differ only in that one has [u] where the other has [ʊ]. We have already seen *fool* and *full,* and we can add *pool* and *pull.* Since [l] affects the preceding vowel, we should add some examples with other consonants following the vowel in question. The past tenses of the verbs *coo,*

2 See Jones (1969:232–36) for further discussion.

shoe, and *woo* are *cooed, shoed,* and *wooed,* all with [u]. These can be contrasted with *could, should,* and *would,* with the lax [ʊ].

For still another pair of vowels, we can look at the tense [e] as in *hate, cake, late* and the lax [ɛ] in *let, bet,* and *west.* The tense versus lax distinction can be observed in pairs of words such as *mate, met; late, let; mace, mess; wage, wedge; played, pled.*

Now let us look at the three tense/lax pairs we have just considered and see how this feature interacts with length. When they are in the same environment (i.e., before the same kind of sound such as voiceless stops or voiced fricatives), the tense vowels are slightly longer than their lax counterparts. Hence, the vowel in *bait* is somewhat longer than that in *bet.* The same holds true for *beet* and *bit* and for *boot* and *foot.* Before a voiceless stop, such as [t], the tense vowels [i, e, u] are slightly longer than the lax [ɪ, ɛ, ʊ].

We thus have two predictable criteria for vocalic length in English:

1. Tense vowels are longer than lax ones in the same environment.
2. All vowels are longer before voiced stops than before voiceless ones; they are longer before fricatives and in word final position than before stops.

According to the first statement, the vowel in *wait* is longer than the one in *wet;* according to the second, the vowel in *wade* is longer than the one in *wait,* and the ones in *way* and *ways* are longer still. What happens if a tense vowel is followed by a voiced stop and the corresponding lax vowel is followed by a voiceless stop, as *wade* and *wet*? Obviously the vowel in *wade* is longer, since both criteria are met. However, what about the reverse situation, in which the tense vowel is followed by a voiceless stop (*wait*) and the lax vowel by a voiced stop (*wed*)? Here the vowel in *wed* is longer than the one in *wait.* The situation is complicated.

A ranking like the following will help to clarify matters:

wet   wait   wed   wade   *wez   ways

There is currently no morpheme *wez,* hence the asterisk. Since it is a potential word, we are including it to make the pattern complete. The vowel in each word is longer than the one to its left, shorter than the one to its right. What this listing indicates is that vocalic length is a matter of degree rather than presence versus absence. We have given six degrees of length. Whereas in the same environment a tense vowel is longer than a lax one, the opposite pattern may result when the environments change. Since length seems to be always predictable from a combination of environment and tenseness, we are not including it as a feature of vowels for English, but we are classifying them as [+tense] or [−tense].

There are still many questions about what is the best way to distinguish the pairs [i, ɪ; e, ɛ; u, ʊ]. As we have seen, the first member of each pair is tenser than the second and also longer when in the same environment. In addition, the first member is slightly higher than the second, and the tense members in English are produced with an off-glide which is absent (or nearly so) from their lax counterparts. Our decision to select tenseness as the most significant of these features may prove to be inaccurate as more languages are studied and more is learned about phonology in general.

Of the other four vowels—[a, æ, o, ɔ]—there are no clear counterparts as there are for those we have been discussing. Both [a] and [æ] are often lax, but tense variants which do not differ in quality are also found. The back [o] is tense. To these we can add the lax [ə], the vowel found at the end of *sofa* and *Cuba.* Also lax is [ʌ] as in *cut, bud,* and *purr.* There are differences between [ə] and [ʌ], but the person making his first acquaintance with phonetics is not likely to hear them. A useful way of distinguishing the two sounds is to say that [ʌ] is found in stressed (i.e., "accented") syllables or in words of only one syllable; [ə] is found only in unstressed syllables. The high back unrounded [ɨ] is heard in some dialects of English in the unstressed syllable of *careless, bracelet,* and the like. It is more distinctive in Turkish and several other languages.

The absence of front rounded vowels is a peculiarity of Modern English and should not be assumed to be true for all languages. French, German, Turkish, Hungarian, and Chinese, for example, have front rounded vowels as well as front unrounded ones. Examples are French *pur, sucre, lune* and German *für, Münster, Tür.* These words have the high front rounded vowel [ü], which is given in some books as [y]. Students are often told to pronounce this sound by positioning the jaw and tongue for [i] and rounding the lips. The mid front rounded [ö] is found in French *jeu, peu* and German *schön, hören.* The low front rounded [œ] is found in such French words as *seul* and *fleur.*

Turkish has rounded and unrounded vowels in both front and back positions. There are four high vowels: front unrounded, front rounded, back unrounded, and back rounded. For such a language the features [+round] and [−round] are indispensable in any discussion of the vocalic system. Table 10.7 gives all of the vowels we have discussed.

Table 10.7. VOWELS

	$\begin{bmatrix} -back \\ -round \end{bmatrix}$	$\begin{bmatrix} -back \\ +round \end{bmatrix}$	$\begin{bmatrix} +back \\ -round \end{bmatrix}$	$\begin{bmatrix} +back \\ +round \end{bmatrix}$
$\begin{bmatrix} +high \\ -low \end{bmatrix}$	[i, ɪ]	[ü]	[ɨ]	[u, ʊ]
$\begin{bmatrix} -high \\ -low \end{bmatrix}$	[e, ɛ]	[ö]	[ə, ʌ]	[o]
$\begin{bmatrix} -high \\ +low \end{bmatrix}$	[æ]	[œ]	[a]	[ɔ]

Consonantal, Vocalic, and Obstruent

At the beginning of the section on vowels, we said that for consonants there is a major obstruction in the oral cavity but for vowels there is not. This statement about consonants is specific enough to satisfy our purposes, but the one about vowels needs refinement.

There are three sounds which we have not yet introduced: [w], the first sound in *wet, wave, work;* [y], the first sound in *you, use, yet, yen, unit;*

[h], in *hot, health, how.* Although it is not definite that [h] belongs with this group, we are following Chomsky and Halle (1968) in placing it here. Some linguists have placed [h] with the fricatives, but this is not altogether satisfactory either.

The sounds [w] and [y]—and perhaps [h]—are often called **glides** because they readily accommodate themselves to the position of the following vowel. By saying *wet, we, woo, wow, warm,* a person can easily see that [w] begins with rounded lips and tongue raised toward the back, but that the tongue glides to the position for the vowel. Similar adjustments can be observed for [y] in *yet, yeast, you, yearn, yarn, yack.*

They are also called **semivowels** because they are partially like vowels, partially like consonants. From the standpoint of production, there is no major obstruction as there is with fricatives and other consonants. At the same time, the tongue is higher than it is for the high vowels [i] and [u]. They are, therefore, between vowels and consonants as far as tongue or jaw height is concerned.

Let us define the feature **vocalic** as belonging to a sound produced with the jaw and tongue no higher than for [i] and [u]. Hence, vowels are [+vocalic]. If the jaw and tongue are higher than for [i] and [u], the sound is [−vocalic]. This includes the consonants (with two exceptions to be mentioned shortly) as well as the glides.

Since [+consonantal] means that there is a major obstruction, we can define vowels as [−consonantal, +vocalic], most consonants as [+consonantal, −vocalic], and the glides as [−consonantal, −vocalic]. There remains a fourth possible combination: [+consonantal, +vocalic]. By the definitions for the articulation of sounds, this combination should be impossible. If there is an obstruction, the tongue and jaw must be higher than for [i] or [u]; hence, there cannot be a vocalic segment which has an obstruction. Early studies of features used acoustic signals rather than articulatory motions for distinctions among features. Since the liquids [r] and [l] are acoustically very much like vowels, they are given the feature combination [+consonantal, +vocalic]. For the ways the liquids function in phonological rules, we want to keep this feature combination even though it is inconsistent with the definition for [+vocalic] when given in articulatory terms. Rather than expand the definition so that it accommodates [r] and [l], we will list them as exceptions. It should be realized that there is nothing really exceptional about the liquids; rather it is our inexact definition and the difficulties of combining articulatory and acoustic criteria which create the problem.

We can group the sounds of a language under the four headings which result from the various combinations of the features vocalic and consonantal:

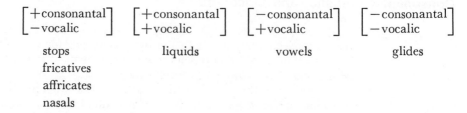

$$\begin{bmatrix} +\text{consonantal} \\ -\text{vocalic} \end{bmatrix} \quad \begin{bmatrix} +\text{consonantal} \\ +\text{vocalic} \end{bmatrix} \quad \begin{bmatrix} -\text{consonantal} \\ +\text{vocalic} \end{bmatrix} \quad \begin{bmatrix} -\text{consonantal} \\ -\text{vocalic} \end{bmatrix}$$

stops	liquids	vowels	glides
fricatives			
affricates			
nasals			

These groups are not of equal size, of course. Under [+consonantal, +vocalic] there are only two members: [r, l]; under [−consonantal, −vocalic] there are three: [y, w, h].

Sometimes another kind of classification is desirable. Since this one is based on auditory criteria, we cannot give articulatory descriptions. The stops, fricatives, and affricates are called **obstruents.** The other sounds—nasals, liquids, glides, and vowels—are called **sonorants.** Since only one term is needed with plus and minus values, we will refer to the obstruents as [+obstruent] and the sonorants as [−obstruent].

Diphthongs

Within each syllable there is one segment which is the most prominent acoustically. This syllable "peak" is usually a vowel, less often one of the other sonorants. Instead of a single vowel, this peak may consist of a combination of vowel and semivowel, known as a **diphthong.**

The vocalic part of *louse* and *house,* for example, is a diphthong which may be represented [aw]. It should be stressed that all vowels and diphthongs are affected by the consonants that follow; hence, no one pronounces the diphthong in *loud* exactly like the ones in *lounge* or *house.* We still represent all three as [aw]. Also, there is much variation among dialects and even within the speech of individuals as to their actual pronunciation of diphthongs as well as vowels. The symbol [aw] will be used for all of them.

Other diphthongs are [ay], as found in *knight, bike, sigh,* and [oy], as in *boy, oil, Lloyd.* As with [aw], there is much variation among speakers of English and even within the speech of an individual. Theoretically, all combinations of vowel plus semivowel are possible, but some such as [öw] are rare.

Because the combinations we have given so far all have the semivowel, or glide, after the vowel, they are often called "off-gliding" diphthongs. There are also "on-gliding" possibilities, with the semivowel first. We find an example in English in [yu] as in *cute, pure,* and the like. In addition to [yu], Russian has [ya, yo, yɛ].

There are currently many unanswered questions regarding diphthongs. Semivowels can be regarded as consonants or as vowels, the latter in particular when they are members of diphthongs. When they follow vowels in a syllable, they are generally regarded as vocalic, and the combination is called a diphthong. When they precede the vowel, the solution is less clear. For example, should [yu], *you,* be classified as a diphthong or as a semivowel with consonantal function plus vowel? The answer depends upon the overall phonological structure of the language in question, and we do not yet know enough about any language to give a very convincing answer.

Another question involves the off-glides found in English with all tense vowels. Some transcription systems write [iy] instead of [i], [uw] instead of [u], and so on. Should tense vowels in English be classified differently from [ay, oy, aw], or should all be treated uniformly as diphthongs?

Features and Natural Classes

Earlier in this chapter, we said that features show the similarities among a group of sounds. The feature [+nasal], for example, belongs to only [m, n, ñ, ŋ]. [+strident] includes [f, v, s, z, š, ž, č, j]. The feature [+anterior] belongs to the front consonants [p, b, t, d, f, v, θ, ð, s, z, m, n, l]. Or we can take combinations of features: [+consonantal, +vocalic] includes the liquids; [−consonantal, −vocalic] the glides; [+consonantal, −vocalic, +continuant], the fricatives. In each of these cases we are grouping together sounds which are similar in production and which function together in phonological processes such as those we will consider in the next two chapters.

The sounds which are defined by a feature or a combination of features constitute a **natural class**. Hence, the nasals are a natural class, as are the strident consonants or the liquids. It may seem at first that any grouping of sounds should constitute a natural class; however, if we try giving the features which [a, f, w] have in common, we see that there is nothing similar about them. They do not constitute a natural class. Similarly, although [r, l] do belong to a natural class, [r, l, k] do not. It does not matter that two members of the group have much in common. For [r, l, k] to be a natural class, there would have to be a feature or combination of features which is common to all.

For a group of sounds to belong to a natural class, they must all share one or more features, and there must be no other sounds that have this feature or combination of features. [m, n] may constitute a natural class, but [+nasal] alone does not define it since [m, n] do not exhaustively list the sounds which have the feature [+nasal]. However, if we give [+nasal, +anterior], then [m, n] comprise a natural class. Both [m] and [n] have the given features, and no other sounds share this combination.

Here are a few additional examples. [u, i] are the high tense vowels in English. If we consider just the vowels for this language, we can describe the natural class as [+vocalic, +high, +tense]. Although they share other features such as [+voice], only three are needed to set them off from other sounds. Another natural class of vowels in English can be described as [+vocalic, −back]. This grouping includes the front vowels [i, ɪ, e, ɛ, æ].

Although the grouping of sounds described by each combination of features in theory produces a natural class, some of them are of questionable importance. By itself, [−nasal] groups together most of the sounds of a language. Whereas nasals usually function in the same way, non-nasals have little in common. For another example, [+anterior] gives a useful grouping of the front consonants, but [−anterior] is by itself of little value. Since there is no obstruction in the production of vowels and glides, they are [−anterior]. Hence, this feature gives a "natural class" composed of palatal and velar consonants, vowels, and glides. It seems most unlikely that these sounds should ever need to be classified together.

Although the use of feature combinations does effectively describe most significant natural classes, it is too broad and permits some that are of questionable worth. This is one area in which linguists need to make refinements. So far, the system has accommodated the groupings linguists wish to make. It should be a fairly simple matter to constrict the theory so that it accommodates only these. Although there are undeniably rich areas for further research in the classification of sounds, this area of linguistics is much better developed than most others.

Exercises

A. List the features that the following pairs of segments share:

1. [k, g]	5. [s, z]	9. [ɪ, ɛ]
2. [f, v]	6. [i, u]	10. [u, ʊ]
3. [m, b]	7. [e, o]	
4. [ð, z]	8. [o, a]	

B. List the ways in which the following pairs differ:

1. [m, n]	5. [i, ɪ]	9. [i, ü]
2. [r, l]	6. [a, ɔ]	10. [d, z]
3. [p, b]	7. [č, ǰ]	
4. [d, g]	8. [s, θ]	

C. Which groups of sounds are specified by the following feature combinations?

1. $\begin{bmatrix} +\text{consonantal} \\ +\text{anterior} \end{bmatrix}$ 2. $\begin{bmatrix} +\text{consonantal} \\ -\text{vocalic} \\ -\text{continuant} \\ -\text{nasal} \end{bmatrix}$

3. $\begin{bmatrix} +\text{consonantal} \\ -\text{vocalic} \\ -\text{coronal} \\ -\text{anterior} \end{bmatrix}$ 4. $\begin{bmatrix} -\text{consonantal} \\ +\text{vocalic} \\ +\text{tense} \end{bmatrix}$

D. If the sounds grouped together constitute a natural class, give the features that distinguish them; if they do not constitute a natural class, do nothing with them.

1. [m, n, ŋ]	4. [y, w, ǰ]
2. [p, b, m, f, v]	5. [i, ɪ, u, ʊ]
3. [s, š, f, č]	6. [u, ʊ, o, ɔ]

E. Each of the following groups will form a natural class if one more sound is added. Supply it.

1. [b, d, ___]	3. [æ, a, ___]
2. [v, ð, ž, ___]	4. [k, g, č, ___]

F. Transcribe the following words into phonetic notation:

1. fit	8. egg	15. seat	22. ship	29. shake
2. feet	9. vet	16. sick	23. sheep	30. shack
3. feat	10. dad	17. seek	24. Shep	31. fish
4. fate	11. vague	18. sack	25. shape	32. bag
5. fact	12. sip	19. sake	26. sheet	33. face
6. fake	13. seep	20. Sid	27. Shick	34. says
7. fib	14. sit	21. gave	28. sheik	35. seize

36. cess	39. sea	42. chef	45. sad	48. vast
37. cease	40. fizz	43. steak	46. shave	49. vest
38. see	41. sheaf	44. dead	47. zigzag	50. best

G. Transcribe the following words:

1. mean	6. sink	11. loose	16. nook	21. move
2. man	7. pink	12. rude	17. nut	22. sure
3. run	8. ping	13. took	18. groom	23. laugh
4. rung	9. null	14. should	19. plaid	24. does
5. sing	10. lose	15. loot	20. pled	25. bank

H. Transcribe the following words:

1. wet	11. few	21. vision	31. teeth
2. hail	12. beauty	22. fishing	32. teethe
3. whale	13. booty	23. measure	33. faith
4. where	14. yes	24. racer	34. thatch
5. wear	15. moo	25. razor	35. these
6. hash	16. music	26. mirage	36. the
7. heel	17. quite	27. dilution	37. bath
8. wheel	18. do	28. delusion	38. bathe
9. who	19. unit	29. composer	39. this
10. whiff	20. use (V)	30. composure	40. thistle

I. Transcribe the following words:

1. breathe	14. white	27. abounding	40. choice
2. nature	15. purely	28. collision	41. fought
3. plowed	16. mule	29. exaggerate	42. sliced
4. residential	17. those	30. voice	43. creature
5. book	18. exact	31. quota	44. moth
6. thigh	19. loathes	32. mighty	45. explosion
7. chord	20. applause	33. said	46. attacked
8. musician	21. wrong	34. sugar	47. pouch
9. champagne	22. appoints	35. suggest	48. pledger
10. leisure	23. badgers	36. of	49. pleasure
11. plumber	24. fox	37. wharf	50. joining
12. view	25. finger	38. English	
13. announced	26. humiliation	39. myth	

chapter 11

Redundancy and Distinctive Features

In the last chapter as we examined the sounds of speech, we saw that a sound such as [t] or [a] is not the result of a single operation such as ringing a bell or blowing a horn, but rather of a complex combination of features. When we hear someone say *bat,* for example, we recognize the [b] as different from the [p] in *pat* by the feature [+voice]. A different feature, [−nasal], distinguishes *bat* from *mat,* and [+anterior] distinguishes it from *gat.* The two features [−continuant] and [−strident] separate [b] from [v] in *bat* and *vat.* Here are several words that differ from *bat* only in different feature selections for the first consonant:

bat	[+voice]		*pat*	[−voice]
bat	[−nasal]		*mat*	[+nasal]
bat	[−nasal, −coronal]		*gnat*	[+nasal, +coronal]
bat	[−continuant, −strident]		*vat*	[+continuant, +strident]
bat	[−continuant, −strident, +voice]		*fat*	[+continuant, +strident, −voice]
bat	[−coronal, +voice]		*tat*	[+coronal, −voice]
bat	[−coronal, −continuant]		*that*	[+coronal, +continuant]
bat	[−continuant, −coronal, −strident, +voice]		*sat*	[+continuant, +coronal, +strident, −voice]
bat	[+anterior, +voice]		*cat*	[−anterior, −voice]
bat	[+anterior, −coronal, −strident, +voice]		*chat*	[−anterior, +coronal, +strident, −voice]

In each pair one or more features differ in a way that causes the speaker of English to consider the items separate words.

Combinatorial Constraints

A complete listing of the features for any sound is quite extensive, as we can see for [z]:

$$
\begin{bmatrix}
+\text{consonantal} \\
-\text{vocalic} \\
+\text{obstruent} \\
+\text{anterior} \\
+\text{coronal} \\
+\text{voice} \\
-\text{nasal} \\
+\text{strident} \\
+\text{continuant}
\end{bmatrix}
$$

Human linguistic capabilities continue to astound students of language, but it seems incredible that anyone might be taking into equal account all of these features for each sound that is produced in normal speech.

As a matter of fact, some of these features are predictable from others, making it unnecessary for all of them to be given the same amount of attention. Take, for example, this combination:

$$
\begin{bmatrix}
+\text{consonantal} \\
-\text{vocalic} \\
+\text{obstruent} \\
-\text{nasal}
\end{bmatrix}
$$

Since obstruents are the non-nasal consonants, all four features are not needed. We can use only [+obstruent] or the other three.

Or take this combination:

$$
\begin{bmatrix}
+\text{consonantal} \\
-\text{vocalic} \\
+\text{strident}
\end{bmatrix}
$$

Since the liquids are not strident in English, we know that if a sound is both [+consonantal] and [+strident], it is also [−vocalic]. This observation would not hold for a language like Czech, which has a strident [r].

If we list just the features that are not predictable for the English [z], we arrive at the following:

$$
\begin{bmatrix}
+\text{obstruent} \\
+\text{anterior} \\
+\text{coronal} \\
+\text{voice} \\
+\text{strident}
\end{bmatrix}
$$

Let us see how we arrived at these. The feature [obstruent] narrows the class of sounds to the stops, fricatives, and affricates. The combination [+anterior, +coronal] limits the sound to the dental obstruents: [t, d, θ, ð, s, z]. If we further restrict the grouping to the sounds which are voiced, we have [d, ð, z]. Of these, only [z] is [+strident]. If we were discussing the [z] in a language which has the dental affricates [tˢ] and [dᶻ], we would have to include [+continuant] as well.

A feature is said to be **distinctive** if it functions in a sound to distinguish one morpheme from another; that is, it is distinctive if it is not predictable. A feature that is predictable is said to be **redundant.** For [z] only the following are distinctive in English:

$$\begin{bmatrix} +\text{obstruent} \\ +\text{anterior} \\ +\text{coronal} \\ +\text{voice} \\ +\text{strident} \end{bmatrix}$$

All other features are redundant.

For another example, let us look at [m], which has these features:

$$\begin{bmatrix} +\text{consonantal} \\ -\text{vocalic} \\ -\text{obstruent} \\ +\text{anterior} \\ -\text{coronal} \\ +\text{voice} \\ +\text{nasal} \\ -\text{strident} \\ -\text{continuant} \end{bmatrix}$$

The feature [+nasal] makes several of the others redundant. First of all, obstruents are defined as the non-nasal consonants; hence, any sound which is [+nasal] is automatically [−obstruent]. Here the definition for one feature precludes a particular combination. A second kind of redundancy results not from definitions but from universal constraints. Since the production of nasals does not permit the kind of friction needed for stridency, there are no strident nasals; [+nasal], then, predicts [−strident]. Another universal constraint is that nasals are normally voiced in all languages, although there are a few exceptions. This means that [+voice] is predictable from [+nasal]. A third kind of redundancy results from the restrictions in particular languages. English, for example, has no nasalized vowels; hence, all nasals are [−continuant]. They are also [+consonantal, −vocalic]. If we are speaking of the [m] in English, German, Russian, and a great many other languages, only the following features are distinctive:

$$\begin{bmatrix} +\text{nasal} \\ +\text{anterior} \\ -\text{coronal} \end{bmatrix}$$

All other features are redundant. [+nasal] limits the class of sounds to [m, n, ñ, ŋ], and [+anterior, −coronal] distinguishes [m] from the other nasals. Redundant features are still present in a segment; they are just not needed to differentiate it from the others.

Let us look at the reasons for redundancy more closely. We said that the definitions preclude certain combinations such as [+nasal] and [+obstruent]. By the convention of the plus and minus values, a sound must be one or the other, not both; it is, therefore, not possible for a sound to be both [+nasal] and [−nasal]. Also, since [−consonantal] means that there is no obstruction, all such sounds are necessarily [−anterior] and [−coronal] because plus values for these two features are defined in terms of the point of obstruction.

More interesting are the combinations which are prohibited by universal constraints. We saw that there are no strident nasals. Similarly, there are no strident vowels. For stridency there must be an obstruction which causes friction, but for vowels there can be no obstruction; [−consonantal, +vocalic] and [+strident] are, therefore, incompatible. Also, vowels must be continuants since there is no obstruction in their production. A segment that is [−consonantal, +vocalic], then, is necessarily [+continuant]. Features of human anatomy make other combinations impossible. A vowel, for example, cannot be both [+high] and [+low]. The tongue is amazingly flexible, but the body cannot be both high and low at the same time.

Finally, there are constraints which apply only to certain languages. In English most fricatives are [+strident], but [θ] and [ð] are not. For those languages which do not have [θ] and [ð], all fricatives may be strident; hence, all sounds which are [+consonantal, −vocalic, +continuant] are redundantly [+strident] as well. For English all vowels are [−nasal], but this restriction is not true for a language such as French, which has nasalized vowels.

Twelve features, each with plus and minus values, yield 4096 potential combinations. Obviously such a large number of significant sounds never occurs in any language. Even if all were possible, no one could perceive or produce that number in normal speech with any kind of efficiency. Some are impossible, and others are merely prohibited for various reasons. Even so, no language uses all that are possible. For example, Modern English has no velar fricatives although they do exist in many languages. Nor does it have front rounded vowels. Some languages have only one liquid. Many do not have the tense/lax pairs such as [i] and [ɪ] found in English or the fricatives [θ] and [ð]. Although languages vary in the exact number they have, few use more than fifty distinctive sounds.

Sequential Constraints

In addition to restrictions on which features may combine to make one segment, there are those on which segments may follow or precede each other. In English there is a word *some*, pronounced [sʌm]. Although there is no word in the language pronounced [zʌm] or [žʌm], the native speaker recognizes the first of these as a potential word. It does not exist now, but there is no reason it could not appear in the future. He also knows that [žʌm] is not a possible English word even though he can pronounce it easily. Since the purpose of linguistic investigation is to account for the native speaker's knowledge of his language, we need to investigate why he accepts [zʌm] but not [žʌm].

Whereas many consonants can occur freely at the beginning of a word, in the middle, or at the end, some are more restricted. In French, [ž] is unrestricted, occurring at the beginning (*jour, jus, jeu*), in the middle (*bouger, léger, plonger*), and at the end (*rouge, singe, large*). But in English [ž] never occurs at the beginning of a word, although it does in the middle (*pleasure, measure, seizure*). For some speakers it occurs at the end of a few French borrowings (*mirage, camouflage, loge,* and the like), but other people use [j] in these words. Some speakers of English, then, have [ž] medially and finally, and others have it only medially; none have it initially. This is the result of historical developments in the language, not of possibility or impossibility of pronunciation. We can predict, therefore, that any word starting with [ž] will be judged impossible for English.

Another consonant which never occurs initially in English or German is [ŋ], although it does in some languages such as Vietnamese. By adding sequential constraints to those on combinations of features within a sound, we can see further redundancy. At the end of a word in English, we need plus or minus values for both anterior and coronal to designate which nasal is intended. In languages which do not permit the velar or palatal nasal initially, all nasals at the beginning of a word are necessarily [+anterior]; hence, [+nasal] and [−coronal] are enough to designate initial [m].

The lax vowels occur freely before consonants but not at the end of a word in English. For some dialects this statement has to be restricted to stressed syllables, since they have [ɪ], for example, in the last syllable of *sincerely, lovely, really,* and similar words. For those dialects that have [i] in this position, most lax vowels never occur finally, regardless of the stress pattern. Thus there are no potential English words [hɪ, mɛ, kæ, bʊ]. The lax [ə] does occur finally, but only in unstressed syllables.

All consonants may occur at the end of a word in English, and all but two may occur initially. It should not be assumed that this freedom is found universally. There are languages in which all syllables consist of a single consonant followed by a vowel; that is, such syllables as [ba, mi, ke] may occur, but none with a consonant at the end: *[bat, mig, ked]. In such languages all words necessarily end with vowels. Chinese is almost this restricted. No obstruent may come at the end of a syllable, but a nasal may. Hence, all Chinese words end with a vowel or a nasal.

Syllables consisting of just the two segments single consonant plus vowel are the most common among the languages of the world. In English we can illustrate them with *see, say, sofa, coffee, Manitoba, Mississippi.* It should be remembered that we are speaking of the pronunciation of these words, not their spellings. This kind of syllable structure in phonetic terms consists of alternations of closing (consonant) and opening (vowel). Many languages have only this kind of syllable; no morpheme begins with a vowel or ends with a consonant. Nor can a word in these languages consist of just a single vowel with no consonant.

Although English has syllables of the type CV (i.e., single consonant followed by a single vowel), it also has CVC syllables: *set, mad, but, patch,* and the like. All obstruents and nasals occur freely at the end of a word or syllable in the language.

No language has syllables consisting entirely of obstruents, although there may be syllables with only vowels for some languages. Hence, there are no syllables or words in any language pronounced [pkb] or [fzdg]. If the reader tries to say such combinations, he soon understands why they do not exist: They are unpronounceable. It is possible for the liquids and nasals to take on a vocalic function since they are not obstruents. In English the last syllable in *cattle, bottle, butter, sitter* may be pronounced without a vowel in it. The liquid [l] or [r] in such words constitutes the entire syllable, and is referred to as **syllabic [r]** or **syllabic [l]**. Similarly, *heaven* and *beaten* may have syllabic [m] and [n] if pronounced [hɛbm] and [bitn]; this is the usual pronunciation for *beaten*. Syllabic liquids and nasals are much more common in some languages than in others. There is a famous sentence in Czech which contains no vowels but has syllabic liquids instead: *Strč prst skrz krk,* meaning "Push your finger through your neck." The reader will gather from the meaning that this is an artificially contrived sentence. Liquids and nasals may function as vowels, but obstruents never do. This is a major reason for setting up the class of sounds known as sonorants, which contrast with the obstruents. All words must contain at least one sonorant.

In many languages, including English, there may be more than a single consonant preceding a vowel. We see two obstruents clustering together in *speak, stop,* and *skip*. If we try [s] with any other obstruent initially, we do not produce possible English words:

[sdik]	[svik]	[sðik]	[sžik]
[sbik]	[sfik]	[szik]	[sčik]
[sgik]	[sθik]	[sšik]	[sʲik]

If [s] occurs at the beginning, the only obstruents that can follow are [p, t, k]. This, of course, is the natural class of voiceless stops. If we try other combinations of obstruents, we likewise produce impossible words for English:

[fted]	[ðsed]	[zged]
[bded]	[tsed]	[gded]
[gbed]	[pked]	[vded]

For English the only possible obstruent clusters that can occur initially are [sp, st, sk].

It should be emphasized that this is an English restriction, not one for all languages. German, for example, does not have [sp] or [st] initially, but it does have [šp] and [št], as in *sparen, Spiegel, Spring, Stadt, stolz, Strauch*. Italian has initial [sp, st, sk] and also [sf] as in *sfortunato, sforzare*. It also has [zv] initially, as in *svelto, sventura*. Russian has such initial obstruent clusters as [gd] and [gv] as well as [pt] and [čt]. From this listing it may appear that just about any combination is possible, but it seems likely that further research will reveal restrictions on which obstruent clusters may occur. Those which we have given, for example, all agree in voicing: Both are voiced or both voiceless. No doubt there are other restrictions.

Although only three combinations of obstruent clusters exist initially in English, there are combinations of obstruent and liquid, nasal, or glide. Such initial clusters as those found in *slum, prick, please, trade, smash, snort, sweat,* and *cute* are certainly possible; however, there are well-defined restrictions, since **tlip* and **rpan* are not possible English words. We will leave the exact details of these restrictions to the exercises at the end of this chapter.

A complete listing of sequential constraints would specify the possible morphemes in a given language in the same way that a complete grammar would specify the possible sentences. The sequential constraints would not limit the morphemes to those which actually exist at some point in history, but would indicate which combinations of segments are possible. This is the kind of information a native speaker possesses. He knows that [flɛd] and [klɛd] are possible English words but that [tlɛd] is not. Although he has never heard [klɛd], he realizes that it is a potential word. For all he knows, it may be in existence. All he can really assert is that it is possible but that he does not know it if it exists. A statement of sequential constraints provides the same information in an explicit manner.

Phonetic and Phonemic Representation

Certain features are predictable, or redundant, because of the presence of other features within the segment; others can be predicted because of the position of the segment in relation to others. There are some features which are always predictable in a given language, such as the following in English.

Most people feel that they are producing the initial consonant in *moon* the same as the one in *mean*, and similarly for the following pairs:

[m] moon	[m] man
[b] boat	[b] bait
[f] full	[f] fill
[k] caught	[k] cot

Careful observation, however, will show that the lips are rounded for the initial consonants in *moon, boat, full,* and *caught,* whereas they are not for *man, bait, fill,* and *cot.* Although there is a slight difference in sound, the speaker of English ignores it and thinks of the rounded [m] in *moon* as the same as the unrounded [m] in *man.* This feature is always predictable in English consonants. If a consonant precedes a vowel that is [+round], it takes on this feature also. If the following potential words are ever added to the language, we will be able to predict whether their initial consonants will be formed with lip rounding or not: [big, fæm, kɪg, rok, lug, sɛk, šɔk]. Whereas lip rounding is a distinctive feature for vowels, it is not for consonants in English.

To take another example, most speakers of English are aware of only one [l] sound and assume that they are pronouncing it the same in *lit* and *gold.* Close attention to the position of the tongue will show that only the tongue tip is raised for the [l] in *lit,* whereas for the [l] in *gold* the tongue is slightly flattened out, so that in addition to the tongue tip, the body is raised as well. The sound in *lit* has often been referred to as the "clear *l*" and the one in *gold* as "dark *l*." Once a person becomes aware of the differences in sound, he can interchange them in *lit* and *gold.* The words are still recognizable, but the pronunciation sounds peculiar, as though a foreigner were saying them. Because the body of the tongue is raised toward (but not touching) the velum, works on phonetics often refer to the [l] in *gold* as **velarized** and represent it [ł]. The fact that speakers of English are not normally aware of the two [l] sounds in their language suggests that this is not a distinctive feature, but rather one which is predictable, such as lip rounding for consonants.

The following pairs of words illustrate one of the environments in which velarized [ł] is found:

[l]	[ł]
lap	pal
lead	deal
loop	pool

Obviously it does not matter whether the vowel in the syllable is front or back, high or low, rounded or unrounded. What is significant is the position of the liquid in relation to the vowel. If we try pronouncing a clear [l] after a vowel, we soon see that this is not possible for English; only the velarized [ł] occurs here.

For another position in which velarized [ł] is found, we can compare the following pairs of words:

[l]	[ł]
land	gland
Lou	blue
late	inflate
loan	Sloan

After a consonant we find [ł] rather than [l].

To achieve a clear distinction between distinctive and redundant features, we should provide an example of them. If we take the two segments [i] and [k] and say that there is another segment before them, we have a word like this: [____ik]. Now if we are told that the first segment is a labial stop, we are unable to predict whether it will be [p] or [b]; that is, the feature of voicing is not predictable in this environment. Similarly, if we are told that the first segment is a liquid, we do not know whether it is [r] or [l] since both [rik] and [lik] are possible. On the other hand, if we are told that the first segment has the features [+consonantal, +vocalic, +anterior], we know that it is [l] rather than [ł]. Velarized [ł] never occurs in this position. Also, if we are told that the first segment is a voiced labial stop, we know that it is [bik] and that the [b] does not have lip rounding. Rounded consonants in English occur only before rounded vowels.

If a feature is unpredictable, its presence in a segment may be used to distinguish one morpheme from another, as we can see from the following pairs:

1. voicing:		tip	dip
2. vowel tenseness:		heed	hid
3. nasality:		mud	Bud

Words which differ by only one segment are called **minimal pairs**. That is, their difference is the minimum possible for distinguishing them.

Minimal pairs provide a useful device for determining which features are distinctive in a language. Since there are such pairs in English as *tip, dip; to, do; town, down; let, led; neat, need,* we know that the voicing contrast between [t] and [d] is significant in distinguishing morphemes in the language. Since the feature [+voice] is unpredictable in obstruents, it is distinctive. Two segments, such as [t] and [d], which can occur in identical environments such as [____aym] and result in different morphemes according to which is selected, are said to **contrast** with each other. As we can see from the following minimal pairs, [t] is in contrast not only with [d], but also with [p, b, k, ǰ, č, l, r, n, h, š, s, z]:

tip	pip	tip	chip	tip	hip
tip	bip	tip	lip	tip	ship
tip	Kip	tip	rip	tip	sip
tip	gyp	tip	nip	tip	zip

We usually speak of two segments such as [t] and [d] as being in *contrast* and of the unpredictable features which distinguish them as being *distinctive.* As we have already seen, voicing in obstruents is distinctive. Other distinctive features include those which designate the point of obstruction (anterior and coronal), as well as continuant, nasal, and the like.

Because a feature is distinctive in one or more segments does not necessarily make it so in all of them. As we saw earlier in this chapter, certain feature combinations make others predictable, as do sequential constraints. Voicing, for example, is distinctive for obstruents, but it is not for sonorants. This is the only feature which distinguishes [p] from [b] or [s] from [z], but it does not serve as the sole distinguishing feature which separates [a, u, m, r] from any other segment.

Some features never produce a contrast in a language. For obstruents in English, lip rounding, unlike voicing, is never distinctive. If we have a vowel that is [+round], the only consonant that can precede it is one that is [+round]. Thus, if we have a dental stop in the position [____om], we know that it will have lip rounding, although we cannot say whether it will be voiced [d] or voiceless [t]. Since either [t] or [d] can occur in the same position in [____om] or [____awn] or [____u], they are in contrast. Rounded and unrounded consonants do not share this freedom of occurrence. It is only in the places that unrounded consonants are prohibited that the rounded ones can occur, and vice versa. They are, therefore, said to **complement** each other, or to be in **complementary distribution.**

By letting X represent some particular environment and Y another, we can illustrate the difference between contrast and complementary distribution as follows:

	CONTRAST	COMPLEMENTARY DISTRIBUTION
X	Either [p] or [b]	Only rounded consonants
Y	Either [p] or [b]	Only unrounded consonants

So that our grammar will distinguish between distinctive and redundant features, we need to establish two levels of phonological representation, similar to underlying and surface structures in syntax. The level which includes all features, redundant as well as distinctive, is called the **phonetic level;** and symbols at this level are enclosed in square brackets such as [p]. Hence, at the phonetic level, we state the following information:

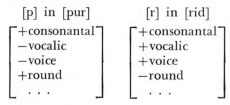

[p] in [pur]

$$\begin{bmatrix} +\text{consonantal} \\ -\text{vocalic} \\ -\text{voice} \\ +\text{round} \\ \quad \cdot \cdot \cdot \end{bmatrix}$$

[r] in [rid]

$$\begin{bmatrix} +\text{consonantal} \\ +\text{vocalic} \\ +\text{voice} \\ -\text{round} \\ \quad \cdot \cdot \cdot \end{bmatrix}$$

The ellipsis points indicate that other features would also be given in a complete representation; we are restricting ourselves to four for the present discussion.

There is a more abstract level, known as the **phonemic level,** at which only unpredictable features are listed. Symbols at this level are enclosed in slash marks: /p/. At the phonemic level we have only the following features given, from the four selected above:

/p/ in /pur/

$$\begin{bmatrix} +\text{consonantal} \\ -\text{vocalic} \\ -\text{voice} \\ \quad \cdot \cdot \cdot \end{bmatrix}$$

/r/ in /rid/

$$\begin{bmatrix} +\text{consonantal} \\ +\text{vocalic} \\ \quad \cdot \cdot \cdot \end{bmatrix}$$

Since lip rounding for consonants is predictable according to the nature of the following vowel, it will never be given at the phonemic level in English. For obstruents, voicing is unpredictable and, therefore, included at the phonemic level; liquids, however, are predictably [+voice], so this feature is not given for them.

We can compare the abstract phonemic level with the underlying level in syntax and the phonetic level with the surface structure. Just as we need transformational rules to relate the two levels in synytax, we need **phonological rules** to relate those in phonology. These will tell us, among other things, that a segment which is [+consonantal] is [+round] if the following vowel is [+round] and that a segment which is [+consonantal, +vocalic] is [+voice].

We can further illustrate phonemic and phonetic representation with the feature of aspiration. When a person says *pat,* he gives a puff of air with the [p], which can be felt if the hand is held in front of the mouth. We call this puff of air **aspiration.** The [b] in *bat,* however, is not aspirated. Examination of the stops shows that the pattern for aspiration runs like this:

ASPIRATED	UNASPIRATED
[p] pit	[b] bit
[t] Ted	[d] dead
[k] cap	[g] gap

The aspirated consonants [p, t, k] form the natural class of voiceless stops, and the unaspirated [b, d, g] are the voiced stops. To indicate aspiration, we can write the symbols like this: [pʰ, tʰ, kʰ]. Or with features we can add [+aspirated].

The addition of more examples shows that the voiceless stops are not always aspirated. In the following words, there is little or no aspiration on the first consonant:

[p] potato, potassium
[t] today, telegraphy
[k] commit, collect

In each of these words the voiceless stop precedes an unstressed vowel.

Another environment in which the voiceless stops are not aspirated can be seen in the following words:

[p] spit, spun, sprint, span
[t] stunt, strip, stack, stiff
[k] scuff, scrounge, skiff, skeptic

In the examples, the stop is preceded by [s].

Since aspiration is predictable in English stops, this feature will not be stated at the phonemic level. A phonological rule will add aspiration to segments which are [−continuant] and [−voice] when they precede a stressed vowel and are not preceded by [s]. Hence, derivations like the following will be found:

Phonemic level:	/pæt/	/bæt/	/pəlís/	/spok/
Aspiration rule:	pʰæt	———	———	———
Phonetic level:	[pʰæt]	[bæt]	[pəlís]	[spok]

The rule of aspiration does not apply to /bæt/ since /b/ is voiced. Although /p/ in /pəlís/ is a voiceless stop, it precedes an unstressed vowel; in /spok/ the /p/ is preceded by an /s/. In neither of these words, therefore, is aspiration applicable.

Some phonological rules apply to many languages, but others apply only to certain ones. Aspiration, for example, is the same in English and German, but it does not exist in the romance languages such as French, Spanish, and Italian. For these languages all stops are unaspirated, regardless of voicing and environment. In some languages such as Chinese and Hindi, aspirated and unaspirated stops are in contrast with each other; aspiration must therefore be indicated at the phonemic level for these languages, since it is not predictable.

To show that several phonological rules may be involved in a derivation, just as several transformations may be needed to convert an underlying to a surface structure, let us look at the following words:

Phonemic level:	/pul/	/kip/	/skræm/	/told/
Aspiration:	pʰul	kʰip	———	tʰold
Vowel length:	pʰu:l	———	skræ:m	tʰo:ld
Velarized [ɫ]:	pʰu:ɫ	———	———	tʰo:ɫd
Phonetic level:	[pʰu:ɫ]	[kʰip]	[skræ:m]	[tʰo:ɫd]

The ordering of the rules is not significant. Using features, we would not mention those of aspiration, length, or velarization at the phonemic level. Rules would add [+aspirated] or [+long] or [+velarized].

In this chapter we have seen several ways in which a feature may be redundant. Some features, such as voicing, are redundant in some segments (e.g., vowels and nasals) but distinctive in others (e.g., obstruents). A feature which is distinctive in some positions may not be in others. For example, at the end of a word in English both anterior and coronal are distinctive for nasals, but at the beginning the feature anterior is redundant since only anterior nasals occur in this position in the language. Finally, there are features such as aspiration and vocalic length which are always redundant in English. To distinguish between redundant and distinctive features, we have established two levels of representation: the phonemic and the phonetic. Phonological rules convert a representation from one level to the other.

Exercises

A. Name the feature or features which distinguish the following pairs of segments:

1. [g, k]   5. [p, f]   9. [i, ü]
2. [t, k]   6. [d, s]   10. [u, o]
3. [ð, z]   7. [i, ɪ]
4. [p, t]   8. [e, o]

B. Which of the following combinations are not possible for English?

1. $\begin{bmatrix} +\text{vocalic} \\ -\text{consonantal} \\ +\text{back} \\ +\text{strident} \end{bmatrix}$ 5. $\begin{bmatrix} -\text{vocalic} \\ +\text{consonantal} \\ +\text{anterior} \\ +\text{strident} \end{bmatrix}$

2. $\begin{bmatrix} +\text{vocalic} \\ -\text{consonantal} \\ +\text{tense} \\ +\text{anterior} \end{bmatrix}$ 6. $\begin{bmatrix} +\text{vocalic} \\ +\text{consonantal} \\ +\text{strident} \end{bmatrix}$

3. $\begin{bmatrix} +\text{vocalic} \\ -\text{consonantal} \\ -\text{tense} \\ +\text{back} \end{bmatrix}$ 7. $\begin{bmatrix} -\text{vocalic} \\ -\text{consonantal} \\ +\text{nasal} \end{bmatrix}$

4. $\begin{bmatrix} +\text{vocalic} \\ -\text{consonantal} \\ -\text{back} \\ +\text{back} \end{bmatrix}$ 8. $\begin{bmatrix} -\text{vocalic} \\ +\text{consonantal} \\ +\text{nasal} \\ -\text{strident} \end{bmatrix}$

C. What features are distinctive for the following English segments?

1. [n]   3. [l]   5. [č]   7. [ʊ]
2. [b]   4. [ð]   6. [æ]   8. [i]

D. At the beginning of a morpheme in English the only possible obstruent clusters are [sp, st, sk]. There are also clusters of [sp, st, sk] plus liquid or glide. Determine which of these exist. Which ones are found only in a few borrowed words?

E. In English, which of the following combinations are possible at the beginning of a morpheme?

1. obstruent + obstruent
2. obstruent + liquid
3. nasal + glide
4. liquid + liquid
5. glide + obstruent

F. All of the following combinations are possible at the beginning of a morpheme in English, but not for all members of the classes involved. For example, *obstruent + obstruent* is permitted only with [s] as the first and [p, t, k] as the second member. List the possibilities for the following:

1. obstruent + glide
2. obstruent + nasal
3. obstruent + liquid
4. nasal + glide

G. Are there any of the following combinations which may occur at the beginning of an English word but not at the end, and vice versa? Are there any that do not occur in either place?

1. [ts]   3. [ŋk]   5. [kw]
2. [py]   4. [vs]   6. [bk]

H. Determine which obstruent clusters may occur in English at the end of a morpheme. Notice that *tax* provides an example of final [ks], but *packs* does not since [k] and [s] are not members of the same morpheme.

I. When words are borrowed from a language with a different set of sequential constraints from those in the borrowing language, adjustments are usually made. Explain what happened to the following initial clusters when the words were incorporated into English:

1. [bd] bdellium   4. [mb] mbakara "buckra"
2. [ps] psalm, psychiatry   5. [ts] tsar
3. [pt] Ptolemy, ptomaine

J. In English which vowels may occur before [ŋ]? Which features of vowels do not contrast in this position?

Suggested Reading

See the list at the end of Chapter 12.

Phonological Rules

In Chapter 11, we saw the need for at least two levels of phonological representation if our grammar is to include the information which a native speaker possesses. The phonetic level includes all features, whether distinctive or redundant; the phonemic level gives only the distinctive or unpredictable features. Phonological rules relate the two levels.

It should not be assumed that a phonetic transcription is a faithful representation of an act of speech. Machines which make visual records of the speech signal show that a person who is speaking does not produce discrete sounds, but rather a continuous flow of varying sound. In saying *pony*, the [p] and [o] are tightly merged. Lip rounding and other features of [o] are found in the [p], and the quality of the [o] is influenced by the nature of the aspirated stop [p]. In the actual acoustic signal it is not possible to say where the [p] ends and the [o] starts. The [o] is also affected by the following [n], being lengthened and taking on a nasal quality. The [n], in turn, is influenced by both the preceding [o] and the following [i]. If phonetic transcription were a faithful representation of the acoustic signal, it would not exist as discrete symbols, but rather as something like a line graph.

Furthermore, phonetic transcriptions ignore differences in speech that result from physical causes, such as the particular makeup of a person's vocal apparatus which makes his speech recognizable even when he is speaking over the radio, talking on the telephone, or standing in another room away from the listener. Phonetic transcriptions do not include the information which tells us the speaker's sex or approximate age or state of health. Nor do they mark clicks made by false teeth or distortions produced by food in the mouth. Machines which record speech acts provide evidence that a person repeating a sentence twenty times does not say it exactly the same way twice, yet a transcription does not show these differences.

A phonetic transcription is more like a written description of a scene than a photograph in that it contains what the transcriber considers to be important rather than a faithful representation of all that is actually said. This is not intended as an apology for phonetics. Quite to the contrary, a transcription system which treated every utterance of "Where is your hat?" as a unique entity would include so much information as to be unusable for linguistic purposes. Unless there is something linguistically significant about the differences, a phonetician will transcribe "Where is your hat?" spoken by twenty different people as though the utterances were identical. His concern is that the people are not saying "Where is your cat?" or "Where is *your* hat?"

Although a phonetic transcription is slightly removed from the physical speech act, it comes closer to it than any other representation linguists use. The phonemic representation is still more selective, including only features which cannot be predicted by phonological rules. In the last chapter, we saw certain types of information which can be supplied by rules. In this one, we will examine a wider variety of examples.

Past Tenses of Verbs

In the chapters on syntax, we did not spell out the pronunciations for past tenses of verbs, but rather left them in the form *Past kick* and the like. There are two ways that we could convert *Past kick* into *kicked*. One is to give the past tense of each verb as part of its dictionary entry; the other is to provide a rule by which past-tense forms are spelled out. The latter is possible only if there is a system which determines the final form. If every verb is idiosyncratic in its past-tense form, we have no choice other than to use the first alternative and give the past tense as part of the dictionary entry for every verb.

If we look at the following forms, there seems to be no system:

Infinitive	*Past Tense*
climb	climbed
sleep	slept
rise	rose
sing	sang
be	was
go	went

We have to ask ourselves whether this list is representative of the verbs in English, and we immediately decide that the answer is no. If we opened any book at a random page and started listing the verbs until we came to some significant number, say three hundred, we would discover that most of them are like *climb* with a past tense spelled *-ed*. Although a more extensive analysis of forms such as *rose, sang,* and the like would perhaps provide some degree of predictability for these past-tense forms, that would take us beyond the scope of this chapter. We will, therefore, treat all verbs which do not form past tense by adding *-ed* as exceptions. In this way we will be following the practice of most dictionaries.

The reader may wonder about those cases in which the regular past tense doubles the preceding consonant before adding *-ed,* as the *p* in *slipped.* A brief inspection of other suffixes added to *slip* shows that the *p* is doubled before any suffix beginning with a vowel (*slipping, slippery*), not just those which designate past tense. We will, therefore, ignore the doubled letters since they are not brought about because of the past-tense morpheme but because of spelling conventions used to indicate that the preceding vowel is lax.

Does the spelling *-ed* reflect a uniform pronunciation in all verbs? If we start with *headed, decided, guided, trotted, plotted, dated,* there does seem to be uniformity. The spelling represents a vowel plus [d], and this vowel is [ə] or [ɪ], depending upon the dialect of the speaker. Because of the spelling, some people may think they are pronouncing the ending [ɛd], but this would give a highly artificial, nonstandard pronunciation not found natively in any variety of English. We could add a great many more words to the six we gave earlier in this paragraph to lend support to our conclusion that the past-tense ending *-ed* stands for [əd] or [ɪd], but we should be as wary of proofs in phonology as we were in syntax. Are there counter-examples?

The words *leased* and *saved* indicate that there are. In *leased* ([list]), the ending *-ed* stands for [t], and in *saved* ([sevd]) it stands for [d]. These, of course, may be rare examples, but a bit of searching shows that they are fairly common. In fact, [əd]/[ɪd], [t], and [d] are all frequently occurring pronunciations for the past-tense ending, and these are the only pronunciations which share this status. We should now see whether there is a system that determines which of the three pronunciations will be found.

Just because we know the pronunciations for the past tenses of the verbs in the preceding paragraphs does not prove that there is a system that determines them. We could have learned each past tense as an idiosyncratic property of each verb, although the number of verbs in the language makes this possibility suspicious. One way of testing to see whether there is a system or not is to select verbs which various speakers of English have not heard before. With verbs currently in the language there is no assurance that we have not heard the past-tense forms, even if we select only uncommon words. The only way we can be sure that we are dealing with words whose past tenses we have never heard before is to select potential words that do not currently exist in the language. So, let us use [klep, kleg, klet]. If there is no system, no one will have any idea about how the past tenses should be pronounced; each person will guess, and there will be no agreement among speakers. Fluent speakers of English do agree, however, on how the past tenses should be pronounced even though they have not heard them before for these words: [klept, klegd, kletəd/kletɪd]. This indicates that there is a system even though a person may not be able to state it.

The fact that we know how the past tenses of [klep, kleg, klet] should be pronounced indicates that such factors as meaning, transitivity, and the like are not the ones that decide whether the past is [t], [d], or [əd]. Since the three words are alike except for their final segments, it seems likely that the final segment is the determining factor. If we add words ending in [p], we find that they, like [klep], all have past tenses in [t]: *clap, slip, drop, grope, mope, snipe.* Those ending in [g] all take past tenses in [d]: *lag, beg, hug, brag.* And those ending in [t] take [əd] or [ɪd], according to the speaker: *trot, pleat, state, shout, loot.*

Let us now see if we can narrow the system further than just stating the last segment and predicting the past-tense ending from it. What specifically in the last segment influences the selection? Why do we have [t] after [p] and not [d] or [əd]? Extending our words for investigation will help:

[əd]/[ɪd]		[t]			[d]	
[t]	trot, state	[p]	clap, slip		[b]	stub, stab
[d]	dread, collide	[k]	lack, bake		[g]	lag, beg
		[f]	stuff, leaf		[v]	shove, shave
		[s]	pass, pace		[z]	hose, realize
		[š]	wish, dash		[ž]	garage, camouflage
		[č]	watch, hatch		[j]	judge, cage
					[ð]	bathe, loathe
					[m]	comb, thumb
					[e]	stay, play

With [t] and [d] as the last segment in a verb, we can soon discover why we do not pronounce the past tense as just [t] or [d]:

Infinitive	*Past*	
[trat]	*[tratt]	*[tratd]
[plit]	*[plitt]	*[plitd]
[stet]	*[stett]	*[stetd]
[šawt]	*[šawtt]	*[šawtd]
[lut]	*[lutt]	*[lutd]

Since English has no double consonants in pronunciation, the double [tt] at the end of the word would not be possible in the system. No one would hear the difference between [trat] and [tratt], thereby making it impossible for the listener to recognize the difference between the infinitive and the past tense. Similarly, the ending [td] violates a restriction in English on which obstruent clusters are possible. To avoid the prohibited final combinations [tt] and [td], we add a vowel: [ə] or [ɪ], according to the dialect of the speaker.

For the verbs whose past tenses are pronounced [t] or [d], it takes very little investigation to determine that the voiceless [t] follows voiceless segments and that the voiced [d] follows those that are voiced. The system is logical. If we had found the reverse situation—[d] after voiceless segments and [t] after those that are voiced—we would have had trouble explaining why the system works as it does.

With aspiration and vocalic length, phonological rules add features that are predictable. They should likewise provide the surface pronunciations of past tenses of regular verbs, since these are also predictable. At the underlying[1] level, all we need to give is *Past*. The following rules will provide the surface pronunciations:

[1] In this derivation and those that follow, we will be using the terms *underlying* and *surface* instead of *phonemic* and *phonetic*. There are three reasons for this less technical terminology. First, *phonemic* has been used with varying meanings in linguistics

1. Replace *Past* + *Verb* with *Verb* + [*d*].
2. If the verb ends in [t] or [d], add the vowel [ə] or [ɪ] before the past-tense ending.
3. Change the past-tense [d] to [t] if the preceding segment has the feature [−voice].

Here are a few derivations:

Underlying:	Past + /pes/	Past + /sayt/	Past + /muv/
Rule 1	pes + d	sayt + d	muv + d
Rule 2	——	sayt + əd	——
Rule 3	pes + t	——	——
Surface:	[pest]	[saytəd]	[muvd]
Spelling:	paced	sighted	moved

Other phonological rules such as aspiration are also applicable between the underlying and surface levels, but we have concentrated on just those which are relevant to the present discussion.

The third rule, which makes the last two segments agree in voicing, involves a process known as **assimilation**. If one segment becomes like another in one or more features, we say that it assimilates to it. In our rule, the [d] assimilates in voicing to the preceding segment, becoming voiceless if it follows a voiceless segment and remaining voiced if it follows one that is voiced. Another example of voicing assimilation in English can be seen in *raspberry*. If pronounced [ræspbɛri], the third segment is an [s], agreeing with the following [p] in being voiceless. However, if the [p] is lost, we get [ræzbɛri], with a [z] which agrees in voicing with the following [b]. Similarly, *louse, worth, north* all end with voiceless consonants. If a suffix beginning with a voiced segment is added—*lousy, worthy, northern*—the final consonant assimilates in voicing to the following segment, becoming voiced in each of these cases.

The rules for providing the surface forms of the past tenses of verbs are like those we encountered in the last chapter in that they give information which is predictable. They are also different in some ways. Instead of just adding redundant features, they actually give the phonetic form [d] to an abstract element; they add a segment, [ə], which is not present at the underlying level; and they change features such as [+voice] to [−voice]. In spite of the fact that these rules are more powerful than those in the last chapter, they still serve to provide predictable information.

Noun Plurals and Other -s Endings

For most verbs, dictionaries give no information about the form for the past tense. They give past tenses for such verbs as *go, swim,* and *freeze,* but

---

publications. The term *underlying* should be less confusing to the reader with some familiarity with phonology than *phonemic* would be. Second, as in syntax, research has not progressed far enough for us to be confident that we have reached the ultimate phonemic level. Finally, many features are ignored in each derivation so that we can concentrate on those rules which are involved in the immediate discussion. The representations marked *underlying* are, therefore, more abstract than surface forms, but they are not necessarily ultimate "phonemic" representations.

say nothing about those which are formed by the rules we discussed in the preceding section. In pronunciation this means representing the past-tense morpheme as [d], adding a vowel if it follows a dental stop, and finally having it assimilate in voicing to the preceding segment. In spelling the ending -*ed* is added. We will not debate whether such words as *hope,* which already end in -*e,* drop this final vowel before adding -*ed* or whether only -*d* is added. Whatever the case, the rules both for spelling and for pronunciation are systematic and fairly simple.

A parallel case can be seen with noun plurals. Dictionaries give plurals for only a handful of words: *sheep, ox, foot, criterion,* and the like. All others are supposedly predictable by rule. If we try forming plurals of a few potential words, we see that there is indeed a system at work. For *glape, glabe, glace* we give *glapes, glabes, glaces,* all with the spelling -*s.* The pronunciations, however, are not uniform: [gleps, glebz, glesəz/glesɪz].

We suspect that there is something in the pronunciation of the noun which allows us to predict the plural form. If this form depended upon the meaning of the noun or such features as animateness, gender, or concreteness, we would not be able to give the plural for a potential word such as [glep] until we knew its meaning or features. The fact that [glep] and [gleb] differ only in the last segment makes us suspect that this is what determines the pronunciation of the plural. Since [p] and [b] differ only in voicing, it seems possible that the phonetic form of the plural morpheme assimilates to the final segment. The two voiceless obstruents [p] and [s] come together, as do the voiced [b] and [z].

If we add other final segments to see which plural form follows, we find that our observations about assimilation hold:

Plural in [s]		*Plural in* [z]		*Plural in* [əz]/[ɪz]	
[p]	top, map	[b]	knob, rib	[s]	guess, loss
[t]	rat, route	[d]	fad, need	[z]	maze, phrase
[k]	ache, tack	[g]	log, rug	[š]	wish, bush
[f]	laugh, puff	[v]	cave, hive	[ž]	garage, mirage
[θ]	myth, faith	[ð]	lathe	[č]	patch, witch
		[n]	nun, tone	[ǰ]	hedge, cage
		[r]	car, tour		
		[i]	bee, knee		

All of the nouns with plurals in [s] end in voiceless segments, and those which take [z] end in segments that are voiced. If we completed the list under [z] by adding the remaining sonorants which can end a morpheme, we would see that this observation continues to be valid. The reader should supply additional words in each line to verify that the words given are truly representative.

We still have the third column to explain. Why do we not add just [s] after the voiceless [s, š, č] and just [z] after the voiced [z, ž, ǰ]? If we attempt this with the illustrative words in the last paragraph, we see that the result is indeed pronounceable. The problem is that English does not permit double consonants for distinctive purposes. The sequence [ss] at the end of a word sounds the same as a single [s] which is prolonged. It has often been said that people could not hear the difference between [mez] and [mezz] in speech at a normal rate. In fact, they probably could if they had learned to listen for this difference. Since the system of English phonology does not include distinctive double consonants, no one has learned to listen for the difference between [mez] and [mezz]. For words ending in [š, ž, č, ǰ] it would be almost impossible to maintain a plural in [s, z] since assimilation would almost invariably convert these into segments identical to those which preceded. For this reason, we add a vowel—[ə] or [ɪ] according to the dialect of the speaker—to provide a phonetic structure in accordance with the restrictions of English.

The six segments [s, z, š, ž, č, ǰ] constitute a natural class, but we need to define it. Four of them are fricatives and two are affricates; the feature [+continuant], therefore, does not belong to all of them. They are all [+strident], but so are [v, f], which do not belong to this group. If we add the feature [+coronal], we can exclude [v, f]. Therefore this combination, [+strident, +coronal], defines the natural class of segments for which we insert a vowel before adding the plural suffix.

We can state rules for providing the surface realization of the plural morpheme in the same fashion as we did for past tenses:

1. Replace *Pl* with [z].
2. Insert [ə] or [ɪ] if this plural suffix follows a segment that is [+strident, +coronal].
3. Change the feature [+voice] to [−voice] in [z] if it follows a segment that has [−voice].

These rules are almost identical to those for forming past tenses. The first one differs only in the segment which is added: [d] for past tense, [z] for plural. The second adds a vowel if this segment is similar to the one it precedes, and the third makes the last two segments agree in voicing. The last rule is part of one which exists in English and a large number of other languages, making obstruent clusters agree in voicing.

For illustrations of the rules for plural formation, we can look at the following derivations:

Underlying:	/layt/ + Pl	/mez/ + Pl	/fæd/ + Pl
Rule 1	layt + z	mez + z	fæd + z
Rule 2	———	mez + əz	———
Rule 3	layt + s	———	———
Surface:	[layts]	[mezəz]	[fædz]
Spelling:	lights	mazes	fads

By using only *Pl* at the underlying level and three phonological rules, we are able to give the phonetic form for all nouns in the language which form their plurals regularly.

The rules are applicable to morphemes other than noun plurals. Listing representative verbs shows that the same system applies for present-tense verbs with third-person singular subjects (*he sings, he seeks,* and the like):

Present in [s]	*Present in* [z]	*Present in* [əz]/[ɪz]
[p] sip, develop	[b] rub, stab	[s] face, pass
[t] get, shout	[d] lead, cloud	[z] close, buzz
[k] shake, hike	[g] shrug, beg	[š] wish, push
[f] stuff, laugh	[v] shove, pave	[ž] camouflage, garage

We do not need to make the list any longer to prove our point. The reader can easily add other examples if he chooses. The following phonetic forms can be derived by our rules:

Underlying:	*Present* + /sɪt/	*Present* + /pliz/	*Present* + /lid/
Rule 1a	sɪt + z	pliz + z	lid + z
Rule 2	————	pliz + ɪz	————
Rule 3	sɪt + s		
Surface:	[sɪts]	[plizɪz]	[lidz]
Spelling:	sits	pleases	leads

This gives the desired forms *he sits, he pleases, he leads.* We give the first rule the number *1a* instead of just *1* because it rewrites *Present* instead of *Plural* as [s].

The same system can be seen in the possessives of nouns:

Possessive in [s]	*Possessive in* [z]	*Possessive in* [əz]/[ɪz]
[p] Philip's, ape's	[b] club's, Deb's	[s] Bess's, Jess's
[t] Kate's, rat's	[d] Dad's, Floyd's	[z] Jones's, Liles's
[k] lake's, Jake's	[g] hág's, Meg's	[š] Flash's, Rush's
[f] wife's, Ralph's	[v] Dave's, love's	[ž] Butch's, witch's

Again, this listing could be extended, and we would do so if this were a new process which no one had investigated before. Derivations for possessives differ from those for noun plurals only in that we write *Poss* as [z] instead of *Pl:*

Underlying:	/dev/ + Poss	/ruθ/ + Poss	/bɛs/ + Poss
Rule 1b	dev + z	ruθ + z	bɛs + z
Rule 2	————	————	bɛs + ɪz
Rule 3	————	ruθ + s	————
Surface:	[devz]	[ruθs]	[bɛsɪz]
Spelling:	Dave's	Ruth's	Bess's

There are still other morphemes which can be accommodated with the rules for plurals: contractions of *is* and *has.* We find the same pattern here. After strident coronal segments we get [əz] or [ɪz]; after other segments we get [s] or [z], agreeing in voicing with the preceding segment. Hence, *Ralph is* without contraction is pronounced [rælf ɪz]; with contraction we get [rælfs], with an [s]. Here are a few other examples:

is *with* [s]	is *with* [z]	is *with* [əz]/[ɪz]
[p] cup's, top's	[b] stub's, knob's	[s] dress's, race's
[t] boot's, bite's	[d] stand's, load's	[z] maze's, hose's
[k] lake's, bike's	[g] bug's, rogue's	[š] wish's, flash's

There may be some question as to whether there really is a contraction after strident coronal segments, since it does not differ in pronunciation from the unstressed, uncontracted *is*. For the sake of uniformity, we are including it.

By having both underlying and surface levels of representation, we are able to state explicitly the phonological information which is predictable in a language. In this way we are stating the system which governs the formation of plurals or past tenses or possessives. This type of representation also accounts for the native speaker's understanding that identical phonetic forms may have different meanings, which is parallel to his recognition of ambiguity in surface syntactic structures. The phonetic form [pæts], for example, can have any of the following meanings:

12.1   **Plural:** There are two *Pats* working in the library.
12.2   **Possessive:** This is *Pat's* sandwich.
12.3   **Present tense:** She hates anyone who *pats* her on the head.
12.4   **Contraction:** *Pat's* in the attic.

The exact meaning, as determined by the syntactic structure, is represented at the underlying level as */pæt/ + Plural, /pæt/ + Possessive, Present + /pæt/,* or */pæt/ + Present + be.* Although all appear phonetically as [pæts], at the underlying level they are distinct, according to the meanings of the morphemes.

Another feature which is stated at the underlying level but not at the phonetic is the morphemic composition of words. The phonetic [tæks] can be one morpheme (*tax*) or two (*tacks*). At the underlying level they are distinguished as */tæks/* for *tax* and */tæk/ + Pl* for *tacks*. Another example of merger at the phonetic level can be seen in [mæks], which is derived from */mæk/ + Possessive (Mack's)* or from the single morpheme */mæks/ (Max).* We can illustrate these forms as follows:

Underlying:	/tæks/	/tæk/ + Pl	/mæks/	/mæk/ + Poss
Rules	———	tæk + s	———	mæk + s
Surface:	[tæks]	[tæks]	[mæks]	[mæks]
Spelling:	tax	tacks	Max	Mack's

It should be noticed that the spelling is closer to the underlying level than to the phonetic. In syntax we saw that one surface form may be recognized by the native speaker as ambiguous, with two or more meanings. We accounted for this understanding by giving a unique underlying structure for each meaning in a sentence such as *He gave the report to the man in the car.*

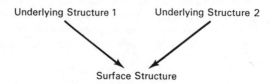

We do the same thing for different words which have the same phonetic form but different morphemic composition, as *tax* and *tacks*:

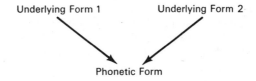

The underlying level in phonology, like that in syntax, expresses the information which the speaker and hearer understand about the sentence or word; the phonetic level, like the surface in syntax, gives the actual form in which it appears.

Nasal Assimilation

As we saw in the preceding sections, the process by which one segment becomes like a neighboring one is known as assimilation. We saw the process illustrated with final [z] and [d] becoming voiceless to agree with the preceding segment.

Further examples of assimilation can be found in nasals. Normally the three nasals of English are in contrast, as in *tam, tan, tang*. It is only at the end of a morpheme, however, that we have full contrast. At the beginning of a morpheme, only the anterior nasals [m] and [n] occur. Before an obstruent, a nasal is even further restricted, as we can see from the following words:

[m] embalm, complain, comfort, embarrass, bombast
[n] enter, sand, ensue, enthusiasm, insure
[ŋ] language, link, sunk, linger, hunger

In the examples, only [m] appears before labials, [n] before dentals, alveolars, and palatals, and [ŋ] before velars. This seems logical, since [m] is labial and [ŋ] is velar. The alveolar [n] naturally occurs before dentals and alveolars; since English does not have a palatal nasal, this position is also filled by [n] in *insure* and before other palatals. There are a few exceptions such as *convict* and *conform,* and some words such as *congress* and *congregate* have alternate pronunciations with [n] or [ŋ]. It should be noticed that in each of these cases the nasal and the following obstruent belong to different syllables and morphemes. At the underlying level it is not necessary to specify the features anterior and coronal for nasals which precede obstruents within a single morpheme. Hence, we can use /N/, a nasal segment unspecified for point of obstruction, and assimilation rules will indicate which one is needed for the phonetic level:

Underlying:	/læNd/	/slʌNbər/	/fɪNgər/	/ræn/	/rum/	/lʌŋ/
Assimilation	lænd	slʌmbər	fɪŋgər	———	———	———
Surface:	[lænd]	[slʌmbər]	[fɪŋgər]	[ræn]	[rum]	[lʌŋ]
Spelling:	land	slumber	finger	ran	room	lung

It should be noted that this rule applies only to nasals which precede obstruents. For words like *ran, room, lung, noon,* and *moon,* the features anterior and coronal have to be given at the underlying level. If we have a

potential word /yeNd/, we know that the nasal must be [n], giving [yend].
However, for nasals in other positions we need more information. /Ned/
could be phonetically [ned] or [med], and /yeN/ could be [yen], [yem], or
[yeŋ]. Nasal assimilation provides an example of features which are predictable in certain environments but not in others.

In Spanish there are two nasals that occur at the beginning of a word:

[m] mismo, mujer, marzo
[n] nieve, noche, nuestro

Within a word and before a vowel, three nasals may be found:

[m] domingo, afirmativo, amigo
[n] animal, bonito, semana
[ñ] montaña, niña, año

In these two positions there are three possible nasals on the surface. Since
[m, n, ñ] are in contrast, they are also found at the underlying level.

Like English and a great many other languages, Spanish has an assimilation rule which makes nasals agree in point of obstruction with a following
obstruent. In this position, [m, n, ŋ] may occur, but not [ñ]:

[m] siempre, también, tiempo, cambiar
[n] pensar, centro, aprender, once, caliente, ancho
[ŋ] nunca, domingo, angosto, banco, blanco, cinco

Although there is variation among dialects and styles of Spanish,[2] for some
varieties of the language the rule of nasal assimilation applies more generally than it does in English. Namely, the rule applies across morpheme
boundaries so that forms such as *conform* and *convict* do not occur. The
rule even applies across word boundaries, particularly with *un* ("a") and the
following noun. Although the following noun phrases all have the article
spelled *un,* the actual nasal is the one given in brackets:

[m] un banco, un billete, un palo, un partido
[n] un tren, un sombrero, un dormitorio
[ŋ] un gato, un color, un club

The article *un* can, therefore, be represented /uN/ at the underlying level.
The surface pronunciation of the nasal is predictable from the initial segment in the following word.

Apart from the palatal nasal [ñ], which exists in Spanish but not in
English, there is one major difference in the system of nasals. Both languages have [m, n, ŋ] on the surface. However, in Spanish [ŋ] never occurs
except before an obstruent, making its surface realization always predictable.
Spanish, therefore, has only /m, n, ñ/ at the underlying level, unlike English, which has /m, n, ŋ/.[3] We can compare the two systems as follows:

---

[2] See Harris (1969:8–18) for a detailed discussion.

[3] Some accounts of English phonology do not give underlying /ŋ/. Chomsky and
Halle (1968), for example, give the final segments in words like *sing* and *wrong* underlying /-Ng/ and later delete the /g/ after nasal assimilation has taken place.

	Spanish	English
Underlying:	/m, n, ñ/	/m, n, ŋ/
Surface:	[m, n, ñ, ŋ]	[m, n, ŋ]

Before obstruents we find only underlying /N/ in both languages.

With nasal assimilation we are giving different representations at the underlying level than at the phonetic, partly because we wish to show that different phonetic forms such as [um, un, uŋ] are related. More importantly, we are showing that a system exists in the language and are stating it.

Vowel Harmony

As can be shown with nasals, some segments may contrast in certain environments but be predictable in others. At the end of a morpheme in English, any of the nasals may occur, but medially we find only those which agree in the features anterior and coronal with the following obstruent. Also, in noun and verb endings the feature of voicing is predictable when two obstruents come together in a cluster. In other positions, this feature is contrastive.

Normally, vowels are unpredictable in a morpheme. In English, for example, we may have any of the vowels of the language in words of one syllable: *beat, bit, bait, bet, bat, boot, boat, bought, but, bite, bout,* and the like. If we did not completely specify each vowel at the underlying level, we would have no way of obtaining the surface form. A representation like /b___t/ with an unspecified vowel would not be possible. Similarly, for words of more than one syllable in English, there are no restrictions on which vowels may follow or precede others. We may have the same vowel following, or it may be different. It is only because we know the following words that we are able to give the vowels which have been omitted: *bull___t, comm___nt, compl___n.* If we take potential words, we are not able to supply the missing vowels: *dogg___p, fl___ket, splant___se.*

In Turkish a slightly different situation is found. For words of only one syllable, the vowel is as unpredictable as it is in English. When there are two or more syllables, however, some features of all vowels but the first can be provided by a rule which is known as **vowel harmony.**

The Turkish vowel system has only two heights: high and non-high:

	$\begin{bmatrix} -\text{back} \\ -\text{round} \end{bmatrix}$	$\begin{bmatrix} -\text{back} \\ +\text{round} \end{bmatrix}$	$\begin{bmatrix} +\text{back} \\ -\text{round} \end{bmatrix}$	$\begin{bmatrix} +\text{back} \\ +\text{round} \end{bmatrix}$
[+high]	i	ü	ɨ	u
[−high]	e	ö	a	o

We are classifying [a] as merely [−high], rather than low, thereby permitting us to merge mid and low into one category.

Although there are a few well-defined exceptions, we will be concentrating here just on the regularities of the system, in the same way as we ignored such English plurals as *geese* and *children.* In Turkish the first vowel in a word is freely selected, but all others in that word agree with it in the feature back. Hence, after a front vowel only other front vowels may follow:

emek   "bread"
mürekkep   "ink"
köpek   "dog"

Back vowels are followed only by other back vowels:

uzatmak   "to reach"
dolap   "cupboard"
dokuz   "nine"

The word for *ink* is *mürekkep,* with all front vowels. A word such as **mü-rakkup* would be impossible since [ü] is front but the other two vowels are back. Similarly, *uzatmak* exists with all back vowels, but **uzitmek* would not be possible with the front [i] and [e] following the back [u].

In addition to agreeing in backness, stem and suffix vowels in Turkish agree in rounding. After an unrounded vowel, only other unrounded vowels may occur. Adding this restriction to the one on backness, we see that the front unrounded [i, e] may be followed only by other front unrounded vowels, namely [i, e]:

"he went"   gitti   *gittü
"master"   efendi   *eföndu

Back unrounded vowels are followed by other back unrounded vowels; i.e., [ɨ] and [a] may be followed only by [ɨ] and [a]:

"I took"   aldɨm   *aldum
"Ankara"   Ankara   *Anköru

With rounded vowels, the situation is slightly more complex. They are followed by high rounded vowels, as would be expected, but also by low unrounded vowels:

"big"   büyük
"neighbor"   komşu
"Friday"   cumā

Except for this slight variation, all vowels in a Turkish word agree with the first one in the features back and round.

Since Turkish is a language with case endings on the nouns, the process of vowel harmony is found here especially. The dative ending is [e] after front vowels, [a] after back. Since these vowels are low, they can follow either rounded or unrounded vowels:

Front

tren	"train"	trene	"to the train"
köprüler	"the bridges"	köprülere	"to the bridges"

Back

adam	"man"	adama	"to the man"
kɨz	"girl"	kɨza	"to the girl"

The genitive case ending is a high vowel plus [n]. If the first vowel is front and unrounded, the ending is [in]:

evler   "the houses"   evlerin   "of the houses"

After front rounded vowels, the ending contains the front rounded vowel [ü], making the ending [ün]:

göz   "eye"   gözün   "of the eye"

Since back vowels are followed by those that are back, we find the back rounded [u] after back rounded vowels:

yol   "road"   yolun   "of the road"

Finally, back unrounded vowels are followed by the back unrounded [ɨ] in the suffix [ɨn]:

adam   "man"   adamɨn   "the man's"

A description of Turkish phonology would not specify the features back and round for vowels in inflectional suffixes since these are determined by the features of the first vowel in the word. Only the feature high would be given at the phonemic level since it alone is unpredictable.

Languages which have vowel harmony present an example of another segment which is predictable in certain environments but not in others. Like nasals which precede obstruents, vowels in Turkish and certain other languages are predictable if they are not in the first syllable of a word. Since this is part of the system which the speakers of these languages know, it should be accommodated in the grammars which are written for these languages.

Phonetic Alternation with Palatals

At the phonetic level there are often two or more sounds such as [l] and [ɫ] or [t] and [tʰ] which are related in a single segment at the underlying level. Features such as aspiration and velarization never provide contrast in English, and the merger at the underlying level is readily understandable. Other features such as voice, anterior, coronal, round, and front may contrast in certain environments but be redundant in others.

Two segments which normally contrast at both the phonetic and underlying levels are [s] and [š]:

[s]	[š]
sip	ship
sue	shoe
sigh	shy
bass	bash
lease	leash
sass	sash

It is clear that there should be a distinction between [s] and [š] at both levels since we need to show that such words as *sigh* and *shy* are unrelated. Yet, the following pairs of words present a problem:

[s]	[š]
face	facial
press	pressure
compress	compression
race	racial
grace	gracious
Greece	Grecian

Whereas there is no reason we should wish to relate pairs such as *sip* and *ship* or *sue* and *shoe*, we would like to show that *face* and *facial* are related words.

The use of regular spelling hides the problem. From the standpoint of pronunciation we are dealing with pairs such as [fes] and [fešəl] or [prɛs] and [prɛšər]. Using a plus mark to designate morpheme boundaries, we can rewrite the pairs under consideration as follows:

[s]	[š]
[fes]	[feš + əl]
[prɛs]	[prɛš + ər]
[kəmprɛs]	[kəmprɛš + ən]
[res]	[reš + əl]
[gres]	[greš + əs]
[gris]	[griš + ən]

The native speaker recognizes such pairs as [fes] and [feš] as related, but our grammar as we have developed it to this point does not provide this information. Since [sɪp] and [šɪp] are unrelated morphemes, contrasting with [s] and [š], there is every reason to expect [fes] and [feš] to be unrelated as well.

In syntax, we saw that information which the native speaker understands is included at the underlying level; similarly, we should expect to explain the similarity between [fes] and [feš] at some level. To do this, we have three possibilities: (1) give both words /s/ at the underlying level, (2) give both of them /š/, or (3) give them some third representation. These possibilities can be illustrated like this.

	1		2		3	
Underlying:	/fes/	/fes + yəl/	/feš/	/feš + yəl/	/fe?/	/fe? + yəl/
Rule	——	feš	fes	——	fes	feš
Surface:	[fes]	[fešəl]	[fes]	[fešəl]	[fes]	[fešəl]

Whichever solution we accept, we are showing the relationship by giving both forms the same representation at the underlying level. (The /y/ in the suffix will be justified presently.)

The third solution has little to recommend it in this case. If [s] and [š] were radically different sounds, we might select for the underlying representation a third which is related to both of them and from which both can be derived; but they differ only in that [s] is [+anterior] and [š] is [−anterior]. Both are obstruent, continuant, strident, voiceless, and so on. Any third sound that we might select for the underlying level would be totally ad hoc and would complicate the description unnecessarily. We are not ruling out solution three for all problems, but just for the one under consideration.

The first two solutions are more attractive. In fact, they are similar to those we examined in the last chapter. The only difference is that whereas [p] and [pʰ] never contrast in English, [s] and [š] do in some morphemes.

If we select the second solution, we will need a rule which will change /š/ to [s]. Under what circumstances would such a rule be applicable? Obviously it is not an unrestricted rule, or we would never find [š] at the phonetic level. Such a rule applied across the board would provide derivations like these:

Underlying:	/feš/	/feš + yəl/	/preš/	/preš + yər/	/šip/	/šʌv/
[s] *rule:*	fes	fes + yəl	pres	pres + yər	sip	sʌv
Surface:	[fes]	[fesəl]	[pres]	[presər]	[sip]	[sʌv]

Whereas this rule would provide the desired [fes] and [pres], it would give the wrong results for [fešəl] and [prešər]. It would give the nonexisting word [sʌv] instead of [šʌv]. The phonetic form [sip] is the English word *seep,* but this derivation would derive *seep* and *sheep* from the same source, as well as give them the same pronunciation at the phonetic level.

We can avoid the problems with *sheep* and *shove* if we restrict the rule to /š/ at the end of a morpheme. Further restricting it to those cases in which a suffix does not follow makes it inapplicable for *facial* and *pressure.* So far, so good; but what about these additional cases: *fish, flush, push, rash?* Each of these words has /š/ at the end of the morpheme, and no suffix follows. There is no way we can derive phonetic *face* and *press* from underlying /š/ and not complicate the situation for those words which end in phonetic [š].

Does the first solution provide a better choice? According to it, both *face* and *facial* have /s/ at the underlying level:

Underlying:	/fes/	/fes + yəl/	/pres/	/pres + yər/
[š] *rule:*	———	feš + yəl	———	preš + yər
Surface:	[fes]	[fešəl]	[pres]	[prešər]

Obviously we cannot let the rule apply unrestrictedly, or all these words would have [š] at the phonetic level. We can limit its application to those cases in which /y/ follows. This will produce the desired results. Such words as *place, rice, lease* will have underlying /s/ and phonetic [s], and *fish, flush, push* will have /š/ and [š]. The [š] rule will be inapplicable in both groups since no /y/ follows.

But isn't this taking extreme liberties with the underlying representation? The solution does produce the desired results, but is there any motivation for it? First of all, is the rule plausible? As we have seen, [s] and [š] differ only in that the first is [+anterior] and the second [−anterior]. A rule which changes only one feature is certainly more likely than one which changes a large number, say the rules needed to convert /s/ to [m]. However, [s] and [θ] differ by only one feature: [s] is [+strident] and [θ] is [−strident]. Is it more likely that /s/ would change to [š] than to [θ] in the given environment? The following /y/ provides the answer. Although the feature system as it is presently given does not capture the similarity as well as it should, we can see it by noticing our tongue position for [y] and then for [θ, s, š]. It is [š] which is the closest in position to [y]. As we have already seen, segments are influenced by those surrounding them; the /s/ in *facial* and similar words changes to [š] to become more like the following segment. This is another example of assimilation.

Is this enough to justify /y/ at the underlying level, a segment which does not occur in any of the given words on the surface? From a historical point of view, the solution is justified. At one time such words as *facial, pressure, gracious, Grecian,* and the like were all pronounced with phonetic [s] plus the glide [y]. Later on a rule was added to the language which changed /s/ to [š] in this position, and then a second rule deleted the /y/. This is parallel to the derivations which we are suggesting here.

Historical explanations are very fine for studies in the development of a language, but can such a solution to our problem be justified strictly from the standpoint of present-day English? As with transformational rules, those in phonology should have some validity. A native speaker of English who knows nothing about the history of the language should have the rule implicitly in his grammar, and the linguist should be able to make it explicit for him—not create something new. Evidence for a rule which converts /s/ to [š] before /y/ can be found in constructions like these:

Bless you.
He tried to kiss you.
We'll miss you.

In normal, unaffected speech, *bless, kiss,* and *miss* all end in [š] in these sentences, whereas in isolation the words end in [s]. A person wishing to provide special stress or create some other effect, of course, can omit the [š] rule and have only [s] in the above sentences. Since this rule is needed in the grammar for cases such as these, it seems justified to use it also for words like *facial, pressure,* and *gracious.*

There are other consonants which may be influenced by a following /y/:

[z]	[ž]
We'll please him.	We'll please you.
His age is surprising.	His youth is surprising.
The book was green.	The book was yellow.

[t]	[č]
Did he meet her?	Did he meet you?
Did he let him go?	Did he let you go?
He hasn't caught it.	He hasn't caught you.

[d]	[j]
Did they feed her?	Did they feed you?
We traded their stamps.	We traded your stamps.
I heard him.	I heard you.

In each case there is the choice of pronouncing the combination as [sy, zy, ty, dy] or as [š, ž, č, ǰ]. It should be noticed that the consonants that precede [y] are the alveolar obstruents. The phonological rule converts each one to the palatal obstruent that agrees with it in voicing and continuance. That is, only the feature anterior (and, for stops, strident) is changed:

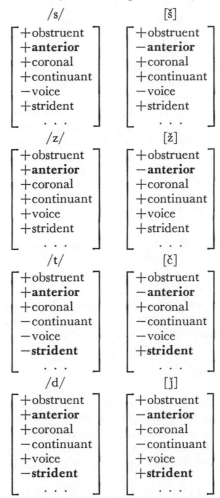

The change from [+anterior] to [−anterior] in each case is brought about to make the consonant palatal, like the following /y/. We call this the **palatalization** rule, since it makes palatals of nonpalatals.

As we saw with /s/ and [š], palatalization is not restricted to the sentence level, but occurs also within a single word. Nor is it limited to words with suffixes. The following provide examples:

Underlying:	/siz/	/siz + yər/	/kəmpoz + yər/
Palatalization:	——	siž + yər	kəmpož + yər
Surface:	[siz]	[sižər]	[kəmpožər]
Spelling:	seize	seizure	composure

Underlying:	/moyst/	/moyst + yər/	/rayt + yəs/
Palatalization:	———	moysč + yər	rayč + yəs
Surface:	[moyst]	[moysčər]	[rayčəs]
Spelling:	moist	moisture	righteous

Underlying:	/prəsid/	/prəsid + yər/	/ɛdyəket/
Palatalization:	———	prəsiǰ + yər	ɛǰyəket
Surface:	[prəsid]	[prəsiǰər]	[ɛǰəket]
Spelling:	proceed	procedure	educate

After palatalization, the /y/ is deleted. Other rules also are performed between the underlying and phonetic levels, but we are concerned only with palatalization here.

In syntax when we had two or more synonymous sentences, we accounted for their relationship by giving them identical underlying structures. We are doing the same thing with phonology. The native speaker recognizes certain pairs of morphemes as related:

[fes]	face	[feš]	facial
[siz]	seize	[siž]	seizure
[moyst]	moist	[moysč]	moisture
[prəsid]	proceed	[prəsiǰ]	procedure

If we had to rely entirely upon phonetic forms, there would be no way to show that [fes] and [feš] belong to the same morpheme. [s] and [š] are normally in contrast, as in *lease* and *leash*. However, we can show the relationship between [fes] and [feš] by giving them the same form at the underlying level and providing a rule which produces the phonetic differences. We are furthermore showing that it is a single process which relates all four alveolars to the corresponding palatals.

Deleted Consonants

In English, such phonetic alternates as [fes] and [feš] are given identical forms at the underlying level. The phonological rule of palatalization accounts for their surface differences.

French has alternate phonetic forms like the following for the pronouns *nous* and *vous*, "we" and "you," respectively:

[nuz]	[nu]
nous avons	nous buvons
nous allons	nous connaissons
nous écrivons	nous plaisons
nous offrons	nous vivons

[vuz]	[vu]
vous avez	vous buvez
vous allez	vous connaissez
vous écrivez	vous plaisez
vous offrez	vous vivez

Not only native speakers of French, but even foreigners with a smattering of the language, recognize [nuz] and [nu] as different forms of the same morpheme. Also, spelling conventions represent both [vuz] and [vu] as *vous* and [nuz] and [nu] as *nous*.

In the illustrative words in the preceding paragraph, we find [nuz] before the same verbs as we do [vuz], and [nu] before the same ones as [vu]. The pattern which is readily discernible is that the forms with final [z] occur before vowels, whereas [nu] and [vu] occur before consonants.

This pattern is not restricted to *nous* and *vous,* as we can see with the possessive plurals:

[mez]	[me]
mes élèves	mes plumes
mes abricots	mes fleurs
mes enfants	mes neveux
mes idées	mes récits
mes observations	mes tours
mes oreilles	mes bagues

The first person singular *mes* occurs as [mez] before vowels, but as [me] before consonants. The same pattern is found with the other possessives: *tes, ses, nos, vos, leurs.* It is also found with the plural of the definite article, *les*: [lez] before vowels, [le] before consonants.

Further examples of the pattern can be found with other words, such as those adjectives which usually precede nouns. *Petit,* "little," is one of these:

[pətit]	[pəti]
un petit idiot	un petit gamin
un petit arbre	un petit cheval
un petit enfant	un petit chiffon
un petit orphelin	un petit parc

These alternations are not unique with pronouns. In fact, we soon see that the pattern is not linked with syntactic information such as part of speech. It is purely phonological.

To show that [nuz] and [nu] or [pətit] and [pəti] are related, we need to give them identical forms at the underlying level. We will then provide a rule to derive their surface realizations. Two possibilities can be suggested: (1) Give /nu/ and /pəti/ at the underlying level and have a rule which adds the final obstruent if a word beginning with a vowel follows. (2) Give /nuz/ and /pətit/ and have a rule which deletes the final obstruent if a word beginning with a consonant follows. With the first possibility, how will we know which obstruent to add? How would we avoid adding [t] to /nu/ and [z] to /pəti/? There is no way. On the other hand, if we accept the second possibility, there are no problems. We merely delete the final consonant if the next word begins with a consonant. Derivations will look like this:

Underlying:	/pətit/ enfant	/pətit/ gamin
Deletion	———	pəti
Surface:	[pətit] enfant	[pəti] gamin
Spelling:	petit enfant	petit gamin
Underlying:	/nuz/ avons	/nuz/ buvons
Deletion	———	nu
Surface:	[nuz] avons	[nu] buvons
Spelling:	nous avons	nous buvons

This is the same procedure we have been adopting with other morphemes which have variant phonetic realizations. As is the case with inflectional endings in English and palatalized consonants, the spelling is closer to the underlying level than the surface pronunciation.

Conclusion

Surface phonetic forms of morphemes often show variation which the native speaker does not consider significant. In English, some plurals are pronounced with [z], whereas others have [s] and still others a vowel plus [z]. The genitive ending for Turkish nouns can contain any of the four high vowels. French has such alternates as [lez] and [le]. If we had to restrict ourselves to the phonetic level, we would find a vast collection of idiosyncratic facts. The variation between [lez] and [le] would be given separately from that between [mez] and [me], as though they had nothing in common.

Many traditional grammars have incorporated a kind of underlying structure in their discussions. Explanations of Turkish vowel harmony or of French consonant deletion (usually referred to as *liaison*), in fact, assume some kind of understood structure which is different from the phonetic realization. Our approach is, therefore, not particularly new. In syntax we saw that traditional grammars often approached the concept of underlying structures in their discussions of understood elements. Both in phonology and in syntax, we are trying to state these underlying abstract structures in a more explicit manner than the traditional accounts did, and we are including some topics, such as palatalization, which were often ignored.

Exercises

A. Use phonological rules to provide the past tenses for the following verbs: *stop, strut, attack, doze, dread.*

B. We said nothing in this chapter about the formation of past participles: (have) *dropped,* (have) *walked,* (have) *headed,* (have) *eaten,* etc. Provide rules for their surface realization.

C. Which underlying consonants would you give for the following words: *confession, confusion, residual, official, legislature*?

D. The following pairs of words are related, but their surface forms differ. What underlying forms and rules could you provide to show the relationships?

1. permit, permissive
2. constant, constancy
3. democrat, democracy
4. president, presidency
5. resident, residency
6. aristocrat, aristocracy

E. Underlying /t/ usually palatalizes to [č], as in *moisture, legislature, presidential.* Yet in some words it becomes [š]: *commission, action, delegation, prohibition.* What rule must apply before palatalization to allow /t/ to become surface [š]?

F. A complete grammar would provide surface syntactic structures with comparative and superlative degrees of adjectives expressed as *rich + comparative* or *rich + superlative.* Phonological rules would provide the suffixes *rich + er* and *rich + est.*

1. State the rules needed for giving phonetic forms to *comparative* and *superlative.*
2. Which of the following adjectives do not follow the rules you have given? Are they just exceptions, or do they follow another set of rules? If they are exceptional, do nothing further with them. If they follow another set of rules, state them and give the conditions under which these rules rather than those for *-er* and *-est* apply.

old	loud	heavy	dangerous
sad	amazed	tranquil	putrid
happy	uncertain	delicious	soft
beautiful	light	safe	dreadful

3. How would you handle the comparative and superlative forms of *good* and *bad?*

G. Is [ə] predictable in the following words?

1. alóne
2. élephant
3. fócal
4. ántelòpe
5. húrricàne
6. consíder
7. hándsome
8. mánifèst
9. achíeve

H. The native speaker of English recognizes *moment* and *momentous* as related forms; *momentous* can be analyzed as *moment + ous.* Yet the surface forms do not indicate this identity: [mómənt] and [mòméntəs]. What underlying vowels would you suggest for *moment* to show the relationship?

Suggested Reading

Brame, Michael K., ed., *Contributions to Generative Phonology.* Austin: University of Texas Press, 1972.

Chomsky, Noam, and Morris Halle, *The Sound Pattern of English.* New York: Harper & Row, Publishers, 1968.

Francis, W. Nelson, *The Structure of American English.* New York: The Ronald Press Company, 1958.

Gimson, A. C., *An Introduction to the Pronunciation of English.* 2nd ed. London: Edward Arnold, 1970.

HALLE, MORRIS, "On the Bases of Phonology," in *The Structure of Language*, ed. Jerry A. Fodor and Jerrold J. Katz. Englewood Cliffs, N. J.: Prentice-Hall, Inc., 1964.

———, "Phonology in Generative Grammar," *Word* 18 (1962): 54–72.

———, *The Sound Pattern of Russian*. The Hague: Mouton, 1959.

HARMS, ROBERT T., *Introduction to Phonological Theory*. Englewood Cliffs, N. J.: Prentice-Hall, Inc., 1968.

HARRIS, JAMES W., *Spanish Phonology*. Cambridge, Mass.: The M.I.T. Press, 1969.

HEFFNER, R-M. S., *General Phonetics*. Madison: University of Wisconsin Press, 1960.

HOCKETT, CHARLES F., *A Manual of Phonology*. Baltimore: Waverly Press, 1955.

JONES, DANIEL, *The Pronunciation of English*. 4th ed. Cambridge: Cambridge University Press, 1966.

JOOS, MARTIN, *Acoustic Phonetics*. Baltimore: Linguistic Society of America, 1948.

LADEFOGED, PETER, *Elements of Acoustic Phonetics*. Chicago: University of Chicago Press, 1962.

MAKKAI, VALERIE BECKER, ed., *Phonological Theory*. New York: Holt, Rinehart & Winston, Inc., 1972.

MALMBERG, BERTIL, *Phonetics*. New York: Dover Publications, Inc., 1963.

POSTAL, PAUL, *Aspects of Phonological Theory*. New York: Harper & Row, Publishers, 1968.

SCHANE, SANFORD A., *French Phonology and Morphology*. Cambridge, Mass.: The M.I.T. Press, 1968.

———, *Generative Phonology*. Englewood Cliffs, N. J.: Prentice-Hall, Inc., 1973.

STANLEY, RICHARD, "Redundancy Rules in Phonology," *Language* 43 (1967): 393–436.

TRUBETZKOY, N. S., *Principles of Phonology*, trans. Christiane A. M. Baltaxe. Berkeley: University of California Press, 1969.

part 4

Acquisition, Change, Variation

chapter 13

Language Acquisition and Language Universals

Our discussions of syntax and phonology have been designed to explore the system that exists in language, but at the sacrifice of the details of its variability. No language is spoken uniformly among all its speakers, nor does any language remain static from one generation to another. In this chapter we will look at the alterations that occur within the language of an individual as he ages, in particular the changes of the first decade of his life. In Chapter 14 we will investigate the ways in which language changes from one period in time to another. Finally, in Chapter 15 we will examine the differences among contemporary speakers of a language. The concept of the preceding chapters that language is systematic will still be maintained. The system merely changes with time, and different groups of people at a given time have slight variations in some of the rules of their language.

The Nature of Language Acquisition

Several reasons for studying the development of language in small children are readily apparent. If we are to teach language skills to children with physical, mental, or emotional problems, we need to know how normal children acquire language. In the past, there has been much wasted effort, money, and time expended by well-meaning teachers who were working with faulty notions of how children should speak at a given age. Those who do not wish to repeat the mistakes of their predecessors need to know a great deal about language in general, and in particular about the development of language in normal children. Those teachers who have been successful in teaching the deaf, the mentally retarded, and other children who need special help have possessed a certain amount of this knowledge.

It is not just for the teachers of exceptional children that a knowledge of language acquisition is essential. Those who teach children in the first few grades or prepare textbooks for them need the same kind of information. In particular, the teaching of reading and spelling can benefit from knowledge of this nature.

But these purposes seem of questionable value to the person who is not concerned with teaching children. It has become apparent, especially within recent years, that we can learn a great deal about the nature of language itself by studying it from various perspectives. By examining the order in which different aspects of the grammar are acquired and comparing the results for children learning various languages, we hope to discover features that are universal in language.

From the time of the birth cry to the end of the first decade of life, there is much similarity among children in all parts of the world in learning to understand and speak their mother tongue. Around the age of three months or earlier they are cooing, by six months they have entered a babbling stage, at twelve months they are saying a few words, and around eighteen months they begin forming two-word sentences. This ordering is as true for Russians as it is for Hottentots, for pygmies as for giants, for girls as for boys, for children of the working class as for those of intellectuals.

The age-old controversy between the environmentalists and the advocates of genetic transmission is as active in discussions of language acquisition as it is in such matters as intelligence and personality. There is much that the environmentalists can point to in arguing their case with language. No one is born with the ability to speak a language. If there is no exposure, the child does not learn to speak. Examples can be drawn from children raised as extra cubs by wolves and other animals, those who are locked up for years in closets or attics, and those who are exposed to no one other than their deaf parents. Without exposure, no one learns a language.

A second argument in favor of environmental influences is that children learn whatever language or languages they are exposed to, regardless of their ancestry. A Chinese infant adopted by Norwegian parents will learn to speak Norwegian fluently and sound like a native. Later, if he learns Chinese as an adult, he will speak it with a foreign accent in spite of the fact that his ancestors spoke the language natively. Or a baby from the Bronx adopted by parents in Santa Fe will have Southwestern speech patterns, and one from Georgia will sound like a New Englander if adopted by a family living in Boston. Students learning a foreign language in school have found that their ancestry is no help to them if they have had no previous exposure to the language. French is as hard for the child whose grandparents came from France as it is for one of American Indian descent—provided that both speak only English when they start studying French. The color of our hair, our height, the shape of our noses, and the length of our index fingers will be like those of at least some of our ancestors; our language will not necessarily be anything like theirs.

For reasons such as these, it seems that language acquisition should be as indeterminate as various traits of a person's character or personality: whether we are courteous, honest, industrious, and the like. These traits are definitely formed in each individual without regard to his biological heritage. A person from a long line of thieves may be the epitome of honesty. Or industrious parents who have worked hard all their lives may have lazy children. The child of a renowned scholar could be a functional illiterate. A child at birth is without language, education, and character traits such as courtesy. Are all of them not acquired through the environment in the same way?

The answer is no. Education is something a person may or may not acquire. Many people live their entire lives without learning even the most elementary aspects of reading and writing. Many graduate from high school and enter college without being able to write a connected paragraph, read and understand a daily newspaper, or perform simple mathematical calculations. Throughout the world there is a wide range in the amount and kind of education people receive. Similarly, people may be honest or not; they may be basically truthful or chronic liars; they may be courteous or rude. But with language there is no choice. Except in the most extreme cases, everyone acquires it. Language is uniform in distribution among all people of the world, from the most advanced in civilization to the most primitive. This is also true for everyone of whom we have any record in the past. There have never been reliable reports of entire tribes who did not have a language or of individuals within a tribe who never learned to talk—unless they were severely retarded, had some physical defect which prevented speech, or were autistic.

It may be supposed that children develop language because it enables them to attain certain needs. If this were so, the neglected child should begin speaking earlier than the one who is pampered. Does a child of eighteen months really have needs which did not exist two months earlier? Why do all children begin talking at about the same age, regardless of where they live? The word *needs* is vague, and no one has yet suggested an objective means of measuring it. Babies cry, yell, squirm, and make gestures to communicate their wishes. So long as these devices are satisfactory, it seems that there would be no reason to learn to speak; yet children who attain their goals by means of nonlinguistic communication learn to speak as early as other children do. Even after they start making sentences, their primary means of communication is nonverbal. At first, children use language only secondarily to impart information or to direct others. Often it is merely a means of playing.

Some people have assumed that children do not begin speaking earlier than they do because of insufficient muscular development. According to this theory, as soon as the muscles controlling the vocal tract are adequately developed, the child begins to speak, forming words at about one year and two-word sentences at one and a half. This assumption can be shown to be wrong. Before children begin making words, they go through a babbling stage, in which they produce practically all of the sounds they will ever use. Children who will later speak English are making not only [a, i, u, s, f, b], but also [θ, ð]—as well as [ü, ö, q] and a great many other sounds which they will never use in speaking. Long before children begin forming words, they are physically capable of producing all of the sounds needed for them. The problem is that they are just sounds during the babbling stage, not segments which function as part of a system. It is cognitive development, not muscular, that is needed. In the same way, both during the babbling stage and the period of forming single words, children utter sequences longer than two- and three-word sentences. Yet they cannot be taught to combine their words into syntactic structures until they are about eighteen months old. *Baby* and *bye-bye* remain separate utterances and are not joined into a unit until the child reaches a crucial age.

Of all the features of language learning, none is more remarkable than that no one is actually taught his mother tongue. We may ask, "But doesn't the mother teach the child to talk?" If we forget our biases about Motherhood, we realize that there is a wide range in the attitudes mothers have toward their offspring. Yet there is relatively little difference in language development between children who are ignored and those whose mothers spend much time talking to them. Even in the latter cases, there is really no concerted effort at teaching language beyond vocabulary items. Especially revealing are those cases in which parents have tried to correct children's syntax or morphology so that they will eliminate double negatives or use the standard forms of verbs, such as *drank* instead of *drinked*. An interesting example is cited in McNeill (1966:69). The child had said, "Nobody don't like me." The mother corrected with, "No, say 'Nobody likes me.' " The child came back with "Nobody don't like me." After eight repetitions, the exasperated mother placed special emphasis on the structure she was trying to teach: "No, now listen carefully; say *'Nobody likes me.'* " Now the child had it figured out: "Oh! Nobody don't *likes* me." Trying to teach a given feature of language before children have reached the right stage for acquiring it is futile. Even if we waited until the children were at the right age for each aspect of grammar we were trying to teach, it would be most unfortunate if they had to rely solely upon our instructions. Linguistic research of the last few decades has shown that we have only scratched the surface in our analyses of language. The gulf between a person's implicit and explicit knowledge of language is so great that there is scarcely a rule that the average person can explain correctly. Whereas learning to read or to add requires expert instruction if people are to become successful in the skills, they are given no real tutoring in learning their first language. In the instances in which a zealous adult does give instructions, they are sketchy and often wrong. Yet all children learn a language, in spite of the absence of teaching or poor efforts at it.

If language is not actually taught in the sense that other skills are, then perhaps the child picks it up through imitation. We have seen that exposure is a sine qua non for language acquisition. Children are normally given no instruction in how to stand, sit, or gesture with their hands and heads; yet they usually develop the traits of their parents or other adults whom they may admire. These are clear examples of learning through imitation. It is true that the only words people learn are those to which they have been exposed, but aspects of grammar and phonology develop even when exposure has been absent, or at best minimal. Jakobson (1968: 14) cites examples of French and Russian children who have not yet acquired [r], but who substitute vocalic length for it: i.e., Russian [ma:ka] for [marka], French [ta:tan] for [tartin]. Yet neither language has vocalic length with phonemic significance. The children have created a contrast between long and short vowels that is not found in the adult language. Another example of departure from the adult models can be found in the case of an English-speaking child who has only voiceless stops at the end of a word (cited in Moskowitz, 1970:436). This pattern possibly reflects the influence of the father, whose native language, German, has a phonological rule which devoices all final stops. To accommodate the English vocabulary, in which voicing is distinctive at the end of a word (*cup, cub; tap, tab*), the child created a system of using voiceless aspirated stops to correspond to those which are voiceless for adults. That is, aspirated [kʰ] was used with *book,* but unaspirated [k] for *bug.* In standard English, aspiration is never contrastive. In the course of this chapter, we will see additional examples of systems in child language which could not be imitated from adults. But this point should not be overemphasized, since a certain amount of imitation obviously does take place. The process of language acquisition is a combination of imitation and creation.

When children reach a critical age, they are apparently predisposed to learn the language or languages to which they are exposed. In some way they separate malformed structures from those which are well constructed and, on the basis of this raw material, develop internalized grammars of the language. The initial grammars they develop must be quite simple, but they are able to revise them periodically to accommodate the new observations they make. Children are not merely mimicking adult sentences as parrots would, but rather are using them to draw generalizations and form their own grammars, from which they can construct original sentences. It seems quite plausible that the desire to construct a grammar and the knowledge of how to go about doing it are innate; children derive the exact details of the language they are learning from the exposure they receive to it.

Lenneberg (1967) has shown that children follow a certain timetable, regardless of the language they are learning. This timetable can be compared with that for the development of various motor skills, but there is no necessary interrelation. There is obviously a certain amount of individual variation among children, but they follow the same milestones in the same order and at approximately the same age. In language this means making vowel-like cooing sounds at about three months, replacing them with syllable-like babbling by six months, and producing words at twelve months. These developments can be compared to supporting the head when in a prone position at three months, sitting alone at six months, and walking with help at twelve months. However, development along the language timetable is much faster than along the one for muscular control. By the age of five or six years, children have mastered the basic core of their language system, whereas they still have a long way to go with their motor skills.

Just as there is a critical age at which children begin to develop a grammar, there is a terminal age, around puberty, after which they are no longer able to do so. Lenneberg (1967) relates this age to the lateralization of function of the hemispheres of the brain. Until about the age of twelve, both hemispheres are equally capable of developing in a given area, but after that time tasks are delegated to one or the other. For most people the left hemisphere governs language. Until the cut-off time, children can learn any language to which they are given sufficient exposure; no special tutoring is needed. They will, furthermore, speak the language like natives, provided that the people they have been listening to are native speakers. After about the age of twelve, mere exposure is not enough. People have to exert a considerable amount of effort to learn a foreign language, and if the teaching is poor they will not be very successful. Even with the same teacher, there will be as wide a span in accomplishment among individuals as there is in their mastery of mathematics or chemistry. Except in rare cases, people who learn another language after the age of twelve or so will always speak it with a foreign accent, and they will occasionally make mistakes in syntax and idiom even if they have worked with the language and lived among native speakers for many years.

Support for linking the formative years for natural language acquisition with the development of the brain can be found in the experience of people who have suffered head injuries, strokes, or surgical removal of part of the brain. If damage occurs while a child is still within the formative years of about two to twelve, regardless of which hemisphere is affected, the other can take on the language function. After the critical age, interference with the left hemisphere results in effects on language which can be reversed only if the source of the interference is removed and the brain resumes its normal functioning. The right hemisphere can no longer take on new tasks, except to a limited degree. During the formative age, people can create a new grammar if need be; after that time, they have to depend on salvaging what is left. In many ways, language acquisition is radically different from the learning of other skills such as playing a musical instrument or repairing watches.

Phonological Acquisition

People who have spent much time with young children are aware that there is a timetable for developing various language skills and that it is not dependent upon external stimuli. If a child of three is not yet potty trained, one's reaction is that the parents have been negligent, not that the child is mentally retarded. However, if a three-year-old is not yet making words, we begin asking what is wrong with him physically, mentally, or emotionally.

Long before babies begin making words, they play with noise. The cooing sounds which have begun by the age of three months are described as "vowel-like." By six months of age, children have entered what is called the babbling stage, in which syllable-like combinations follow one another. These combinations are similar to consonant plus vowel units in adult speech: [ta da ti du]. The children are not communicating with their babbling, but rather are playing with the noises they can make. They make a wide variety of sounds that resemble consonants and vowels in adult languages, but there is no system to them and they do not combine to form referential units. Sounds are not used functionally until children are between nine and twelve months of age.

Even before the first words are produced, the features of intonation are developed: the changes in pitch, stress (accent), and pause which distinguish a phrase or a sentence in English from a list of words, or the rising, falling, and other changes in pitch which can distinguish one morpheme from another in a language such as Chinese. Weir (1966:157) cites a study of an infant in a Polish speech community that had recognizable Polish intonations by the fifth month, even though the babbling did not produce morphemes of any language. There has been very little research conducted on the development of intonation patterns, but there is much agreement that babbling begins to sound like sentences before the child forms words.

The first significant work in child phonological acquisition was Roman Jakobson's *Kindersprache, Aphasie und allgemeine Lautgesetze* (1941). The work has been translated into English by Allan R. Keiler under the title *Child Language, Aphasia and Phonological Universals* (1968). Although certain refinements in Jakobson's conclusions are needed, the work is still considered basically sound and remains a classic. This work furnishes the basis for the following discussion.

The first phonological contrasts children make which can be considered systematic are between consonantal and vocalic segments. The consonantal segment is typically a stop which is anterior, but since there is only one phonemic consonant at this stage, it may vary in exact realization as [p, t, m]. The vowel can be given as [a], but since it does not contrast with other vowels, it may not be precisely like the adult [a]. In terms of features, we say that the child has acquired two segments, one which is [+consonantal] and the other [−consonantal]. At this first stage [ba ba], [da da], and [ma ma] are variants of the same morpheme. The contrast is between complete opening of the vocal tract with the vowel and complete closure with the stop.

The second contrast that is learned is between nasal and oral consonants. That is, the features [+nasal] and [−nasal] are acquired. [ba ba] and [da da] are still not in contrast, but [ma ma] is different. We can list the distinctive features as follows:

$$
\begin{array}{cccc}
[\text{b} & \text{a}] & [\text{m} & \text{a}] \\
\begin{bmatrix} +\text{consonantal} \\ -\text{nasal} \end{bmatrix} & [-\text{consonantal}] & \begin{bmatrix} +\text{consonantal} \\ +\text{nasal} \end{bmatrix} & [-\text{consonantal}]
\end{array}
$$

The actual realization is not necessarily [b] in the case of the [−nasal] consonant. It may be [β] or [p] or even [t] or [d]. The important features are [+consonantal] to distinguish it from [a] and [−nasal] in opposition with [m].

Third in the listing of contrasts is between labials and dentals; that is, the feature coronal is added. Now [pa pa] contrasts with [ta ta] and [ma ma]. The single feature [−consonantal] is all that is distinctive about the vowel even though we could classify it as [+voice], [−strident], and [+low].

For the three consonantal segments, the features consonantal, nasal, and coronal are needed.

Jakobson (1968:48) notes that not only do children develop contrasts in the order given, regardless of which language they are learning, but that these contrasts are found in all languages of the world. All languages have at least three consonants: a nasal, a labial, and a dental.

After these first consonantal contrasts are added, the child distinguishes between a low and a non-low vowel. The low vowel can be written [a], but the non-low one may be realized as [i, u, e, o]. A word of caution is in order. There is a certain amount of danger in representing these phonemes with the symbols we use for languages which have a larger number of contrasts. When there are only two vowels, the child is making only one distinction between them. So long as the vowel other than [a] is non-low, its exact shape is unimportant. *Baby* may come out as [be be] or [bi bi].

A third vowel is added next, either similar to [u] or to [e]. If the first is added, the system looks like this:

$$[i] \qquad [u]$$

$$[a]$$

The feature distinguishing [i] and [u] is back versus front. If the [e]-like vowel is the third one added instead of [u], the system is as follows:

$$[i]$$
$$[e]$$
$$[a]$$

In addition to the feature low versus non-low, this system now includes high versus non-high. Since there is no tense/lax contrast yet in the system, either variant may occur. Jakobson (1968:49) gives these as the two types of vowel systems which are the most basic. No language has fewer than three vowels, distinguished either by three degrees of height or by two of height and front versus back.

One word of caution reappears frequently in discussions of child language, namely that features are not acquired individually. While children are working on the distinction between coronal and noncoronal stops, they are still perfecting the differentiation between nasal and non-nasal consonants. There is considerable overlapping, yet there is an óverall order in which features are acquired.

The acquisition of stops, for example, always precedes that of fricatives. There are no records of children who master [s, z, š, ž, x] before they do [p, b, t, d, k, g]. Various studies of the language of children between two and two and a half (e.g., Weir, 1962; Moskowitz, 1970) show that the stops are all fairly stable while only the fricatives are still being learned. This means that for consonantal segments which are [−continuant], the features of voicing and those which determine place of obstruction are reasonably well established. Cited in Moskowitz (1970:428) are the following uses of stops by a twenty-six-month-old child. The figures indicate the number of occurrences of each phoneme in the materials studied:

Phoneme	Correct realizations	Substitutions
[p]	26	3
[t]	112	42
[k]	75	13
[b]	66	8
[d]	56	41
[g]	28	4

Two of the figures under substitution need comment. Of the 42 substitutions for [t], 33 are omissions in final position. Many of the substitutions for [d] are found in the word *daddy,* in which the intervocalic stop is omitted altogether. Except for these cases, there is very little substitution for stops.

Among all consonants, those formed with obstruction in the front part of the mouth occur before those in the back. In terms of features, this means that [+interior] appears before [−anterior]. The stops [p, b, t, d] are added to the inventory before [k, g] are; of the nasals, [m, n] are added before [ŋ]. Before the addition of palatals and velars, children substitute anterior consonants for them, usually dentals. Jakobson (1968:47n) cites substitution of *tut* for *cut* in English, *tata* for *caca* in French, *tata* for *kaka* in Serbian, *taal* for *kukal* in Estonian. He notes the same substitution in Japanese.

Especially interesting for our purposes are Jakobson's comparisons of the order of the child's acquisition of phonemes to the phonological systems of the languages of the world. We saw earlier that all languages have at least the contrast of oral versus nasal and labial versus dental consonants, which is one of the earliest contrasts found in children. The acquisition of stops prior to fricatives likewise has its counterpart in that no languages have been found without stops, but some lack fricatives. We can predict, then, that if a phonological system has fricatives, it also has stops. The reverse does not hold, since there may be stops without fricatives. Similarly, the presence of back consonants presupposes the presence of those at the front. Children acquire labials and dentals before palatals and velars, and there are languages with only front consonants. Conversely, there are no languages with only velars and palatals but no labials or dentals. Voiced consonants presuppose those which are voiceless, and affricates presuppose the corresponding fricatives. These observations hold for all phonological systems, whether they are those of a child whose system will later be expanded or those of fully developed adult languages.

Studies since the time of Jakobson's monograph support his conclusions. In Weir (1962), the two-and-a-half-year-old child had virtually mastered the stops. The fricatives were still being learned, with those that are voiced less stable than their voiceless counterparts. For the language of the twenty-six-month-old child reported in Moskowitz (1970), the stops were stable, but the only fricatives that had been mastered were [s] and [f]. The voiced fricatives [v, z, ð] were still in the process of being acquired.

Of the vowels, we saw that the first three are in one of these patterns:

[i]	[u]	[i]
		[e]
[a]		[a]

Several observations are made in Jakobson (1968) about further additions. Contrasts may not be added at one level before they are added at the higher level. For the second system above, the distinction of front versus back may be added to the mid position only after it has been added to the high. That is,

$$[i] \qquad\qquad [u]$$
$$[e]$$
$$\qquad [a]$$

is a possible expansion, but

$$[i]$$
$$[e] \qquad\qquad [o]$$
$$\qquad [a]$$

is not. Similarly, contrasts in low vowels presuppose those in the ones that are higher. These contrasts may involve front versus back, tenseness, or other distinctions. Also, contrasts in unrounded vowels must precede those in rounded. To the basic triangle

$$[i] \qquad\qquad [u]$$
$$\qquad [a]$$

the acquisition of [e] must precede that of [o]. These restrictions are found among the languages of the world as well as in the order of the child's acquisition. There are languages with contrasts among high vowels which are not found in those at lower levels, but the reverse does not occur. There are languages with [e] and not [o], but not vice versa.

Whether vowel or consonant, those phonemes that are rare among languages are also the ones that the child adds last. These include front rounded vowels, nasalized vowels, a second liquid, the Czech strident [r], and the English [θ, ð].

Also among sequential constraints we find similarities between the child's order of acquisition and the systems among fully developed languages. The syllable structure most often found throughout the world is CV. The frequent omission of final consonants among children is no doubt an effort to preserve this type of syllable. Clusters of obstruents or obstruent plus liquid, nasal, or glide are simplified at first. The greater the departure from the basic CV pattern, the rarer the syllable structure is among languages.

When we find children acquiring phonemes in an order which parallels that of their frequency among the languages of the world, we suspect that we are dealing with features that are universal. This suspicion is especially strong when we realize that this sequence is found regardless of the language which the child is learning. When we add to this information the observation that people who experience partial loss of their language abilities because of aphasia lose phonemes in the reverse order from which they were attained (i.e., those that are attained last are lost first), the argument for universals seems most appealing. Research in language acquisition and in universals is not yet advanced enough to provide us with anything more than possibilities, but this is a rich area for learning about the nature of language.

In concluding our discussion of the acquisition of phonology, let us return to the issue of imitation. Obviously some imitation occurs, or how would children know whether to use retroflex, tongue-trilled, or uvular [r], for example? But imitation alone is not enough. People do not produce discrete segments when they speak, but rather sounds which merge into one another. There is also much variation in the actual execution of sounds, yet adults hear them as the same. How are children to know which variations are meaningful and which ones are not? How are they to know that [k] in *skip* is "the same" as the one in *cope* in spite of the differences in aspiration, lip rounding, and tongue position? How are Hindi children to know that aspiration is distinctive, but English children to know that it is not for their language? Children learn to ignore certain features as well as the mistakes which they hear. It is highly questionable that they could do all this by mere imitation.

The imitation theory would also lead us to assume that phonemes are acquired in the order of their frequency. Those which occur the most often in the language would be added first, and the rarer ones last. Yet we find the same ordering among all children, and the languages they are learning vary considerably in the frequency of their segments. A study for English (cited in Moskowitz, 1970:429) lists the order of frequency for the fricatives as follows: [s, ð, z, v, f, š, θ, ž]. Yet the English-speaking child acquires [f] before the voiced [ð, z, v]. A purely environmental explanation of phonological acquisition leaves many unanswered questions.

The Acquisition of Syntax and Inflections

Since the early 1960s, when scholarly studies of language acquisition began appearing in sizable numbers, linguists have looked upon children's internalized grammars not as incomplete copies of adult grammars, but rather as independent creations. Children make hypotheses in response to the language they are exposed to, following whatever innate devices they may possess regarding what a language may be like. These hypotheses are the basis of their first grammars, which are like some aspects of adult grammars. These first grammars fulfill the same functions as any other internalized grammar in that they account for the children's ability to produce and understand sentences, most of which are new. As time passes, children add rules to their grammars and modify earlier ones. This process of revision and addition continues until the grammars are essentially like those of the adult. If we spoke of children's sentences according to adult grammars, we would see many mistakes, just as we would if we discussed a football game in terms of the rules for basketball. A more interesting observation would be to consider children's sentences according to their own grammars, not by some set of rules which they are not following.

Children start with one-word utterances, followed by those of two words, then those of three, and so on. With an utterance of one word, a child is merely naming, not creating a syntactic structure. Furthermore, two or more words in succession that are merely compounded or members of a list do not constitute a syntactic structure: *duck, ball, block*. On the other hand, two words that relate as subject and verb, modifier and noun, or verb and object clearly do have a syntactic function.

The earliest age at which children form two-word syntactic structures is usually around eighteen months. These earliest sentences lack prepositions, articles, auxiliary verbs, and inflectional endings such as past tense, plural, present participle, and the like. For children learning languages other than English, the first sentences do not contain markers for gender, case, aspect, and other grammatical categories. Although these early structures are in many ways impoverished according to adult standards, there is no reason to classify them as incomplete. They are complete according to the system of rules they are following; they are also systematic.

During the early 1960s, several students of language acquisition noticed that these first two-word sentences contained words which could be placed into classes. They resisted giving traditional parts-of-speech labels to the classes since their use would suggest more of a correspondence between adult grammars and those of children than was warranted. Also, the classes did not relate very well to any particular part-of-speech categories. Since three groups working independently at Harvard University, Walter Reed Army Hospital, and the University of California at Berkeley arrived at basically the same system, their results attracted considerable interest. Because they were working independently, they gave different names to the two classes of words in children's sentences. We will follow McNeill (1966:20) in calling them **Pivot** and **Open.**

The words in the Pivot class from the study of Braine (cited in McNeill, 1966) include *allgone, byebye, big, more, pretty, my, see, night-night,* and *hi.* In the material examined, these words occur frequently, but their number is small. The much larger class of Open words includes *boy, sock, boat, fan, milk, plane, shoe, vitamins, hot, Mommy, Daddy,* and the like. The distinction is basically between nouns (Open) and non-nouns (Pivot), but there are obvious reasons for not using these terms, such as the inclusion of *hot* under the Open class. In the material examined, a word in the Open class could occur as a single-word sentence, but members of the Pivot class could not. Also, two words from the Open class could form a syntactic unit, but not two from the Pivot class. Possible sentences combining Pivot and Open words according to the restrictions of the grammar are *See boat, Allgone milk, My shoe, Pretty plane,* and the like. The list of vocabulary items varied from child to child, as it should, since this aspect of language learning depends upon exposure, and children in different homes naturally are exposed to different words.

An especially interesting discovery of the studies cited in McNeill (1966:24) is that the sentences could not be mere imitations of adult speech. The several hundred sentences produced spontaneously by each child would demand an unbelievable capacity for memorization if the child lacked creative ability. By *spontaneous* sentences, we are excluding those in which the child repeats what someone has just said. Even more revealing are structures which the child could not have heard because they violate rules in adult grammars. The ordering *Allgone milk* is the reverse of what the adult would say: *(The) milk (is) all gone.* The child clearly has a system of rules which permits him to create structures.

Studies of syntactic acquisition have been conducted for children in various countries. One is the diary kept by the Soviet linguist Aleksandr N. Gvozdev on the speech of his son up until his ninth year (1921 to 1929). Studying this extensive record in light of current developments in linguistics, Slobin (1966) discovered that there was a clear classification of words into Open and Pivot classes and that the rules for their combination were identical to those of the child learning English. What is especially interesting about this discovery is that the surface structures of adult English and Russian are not alike. Whereas English uses word order as the primary signal for syntactic structures, Russian uses inflections primarily and word order only secondarily. Yet the first two-word sentences by the Russian child were as lacking in inflectional endings as were those of American children, and both used the same principles for combining words into syntactic structures.

Also, the Russian child was observed experimenting with combinations, taking one Pivot word and introducing various members of the Open class (Slobin, 1966:133). This experimentation reminds us of the later study of Ruth Weir, who recorded and studied the pre-sleep monologues of her first child when he was two and a half years old. One example, in which the child was practicing the adjectives *big* and *little,* is given as follows (Weir, 1962:118):

> Hi big Bob.
> That's Bob. That's Bob.
> Big Bob. Big Bob. Big Bob.
> Little Bob.
> Big and little.
> Little Bobby.
> Little Nancy.
> Big Nancy.
> Big Bob and Nancy and Bobby.
> And Bob.

At two and a half, this child was obviously more advanced than the Pivot and Open stage of syntactic development, as the sentences show. The monologue of another child talking to himself before going to sleep is reported by King (1969:72). This child was three and a half.

> Cat (many times)
> Two (many times)
> Bats
> The cat sees two bats.

Another example from the same source is

> Pig (many times)
> Big
> Sleep
> Big pig sleep now.

Neither "The cat sees two bats" nor "Big pig sleep now" had occurred in the speech of adults talking to the child. The playful practicing of the Russian child and that described by Weir and by King are clear evidence that children do not simply imitate sentences they hear but rather have developed a device for original creation.

More recently, some linguists (e.g., Bloom, 1970, 1973; Gruber, 1973) have found the Pivot and Open classification inadequate. There are too many exceptional sentences in the speech of some children. More seriously, it has some of the weaknesses that a grammar of adult language possesses if it does not go beyond surface structures. *Mommy sock,* for example, can mean *Mommy('s) sock* or *Mommy (is putting the) sock (on me)*. In either case, *Mommy* and *sock* are merely two members of the Open class.

In Brown (1973:454) we find the following examples of syntactic relations in two-word sentences:

Attributive: Big train, Red book, etc.
Possessive: Adam checker, Mommy lunch, etc.
Locative: Sweater chair, Book table, etc.
Locative: Walk street, Go store, etc.
Agent-Action: Adam put, Eve read, etc.
Agent-Object: Mommy sock, Mommy lunch, etc.
Action-Object: Put book, Hit ball, etc.

Underlying representations of these sentences in terms of case grammar certainly seem worth investigating. This approach has been suggested by several linguists, but so far no full-scale study has been made. Tense and auxiliary verbs are missing from children's speech at this age, and there is no indication that they have any meaning for them in the sentences of others; we therefore do not give a modality constituent. Otherwise, *Eve read* looks very much like *Eve is reading* on a case-grammar tree:

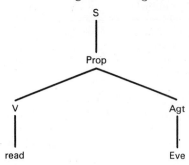

For an action-object structure such as *Hit ball,* we can provide the following tree:

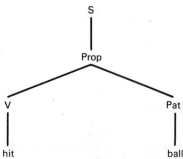

The other examples can be derived in a similar manner.

Since the grammar at this stage permits structures of not more than two words, some of the classifications found in adult grammars are not found in those of children. A verb, for example, takes only one case category: an agent, a patient, or a locative. A possible exception is the sentence in which there is no verb, but rather two case categories (e.g., *Mommy lunch* or *Sweater chair*). We could say that these sentences have underlying verbs which are deleted, but this approach is drawing too much on adult grammars. It is safer to say that underlying structures at this stage of development contain either a verb and a case category or else two case categories.

Except for subject placement, there are no transformations during the two-word stage. It seems most unlikely, then, that attributive adjectives and possessive nouns are derived from relative clauses as they are in adult grammars. No convincing suggestions have been offered for their derivation, but something elementary seems probable. Transformations begin appearing later, as the grammar increases in complexity.

At the three-word stage of syntactic development, the child is no longer restricted to two constituents, but rather can have a verb and two case categories, such as agent and patient, as in *Bob hit ball*. Seen from the perspective of case grammar, this expansion is more systematic than a mere addition of another word. Even at this early stage of syntactic development, an analysis which goes deeper than surface ordering is needed.

As for other structural elements, inflectional suffixes appear before prepositions do, and auxiliary verbs come even later. Whereas the ordering appears to be determined at least in part by cerebral maturation, studies which link cognitive and syntactic development are scant. If a definite relationship can be established, the fact that children in all language groups acquire syntactic structures in the same order will be less mysterious. We will still have syntactic universals, but there will be an explanation for them.

As with phonology, those syntactic and inflectional structures which are universal among the languages of the world are acquired first, those that are the rarest, last. It appears that all languages use word order for syntactic purposes, although it may be of secondary importance in some of them. It is no surprise, then, that word order is the first syntactic device acquired by children, regardless of the language they are learning. Slobin (1966:134) found that word order is as inflexible with Russian children at the first stages of syntactic development as it is with those learning English. None of the freedom of ordering of adult Russian is found in the young child. Since all languages do not have inflectional suffixes, these are acquired later than word order.

There is some question as to the age at which children have mastered the syntax and inflections of their language. McNeill (1966:15) gives the average beginning age for syntactic acquisition as one and a half and the average age for completion of the basic principles as three and a half—a two-year period. McNeill is not saying that three and a half is the age at which children have mastered all details of syntax, even if they have by then learned more about it than they will in the rest of their lives. Others have given five or six as the age at which children have acquired most of the syntactic, phonological, and inflectional details of their language—but the word *most* needs to be emphasized. Slobin (1966:140) says that some morphological details of Russian are not mastered by children until they are around eight years old. Carol Chomsky (1969) has shown that some children learning English have not learned certain structures until they are well past kindergarten. Some children of seven and eight have not yet mastered structures like *The doll is easy to see* or *John is easy to please.* In experiments they interpreted these structures as they would *John is eager to help,* in which the subject of the main verb is understood as coreferential with the deleted subject of the infinitive. Hence, they thought that *The doll is easy to see* meant something like *The doll can see easily.* Similar structures which some children had not yet learned were the difference between *Ask Joe what to feed the doll* and *Tell Joe what to feed the doll* and more complex sentences with *ask* and *tell* when an infinitive follows. Some children as old as ten had not yet mastered all of the infinitival structures which were included in the testing. We could add certain literary structures, such as participial and absolute phrases, which are learned only after a person is reading reasonably sophisticated material. Some people never learn these structures.

Conclusion

Language acquisition is not a process of merely imitating utterances or responding to stimuli. Regardless of the language they are learning, children develop phonological, syntactic, and inflectional details according to a time-table which is often at variance with the frequency and kinds of structures to which they are exposed. This timetable is seemingly universal and related to cerebral maturation.

During the formative period starting with eighteen months to two years and ending around twelve or thirteen years, children can develop a grammar of any language to which they are given adequate exposure. After that time, only minor modifications can be made. As with adult grammars, we are more interested in the system that governs the language than we are in individual sentences.

Suggested Reading

Bloom, Lois, *Language Development: Form and Function in Emerging Grammars.* Cambridge, Mass.: The M.I.T. Press, 1970.

Brown, Roger, *Psycholinguistics: Selected Papers.* New York: Free Press, 1970.

Chomsky, Carol, *The Acquisition of Syntax in Children from 5 to 10.* Cambridge, Mass.: The M.I.T. Press, 1969.

Ferguson, Charles A., and Dan Isaac Slobin, eds., *Studies of Child Language Development.* New York: Holt, Rinehart & Winston, Inc., 1973.

Greenberg, Joseph H., ed., *Universals of Language.* 2nd ed. Cambridge, Mass.: The M.I.T. Press, 1966.

Jakobson, Roman, *Child Language, Aphasia and Phonological Universals,* trans. Allan R. Keiler. The Hague: Mouton, 1968.

LENNEBERG, ERIC H., *Biological Foundations of Language.* New York: John Wiley & Sons, Inc., 1967.

————, ed., *New Directions in the Study of Language.* Cambridge, Mass.: The M.I.T. Press, 1964.

MENYUK, PAULA, *Sentences Children Use.* Cambridge, Mass.: The M.I.T. Press, 1969.

SMITH, FRANK, and GEORGE A. MILLER, eds., *The Genesis of Language.* Cambridge, Mass.: The M.I.T. Press, 1966.

WEIR, RUTH HIRSCH, *Language in the Crib.* The Hague: Mouton, 1962.

chapter 14

Change in Language

Linguists have many interesting areas of research open to them as they try to discover which features of phonology and syntax are universal. Whatever areas they investigate, however, there are two statements about language which are not open to question: (1) language has existed among all people in all cultures as far back as we have records, and (2) all living languages change.

The second statement may seem questionable to many people who cannot remember a time in which they spoke much differently from the way they do today. If they have saved letters which they wrote a number of years ago, they are unable to see any changes. Nor do the old movies shown on television use language which seems particularly archaic apart from a few words such as *natch* as a clipping of *naturally* and *you bet your boots* as a phrase signaling agreement. If they are aware that elderly people use words, pronunciations, or constructions different from theirs, they probably attribute the oddities to senility or limited education. Adults usually are aware of the language of teenagers, but they often consider it a perversion brought on by an age of permissiveness. Some adults attribute the peculiar characteristics of teenage language to teenagers' liberal use of slang. They may even remember their own youth during the 1940s with *hep cat, hubba hubba, swell, in the groove,* and *the cat's meow.* Those who entered their teens during the 1950s remember *cool, way out,* and *gone.* As they left their teens behind, they abandoned most of their slang, as they did panty raids and pajama parties.

Linguists would agree that much of the language of teenagers consists of ephemeral slang and that some of the features of the speech of the elderly are the result of senility. They would also discover some features which teenagers will carry with them throughout life and some features which the elderly have had since they were young. Although language changes fairly slowly, if we compare the usages of people from different generations we can find enough evidence of change to assure ourselves that our language, like that of the past, is not remaining static.

As we look at the written records of any language that has had a writing system for several centuries, we see ample evidence of change. Speakers of Modern English need a glossary if they are to read Shakespeare well; they find one essential if they try to read Chaucer. They are unable to read *Beowulf* in the original unless they have studied Old English, their language a thousand years ago.

We do not have to look very far back to find evidence that a spoken language is not standing still. In the last decades many words have been added to the English vocabulary, such as *fan-jet, flashcube, brain drain, biodegradable, defoliant,* and the like. People may remember when they stopped saying [grizi] and began saying [grisi], or they may have changed from [iðər] to [ayðər] or from [ɛnvəlop] to [anvəlop]. Since most people feel insecure about their language, they probably feel that their earlier pronunciation was wrong and the new one right. Linguists do not see such changes in black and white terms, but rather as trends in the language as a whole. They also see the variant pronunciations [dyu, nyu, tyuzdi, tyun] or [du, nu, tuzdi, tun] as the continuation of a change which began during the seventeenth century. They see nothing perverse in reducing initial [hw] to [w] so that such pairs as *where, wear; which, witch; while, wile* are homonyms, since they know that this is a change which began in England during the Middle Ages. Variation within a language is often evidence that a change is in progress.

Some people are appalled that their language is changing. This is especially true if they disapprove of other changes which are occurring in their world. For various languages there have been concerted efforts by academies, lexicographers, and others to arrest change and to purify the language of the alterations which occurred in the past. Samuel Johnson in the preface to *A Dictionary of the English Language* (1755) wrote a most sensible comment on change:

> Those who have been persuaded to think well of my design, require that it should fix our language, and put a stop to those alterations which time and chance have hitherto been suffered to make in it without opposition. With this consequence I will confess that I flattered myself for a while; but now begin to fear that I have indulged expectation which neither reason nor experience can justify. When we see men grow old and die at a certain time one after another, from century to century, we laugh at the elixir that promises to prolong life to a thousand years; and with equal justice may the lexicographer be derided, who being able to produce no example of a nation that has preserved their words and phrases from mutability, shall imagine that his dictionary can embalm his language, and secure it from corruption and decay, that it is in his power to change sublunary nature, or clear the world at once from folly, vanity, and affectation.

The only time a language stops changing is when there are no longer people who speak it.

From an objective standpoint, it is not possible to say that change makes a language better or worse. Would Chaucer have been a better poet if he had used twentieth-century English, or would Milton have written better if he had used Middle English? If these questions seem ridiculous, so should any claims that our language is decaying or rising to higher excellence. As scholars we are interested in learning which aspects of language change, what directions changes take, and why they occur. These will be the topics considered in this chapter.

Lexical Change

The most common type of change in language is the alteration of a single lexical item rather than a rule of the grammar. A new word may be added, or one may become obsolete; a feature such as transitivity may be changed, or a new dimension in meaning may be added. This is the kind of change in language which people are most aware of, and it is the easiest to document. It is also the most superficial in that it has little effect on the language as a whole.

1. BORROWING. As people discover new products, new ideas, or new ways of doing things, they need words to talk about them. When Roman and Irish missionaries brought Christianity to the Anglo-Saxons, they also introduced many words from Latin. With a new religion there were officials, services, and concepts which had to be discussed. Such words as the following were, therefore, borrowed: *pope, bishop, priest, abbot, nun, angel, altar, candle, disciple, hymn, psalm, shrine, martyr, church.* (All words are given in their Modern English spellings.) Some of these, such as *church* and *psalm,* had been borrowed earlier by the Romans from Greek, but English received them by way of Latin.

In the realm of foods and cooking, English has borrowed a large number of words from French. During the Middle English period such words as these entered the language: *dinner, supper, broil, baste, appetite, salmon, sardine, pork, beef, veal, mutton, poultry, grape, orange.* In many cases these imports did not reflect new products or ways of preparing them, but rather a new French-speaking aristocracy in the country. The English have probably always admired French cooking, and later borrowings reflect techniques and foods which were imported: *crêpes suzettes, crème vichysoisse, meringue glacé, consommé, bouillon, hors d'oeuvres, sautée, soufflé,* to name only a few of the most common. On the menu in a French restaurant many additional examples can be found.

English is by no means unique in its borrowing from other languages. French has imported such English words as *smoking* ("dinner jacket"), *redingote* (i.e., "riding coat"), *bifteck* ("beefsteak"), *five-o'clock*[1] ("afternoon tea"). These have been in the language for many years. More recent borrowings are much more numerous:

---

[1] An anonymous reviewer of this book has kindly informed me that although this term is still found in dictionaries, most French people say *le goûter.*

baby sitter	hamburger	pop
beatnik	hit parade	pressing
breakfast	jazz	pub
bulldozer	management	rock
business man	man made	self-service
chewing gum	one-man show	tanker
drug store	parking	traffic
flashback	pipeline	weekend

Some of these may be short-lived, but all can be found in current French publications. Because of the number, a new word has been coined to describe French with copious borrowings from English: *franglais.*

Some Frenchmen became so disturbed by these importations from their island neighbors and the Coca Cola culture across the Atlantic that in 1970 Premier Jacques Chaban-Delmas set up a commission to study the problem. As a result, some 350 words have been banned and red-blooded French words coined to replace them. The decision, of course, was influenced by such political and economic features as England's threat as a new member of the Common Market and the decline of France as a world power. It will be interesting to see whether this attempt to legislate language will be more successful than those of the Académie française, of English purists during the eighteenth century, or of the dozens of other efforts in this direction.

Borrowing is found in all parts of the world, but it is limited by the degree of contact with other languages. During the sixteenth century, English borrowed many words from French and Italian because Englishmen were frequently in contact with speakers of these languages. In Korean we find many words borrowed from Chinese and Japanese but few before this century from European languages. Russian has borrowings from Mongol, but none from the American Indian languages. Contact with a language does not have to be through living speakers. Many languages in recent times have borrowed heavily from Classical Greek and Latin although there are no longer any native speakers of these languages. The minimum prerequisite for word borrowing is that the two languages involved be in reasonably close contact.

But contact alone is not enough. The speakers who are borrowing must have a high enough regard for the speakers of the other language to consider them worthy of imitation, both in product and vocabulary. During the early settlement of what is now the United States, the English-speaking settlers had a great deal to learn about surviving in a strange environment. Since the Indians were successful in this endeavor, the earliest colonists looked to them for advice. From the seventeenth century, we find borrowings in English from the various Amerindian languages: names of trees (*hickory, pecan, persimmon, sequoia*), of animals (*raccoon, skunk, opossum, moose*), of food (*hominy, succotash, pemmican*), of Amerindian culture (*totem, powwow, papoose, squaw, moccasin, tomahawk, wigwam*).[2] After the seventeenth century, when relations between the English-speaking settlers and the Indians had changed, borrowing practically ceased. For large-

2 See Marckwardt (1958:22–33) for a fuller listing.

scale borrowing to occur, the borrowers must respect the people they are borrowing from.

The notion of respect or prestige is not necessarily related to intrinsic worth or cultural advancement, but rather to nonlinguistic reactions and biases. A conquered people may borrow words from the language of the conqueror, but the reverse almost never occurs. When the Angles, Saxons, and other Germanic tribes conquered Britain during the fifth century, they found Romanized Celts whose level of civilization was undoubtedly far superior to theirs. Yet other than place names, we find only a handful of Celtic borrowings in Old English. Either there was too wide a cultural gap for the conquerors to make use of Celtic institutions, or prejudices were too strong for borrowing to exist. Similarly, we find relatively few borrowings in American English from the various African languages, and none from Hebrew and Yiddish into German during the Hitler era.

The usual course of borrowed words is for them to be so completely assimilated into the language that native speakers are unaware of their not being native. Here are some examples from English:

Native	Borrowed
floor	ceiling
tongue	face
arm	stomach
door	table
window	chair

The borrowed words from French all seem as typically English as do those which are native.

In fact, such words as *table* and *face,* which had [a] at the time of borrowing, went through a sound change in English during the fifteenth century which raised and fronted the vowel to [e]. Along with native *name, gate, bake* we find *face* and *table* undergoing the same change in pronunciation. Another example can be drawn from German, which at an early date borrowed the Latin *palatium,* "palace." Early in the Old High German period, initial [p] became the affricate [pᶠ]. The following examples show the change in German; the English cognates show the unchanged consonant:

German	English cognate
Pfund	pound
Pfeffer	pepper
Pfeife	pipe
Pfahl	pole
Pflanze	plant

Since *palatium* was apparently well assimilated at the time of the sound change, it became *Pfalz.* Like English *face* and *table,* the German example no longer seemed foreign; it therefore went through the same sound change as the words which were native to the language.

All words, of course, do not become immediately assimilated into a language. This is especially true of technical terms which are used by a limited number of specialists in a given field. The following Latin borrowings in English still seem like foreign words, as evidenced by the retention of their original plurals:

Singular	*Plural*
larva	larvae
nebula	nebulae
vertebra	vertebrae
fungus	fungi
radius	radii
memorandum	memoranda
vortex	vortices
cicatrix	cicatrices

Others pass into the common vocabulary and take on the regular English plural, such as the following from various languages: *stadium, campus, bandit, opera, hippopotamus, gymnasium.* With the native plural formation, the words no longer seem like borrowings.

In Weinreich (1963:44) we find further examples of borrowed words which have undergone naturalization by the addition of native inflectional endings. When borrowed by American Polish, English *bootlegger* took on the regular Polish case endings, so that "one of the bootleggers" appears as *jeden z butlegerów,* with the genitive plural ending. Also in American Polish we find *rokińczer-ować,* "to rock in a rocking chair." A Greek ending is seen in the following borrowings in American Greek: *bossis* ("boss"), *bommis* ("bum"), *grihonnis* ("greenhorn"). In American Yiddish the verb *to bother* appears as the infinitive *badern* and with personal endings as *er hot gebadert,* "he bothered." Each of these examples shows assimilation of a borrowed word to native patterns.

Whether a borrowed word retains its foreign feel or is completely naturalized, it has no more effect on the language than an enlargement of the dictionary. *Soup* and *consommé* are both borrowings from French, the first totally assimilated, the second retaining an exotic tone. The addition of neither word caused changes in any of the rules of English. We use the same articles (*the, this*) as we do with the native words *water* and *beer.* We use *it* as a pronominal replacement for both the borrowed *soup* and the native *water.* Both native and borrowed words undergo the same transformations, such as subject placement.

In some instances there are effects of large-scale borrowing, particularly in phonology. For centuries English did not have [ž]. Then the palatalization rule was added during the Early Modern English period, converting /z/ to [ž], and another rule deleted /y/. Since the combination /zy/ occurred only in the middle of a word, this is the only place that [ž] emerged. We still do not have this sound at the beginning of an English word, but for many people it occurs at the end in such French borrowings as *beige, mirage, massage, camouflage, barrage, loge,* and the like. Other people have resisted this foreign influence and pronounce all of these words with final [j].

A similar influence can be seen in French, which has no native words beginning with [ps], yet there are several borrowings from Greek which are pronounced with this initial obstruent cluster: *psalmist, psaume, pseudo-, psyche, psychologie*. Similarly, initial [pt] occurs in French only in Greek borrowings: *ptérodactyle, ptôse*. English has also borrowed all of these words, but has converted them to conventional English patterns. Since the only initial obstruent clusters which are permitted in English are [sp, st, sk], the clusters [pt, ps] are reduced by dropping the [p]. A few non-native clusters are heard also in rare words such as *tse-tse* and *sclerosis*.

In none of these cases do we find the borrowed cluster extended to other words in the language. If new words were coined in English with final [ž] or in French with initial [pt], we would say that the borrowings had affected the rules for sequential constraints in these languages. So long as examples are restricted to a handful of foreign borrowings, there is no real effect on the rules of the language.

2. CREATION OF NEW WORDS. Borrowing words for new concepts, institutions, or products is a viable process provided that the needed words already exist in some other language. Since the culinary arts had been thriving in France for centuries, it was only natural that English should borrow French cooking terms along with the processes. But borrowing is not a handy source for naming products which are newly invented, not merely transplanted. Such was the case with the automobile industry when it developed in the English-speaking world. Since there was no language which had already provided names for the various parts of the car, they had to be coined from elements in English.

One possible means of creating new words is to make them up from scratch. Because they have to follow the constraints of the language, such forms as *tlimp, ngack, pdill,* and *tsend* are not possible for English. Yet there are hundreds of possible morphemes which do not currently exist in the language: *trunt, quap, beab, pliss,* and the like. Any of these could have been used to name parts of the car, but none were selected. Nor are they usually found as names of new products such as breakfast cereals. Except for a handful of totally new formations such as *kodak, nylon,* and possibly *gas,* most new words are formed by new combinations of morphemes which are already in existence. It is easier for people to remember familiar morphemes in a new arrangement than totally new words.

The most prolific process of word formation in English is **compounding**. By this process, two morphemes which can function independently as complete words are joined together: *floorboard, steering wheel, seat belt, shoulder harness, dashboard, hub cap*. As can be seen from these examples, English is inconsistent in spelling compounds solidly or with a space between the parts. There is even a third spelling: with a hyphen, as in *cross-reference*. In most cases the better dictionaries are in agreement on the spelling of a given compound, but occasionally it is possible to find three different spellings given in three equally reputable works.

To give some idea of the scope of compounding, we can list the following examples from various types of activities: *fail-safe, fan-jet, airbus, anchor man, ape hanger* ("a high handlebar on a motorcycle"), *area code, zip code, flashcube, garage sale, asphalt jungle, doggie bag, brown bagger, cash bar, booze hound, bar fly, fruit fly, brain drain, cable TV, carbon dating, credit card, charge-plate.* It is hard to find an area of the English vocabulary which does not contain a large number of compounds.

A second process of word formation is known as **affixing:** the formation of a word by the addition of a suffix, prefix, or infix to another morpheme. An infix, as the name suggests, is added within another morpheme, rather than after or before it, as is the case with suffixes and prefixes. A few examples of fairly recent creations by means of affixation are *biodegradable, de-escalate, defoliant, astrodynamics, beautification, apolitical, antiperspirant.* Some affixes become a fad and lead to large numbers of new creations. One example is *anti-,* which had existed in the language for many years in such words as *antiseptic, antifreeze,* and *anticlimax.* During the 1950s and 1960s, the prefix attained great popularity, leading to the creation of new words and to the increased use of others which had been relatively obscure: *anti-war, anti-story, anti-hero, antiachiever* ("a recalcitrant student who refuses to achieve"), *antigravity, antinovel, antipoverty,* and so on. Earlier fads witnessed the proliferation of new words with the suffixes *-ize* and *-wise.*

Other means of forming new words involve **clipping** (*disco* from *discotheque, fan* from *fanatic, pants* from *pantaloons*), **blending** (*Europass* from *European rail pass, Medicaid* from *Medical Aid*), **acronomy** (*ABM* from *Antiballistic missile, LSD* from *lysergic acid diethylamide, laser* from *light amplification by stimulated emission of radiation*), **back formation** (i.e., the clipping of what appears to be an affix, as *to lase* from *laser, abort* from *abortion, escalate* from *escalator*), **creations from proper names** (*curium, Teddy bear, peeping tom, levi's*), **onomatopoeic creations** (*swoop, plunk, pop*), and **functional shift** from one part of speech to another without the addition of affixes (noun to verb: *to bug, to knee;* verb to noun: *a flyby, a happening, a hold*).

The lexicon can be changed by the loss of words as well as by their addition. Many new coinages are very short-lived, but others remain in the vocabulary for many years. One of the most common causes for the loss of vocabulary items is the discontinuation of the object they name. *Soap flakes* is already obsolete, and *wash board, running board,* and *rumble seat* are on the way out. Many teenagers do not know the following terms for items of women's clothing: *fascinator, snood, peddlepushers, step-ins.* Most of them know what a *bustle* and *bloomers* are, but they find the words quaint. Nor do they know what *clocks* in a pair of socks might be. Even a cursory inspection of a glossary to the works of Shakespeare or Chaucer reveals abundant examples of words which are no longer part of the English vocabulary.

3. Shifts in Meaning. More productive as a means of enlarging the vocabulary than borrowing and creating new words from native elements is expanding the meaning but not the form of a word that already exists in the language. Before the invention of the automobile, the word *bumper* already existed as "the buffer of a railway carriage." The earliest citation given in the *Oxford English Dictionary* is 1839. An earlier meaning had existed since the seventeenth century: "A cup or glass of wine, etc., filled to the brim, *esp.* when drunk as a toast." Perhaps this cup or glass was called a *bumper* because it was "bumped" in toasting. For the front and rear bumpers on an automobile, it was a simple process to extend the meaning

of the word. Other words already in existence whose meanings were extended to cover objects on the automobile are *starter, muffler,* and *pedal.*

Texts in historical linguistics traditionally give at least four processes by which words change in meaning. By **amelioration,** a word is assigned to a more favorable class of objects than previously. The word *fond* originally meant foolish. *Nimble* comes originally from Old English *niman,* "to take." It now means adroit. The opposite of amelioration is **pejoration.** By this process, a word becomes attached to a less favorable class of objects than previously. A *hussy* was at one time a housewife, and *to counterfeit* meant to imitate anything. Both words have unfavorable connotations today, although they were once neutral.

A different type of classification involves changes in the number of objects named. If a word refers to a larger class of objects than previously, it has undergone **generalization.** A *place* was originally the same thing as a plaza, and a *butcher* was a person who slaughtered goats. A *bikini* was at one time a swimming garment for women; it is no longer restricted by sex. In the opposite direction, a word can undergo **specialization** and refer to a smaller class of objects. A *wife* was originally any woman, a *deer* was any animal, and *disease* was lack of ease for any reason. A word may undergo amelioration or pejoration and at the same time generalization or specialization. As we saw in the last paragraph, *counterfeit* has undergone pejoration; it has also been specialized in meaning.

More important for the purpose of expanding the vocabulary are metaphoric extensions of words. A congressman's beliefs may remind us of the peacefulness of a dove or of the aggressiveness of a hawk. Instead of coining a new word to refer to him, we extend the meaning of *dove* or *hawk.* Similarly, if a person's actions strike us as cowardly, we call him *chicken.* Other animal names which have been extended to humans include *bear, bull, ox, mouse, moose, jackass, fox,* and so on. There is hardly an animal name that has been overlooked. The associations in most cases are clear. Other metaphoric extensions include *acid, bomb* (in football), *cameo* (in movies), *cage* (a dress), *clad* (coin), *digger* (in a hippie commune), *granny* (gown), *grass, head,* and the like.

4. THE NATURE OF LEXICAL CHANGE. When there are large numbers of words added to a lexicon by borrowing, new formation, or semantic expansion, there are sometimes changes in the rules of the grammar. The rules for stress assignment in Modern English, for example, almost certainly result from the large number of borrowed words from Latin and French. Unless there is some such effect in the rules, borrowing has no more influence than that it enlarges the vocabulary.

There are good reasons for asking whether such processes of word formation as compounding and affixation should be treated as nothing more than lexical addition like borrowed words, or whether they should be considered as the output of productive rules. Both compounds and derived words are understood in ways that *avocado, tulip,* and *honest* are not. A *horse doctor* is "a doctor who treats horses," and a *horse opera* is "an opera which is about horses." Many compounds have the same meaning as possessives: *frog legs, goose liver, chicken breast, ox tail, horse meat.* In each of these examples, we can take the second element, such as *meat* in *horse meat,* and add an *of* phrase: *meat of a horse.* In like manner, in *Bill's cancellation of his subscription, cancellation* is understood to be in the same relationship to the nouns *Bill* and *subscription* as the verb *cancel* is in *Bill cancelled his subscription.* Linguists are still debating over how to handle this information. If compounds and affixed words are derived by transformations or some other process, their addition is of no more importance than the creation of a new sentence. They are not real expansions of the vocabulary in the sense that *sputnik* and *charisma* are.

In addition to changes which result in the addition of new lexical items or the loss of old ones, there are changes in features. In Shakespeare's time, the verb *to fall* could be transitive, as seen in *Richard III*:

> Tomorrow in the battle think on me,
> And fall thy edgeless sword. (V, iii, 135–6)

Or this example from *As You Like It*:

> The common executioner,
> Whose heart th' accustom'd sight of death makes hard,
> Falls not the axe upon the humbled neck
> But first begs pardon. (III, v, 3–6)

The verb is no longer transitive. Today we have to say something like "let the axe fall," with an intransitive use. A verb whose dictionary entry at one time specified it as transitive has now been changed. Nouns with plurals formed by means other than the rules of Modern English are given in the lexicon with the plural as an exceptional feature. Hence, at one time *curriculum* and *stadium* were given with the plurals *curricula* and *stadia,* forms which were perfectly regular in Latin but which for English are exceptional. When *stadia* gave way to *stadiums,* the lexical entry lost the irregular feature, and the word was then allowed to form its plural according to the rules of the language. *Curriculum* is showing signs of similar regularization.

Addition and Loss of Rules

More influential than alterations in individual lexical items are the changes which occur in the rules of a language. Since most rules apply to large numbers of possible morphemes or structures, a change in this part of the grammar can have a widespread effect on the language as a whole, whereas a change in the lexicon affects only a single morpheme.

By the middle of the seventeenth century, a phonological rule was added in English which resulted in the loss of [t] at the phonetic level when it occurred between consonants. We see the effects of this change in such words as *mortgage* and *Shaftsbury,* where an obstruent follows; the spelling reflects the earlier pronunciation before the rule was added. Before a nasal we find original [t] lost in such words as *Christmas, chestnut, Westminster.* Before syllabic [l] we see the change in *bustle, gristle, wrestle, epistle, castle, thistle,* and the like. It does not occur if the [l] is in a different morpheme from [t]: *costly, ghastly, beastly.* It should be noted that the restriction depends upon morphemic division, not the syllable. In *wrestler,* the [t] is lost because the [l] is in the same morpheme. If we were depending upon syllable division, we would have no way of explaining why the rule applies in *wrestler* but not in *costly,* both of which have [t] and [l] in separate syllables.

Let us limit ourselves to one aspect of the rule: [t] before syllabic nasals. Since the following words have [t] between consonants (syllabic [n] follows), they are pronounced without [t]: *soften, often, fasten, hasten, listen, glisten, moisten.* Since adults are no longer able to make major revisions of their internalized grammars, they cannot change the underlying forms of these words, but will merely add a rule which deletes /t/. Simplifying the underlying forms and derivations so that we can concentrate exclusively on this rule, we can provide forms like these:

Underlying:	/fæst + n/	/hest + n/	/moyst + n/
/t/ deletion:	fæs + n	hes + n	moys + n
Phonetic:	[fæsn]	[hesn]	[moysn]
Spelling:	fasten	hasten	moisten

These adults will continue to have an underlying /t/ in all of these words, the same as they had before they added the deletion rule.

Children learning the language have considerably more flexibility. They are not limited to particular structures, but can develop their grammars according to the language as they are exposed to it. To get phonetic [fæsn, hesn, moysn], they have the choice of developing underlying forms without /t/ or maintaining the same forms as members of the earlier generation: underlying /t/ and a rule which deletes it in the appropriate environment. Since children are not linguists who have specialized in historical developments in the language, their decision will not be based upon past forms of the words, but rather upon the information which is available to them. Also, they will develop the needed forms and rules before they learn the spellings of the words which are involved; hence, the letter *t* will have no influence.

For words such as *fasten, hasten,* and *moisten,* they will know related words which have phonetic [t]:

Without [t]	*With* [t]
soften	soft
fasten	fast
hasten	haste
moisten	moist
often	(oft)
listen	(list)

Since they probably will not know the obsolete *oft* or *list,* they are given in parentheses. For the rest of the words, there will be the problem of showing that [fæst] and [fæsn] are related. Since *fasten* means "to make fast," it is unavoidable that it will be recognized as *fast* with a suffix added. Yet the surface forms are [fæs] in *fasten* and [fæst] in *fast.* The presence or absence of a phoneme can indicate two completely different morphemes, as we can see with [bes] and [best], *base* and *baste.* The obvious answer is that for [fæs] and [fæst] there should be identical underlying forms. The children, therefore, will incorporate a /t/ deletion rule into their internalized grammars and not alter the underlying representations of *fasten, hasten,* and similar words.

The rule which deletes /t/ before syllabic nasals resulted in different phonetic forms than existed before the rule was added. The change was entirely in the phonological rules, not in the underlying representations. People today have the same underlying forms as did those before the rule was added. Their surface forms are different because they have a rule which was not previously there.

For another example of a rule which was added to a language without affecting underlying forms, let us look at final obstruents in German. In the neighborhood of the year 1000, a rule was added which made all obstruents in final position voiceless. Before the rule was added, the following derivations could be found (as usual, including only the relevant details):

Underlying:	/gibe/	/gab/	/binde/	/band/	/birge/	/barg/
Rules:	———	———	———	———	———	———
Surface:	[gibe]	[gab]	[binde]	[band]	[birge]	[barg]
Meaning:	"I give"	"I gave"	"I bind"	"I bound"	"I hide"	"I hid"

The new rule made all obstruents at the end of a word voiceless; it did not affect those in other positions. Hence, adults who added the rule would have different phonetic realizations for some words than they had previously:

Underlying:	/gibe/	/gab/	/binde/	/band/	/birge/	/barg/
Devoicing:	———	gap	———	bant	———	bark
Surface:	[gibe]	[gap]	[binde]	[bant]	[birge]	[bark]
Meaning:	"I give"	"I gave"	"I bind"	"I bound"	"I hide"	"I hid"

Since adults are severely limited as to the kinds of changes they can make, they did not alter their original underlying forms, but rather derived their new surface forms by means of a devoicing rule.

Children learning German would find no reason to provide different underlying forms from their parents in words like [gap, bant, bark]. Because of the alternation between voiced and voiceless stops in related forms of the same words, they would maintain the older underlying forms. The same system continues into Modern German, which is rich in alternates of this kind. Here are a few examples:

	Voiceless	*Voiced*
Plurals:	[kɔrp] basket	[körbə] baskets
	[lit] song	[lidər] songs
	[tak] day	[tagə] days
Possessives:	[rawp] robbery	[rawbəs] of robbery
	[kɪnt] child	[kɪndəs] child's
	[könɪk] king	[könɪgəs] king's
Derivatives:	[urlawp] leave	[urlawbər] soldier on leave
	[nɔrt] north	[nɔrdɪš] northern
	[krik] war	[krigər] soldier
Verb forms:	[grup] I dug	[grabən] to dig
	[fant] I found	[fɪndən] to find
	[flok] I flew	[fligən] to fly

As with the deletion of /t/ in English, the German change from voiced to voiceless obstruents at the end of a word added a rule to the phonological component and hence affected the surface forms of many words, but it did not alter their underlying forms.

Change does not have to result from the addition of a rule; it can also result from the loss of one. Old English had a syntactic rule that placed verbs which were in dependent clauses at the end of the clause. We find examples like the following:

14.1
> *God   saw   then [that it good was].*
> God geseah þa   þæt hit god **wæs**.

14.2
> [*Because (the)   Picts   women (did) not have*], (they) asked (for) them
> Mid þy   Peohtas wif   **næfdon**   bædon   him
> *from (the)   Scots.*
> fram   Scottum.

At the time of the extant written records of Old English, the rule was optional. For example, in *The Voyages of Ohthere and Wulfstan,* we find the first sentence below with the rule applied, the second without it. These are consecutive sentences in the text.

14.3
> *Ohthere   said (to) his   lord,   Alfred (the)   king,*
> Ohthere sæde   his hlaforde, Ælfrede   cyninge,
> [*that he (of)   all   Northmen   farthest north dwelt*].
> þæt he   ealra Norðmonna norþmest **bude**.

14.4
> *He   said [that he dwelt on the   land   northward*
> He cwæð   þæt he **bude** on þæm lande norþweardum
> *along the west sea*].
> wiþ þa Westsæ.

The rule which extraposed the verb in dependent clauses was operative throughout the Old English period, but as an optional rule. Early in the Middle English period (c. 1100 to c. 1500), the rule was lost. Using Modern English spellings, we can illustrate the effect. While the optional rule was still in the language, either of the following was possible:

14.5a   God saw [that it good was].
   b   God saw [that it was good].

After the rule was lost, only the second of these was possible. It should be noted that Modern German has retained the rule, but English has lost it.

Changes in Underlying Forms

The addition or loss of a phonological rule in itself does not affect underlying representations of morphemes any more than an addition or loss of transformational rules changes underlying syntactic structures. In both cases, only surface forms are affected. For the examples we have considered so far, there is enough evidence from related words or alternate syntactic structures for children acquiring the language to incorporate the same set of underlying forms and rules in their grammar as members of older generations had.

This is not always the case. In King (1969:47), we find an interesting development of the German final devoicing rule. Apparently all of the dialects of German added this rule between A.D. 900 and 1200, but at a later time some of them lost it. For example, the early dialect of German which became Yiddish apparently went through the following stages:

Stage One

Underlying:	/lid/	/lidər/
Rules:	———	———
Surface:	[lid]	[lidər]
Meaning:	song	songs

The devoicing rule was then added:

Stage Two

Underlying:	/lid/	/lidər/
Rules:	lit	———
Surface:	[lit]	[lidər]
Meaning:	song	songs

Later the devoicing rule was lost:

Stage Three

Underlying:	/lid/	/lidər/
Rules:	———	———
Surface:	[lid]	[lidər]
Meaning:	song	songs

This is the situation in many dialects of Modern Yiddish. The surface forms of Stage One are found once again, with voiced obstruents in word-final position. Since the devoicing rule did not affect underlying forms, it is natural that the earlier surface forms reappeared.

There were some words, however, that did not have alternation on the surface between voiced and voiceless obstruents of the nature of [lit] and [lidər]. Examples from Modern Yiddish cited in King (1969:47) include *avek*, "away," *hant*, "hand," and *gelt*, "money." Apparently what happened is that during the period in which the devoicing rule existed in the language, the underlying forms of these words changed. Hence, the following developments took place with two divisions of Stage Two, before and after the change in underlying forms:

Stage One

Underlying:	/lid/	/lidər/	/avɛg/	/hand/	/gɛld/
Rules:	———	———	———	———	———
Surface:	[lid]	[lidər]	[avɛg]	[hand]	[gɛld]
Meaning:	song	songs	away	hand	money

The devoicing rule was added:

Stage Two (Early)

Underlying:	/lid/	/lidər/	/avɛg/	/hand/	/gɛld/
Rules:	lit	———	avɛk	hant	gɛlt
Surface:	[lit]	[lidər]	[avɛk]	[hant]	[gɛlt]
Meaning:	song	songs	away	hand	money

Some underlying forms were changed:

Stage Two (Late)

Underlying:	/lid/	/lidər/	/avɛk/	/hant/	/gɛlt/
Rules:	lit	———	———	———	———
Surface:	[lit]	[lidər]	[avɛk]	[hant]	[gɛlt]
Meaning:	song	songs	away	hand	money

The devoicing rule was lost:

Stage Three

Underlying:	/lid/	/lidər/	/avɛk/	/hant/	/gɛlt/
Rules:	———	———	———	———	———
Surface:	[lid]	[lidər]	[avɛk]	[hant]	[gɛlt]
Meaning:	song	songs	away	hand	money

This means that in the modern period, after loss of the devoicing rule, some words such as *avek, hant,* and *gelt* still had phonetic voiceless obstruents at the end because their underlying forms had been altered.

For another example, let us look at a change which occurred at a time before English, German, Dutch, Swedish, Danish, Icelandic, Norwegian, and related languages split up. We call the language at that time **Germanic.** Before that it belonged to a larger group known as **Indo-European,** which included Italic (from which Latin developed), Greek, Celtic, Slavic, and several other groups of languages. At the time of development from Indo-European to Germanic, several rules were added which affected the obstruent system of the language. This change is often called the **Germanic consonant shift** or **Grimm's Law,** after the early nineteenth-century German linguist and collector of fairy tales who described it.

The late Indo-European obstruent system apparently contained only one fricative but a large number of stops. One group of these, the labiovelars, merged with the velars in Germanic; we will, therefore, not consider them in the discussion which follows. Leaving out the labiovelars, we can give the following obstruent system for late Indo-European:

	Labials	Dentals	Velars
Aspirated stops	[bʰ]	[dʰ]	[gʰ]
Unaspirated stops			
Voiceless	[p]	[t]	[k]
Voiced	[b]	[d]	[g]
Fricative		[s]	

This system, which was arrived at during the nineteenth century, does not conflict with any of the phonological universals which have been recently suggested. Wherever there are velars, there are corresponding dentals or labials. The presence of fricatives presupposes the presence of stops, but not necessarily vice versa. A system which has nine fricatives and only one stop would be unlikely to occur, but this one, though unbalanced, is possible. Also, a dental fricative without a velar is possible; when there is only one fricative, it should not be [x] but a front one. Finally, since voiceless obstruents are more natural than voiced, we would expect a single fricative to be [s] instead of [z] or [ð].

Although the final results of Grimm's Law are clear, the absence of written records from the time it was in progress makes the order of changes a problem. Scholars do not agree on the exact sequence of events, but that does not affect the issue we are illustrating. One possible sequence is as follows.

First, a rule was added which aspirated all voiceless stops except those which were preceded by an obstruent. That is, [p, t, k] became [pʰ, tʰ, kʰ] unless they were the second member of an obstruent cluster such as [sp, st, sk]. This changed the obstruent system to the following:

	Labials	*Dentals*	*Velars*
Aspirated stops			
Voiceless	[pʰ]	[tʰ]	[kʰ]
Voiced	[bʰ]	[dʰ]	[gʰ]
Unaspirated stops			
Voiceless	[p]	[t]	[k]
Voiced	[b]	[d]	[g]
Fricative		[s]	

Using just the dentals, we can illustrate the change with the following derivations:

Underlying:	/dʰe/	/trei/	/stel/	/ed/	/sed/
Grimm's Law 1:	——	tʰrei	——	——	——
Surface:	[dʰe]	[tʰrei]	[stel]	[ed]	[sed]
English form:	do	three	still	eat	sit

The underlying and surface forms are for roots only, since inflectional and other suffixes would merely complicate the derivations with morphemes not related to our illustrations. Also, vowel changes and other developments are not included.

Next, a rule was added which changed all aspirated consonants from [−continuant] to [+continuant]. That is, aspirated stops became the corresponding fricatives. The voiced members retained voicing and place of obstruction:

[bʰ]	became	[β]
[dʰ]	became	[ð]
[gʰ]	became	[γ]

Similarly, with the voiceless aspirates:

[pʰ]	became	[φ]
[tʰ]	became	[θ]
[kʰ]	became	[x]

Now, using the same derivations as before, we can illustrate the effects of the second rule of Grimm's Law:

Underlying:	/dʰe/	/trei/	/stel/	/ed/	/sed/
Grimm's Law 1:	———	tʰrei	———	———	———
Grimm's Law 2:	ðe	θrei	———	———	———
Surface:	[ðe]	[θrei]	[stel]	[ed]	[sed]
English form:	do	three	still	eat	sit

The initial [θr] of *three* now sounds like English.

A third rule made all stops voiceless. No other features were changed:

[b]   became   [p]
[d]   became   [t]
[g]   became   [k]

Adding this rule to our derivations, we find

Underlying:	/dʰe/	/trei/	/stel/	/ed/	/sed/
Grimm's Law 1:	———	tʰrei	———	———	———
Grimm's Law 2:	ðe	θrei	———	———	———
Grimm's Law 3:	———	———	———	et	set
Surface:	[ðe]	[θrei]	[stel]	[et]	[set]
English form:	do	three	still	eat	sit

The changes in vowels which eventually gave the Modern English forms were not part of Grimm's Law; some of them, in fact, did not occur until many centuries later. We need one more change: initial [ð] to [d], which occurred later than Grimm's Law. Otherwise, the consonants are the ones we find in Modern English.

As a result of Grimm's Law, the obstruent system changed to the following:

	Labials	*Dentals*	*Velars*
Stops			
Voiceless	[p]	[t]	[k]
Fricatives			
Voiceless	[φ]	[θ], [s]	[x]
Voiced	[β]	[ð]	[γ]

There was also a [z] from another source, Verner's Law, which should probably be included in Grimm's Law. We have omitted it here to simplify the presentation. This system with more fricatives than stops was unstable, and later rules changed the voiced fricatives in many environments to voiced stops, as we saw with *do*. Since this change is not part of Grimm's Law, we will say nothing further about it.

At one time, linguists speculated that the changes effected by Grimm's Law must have occurred over many centuries. This assumption was based on the then popular belief that all changes in language are gradual. Recently this belief has been challenged, but there is as yet no very convincing evidence to prove that changes do or do not occur gradually. To simplify our illustration, let us assume that all three rules were added during the lifetime of a single generation. The adults of this generation would be able to do nothing more than add a set of rules to their grammars, keeping their original underlying forms. For later generations, there would be no variant surface forms of morphemes to justify more abstract underlying forms. Instead, the surface consonants from the preceding generation would become their underlying consonants. Instead of having an underlying form like /trei/ for *three* and then a set of rules to convert it to [θrei], they would have underlying /θrei/. There would be no reason for them to incorporate the rules of Grimm's Law into their grammars. Hence, there would be a change in underlying forms. In case the three rules were not added at the same time, the eventual result would be the same as we have given. The difference would be that there would be intervening generations of speakers with the intermediate forms we have given in our derivations. Eventually there would be a group of people with underlying /θrei/.

During the nineteenth century, when students of language recognized only surface structures, change in language was looked upon as something that occurred at a given point in time and then was finished. We still say that the actual change occurs in this way, but that it may be in the rules rather than in underlying forms. If so, the underlying forms remain unaltered, and a rule containing the essence of the change remains in the grammar. We see important reasons for distinguishing between changes in underlying representations and changes in the rules of a grammar.

Changes in Rules

As we have seen, it is possible for a rule to be added to or lost from a grammar, affecting the surface structures of sentences but not their underlying forms. It is also possible for underlying forms to be changed, generally as the result of rules such as Grimm's Law which do not provide enough data for the child learning the language to incorporate the underlying forms of adults. In addition to changes in underlying forms and those which increase or decrease the number of rules, there are modifications of rules. This kind of change does not add a new rule or drop one, but rather alters some aspect of a rule that is in the grammar.

Early in the Old English period, there was a rule which converted /sk/ to [š] whenever a front vowel followed. Before this rule was added, the following surface forms resulted:

Underlying:	/skɪp/	/skɪn/	/skɔrt/	/skuːr/	/skriːn/
Rules:	———	———	———	———	———
Surface:	[skɪp]	[skɪn]	[skɔrt]	[skuːr]	[skriːn]
Spelling:	scip	scin	scort	scur	scrin
Modern:	ship	shin	short	shower	shrine

After its addition, these derivations could be found:

Underlying:	/skɪp/	/skɪn/	/skɔrt/	/skuːr/	/skriːn/
Rules:	šɪp	šɪn	———	———	———
Surface:	[šɪp]	[šɪn]	[skɔrt]	[skuːr]	[skriːn]
Spelling:	scip	scin	scort	scur	scrin
Modern:	ship	shin	short	shower	shrine

At this point phonetic [sk] and [š] were in complementary distribution, [š] occurring only before front vowels, [sk] everywhere else. There would, therefore, be no /š/ at the underlying level; rather, surface [š] would be derived from /sk/ by a phonological rule.

By the time of most of our extant written records of Old English, this rule had become more general. Instead of applying just to those instances of /sk/ which preceded front vowels, it came to apply to /sk/ regardless of what followed: front vowel, back vowel, or liquid. The speakers who added this generalized version of the rule had derivations like these:

Underlying:	/skɪp/	/skɪn/	/skɔrt/	/skuːr/	/skriːn/
Rules:	šɪp	šɪn	šɔrt	šuːr	šriːn
Surface:	[šɪp]	[šɪn]	[šɔrt]	[šuːr]	[šriːn]
Spelling:	scip	scin	scort	scur	scrin
Modern:	ship	shin	short	shower	shrine

Future generations learning the language would hear [š] in all of these words and no alternations with [sk]. They would, therefore, have no reason to retain the rule or the underlying forms with /sk/. Instead, their derivations would be as follows:

Underlying:	/šɪp/	/šɪn/	/šɔrt/	/šuːr/	/šriːn/
Rules:	———	———	———	———	———
Surface:	[šɪp]	[šɪn]	[šɔrt]	[šuːr]	[šriːn]
Spelling:	scip	scin	scort	scur	scrin
Modern:	ship	shin	short	shower	shrine

This generalization of the rule to all environments led to the reformation of underlying forms and the loss of the rule.

We know that it was lost because later words with /sk/ were borrowed from Old Norse, and they occur with surface [sk], not [š]: *skin, skirt, skull,* and the like. We have also borrowed words from other sources which have surface [sk]: *schedule, scheme, scherzo, schizophrenia,* and the like. The first of these, *schedule,* has recently changed to initial [š] in some dialects of British English, but this is a sporadic change of a single lexical item. If English still derived surface [š] from underlying /sk/, we would have a large number of exceptional words which would have to be marked in the lexicon as foreign borrowings that are not subject to the rule.

A rule that is generalized does not have to lead to loss. For example, if a dialect of German had devoicing of final fricatives, it would have a rule that applied to segments which were [+obstruent] and [+continuant]. If this rule were generalized to apply to the larger class of fricatives and stops, the feature continuant would no longer be in the rule. Since the rule would apply only to those obstruents in final position, there would be alternations between forms with final suffixes and those without them; hence, the rule would remain in the language. It would merely apply to a larger class of segments.

The Explanation of Change

Linguistic literature of the past two centuries contains many descriptions of changes that have occurred in languages, but it is rare that anyone tries to explain why a change occurs or what limits exist regarding change.

The earliest attempts were guesswork. It was suggested, for example, that the consonant changes brought about by Grimm's Law and the later Old High German shift occurred because the Germanic people were living at a high altitude and their breathing habits caused the changes. Other explanations said that the Germanic people were robust and forceful and that their way of life led to a more vigorous habit of speaking. These explanations are pure fancy. There is no way of knowing where the Germanic tribes were at the time of the first consonant shift, but there is reasonably good evidence that they were on the lowland near the Baltic Sea, not in the mountainous regions of southern Germany. Nor is there any evidence that the lifestyle of a group of people affects their phonological rules. In the course of history, there have been people on all continents as aggressive as the Germanic tribes were, and none of them experienced phonological changes like Grimm's Law.

Aspects of the climate certainly affect the vocabulary, resulting in differences between languages in tropical zones and those in arctic regions, between those on the plains and others in the mountains, or between those in a desert and others in a rain forest. But there have been no convincing arguments offered to prove that humidity, altitude, heat, or other climatic features affect such aspects of language as phonology or syntax. Popular explanations that people in a hot climate become lazy and talk slowly in contrast to their fast-talking northern neighbors simply do not stand up under the facts. Nor do people in climates that are excessively humid or arid develop nasalized vowels because of their swollen nasal passages.

Anatomical and personality traits are likewise unsupported causes of change which have been suggested in the past. There is some variation among the various races as to the shape of the nose and jaw or the size of the lips. None of these differences, however, is great enough to cause noticeable variations in speaking. Also, it is questionable that any character trait can be attributed to all speakers of any language; even if it could, there is no evidence that energetic people, for example, develop different rules from those who are lazy. No differences in rules have been recorded which result from regularly eating dinner early at five in the afternoon or late at ten in the evening, from being scrupulously punctual or habitually late, from being peaceful or warlike. Early explorers in America, the South Seas, Asia, and Africa came home with all kinds of fanciful reports on the languages and customs of the people they encountered. Their impressions of language were generally of little value.

After a change has started, it is possible to trace its spread. Whether we are speaking of a change in the lexicon or in the rules of a language, there are many studies which document the borrowing process. Yet this does not tell us why the change originated in the first place.

Some phonological changes occur because of assimilation. For example, palatalization is the result of the assimilation of non-palatals to the palatal position of /y/. Changes that are the clear result of assimilation obviously originate because they promote a more natural, easier pronunciation. However, only part of the changes in any language are assimilatory in nature. Grimm's Law cannot be explained in this way, nor can the Old English changes in word order.

For the actual causes of most changes in language, we are in little better position to give satisfactory answers than linguists were a century ago. Yet with the study of universals, we are better able to say which kinds of changes are more likely than others. It is not probable that a change will remove all the front vowels in a language and leave only those in the back, nor that one will convert all stops into fricatives. In either case only one feature is involved; but in spite of the simplicity of the change, the result would be one which violates universal constraints on what is a possible phonological system. The direction of changes is usually toward making the language adhere more closely to universal constraints, not moving it further away from them. For example, in most of the Germanic languages the earlier fricatives [ð, θ] have been replaced by the corresponding stops; English is exceptional in not changing. Another example can be seen with the voiced aspirated stops, which are rare among the languages of the world. The Indo-European series [bʰ, dʰ, gʰ] became the corresponding voiced fricatives in Germanic. In Greek and Italic they became the voiceless aspirated stops [pʰ, tʰ, kʰ]. In Slavic and Celtic they lost aspiration, becoming [b, d, g]. Only in Indic did the voiced aspirates remain, and there only with the anterior stops. There is a clear tendency among all languages to make changes in the direction of the more usual systems.

Even after we discover the universal constraints in language, there will still be many unanswered questions. The trend is from the unusual to the universal, but this does not explain how the unusual state came about in the first place. If voiced aspirated stops are less normal than those that are voiced and unaspirated or voiceless and aspirated, then why did Indo-European develop them in the first place? If the dental fricatives [θ, ð] are uncommon, why did they develop through Grimm's Law?

Other questions involve a situation in which two languages have the same rules in some part of the grammar, yet one language makes a change and the other does not. For example, when Old English changed /sk/ to [š], why did Old Norse not make the same change? Both had the same phonological patterns. Also, why does a change occur at one time rather than another? The conditions for palatalization in English had existed for centuries before the process actually appeared. Why do we find it in the seventeenth century and not earlier? Why did it not wait until the twentieth century? Why did it occur at all?

Until the middle of the twentieth century, linguists were generally content with describing change. Today we are still interested in description, but we also would like to explain it. We could draw a rough parallel to a doctor describing a patient's symptoms or diagnosing the cause of them. The description is always easier than the explanation. Linguists today know a great deal more than their nineteenth-century predecessors did about the nature of language and the developments that a language undergoes in time. Yet the many questions which we still cannot answer point to a large number of interesting studies for linguists of the future. Specialists in historical linguistics will find many problems yet to be solved.

Suggested Reading

BLOOMFIELD, LEONARD, *Language.* New York: Holt, Rinehart & Winston, Inc., 1933.

DOBSON, E. J., *English Pronunciation 1500–1700.* 2nd ed. Oxford: Clarendon Press, 1968.

HOCKETT, CHARLES F., "Sound Change," *Language* 41 (1965): 185–204.

HOENIGSWALD, HENRY M., *Language Change and Linguistic Reconstruction.* Chicago: University of Chicago Press, 1960.

JESPERSEN, OTTO, *A Modern English Grammar on Historical Principles.* Copenhagen: Ejnar Munksgaard, 1909–1949.

KING, ROBERT D., "Functional Load and Sound Change," *Language* 43 (1967): 831–52.

———, *Historical Linguistics and Generative Grammar.* Englewood Cliffs, N. J.: Prentice-Hall, Inc., 1969.

KIPARSKY, PAUL, "Linguistic Universals and Linguistic Change," in *Universals in Linguistic Theory,* ed. Emmon Bach and Robert T. Harms. New York: Holt, Rinehart & Winston, Inc., 1968.

KÖKERITZ, HELGE, *Shakespeare's Pronunciation.* New Haven, Conn.: Yale University Press, 1953.

LEHMANN, WINFRED P., "A Definition of Proto-Germanic: A Study in the Chronological Delimitation of Languages," *Language* 37 (1961): 67–74.

———, *Historical Linguistics, An Introduction.* 2nd ed. New York: Holt, Rinehart & Winston, Inc., 1973.

LUICK, KARL, *Historische Grammatik der Englischen Sprache.* Cambridge, Mass.: Harvard University Press, 1964.

MARTINET, ANDRÉ, *Économie des changements phonétiques.* 3rd ed. Berne: A. Francke, 1970.

PAUL, HERMANN, *Prinzipien der Sprachgeschichte.* Tübingen: Max Niemeyer Verlag, 1920.

PENZL, HERBERT, "The Evidence for Phonemic Changes," in *Studies Presented to Joshua Whatmough on His Sixtieth Birthday,* ed. Ernst Pulgram. The Hague: Mouton, 1957.

POSTAL, PAUL M., *Aspects of Phonological Theory.* New York: Harper & Row, Publishers, 1968.

TRAUGOTT, ELIZABETH CLOSS, *A History of English Syntax.* New York: Holt, Rinehart & Winston, Inc., 1972.

WEINREICH, URIEL, WILLIAM LABOV, and MARVIN I. HERZOG, "Empirical Foundations for a Theory of Language Change," in *Directions for Historical Linguistics,* ed. W. P. Lehmann and Yakov Malkiel. Austin: University of Texas Press, 1968.

WYLD, HENRY CECIL, *A History of Modern Colloquial English.* Oxford: Basil Blackwell, 1956.

chapter 15

Contemporary Variation

For all languages about which we have very much information, two facts can be stated without exception. First, as we saw in the last chapter, all living languages change with time. A language ceases to change only when there are no longer any speakers of it. Second, the internalized grammars of the speakers of a language are not uniform. People from different geographical regions do not produce exactly the same kinds of syntactic and phonetic structures, nor do they have all of the same vocabulary items. Differences can also be found among people within a single geographical region who are separated from one another because of economic, racial, religious, or other social factors. Even within the language of one individual, certain rules are used with formal styles which are not found in the more casual. In this chapter we will be concerned with these variations which exist in languages at a given point in time.

Individual Contextual Styles

We all experience situations in which we are more relaxed than in others. When speaking before a group of people or being interviewed for a job, we are normally conscious of our speech and use words, pronunciations, and constructions which we consider to be the best English, Danish, Japanese, or whatever language we are speaking. If we are talking to a stranger at a bus stop, we are more at ease than we are in an interview, and with friends we are still more relaxed. With very close friends and members of our family, we do not think about our language at all.

Such changes in individual contextual styles have long been noticed by good playwrights and fiction writers. In the first act of *King Lear,* we find Goneril catering to her father's desire for flattery with language that is highly formal:

> Sir, I love you more than word can wield the matter;
> Dearer than eyesight, space, and liberty;
> Beyond what can be valued, rich or rare;
> No less than life, with grace, health, beauty, honour;
> As much as child e'er lov'd, or father found;
> A love that makes breath poor, and speech unable.
> Beyond all manner of so much I love you. (I, i, 54–60)

The claims are so exaggerated as to be unbelievable, yet the vain, doddering old king is pleased. The language is as extravagant as the claims. Later, when Goneril is alone with her sister Regan, she shifts from her formal style to one that is unadorned:

> Gon. Sister, it is not little I have to say of what most nearly appertains to us both. I think our father will hence tonight.
> Reg. That's most certain, and with you; next month with us.
> Gon. You see how full of changes his age is. The observation we have made of it hath not been little. He always lov'd our sister most, and with what poor judgment he hath now cast her off appears too grossly. (I, i, 283–90).

Although there is much in the language that is now archaic, it is probably close to the casual, un-self-conscious speech of royalty in Shakespeare's day (even though not that of Celtic Britain). Much of the shift in style is effected by changing from poetry to prose, but there are other differences as well. Throughout Shakespeare's plays we find similar variations in style. Obviously Shakespeare's real-life contemporaries did not speak in poetry, even for the most formal occasions, yet Shakespeare clearly indicated that people did not talk the same way when speaking to a king as they did when speaking to one of their peers.

Even today there are certain people to whom we show special respect by the use of such honorifics as *Sir, Your Honor, Your Grace, Your Majesty, Your Eminence, Mr. President,* and the like. Whereas highly ornate language is frowned upon even when speaking to a chief of state or a high-ranking churchman, most people are fairly self-conscious of their speech in such situations and avoid many words, phrases, and pronunciations that they use with close friends. Less elevated than *Your Honor* and similar honorifics, but still formal are such titles as *Dr. Carson, Professor Eubanks, Mr. Webster,* and *Mrs. Lawrence,* as opposed to *Sally, Lucille,* and *John.* Even within the use of first names, there is a difference in formality between *Robert, Elizabeth, Andrew, Constance* and the shortened *Robbie, Liz, Andy, Connie.* With members of the family, *Mother* and *Father* are more formal terms than *Mom* and *Dad.* In many languages there are special pronouns which are used for close friends, relatives, and children (German *du,* French *tu,* Russian *ty*) as opposed to people with whom one is less intimate (German *Sie,* French *vous,* Russian *vy*). The use of honorifics, nicknames, or special pronouns can say a great deal about the formality of the relationship between people, but these are not the only signals. They are accompanied by characteristic usages in vocabulary, syntax, and phonology.

One of the earliest attempts to define the various contextual styles is found in G. P. Krapp's *The Knowledge of English* (1927). Several approaches to the subject followed in the next decades, but the one which has received the widest attention is Joos (1962), in which we find the following five classifications with an example for each:

> *Frozen:* In my opinion he is not the man whom we want.
> *Formal:* I believe he is not the man we are looking for.
> *Consultative:* I don't think he's the man we're looking for.
> *Casual:* I don't think he's our man.
> *Intimate:* I'm afraid you've picked a lemon.

Such phrases as *in my opinion* and *I believe* are more formal than *I don't think. Whom* is more formal than *that* or the deleted relative. The non-shifted *for* in a relative clause is a sign of informality. *He's our man* is highly informal, and *a lemon* is slang.

Noticing that contextual styles are often accompanied by variations in tempo, Harris (1969:7) borrowed terms from music to name the styles for Spanish. He called the most formal **largo,** since it is also the slowest. This is the style a speaker of Spanish uses when talking with people who may have trouble understanding him, such as foreigners. It is overprecise and somewhat artificial. The second style, **andante,** is still moderately slow and careful. Unlike largo, it is natural. This style is similar to Joos' formal, which is used for a lecture or formal speech. More informal is **allegretto,** which is also faster. The last style is **presto,** "very fast, completely unguarded."

Five levels as given by Joos, or four as given by Harris, are certainly more adequate than just two (formal and informal), but it is probably impossible to give a really precise classification. Contextual styles shade into one another so gradually that it is normally difficult to state which one people are using—apart from the observation that they are using a form of language which is more formal or less formal than they used previously. Nor do people begin with one style and adhere to it; there is much shifting.

If linguists are to describe language, should they try to include all contextual styles, or should they limit themselves to one? If they decide to use only one, which should it be? All, with the possible exception of the most formal and artificial, are legitimate forms of the language. If one of these were pure in some sense and the others corruptions of it, then we would study the pristine style and ignore the others or at best mention them in an appendix on language pathology. This is the view of the man on the street, but it can easily be shown to be wrong. Even the most casual of speech forms are as highly structured as the most formal. They differ in the rules that are used, but the informal styles follow their rules as rigidly as the formal styles do theirs. If linguists limit themselves to any one style, they present a skewed picture of language.

In an attempt to elicit structures and pronunciations from various contextual styles, William Labov (1966) has used several techniques. The more formal styles are fairly easy to study. A linguist can ask a person to read a list of words which includes such pairs as *pen, pin; hoarse, horse; god, guard* to see whether they are distinguished or not. A word list leads people to a very careful style in which they often give what they consider to be the correct pronunciation, rather than the one they actually use.

Still formal, but less so than the reading of word lists, is the interview between linguist and the person whose language is being studied. The exact level of the speech in the interview depends upon the personality and skill of the interviewer, but it is always rather formal. It is of necessity a conversation between strangers in which a microphone is present. Yet the interviewee creates his own sentences and does not have his attention called to particular words or structures. Even in the interview, the style may become more chatty if the person being studied offers the linguist something to eat or drink or if they talk off the cuff when parting. When asked to relate some incident from their past, many people lose much of their restraint and shift to a relaxed style. Or when reciting sayings from childhood, they have to give their normal pronunciation or the rimes are imperfect. At the interview, then, various styles can be elicited.

A third situation exists when the person is asked to read a story or other passage which the linguist has prepared. A person reading aloud is reasonably careful, but the rate of normal reading prevents him from thinking very long about correct pronunciations. If the passage is interesting, the person may use a style which is less formal than the one in the interview.

The more casual styles are harder for the linguist to obtain since they are usually reserved for relatives and close friends. During the course of an interview, there may be an interruption while the person being interviewed speaks to a member of the family or answers the telephone. Labov has also attempted to lessen the artificiality of the interview by using as the interviewer a person who has worked with the subjects for some time and who has gained their confidence. Then the interview situation consists of a small group of peers, such as members of a teenage club, and the interviewer. Although they are aware of the microphones, their speech is more relaxed as they talk to and argue with one another than it would be if they were speaking with a stranger.

As speakers change styles, Labov noticed that they also alter their tempo, pitch, volume, and breathing (1966:110). The more formal styles are marked by fairly slow tempo, low pitch, and moderate volume. The changes in tempo are the same ones noticed by Harris in his classification of Spanish styles as largo, andante, allegretto, and presto.

All aspects of language vary according to the contextual style. Let us look briefly at vocabulary, then proceed to phonology and syntax. Many words never appear in the informal styles; some, in fact, are so formal that they rarely appear in speech at any level, but are largely confined to formal writing: *cogitate, fratricide, felicitations, remonstrate, veracity, pusillanimity,* and the like. Such words as *twilight, journey,* and *voyager* are now rare in conversation. At the other end of the continuum of formality, pet names for members of the family, special terms used by lovers, and words which have significance to a few close friends are found only in intimate speech. Slang is highly informal. Some words and phrases such as *a lot of, stupid, flabbergasted,* and *a mess* are found in all levels of speech except the most formal, but they rarely occur in writing other than conversation in fiction.

As for phonology, the most obvious differences among styles do not involve the presence or absence of certain rules, but rather the frequency of application of those which are optional. In most environments, palatalization in English is obligatory. Whether a person is using the most formal or the most casual style, he has surface [š] in such words as *issue, pressure, sugar,* and the like. Across word boundaries, the rule is optional. In the most formal speech, it occurs in such constructions as *can't you, would you, raise you,* and the like, but less often than it does in informal situations. It normally occurs in casual speech, but even here it is not found consistently. The difference is one of relative frequency. Palatalization across word boundaries in English occurs in all styles, but more frequently in informal than in formal. Linguists in the future will perhaps be able to provide us with figures which state the frequency with which a variable such as palatalization occurs with each style—that is, perhaps something like .75 for one style but .25 for another.

For another example of phonological variation within the speech of a given individual according to the contextual style, let us look at the voiced stops in Spanish. For many dialects there is surface alternation between voiced stops and fricatives, which are in complementary distribution. The voiced stops [b, d, g] appear initially (*bajo, blusa, doce, grande, gustar*) and after nasals (*diciembre, aprender, inglés*). After a vowel the voiced fricatives [β, ð, γ] are found: *saber, abril, adiós, ciudad, negativo, negro.* Hence, only the stops appear at the underlying level, the voiced fricatives being derived by a phonological rule:

Underlying:	/blusa/	/saber/	/dose/	/siudad/
Rule:	———	saβer	———	siuðað
Surface:	[blusa]	[saβer]	[dose]	[siuðað]
Spelling:	blusa	saber	doce	ciudad

Harris (1969:38) has pointed out a variation of the rule which is governed by contextual style. For the careful andante style, the stops are found at the beginning of a word, regardless of the environment. Hence, for *Beatriz babea,* "Beatrice slobbers," the careful style gives the stop [b] for the first consonant in both words but the fricative [β] for the second consonant in *babea.* The more casual and faster allegretto style extends the fricative rule to word-initial positions unless they are at the beginning of an utterance. In this style, *Beatriz babea* has a labial stop only in *Beatriz* since it alone begins the utterance. Both labials in *babea* are voiced fricatives. The informal style has extended the rule to a larger environment.

Turning finally to syntax, English has deletion for all styles in structures such as these:

15.1 Brenda wants (Brenda) to go with us.
15.2 (You) catch me if you can (catch me).

Although there is always a certain amount of redundancy in language, we remove part of it according to what we think the reader or listener knows. In the case of subjects of embedded infinitives and gerunds, deletion is obligatory under certain conditions which apply for all speakers of English. Similarly with the subject of an imperative, the form of the sentence demands that *you* be deleted unless it is the vocative as in "You, come here." Repeated structures are normally deleted, whether the second occurrence is in the same sentence as the first or not:

15.3   Polly heard the news, but I didn't (hear the news).
15.4   Can she sing well? Yes, she can (sing well).

Deletion may be performed because the information is shared by speaker and listener through past experience or the present situation. For example, if Robert enters the room in which Tom is sitting, he may say, "Not at home," instead of "Ann was not at home" if Tom knows that he went to see Ann. Or a person sipping a cup of coffee may say "Hot" instead of "The coffee is hot" if the addressee sees him holding the cup to his lips. In each of these cases the underlying structure contains all understood information; the speaker deletes everything which he thinks the listener already knows, whether it is from a previous sentence, prior knowledge, or a shared situation. The more informal the style, the more deletion of this nature. The degree of formality corresponds to a large extent to the shared information of speaker and listener. The most formal styles assume little shared knowledge beyond that which is actually contained in the spoken or written sentences. Writing is necessarily more formal than speech because it lacks most nonverbal signals. Hence, there is less deletion in writing and formal speaking than in the casual styles. The better people know each other, the more casual they can be in speaking, and the more they can delete.

Since all aspects of language vary according to the contextual style, we find features of syntax and phonology interacting. For example, with a careful formal style of speaking, a person may use little palatalization between words and little deletion. *What did you do?* may be pronounced [hwat dɪd yə du], or [hwadɪd yə du]. With a more casual style, palatalization and contraction may produce [hwajədu]. Likewise, *What are you doing?* with deletion of the unstressed *are* and palatalization, may be pronounced [hwačə-duɪn] in informal situations.

Pronoun case forms provide another example of differences among contextual styles. In English there is a rule which assigns an objective case marker to pronouns that follow prepositions and transitive verbs but to no others. This rule accounts for the form of the italicized pronouns in the following sentences:

15.5   She threw the ball to *me*.
15.6   I walked beside *him*.
15.7   They chose *us*.
15.8   We saw *her*.

Since the rule applies only to pronouns following transitive verbs, it is inapplicable in sentences like the following:

15.9a   It is *I*.
15.10a   These are *they*.

This is the rule for the more formal styles. For many people, the rule is generalized for informal styles so that the objective case marker is added after all verbs, not just those that are transitive. For these styles, the following surface forms result:

15.9b   It's *me*.
15.10b   These are *them*.

For people who have pronoun forms like those in the *a* versions for the formal styles and objective forms like those in *b* for informal, the difference is in the limits on the rule, not in the presence or absence of a rule.

The various contextual styles differ from one another in the nature of their rules and often in the degree to which optional rules are applied. The informal styles are not just careless speech, but rather the results of grammatical rules that differ in some ways from those of the more formal styles. The best style is the one that is the most appropriate for the purpose to which it is employed. A person yelling in formal English at a ball game would sound foolish. A salesman hitting a level too formal or too informal would have little persuasive force. Formal styles would be ineffective for courtship and seduction. A very casual style at a job interview or at a formal speech would be out of place. Styles are appropriate or not for the situation; they are not intrinsically good or bad.

Regional Variation

Everyone is aware that all speakers of the same language do not sound alike. A Norwegian can tell what part of Norway others are from by listening to them talk. It is possible to distinguish an Irishman, an Englishman, an Australian, and an American from one another. An Englishman from Yorkshire does not sound like a Londoner if both are using their regional speech. To naive observers, everyone outside of their province speaks with an accent; only they themselves and their friends do not sound peculiar. People with broader experience realize that there is no such thing as a "pure" and unaccented form of language. There are merely various regional forms, all of which are equally systematic; and everyone uses a regional form, even though chauvinists will not admit that their form of speech is anything but universal and correct. Linguists use the word **dialect** to refer to any variety of language, regional or social. In this usage, the term is not pejorative, since everyone speaks a dialect.

There have been many fanciful explanations for the existence of regional dialects, most of them identical to those for change in language: climate, character traits, and the like. It is more sensible to look upon dialects as the result of linguistic change which spreads unevenly. If a new word or rule is added to the internalized grammars of some people and it eventually spreads to those of all other speakers of the language, the result is looked upon as nothing more than a change in the language as a whole. But many changes are not adopted by all speakers. For example, the addition or loss of a rule may occur in England but not spread to any other English-speaking country. Similarly, a change which originates in New England, in northeastern Illinois, or in New Zealand may go no farther than the original area. If several changes are limited to a given geographical area, the origin of speakers is readily recognizable. They will recognize others as outsiders; and if they travel to another region, their speech will set them apart from the natives there.

A question which has long intrigued students of language is why a change does not spread uniformly to all speakers. Before modern transportation and communication systems made virtually all parts of the world accessible, most people had only limited contact with language outside their immediate region. For example, the Atlantic Ocean did not completely block contact between England and the American colonies, but it severely restricted it for all but a few people. The same separation existed for speakers of French, Spanish, and Portuguese in Europe and in the Americas. The separating element does not have to be so large as an ocean. A major river can have the same effect, as can a mountain range or a political boundary. Whatever the cause, if people have only limited contact with the language outside their own area, they will not adopt many of the changes that originate elsewhere, and many of the changes which are initiated with them will not go beyond their boundaries.

Inadequate exposure to a linguistic change is one reason for a group of people not to adopt it. On the other hand, even when there is a great deal of exposure there is no certainty that the change will be accepted. People may be inundated with certain words, pronunciations, and syntactic structures and reject them for their own use because they do not wish to emulate those among whom the change originated. For people to adopt a change, they must feel that the people from whom they are borrowing have prestige, or at least they must be neutral toward them. During the years following the American Civil War, many Southerners had frequent contact with Northern speech through the carpetbaggers; yet because of feelings of hostility, they did not choose to incorporate any of the rules found in the grammars of the intruders. Although evidence is scarce, it is doubtful that many of the carpetbaggers who eventually returned North carried back with them features of Southern speech. On the other hand, when there is a great deal of respect for the people of a particular area, there is borrowing. This was true in earlier times with the language of London, Paris, Boston, Charleston, New Orleans, and other culture centers, whose vocabulary and rules were adopted by people outside their immediate areas. A dialect that is widely emulated is known as a **prestige dialect.** In the United States there is no single city whose speech is admired in all parts of the country, but the language spoken by announcers and hosts on national television and radio programs is respected by people in all sections. For many people in England, the language heard on the BBC constitutes a prestige dialect, but there are others who reject it.

For a few examples of regional variation, let us examine some rules of phonology. Sometime after the settlement of the American colonies, speakers of English in the new world added a phonological rule to their grammars which converted /t/ to the voiced [d] in intervocalic position if the preceding vowel was stressed. Hence, earlier [wátər] became [wádər]. The rule did not affect words like *atone;* the vowel before the [t] is not stressed. It is only in American English that the rule was added. Either speakers of English in Great Britain did not have enough exposure to the change, or else American English did not have enough prestige for them to wish to add the rule. The rule did not affect underlying representations, since people still have the choice of applying it or not, according to the contextual style. Hence, *water, better, butter, little, pity,* and the like can have a surface [t] or [d] depending upon whether the voicing rule has been applied. Also, with shift in stress there are surface manifestations such as *pólitics* with [t] but *political* with [d]. Further evidence for underlying /t/ can be found in such alternates as *bat, write, cute,* and *forget* with surface [t], but *batter, writing, cutest,* and *forgettable* with [d]. Hence, both Englishmen and Americans have the same underlying forms in *butter, writing, putting,* and the like. Their surface forms differ because of the voicing rule that is found in American English but not in British.

No living dialect remains the same from one period of time to another, and British English is no exception. Various words ending in the spelling *-ile* have undergone a change in many British dialects during this century so that *missile, fertile, projectile,* and other words now have a secondary stress on the last syllable, which is pronounced [ayl]. Since British English has considerable prestige for many Americans, there is evidence that this change is spreading, at least in some words such as *projectile.*

One of the most characteristic features of some British dialects is the absence of surface [r] in such words as *murder, beard, beer,* and the like. During the second half of the eighteenth century, a rule was added to the London dialect, deleting /r/ if a vowel preceded and a consonant or word boundary followed. After the addition of the rule, the surface forms of the following words had no [r] in the dialect that was affected: *beard, heart, mourn, farm.* In each of these, a vowel precedes the /r/, and a consonant follows. The rule also deleted /r/ at the end of a word, provided that it was preceded by a vowel: *sir, fear, fur, war.* It did not apply if /r/ was not preceded by a vowel; hence, *red, run, rob, pretty, try, drone* had surface [r]. Nor did it apply if a vowel followed: *carry, very, hurry.* The environment for deletion can be summarized as follows:

Deletion of /r/	No deletion of /r/
beard	red, try
sir	carry

Eventually the environment for deletion was modified. Word boundaries were disregarded, so that a word ending in /r/ had surface [r] if the next word began with a vowel (*Dear Ann*), but no [r] if it began with a consonant (*Dear John*).

This rule spread to the prestige British dialects and to those dialects of American English whose speakers still looked upon British institutions with favor: New England, New York City, and the coastal South. Those dialects which did not add the rule either had insufficient exposure to it, or else their speakers did not care to sound like Londoners.

We might ask whether the rule which deleted postvocalic /r/ remained in the internalized grammars or whether it resulted in new underlying forms. That is, for such words as *older, labor,* and *mother,* does the Bostonian have different underlying forms from the Chicagoan? There are good reasons for saying that all dialects of English have underlying /r/ in all of these words and that the surface differences are the result of a deletion rule found in some dialects. Without this situation, a word like *poor* would have two underlying forms, one with /r/, the other without; yet the presence or absence of surface [r] has nothing to do with the word *poor* itself, but rather with what follows. No one would recommend giving *poor me* the underlying form /puə/ but *poor us* /pur/. The presence or absence of surface [r] is predictable, and the native speaker recognizes [puə] and [pur] as alternate forms of the same morpheme. The same problem exists with words that take suffixes. Unless a word beginning with a vowel follows, there is no surface [r] in the dialects concerned for the following words: *pore, pure, adore.* Yet with *porous, purest,* and *adorable* there is surface [r]. Setting up underlying forms like /poə/ as opposed to /por + əs/ would indicate that the differences between *pore* and *porous* are not predictable or that /poə/ and /por/ are totally different morphemes.

There is still another reason for giving all dialects underlying /r/. Along with the deletion of /r/, the preceding vowel is lengthened and tensed; after certain vowels [ə] is added. Hence, in the [r]-less dialects, *bunny* has a lax vowel after [b], but *Bernie* has one that is tense and lengthened. If *Bunny* is a person's name, no one from the [r]-less dialects is confused between "Did you see Bunny?" and "Did you see Bernie?" Yet the two words differ only in the first vowel. Similarly, no one confuses "I'm going to the party" with "I'm going to the pottie." If these dialects did not have underlying /r/ in *Bernie* and *party,* these words and others like them would have to be given underlying tense and lengthened vowels. This solution would be most undesirable since length is not distinctive anywhere else in Modern English, nor do tense and lax /ʌ/ or /a/ contrast. These features would occur at the underlying level only in the [r]-less dialects, and in them only in those words which have [r] in other dialects.

With underlying /r/, the following derivations can be given for the [r]-less dialects:

Underlying:	/lʌrn/	/hær kom/	/hær + i/	/parti/	/lɔrə/
/r/ Deletion:	lʌ:n	hææ kom	———	pa:ti	———
Surface:	[lʌ:n]	[hææ kom]	[hæri]	[pa:ti]	[lɔrə]
Spelling:	learn	hair comb	hairy	party	Laura

It is only on the surface that these dialects are [r]-less; at the underlying level they have the same representations as the other dialects of English.

With the /r/ deletion rule, we can see an example of uneven spread of a change. The rule was added to the grammars of some speakers of English but not to those of others. The presence or absence of the rule is generally defined along geographical lines. But even within those dialects that have the rule, all aspects are not exactly alike. The presence of word boundaries, for example, is not treated the same way in all [r]-less dialects. In England and New England, if the following word begins with a vowel, a final /r/ is not deleted. The surface forms of the words in the left column, therefore, have [r], whereas those in the right do not:

With [r]	*Without* [r]
Mother is	Mother was
Dinner at six	Dinner with music
Four of us	Four loons

In New York City and the southeastern part of the United States, word boundary is treated the same as a consonant in requiring deletion. Regardless of what follows in the next word, *mother, dinner, four,* and the like do not have surface [r]. Both *dinner at six* and *dinner with music* are [r]-less.

Even within a given region, there are variations in the rule. The prestige dialects of the southeastern part of the United States have [ə] in place of /r/ in *door, lure, ear*: [doə, luə, iə]. There are other dialects in this region which do not have [ə], especially after [o]. For them, *more, door, pour* are [mo:, do:, po:]. People reveal a great deal about their regional and social origins when they say [mor], [moə], or [mo:].

Still another aspect of the /r/ deletion rule varies among the [r]-less dialects. For England and New England, there is a rule that adds [r] in certain environments, namely after words ending in [ə] when the next word begins with a vowel. This rule is obviously the result of the condition on the rule which does not delete final /r/ if the next word begins with a vowel. Hence, *father is* is on the surface [faðər ɪz], but *father went* is [faðə wɛnt]. The surface pattern which emerges is schwa plus consonant or glide in the following word or schwa plus [r] plus vowel. Hence, *the sofa was* has the same pattern as *father was*:

> [faðə   waz]
> [ðə   sofə   waz]

But *father is* does not delete the /r/:

> [faðər   ɪz]

It is at this point that the [r] addition rule applies to a word like *sofa*:

> [ðə   sofər   ɪz]

Such derivations produce a suspiciously complicated grammar. They probably reflect the state of the speakers who originally added the rules, but not those of later generations. There is no reason to assume that a person hearing [faðə waz, faðər ɪz] and [ðə sofə waz, ðə sofər ɪz] obtains underlying forms /faðər/ and /sofə/, with an /r/ deletion rule which applies to /faðər/ and an [r] addition rule for /sofə/. One of two choices seems probable. The underlying form /faðər/ seems sound, but /sofə/ may not be. Perhaps people in these dialects have underlying /sofər/. Then only the /r/ deletion rule is needed; there is no [r] insertion. The second possibility is that our explanation of [r] before a word beginning with a vowel may be wrong. It could be that all of these dialects delete /r/ before a word boundary if a vowel precedes, regardless of what follows. Hence, underlying /r/ is deleted in *father* whether the next word begins with a vowel or a consonant. Then an [r] addition rule adds the [r] in both *father* and *sofa* if the next word begins with a vowel. That is, at the time the addition rule is applicable, it adds [r] after final schwa if the next word begins with a vowel. At this point *father* and *sofa* are [faðə] and [sofə]. Because of the scarcity of evidence, we will not try to choose any of these explanations as the correct one: (1) underlying /faðər/ with a deletion rule which does not recognize word boundaries and /sofə/ with an [r] addition rule, (2) underlying /faðər/ and /sofər/ with a deletion rule but none for addition of [r], (3) underlying /faðər/ and /sofə/ with a deletion rule which recognizes word boundaries, and also an [r] addition rule which adds [r] to both *sofa* and *father* if the next word begins with a vowel.

The prestige of linguistic rules shifts as do all other aspects of language.

Apparently the /r/ deletion rule originated among the Cockney speakers of London. It was, therefore, not fashionable among upper-class Londoners. John Keats was attacked by the *Edinburgh Review* for his use of Cockneyisms in *Endymion*. For example, he rimed *Thalia* and *higher:* [θəláyə] and [háyə]. The deletion rule eventually gained prestige among speakers of other dialects, and it spread. There is no reason to believe that the original settlers of the American colonies had the rule, but some of them later borrowed it from the English. It appeared first among the upper classes in eastern New England, New York, and the coastal South, and eventually spread to most of the other classes in these areas. Possibly the development in New York came from New England, rather than from England directly. Some isolated spots such as Martha's Vineyard did not adopt the rule, nor did speakers in several other dialect areas.

During the third quarter of this century, many of the middle-class speakers of English in New York City have decided that their [r]-less pronunciations are not so admirable as their ancestors felt. There is, therefore, a tendency to try to remove the rule. Having noticed this tendency, William Labov in 1962 made a systematic study of the change (Labov, 1966). Preliminary studies indicated that the prestige of pronunciations with surface [r] does not exist among all speakers of English in New York City, but rather that it is linked with social stratification. The upper middle classes seem to favor pronunciations with surface postvocalic [r], whereas the lower classes do not. Since salespeople in department stores normally use the form of language found among their customers, they were selected as subjects for investigation. Labov wanted their responses to be as un-self-conscious as possible, and he was also interested in distinguishing uses among contextual styles.

The phrase selected for elicitation was *fourth floor*. In *fourth* the postvocalic /r/ precedes a consonant; in *floor* it comes before a word boundary. The interviewer collected his data by asking for directions such as "Where are women's shoes?" or some other department on the desired floor. The salesperson responded with "Fourth floor" in a normal tone since this is a typical request. Whereas the style was not intimate, it was much more casual than it would have been if the person had known his language was being studied. The interviewer then leaned forward as though he had not understood and said, "Excuse me?" The salesperson responded in a more deliberate style, "Fourth floor," or sometimes just "Fourth." For interviews on the fourth floor, the question was "Excuse me, what floor is this?" For most of the speakers interviewed, there were four potential positions for surface [r], two in each style.

The interviews were conducted in three New York department stores which attract customers from different social groups: Saks Fifth Avenue, Macy's, and S. Klein. A total of 264 salespeople were interviewed: 68 from Saks, 125 from Macy's, and 71 from S. Klein. In all three stores there were some responses with surface postvocalic [r] and some without it, but there was a clear scale. Below are the percentages of replies in which all four words contained surface [r] and those in which one or more words contained it:[1]

---

[1] All figures are from Chapter 3 of Labov (1966).

	Saks	Macy's	S. Klein
All [r]	30%	20%	4%
Some [r]	32%	31%	17%
Total	62%	51%	21%

In Saks, almost two-thirds of the salespeople used surface [r] in at least some of the words, as opposed to S. Klein, where only about one-fifth used it. Macy's, as expected, fell in between, but leaned toward the norm of Saks.

Even more revealing was the difference between the two styles:

		Saks	Macy's	S. Klein
Casual				
	Fourth	30%	27%	5%
	Floor	63%	44%	8%
Careful				
	Fourth	40%	22%	13%
	Floor	64%	61%	18%

It should be noticed that in all three stores there is an increase in pronunciation with surface [r] at the more careful style. Interestingly enough, on *floor* the Saks employees showed almost no change, but the Macy's people in the careful style came up almost to the level used at Saks.

The prestige model for postvocalic [r] is shifting in New York in the reverse direction from the way it must have shifted during the early part of the nineteenth century. At that time the [r]-less pronunciations were the admired forms, and apparently for a time the upper classes were [r]-less and the lower classes [r]-full. Eventually the deletion rule spread to all classes in the city. Now the situation has changed. The tendency is for the upper classes to approach an [r]-full pronunciation while the lower maintain the [r]-less.

A question which linguists are asking is whether all dialects of a language have the same underlying phonological and syntactic forms but different rules to provide the surface variations. There have been only a few dialect features studied from the standpoint of underlying representations, but all of these show difference only at the surface level. It seems reasonable that all dialects of a language have the same underlying representations, but it is too early to say anything very definite.

Social Variation

Because changes do not spread evenly among all speakers of a language, it is possible to find differences that are limited geographically. For a language such as English, which is spoken in many parts of the world, there are national differences that distinguish Englishmen, Australians, South Africans, Americans, and others from one another. Within each country there are further distinctions. An American from eastern New England, one from Georgia, and a third from Arizona do not sound alike. Even within a single region there are differences. A Midwesterner is readily distinguishable from a person from New England, the South, and the Pacific Northwest, but Midwestern speech is far from uniform. Even within a single state such as Ohio, Indiana, or Illinois, there are differences in speech which follow geographical lines. Claims made by some native St. Louisans that they can hear a difference between the speech of people from the northern part of St. Louis County and those from the southern part may be exaggerated—but again, they may not be. We have to come down to a very small, closely-knit area in any language before we cease to find regional variation. In each area there are conservative features that other regions possessed at one time and since have lost; there are also innovative features which are not found in some of the other dialects of the language. It is the exact combination of conservative and innovative features—vocabulary items and rules of phonology and syntax—which makes the language of each region unique.

A change in language does not spread uniformly if all speakers do not have adequate exposure to it or if some people do not want to sound like members of the group who have accepted the change. These inhibiting factors can promote variation among speakers of a language within a single geographical region as easily as they do among those from different regions. The fact that people live within a few miles—or even a few yards—of one another does not mean that they have any real contact. People form cliques based on economics, social interests, race, religion, ethnic background (which does not necessarily fall along racial lines), and other differences. At one time these separating factors, which we will group together under the term *social,* were determined by one's family. A child born to a family of aristocrats was also of the aristocracy, as were his children and grandchildren. Similarly, a peasant was born into the lower classes, and it was reasonably certain that his descendants would likewise be peasants. During the Middle Ages, and even for several centuries later, the class distinctions in Europe were fairly clear-cut, even with the emergence of the middle class. Social variation in language was also well defined.

With the changes of recent centuries, however, social divisions have become extremely complicated. Social mobility is so common in many countries that it is impossible to predict which group a person's descendants will belong to, and large-scale immigration has made it certain that no group will be homogeneous. These changes in the social structure do not mean that social distinctions have ceased to exist. They are very much present, only vastly more complicated than ever before.

Most people are aware that a chemical engineer and a bank president may sound very much alike when they are discussing politics or sports and that neither sounds like most factory workers. Some people associate various character traits with these social variations in speech. People may have difficulty persuading a salesman to extend credit to them if the salesman believes that people from their social class are not dependable. College professors often find that they are overcharged or given shoddy service when they have their cars repaired. Their speech does not convince the service manager that they know anything about mechanics. Parents may object to the friends their children choose or to a prospective son- or daughter-in-law on grounds of speech.

It is popularly assumed that these social variations in language result from education or the lack of it. To a degree there is some evidence that would suggest such a belief. Most people in the upper echelons finish high school, at least. Yet this explanation is questionable when we consider the vast differences among educational systems. White, middle-class, suburban high-school graduates of comparable intelligence may show no similarities whatsoever in what they have learned. Graduates from some schools have received excellent instruction, as evidenced by their scores on college entrance examinations and their performance in prestige universities. Those from other schools are so poorly prepared that it is only a slight exaggeration to say that they show no evidence of having gone beyond the fourth grade. When students go through six years of secondary English without evidence that they have learned anything about composition, literature, reading, or the English language, it hardly seems reasonable that the absence of double negatives in their speech is the result of this system. Many school systems are given credit which they do not deserve. Some people do not use double negatives and other stigmatized forms such as *ain't, hisself, have ate, have froze,* and the like because the language of their friends does not contain these forms, not because the schools have weeded them out.

Until recently, there was a general belief that Standard English was the pure form of the language and that any deviations from it were the result of depravity or the absence of logical thinking. Although linguists have only begun the study of nonstandard English, they have learned enough to refute the earlier belief in the purity of any form of language. Social dialects of a language are very much like those of a regional nature or contextual styles in that all are governed by sets of rules which are about as rigid in one dialect as in another. All dialects probably have the same underlying structures but differ on the surface because of differences in phonological and syntactic rules. Members of different social groups have differences in their grammars because changes do not spread evenly. As with regional variation, a change does not affect all speakers of a language—either because they are not exposed to it or because they consciously reject it.

If all speakers of nonstandard dialects talked alike, our task of describing their grammars would be easy. We could follow a procedure similar to the one we used for comparing surface [r] in various regional dialects of English. Unfortunately for the linguist, it is almost impossible to isolate a group of speakers and say that their speech is homogeneous enough to constitute a particular social dialect. There is unquestioned social stratification that is reflected in language, but segmenting the strata is no easy matter for sociologists or linguists.

The nonstandard dialect which has received the most research in recent years is that of working-class black Americans. As with any large group of people, there is variation among members of the group, but it has been shown that there are features of the language of working-class blacks which are different from those of middle-class blacks and whites. This dialect also contains many of the rules found in other dialects of English; in fact, a complete analysis would probably reveal that most of the rules are the same. It should be stressed that all black Americans do not speak this dialect, but there are large numbers who do. It is often called **Black English.**

As with all other varieties of language, we are interested in discovering the origins of Black English. One early theory is easily disproved: namely, that it resulted from anatomical features. Noticing that Black English lacks surface postvocalic [r] and that many blacks have thick lips, some early theorists saw a cause-and-effect relationship. But there is much variation among speakers of Black English as to lip size, many of them with thinner lips than some whites. When one asks what role the lips play in the articulation of [r], the issue becomes ludicrous. If any phonological feature were affected by lip size, one would expect it to be the labials. The only known cases in which anatomical features have affected the phonology of a language are those individuals who have cleft palates or some other defect, or those tribes which practice lip mutilation and have lost all labial consonants (e.g., as cited in Jakobson, 1968:48). There are some physical variations among the people of the world in the make-up of their speech-making apparatus, but none that are great enough to cause any noticeable differences in speech. The most obvious evidence for discrediting the belief that anatomical features cause variation in language is that large numbers of black Americans speak Standard English.

Another extreme view from earlier years was that Black English did not exist. Holders of this belief said that there were no differences in speech between blacks and whites of the same economic class in a given community. They pointed, for example, to the surface absence of postvocalic [r] in the English of the coastal South, both black and white. The absence of [ə] in *more, pour, door* was found in the speech of whites and blacks of similar economic and social status. Yet there is a difference between finding some features which are the same and saying that there are no differences between two groups of speakers. Both blacks and whites have long insisted that they could tell the race of a telephone caller by just listening to him. The only people they could not identify were those blacks who spoke Standard English. Today there is no real question about the existence of Black English. It does exist.

At least part of the origins of Black English must have been with various dialects of English spoken by whites. For those features which are identical in Black English and a white dialect with which it could have had close contact, such an explanation is plausible. When there is no white dialect with the given feature from which the black dialect could have borrowed, such an explanation seems forced. The presence of a feature in a rural dialect of England but found nowhere else except in Black English is hardly evidence for borrowing. There is always the possibility, of course, that a white dialect of American English once had the feature and that it has since vanished without being documented, but this is not very convincing. Some features of Black English no doubt had their origin in the American English of the whites with whom they came in contact, but all of the features could not have this origin.

A more recent theory sees many features of Black English as survivals of rules from languages which blacks of the seventeenth and eighteenth centuries spoke before they learned English. We know that adults learning a foreign language even under ideal conditions find it impossible to avoid introducing features of their native language into the one they are learning.

Even adults who have received systematic training from proficient teachers speak the new language with a foreign accent and use syntactic structures which belong to their mother tongue rather than to the new one they are learning. Black slaves learning English as adults would be too old to learn the new language from exposure alone, and there is no reason to believe that there was ever an attempt to use the most scientific methods in teaching the foreign language to them. They obviously carried over into English many features from their West African languages.

With later immigrants from Italy, France, Germany, and other European countries, it was normally only the original settlers who spoke English with a foreign accent. Their children born in the United States usually had enough contact with native speakers of English for them to develop unaccented forms of the language. Those born in this country and their descendants developed native-speaker grammars, not grammars like those of their parents. Even with immigrants who speak European languages, however, there is no guarantee that their children will be exposed to native speakers. A family may settle in an area in which all other families are from the same country. Because of the heavy concentration of Scandinavian settlers in Minnesota, for example, many children born there continued to use Swedish intonation patterns when speaking English. In the southwestern states, social and economic factors restrict the outside contacts of people of Latin American descent. It is not unusual, therefore, for children of the second and third generation to speak a form of English which is highly influenced by Spanish. An even more extreme situation existed with blacks in pre–Civil War times, and for vast numbers even until the present. It seems possible that the first slaves developed a form of English which was influenced by features of their original languages. Their descendants had little exposure to English other than that spoken by other blacks; the African influence, therefore, became a permanent feature of their language. Until more studies have been made of West African languages, such an origin for features of Black English has to remain an interesting possibility for which we presently have little evidence.

A similar source has been suggested in the Pidgin English of the seventeenth century. The word *pidgin* is a development of the word *business;* **pidgin languages,** therefore, are business or trading languages. Although they are always spoken as second languages, their structures are as systematic as first languages are. When a pidgin language becomes the principal language of a group of people and the one their children learn natively as their first language, it is known as a **creole language.** There is evidence that Pidgin English was in use among slave traders and others during the seventeenth and eighteenth centuries. It would certainly be possible for the original slaves to have learned this variety of English rather than that of their masters, and then to have passed it along as a creole language to their descendants. Since the slaves in any given location probably spoke a variety of languages, the English creole may have been the only one they had in common, and therefore this is the language which survived. Like the theory which attributes features of Black English to survivals of forms from African languages, this one is hampered by lack of evidence. If the theory could be proved, most linguists would be delighted, since it would give evidence for a cause of change which has been speculated about many times in the past but never proved. It is not enough to find similar rules in Black English and seventeenth-century Pidgin English or West African languages. There must be evidence of transmission and continuity.

It is not clear that there is only one origin for all features in Black English: dialects spoken by whites, African languages, or Pidgin English which became a creole. All three could have been important. Even if we could establish one of these as more important than the others in the origins of the dialect, we would be overlooking something very important if we attributed all features of Black English to it: namely, the fact that all forms of language change. Many of the rules of Black English are identical to those in other varieties of English and no doubt to those in African languages and Pidgin English. It is also true that every one of them could have developed independently. There is no reason to believe that any dialect of any language is so impoverished in creativity that it cannot change the rules of its grammar. The speakers of Black English have often been isolated from other speakers of English; hence, changes which originated among them would not always spread outside their areas, and vice versa. The prestige element would also have been influential. Most people find it more desirable to sound like their friends than like outsiders. Those blacks who had sufficient exposure to middle-class white English may have had no desire to learn it.

A characteristic of Black English phonetic forms which has often been noticed is the simplification of final consonant clusters:

Obstruent + Obstruent	*fast*	[fæs]
Nasal + Obstruent	*mind*	[mayn]
Liquid + Obstruent	*hold*	[hol]

This pattern is found only when the two segments agree in voicing. Such clusters as [ŋk] or [lt], as in *thank* and *wilt,* do not simplify. Since consonant clusters are less normal among the languages of the world than single consonants are, it seems quite reasonable that Black English would have added a rule which reduces the clusters. The speakers making the innovation would have had underlying clusters in final position but a rule which deleted the second consonant:

Underlying:	/fæst/	/græsp/	/kræft/	/wayld/	/θæŋk/
Deletion rule:	fæs	græs	kræf	wayl	———
Surface:	[fæs]	[græs]	[kræf]	[wayl]	[θæŋk]
Spelling:	fast	grasp	craft	wild	thank

The deletion rule does not apply to *thank,* since /ŋ/ and /k/ do not agree in voicing.

One may ask whether the eventual outcome of the change was just an added rule to the phonological component of the grammar with no alteration of underlying forms, or whether later generations changed their underlying forms to /fæs/, /græs/, /kræf/, /wayl/, and the like. The answer in most changes such as this rests on whether there are surface alternations or not. With Grimm's Law there were no morphemic alternants on the surface, some with and others without shifted consonants; they all shifted.

Hence, the underlying forms were affected. With a rule such as palatalization in English, however, there were surface alternants such as *press* and *pressure* so that the simplest grammar is still one without palatalized consonants at the underlying level. Palatalization did not affect underlying representations; rather, it remained in the language as a phonological rule. In Black English, in addition to such words which have simplified consonant clusters on the surface, there are morphemic alternants with unsimplified clusters, namely when a suffix beginning with a vowel follows:

Simplification	*No Simplification*
[fæs] the fast man	[fæstɪs] the fastest man
[æk] act	[æktɪn] acting
[koɫ] cold	[koldə] colder
[bʌs] bust ("burst")	[bʌstɪd] busted

On the basis of such surface variations as these, Wolfram (1969:65) has presented convincing evidence that the correct underlying forms are with the clusters but that the deletion rule has remained in the language to simplify final clusters on the surface. Otherwise there would be no systematic way to explain why *fast* appears as [fæs] and *fastest* as [fæstɪs]. It should be noted, by the way, that the cluster in the suffix of *fastest* correctly shows simplification. The alternation between [fæs] and [fæst] is as systematic as that between [prɛs] and [prɛš] in *press, pressure.* If they were represented differently at the underlying level, we would be saying that the surface forms are idiosyncratic. A more reasonable solution is to have underlying clusters.

A second characteristic which has been noticed among many speakers of Black English is the absence of past-tense markers on verbs. The following surface forms are found:

guess	[gɛs]	guessed	[gɛs]
clap	[klæp]	clapped	[klæp]
cough	[kɔf]	coughed	[kɔf]
push	[puš]	pushed	[puš]
cook	[kʊk]	cooked	[kʊk]
move	[muv]	moved	[muv]
comb	[kom]	combed	[kom]
own	[on]	owned	[on]
tease	[tiz]	teased	[tiz]
roll	[rol]	rolled	[rol]
judge	[jʌǰ]	judged	[jʌǰ]

In most sentences of English, time adverbials and other words are more important in designating time than is the tense of the verb. In a sentence such as "We helped him yesterday," we can remove the tense on the verb, giving "We help him yesterday" and lose none of the semantic content of the sentence. Although many sentences do not contain time adverbials, the overall context of the discourse or an earlier sentence provides the time reference unambiguously. Verb tense is, therefore, usually redundant.

Does Black English have tense? The examples which we gave in the preceding paragraph do not contain any indication of it on the surface, but a form such as *clapped* would yield a final cluster that would be deleted. Two possible explanations exist:

	A	B
Underlying:	/klæp/ + Past	/klæp/
Past tense:	klæpt	———
Deletion:	klæp	———
Surface:	[klæp]	[klæp]
Spelling:	clapped	clapped

The first solution, A, assumes that there is an underlying past-tense morpheme but that the deletion rule removes it as it would any other final cluster. The second, B, gives no past-tense morpheme at the underlying level. Wolfram (1969:73) favors the first solution because of the parallels between surface forms such as *clapped* and *apt,* both lacking [t]. Unfortunately we cannot compare the surface forms we have given with past tenses in which the final cluster does not agree in voice; the rules for English past-tense formation insure agreement in voicing.

One of the most frequently noticed characteristics of Black English is the absence of *be* in many positions in which it is found in other dialects of the language:

15.11   She a teacher.
15.12   You silly.
15.13   It in the yard.
15.14   We going with you.
15.15   It gonna snow.

Although other dialects of English also delete *be* in certain environments such as relative clauses and various constructions in very casual speech, those illustrated by 15.11–15 are distinctive with Black English. Some people have seen a parallel with various creole languages and have therefore said that sentences such as 15.11–15 have no underlying *be*.

Yet there are sentences in which *be* does occur in surface structures of Black English:

15.16   I was small.[2] (past tense)
15.17   I'm tired. (first-person *am*)
15.18   You got to be good. (infinitive)
15.19   Be cool. (imperative)
15.20   Are you down? (question)

It is only *is* and *are* which are regularly not present in surface structures, and there are certain structures, such as questions, in which they appear. An especially interesting structure in which *is* and *are* appear on the surface is the emphatic sentence:

15.21   First speaker: "He not late."
         Second speaker: "He *is* late."
15.22   First speaker: "I not going."
         Second speaker: "You *are* going."

2 Examples 15:16–20 are from Labov (1969).

The presence of *be* in such surface structures as 15.16–22 lends strong support to giving it at an underlying level for sentences 15.11–15 as well but having it deleted.

William Labov (1969) has noticed that Black English deletes *be* in the environments in which Standard English contracts:

	Black English	*Standard English*
15.23	He late.	He's late.
15.24	They over there.	They're over there.
15.25	She going with us.	She's going with us.

Those positions in which Standard English does not permit contraction are also impossible for deletion in Black English:

	Black English	*Standard English*
15.26	*There it.	*There it's. (There it is.)
15.27a	***Who** he?	***Who's** he?
b	Who **he?**	Who's **he?**

The rules for contraction are complicated, and they need not concern us here. What is important is that contraction and deletion are alike in places of occurrence. Both are, furthermore, optional rules. They occur more often if a pronoun precedes than if a noun does. They are also more likely to occur if a verb ending in *-ing* follows than if an adjective does, and they are more likely if an adjective follows than if a noun does. Such parallels between the two rules seem hardly coincidental.

Labov (1969) suggests giving underlying *be* for Black English in the same positions as it would occur in other dialects. A derivation like the following would provide surface forms without *be:*

Underlying:	/hi ɪz let/
Contraction:	hiz let
Deletion:	hi let
Surface:	[hi let]
Spelling:	He late

Between the underlying form and contraction there are rules for stress placement and reduction of certain vowels to [ə]. Contraction applies optionally to [ə] in certain environments. Labov shows that there is a deletion rule in Black English for /z/ and /r/ which is needed for other forms. Since /m/ does not delete, surface forms with *am* appear, but those with *is* and *are* do not. The past-tense forms *was* and *were* are blocked from contracting and thus from deleting because of the initial /w/. Since contraction applies only to unstressed [ə], such emphatics as "He *is* late" do not contract or delete. Labov's phonological rules account for the absence of *be* in some surface structures of Black English.

Returning to the various arguments about the origins of Black English, we see several characteristics and rules which could have been adopted from other dialects of English, from African languages, or from a creole English. In each case there is no reason to say that the modern developments could not have arisen in Black English independent of any other language. Each of the rules we have examined illustrates universal principles of language change.

Conclusion

As was stated in the Preface, no topic in this book has been covered exhaustively, and language variation is no exception. This is an area which linguists of the future can find practically unexplored as they study it along the lines of current linguistic theory. Most of the earlier studies do not go beyond the stage of collecting interesting data.

The notion that language is systematic holds true not only for the standard dialect, but also for other forms: developing grammars of children, language at various periods, contextual styles, regional and social dialects. The differences we find in the various dialects of a language are the result of differences in the rules of each group. The grammar of any one group seems to be as systematic as that of any other. The same holds for logic and adherence to tradition or acceptance of innovation. Most of the differences we find among the dialects of a language are confined to the rules and surface representations. It may be that all dialects of a language have the same underlying structures, but linguistic research is not far enough advanced at present to give a definitive statement.

Suggested Reading

ALLEN, HAROLD B., and GARY N. UNDERWOOD, eds., *Readings in American Dialectology*. New York: Appleton-Century-Crofts, 1971.

ATWOOD, E. BAGBY, *A Survey of Verb Forms in the Eastern United States*. Ann Arbor: University of Michigan Press, 1953.

BROOK, G. L., *English Dialects*. 2nd ed. London: Andre Deutsch, 1965.

GLEASON, H. A., JR., *Linguistics and English Grammar*. New York: Holt, Rinehart & Winston, Inc., 1965.

JOOS, MARTIN, *The Five Clocks*. Bloomington: Indiana University Research Center in Anthropology, Folklore, and Linguistics, 1962.

KEYSER, SAMUEL JAY, Review of *The Pronunciation of English in the Atlantic States* by Hans Kurath and Raven I. McDavid, Jr., *Language* 39 (1963): 303–16.

KURATH, HANS, *A Word Geography of the Eastern United States*. Ann Arbor: University of Michigan Press, 1949.

KURATH, HANS, and RAVEN I. McDAVID, JR., *The Pronunciation of English in the Atlantic States*. Ann Arbor: University of Michigan Press, 1961.

LABOV, WILLIAM, *Language in the Inner City*. Philadelphia: University of Pennsylvania Press, 1972.

———, *The Social Stratification of English in New York City*. Washington, D. C.: Center for Applied Linguistics, 1966.

———, *Sociolinguistic Patterns*. Philadelphia: University of Pennsylvania Press, 1972.

MARCKWARDT, ALBERT H., *American English*. New York: Oxford University Press, Inc., 1958.

McDAVID, RAVEN I., JR., "The Dialects of American English," in *The Structure of American English* by W. Nelson Francis. New York: The Ronald Press Company, 1958.

MENCKEN, H. L., *The American Language*. Abridged by Raven I. McDavid, Jr. New York: Alfred A. Knopf, Inc., 1963.

PYLES, THOMAS, *Words and Ways of American English*. New York: Random House, Inc., 1952.

SLEDD, JAMES H., "Breaking, Umlaut, and the Southern Drawl," *Language* 42 (1966): 18–41.

WOLFRAM, WALTER A. *A Sociolinguistic Description of Detroit Negro Speech*. Washington, D. C.: Center for Applied Linguistics, 1969.

Bibliography

The entries in this bibliography are restricted to the works cited in the book. For more extensive listings, see the suggested readings at the end of each chapter.

BACH, EMMON. 1964. *An Introduction to Transformational Grammars*. New York: Holt, Rinehart & Winston, Inc.

BEVER, T. G., and D. T. LANGENDOEN. 1972. "The Interaction of Speech Perception and Grammatical Structure in the Evolution of Language," in *Linguistic Change and Generative Theory*, ed. Robert P. Stockwell and Ronald K. S. Macaulay. Bloomington: Indiana University Press.

BLOOM, LOIS. 1970. *Language Development: Form and Function in Emerging Grammars*. Cambridge, Mass.: The M.I.T. Press.

———. 1973. "Why Not Pivot Grammar?" in *Studies of Child Language Development*, ed. Charles A. Ferguson and Dan Isaac Slobin. New York: Holt, Rinehart & Winston, Inc.

BROWN, ROGER. 1958. *Words and Things*. Glencoe, Ill.: Free Press.

———. 1973. "The First Sentences of Child and Chimpanzee," in *Studies of Child Language Development*, ed. Charles A. Ferguson and Dan Isaac Slobin. New York: Holt, Rinehart & Winston, Inc.

CHAFE, WALLACE L. 1971. "Directionality and Paraphrase." *Language* 47: 1–26.

CHOMSKY, CAROL. 1969. *The Acquisition of Syntax in Children from 5 to 10*. Cambridge, Mass.: The M.I.T. Press.

CHOMSKY, NOAM. 1964. "On the Notion 'Rule of Grammar,' " in *The Structure of Language*, ed. Jerry A. Fodor and Jerrold J. Katz. Englewood Cliffs, N. J.: Prentice-Hall, Inc.

————. 1965. *Aspects of the Theory of Syntax.* Cambridge, Mass.: The M.I.T. Press.

————. 1970. "Remarks on Nominalization," in *Readings in English Transformational Grammar,* ed. Roderick A. Jacobs and Peter S. Rosenbaum. Waltham, Mass.: Ginn and Company.

————. 1971. "Deep Structure, Surface Structure, and Semantic Interpretation," in *Semantics,* ed. Danny D. Steinberg and Leon A. Jakobovits. Cambridge: Cambridge University Press.

————. 1972. "Some Empirical Issues in the Theory of Transformational Grammar," in *Goals of Linguistic Theory,* ed. Stanley Peters. Englewood Cliffs, N. J.: Prentice-Hall, Inc.

CHOMSKY, NOAM, and MORRIS HALLE. 1968. *The Sound Pattern of English.* New York: Harper & Row, Publishers.

CURME, GEORGE O. 1935. *Parts of Speech and Accidence.* Boston: D. C. Heath & Company.

FRIES, CHARLES C. 1940. *American English Grammar.* New York: Appleton-Century-Crofts.

GREENBERG, JOSEPH H. 1966. "Some Universals of Grammar with Particular Reference to the Order of Meaningful Elements," in *Universals of Language,* ed. Joseph H. Greenberg. 2nd ed. Cambridge, Mass.: The M.I.T. Press.

GRUBER, JEFFREY S. 1973. "Correlations Between the Syntactic Constructions of the Child and of the Adult," in *Studies of Child Language Development,* ed. Charles A. Ferguson and Dan Isaac Slobin. New York: Holt, Rinehart & Winston, Inc.

HARRIS, JAMES W. 1969. *Spanish Phonology.* Cambridge, Mass.: The M.I.T. Press.

HILL, ARCHIBALD A. 1958. *Introduction to Linguistic Structures.* New York: Harcourt Brace Jovanovich, Inc.

HOUSE, HOMER C., and SUSAN EMOLYN HARMAN. 1950. *Descriptive English Grammar.* 2nd ed. Englewood Cliffs, N. J.: Prentice-Hall, Inc.

JACKENDOFF, RAY S. 1972. *Semantic Interpretation in Generative Grammar.* Cambridge, Mass.: The M.I.T. Press.

JAKOBSON, ROMAN. 1960. "Closing Statement: Linguistics and Poetics," in *Style in Language,* ed. Thomas A. Sebeok. Cambridge, Mass.: The M.I.T. Press.

————. 1968. *Child Language, Aphasia and Phonological Universals,* trans. Allan R. Keiler. The Hague: Mouton.

JESPERSEN, OTTO. 1924. *The Philosophy of Grammar.* London: Allen and Unwin.

————. 1949. *A Modern English Grammar,* Vol. VII. Copenhagen: Ejnar Munksgaard.

————. 1964. *Language: Its Nature, Development and Origin.* New York: W. W. Norton & Company, Inc.

Jones, Daniel. 1969. *An Outline of English Phonetics*. 9th ed. Cambridge: Heffer.

Joos, Martin. 1962. *The Five Clocks*. Bloomington: Indiana University Research Center in Anthropology, Folklore, and Linguistics.

Katz, Jerrold J., and Jerry A. Fodor. 1963. "The Structure of a Semantic Theory," *Language* 39 (1963): 170–210.

Katz, Jerrold J., and Paul M. Postal. 1964. *An Integrated Theory of Linguistic Descriptions*. Cambridge, Mass.: The M.I.T. Press.

King, Robert D. 1969. *Historical Linguistics and Generative Grammar*. Englewood Cliffs, N. J.: Prentice-Hall, Inc.

Kiparsky, Paul, and Carol Kiparsky. 1970. "Fact," in *Progress in Linguistics*, ed. Manfred Bierwisch and Karl Erich Heidolph. The Hague: Mouton.

Koutsoudas, Andreas. 1966. *Writing Transformational Grammars*. New York: McGraw-Hill Book Company.

Labov, William. 1966. *The Social Stratification of English in New York City*. Washington, D. C.: Center for Applied Linguistics.

———. 1969. "Contraction, Deletion, and Inherent Variability of the English Copula," *Language* 45 (1969): 715–62.

Lakoff, George. 1970. *Irregularity in Syntax*. New York: Holt, Rinehart & Winston, Inc.

———. 1971. "On Generative Semantics," in *Semantics*, ed. Danny D. Steinberg and Leon A. Jakobovits. Cambridge: Cambridge University Press.

Langacker, Ronald W. 1968. "Observations on French Possessives," *Language* 44 (1968): 51–75.

Lees, Robert B. 1960. *The Grammar of English Nominalizations*. Bloomington: Indiana University Research Center in Anthropology, Folklore, and Linguistics.

Lenneberg, Eric H. 1967. *Biological Foundations of Language*. New York: John Wiley & Sons, Inc.

Liles, Bruce L. 1971. *An Introductory Transformational Grammar*. Englewood Cliffs, N. J.: Prentice-Hall, Inc.

Maclay, Howard. 1971. "Overview," in *Semantics*, ed. Danny D. Steinberg and Leon A. Jakobovits. Cambridge: Cambridge University Press.

Marckwardt, Albert H. 1958. *American English*. New York: Oxford University Press, Inc.

McCawley, James D. 1968a. "Concerning the Base Component of a Transformational Grammar," *Foundations of Language* 4 (1968): 243–69.

———. 1968b. "The Role of Semantics in a Grammar," in *Universals in Linguistic Theory*, ed. Emmon Bach and Robert T. Harms. New York: Holt, Rinehart & Winston, Inc.

McNeill, David. 1966. "Developmental Psycholinguistics," in *The Genesis of Language*, ed. Frank Smith and George A. Miller. Cambridge, Mass.: The M.I.T. Press.

Moskowitz, Arlene I. 1970. "The Two-Year-Old Stage in the Acquisition of English Phonology," *Language* 46 (1970): 426–41.

Postal, Paul M. 1971. *Cross-Over Phenomena*. New York: Holt, Rinehart & Winston, Inc.

Roberts, Paul. 1964. *English Syntax*. New York: Harcourt Brace Jovanovich, Inc.

———. 1968. *Modern Grammar*. New York: Harcourt Brace Jovanovich, Inc.

Rosenbaum, Peter S. 1967. *The Grammar of English Predicate Complement Constructions*. Cambridge, Mass.: The M.I.T. Press.

Ross, John Robert. 1970. "On Declarative Sentences," in *Readings in English Transformational Grammar*, ed. Roderick A. Jacobs and Peter S. Rosenbaum. Waltham, Mass.: Ginn and Company.

Sapir, Edward. 1921. *Language*. New York: Harcourt Brace Jovanovich, Inc.

Slobin, Dan I. 1966. "The Acquisition of Russian as a Native Language," in *The Genesis of Language*, ed. Frank Smith and George A. Miller. Cambridge, Mass.: The M.I.T. Press.

Smith, Carlota S. 1964. "Determiners and Relative Clauses in a Generative Grammar of English," *Language* 40 (1964): 37–52.

Stockwell, Robert P., et al. 1973. *The Major Syntactic Structures of English*. New York: Holt, Rinehart & Winston, Inc.

Weinreich, Uriel. 1963. *Languages in Contact*. The Hague: Mouton.

Weir, Ruth Hirsch. 1962. *Language in the Crib*. The Hague: Mouton.

———. 1966. "Some Questions on the Child's Learning of Phonology," in *The Genesis of Language*, ed. Frank Smith and George A. Miller. Cambridge, Mass.: The M.I.T. Press.

Wolfram, Walter A. 1969. *A Sociolinguistic Description of Detroit Negro Speech*. Washington, D. C.: Center for Applied Linguistics.

Index